connect®

McGraw-Hill Connect® is a high[...]
use homework and learning ma[...]
that utilizes learning science an[...]
adaptive tools to improve studen[...]

Homework and Adaptive Learning

- Connect's assignments help students contextualize what they've learned through application, so they can better understand the material and think critically.

- Connect will create a personalized study path customized to individual student needs through SmartBook®.

- SmartBook helps students study more efficiently by delivering an interactive reading experience through adaptive highlighting and review.

Over **7 billion questions** have been answered, making McGraw-Hill Education products more intelligent, reliable, and precise.

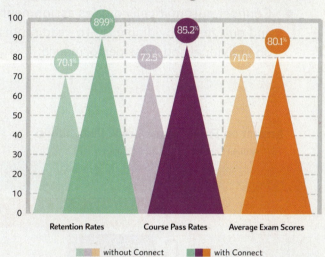

Connect's Impact on Retention Rates, Pass Rates, and Average Exam Scores

- 70.1%, 89.9% — Retention Rates
- 72.5%, 85.2% — Course Pass Rates
- 71.0%, 80.1% — Average Exam Scores

without Connect / with Connect

Using **Connect** improves retention rates by **19.8 percentage points**, passing rates by **12.7 percentage points**, and exam scores by **9.1 percentage points**.

73% of instructors who use **Connect** require it; instructor satisfaction **increases** by 28% when **Connect** is required.

Quality Content and Learning Resources

- Connect content is authored by the world's best subject matter experts, and is available to your class through a simple and intuitive interface.

- The Connect eBook makes it easy for students to access their reading material on smartphones and tablets. They can study on the go and don't need internet access to use the eBook as a reference, with full functionality.

- Multimedia content such as videos, simulations, and games drive student engagement and critical thinking skills.

©McGraw-Hill Education

Robust Analytics and Reporting

- Connect Insight® generates easy-to-read reports on individual students, the class as a whole, and on specific assignments.

- The Connect Insight dashboard delivers data on performance, study behavior, and effort. Instructors can quickly identify students who struggle and focus on material that the class has yet to master.

- Connect automatically grades assignments and quizzes, providing easy-to-read reports on individual and class performance.

©Hero Images/Getty Images

Impact on Final Course Grade Distribution

without Connect		with Connect
22.9%	A	31.0%
27.4%	B	34.3%
22.9%	C	18.7%
11.5%	D	6.1%
15.4%	F	9.9%

> More students earn **As** and **Bs** when they use **Connect**.

Trusted Service and Support

- Connect integrates with your LMS to provide single sign-on and automatic syncing of grades. Integration with Blackboard®, D2L®, and Canvas also provides automatic syncing of the course calendar and assignment-level linking.

- Connect offers comprehensive service, support, and training throughout every phase of your implementation.

- If you're looking for some guidance on how to use Connect, or want to learn tips and tricks from super users, you can find tutorials as you work. Our Digital Faculty Consultants and Student Ambassadors offer insight into how to achieve the results you want with Connect.

Organizational
Behavior

Steven L. McShane
University of Victoria (Canada)

Mary Ann Von Glinow
Florida International University

McGraw Hill Education

ORGANIZATIONAL BEHAVIOR: FOURTH EDITION

Published by McGraw-Hill Education, 2 Penn Plaza, New York, NY 10121. Copyright © 2019 by McGraw-Hill Education. All rights reserved. Printed in the United States of America. Previous editions © 2016, 2014, and 2012. No part of this publication may be reproduced or distributed in any form or by any means, or stored in a database or retrieval system, without the prior written consent of McGraw-Hill Education, including, but not limited to, in any network or other electronic storage or transmission, or broadcast for distance learning.

Some ancillaries, including electronic and print components, may not be available to customers outside the United States.

This book is printed on acid-free paper.

1 2 3 4 5 6 7 8 9 0 LWI 21 20 19 18

ISBN 978-1-259-92767-6 (bound edition)
MHID 1-259-92767-9 (bound edition)

ISBN 978-1-260-15762-8 (loose-leaf edition)
MHID 1-260-15762-8 (loose-leaf edition)

Director: *Michael Ablassmeir*
Product Developer: *Anne Ehrenworth*
Marketing Manager: *Debbie Clare*
Content Project Managers: *Harvey Yep (Core)/Keri Johnson (Assessment)*
Buyer: *Sandy Ludovissy*
Design: *Jessica Cuevas*
Content Licensing Specialist: *DeAnna Dausener (Image and Text)*
Cover Image: *©Rawpixel.com/Shutterstock*
Compositor: *Aptara®, Inc.*

All credits appearing on page or at the end of the book are considered to be an extension of the copyright page.

Library of Congress Cataloging-in-Publication Data

Names: McShane, Steven Lattimore, author. | Von Glinow, Mary Ann Young, 1949-
    author. | Von Glinow, Mary Ann.
Title: Organizational behavior / Steven L. McShane, University of Western
    Australia, Mary Ann Von Glinow, Florida International University.
Other titles: Organisational behavior
Description: Fourth Edition. | Dubuque, IA : McGraw-Hill Education, 2019. |
    Revised edition of the authors' Organizational behavior, ©2005.
Identifiers: LCCN 2017058678 | ISBN 9781259927676 (paperback : alk. paper) |
    ISBN 1259927679 (alk. paper)
Subjects: LCSH: Organizational behavior. | BISAC: BUSINESS & ECONOMICS /
    Organizational Behavior.
Classification: LCC HD58.7 .M42 2018b | DDC 658–dc23 LC record available at
    https://lccn.loc.gov/2017058678

The Internet addresses listed in the text were accurate at the time of publication. The inclusion of a website does not indicate an endorsement by the authors or McGraw-Hill Education, and McGraw-Hill Education does not guarantee the accuracy of the information presented at these sites.

www.mheducation.com

about the
Authors

Steven L. McShane

Steven L. McShane is adjunct professor at the Peter B. Gustavson School of Business, University of Victoria (Canada). He previously held the positions of professor at Simon Fraser University Business School in Canada and professor of management at the University of Western Australia Business School. He currently teaches in the Shanghai Jiao Tong University IMBA program. Early in his career, Steve taught at Queen's University in Canada. Steve has received awards for his teaching quality and innovation, and receives high ratings from students in Perth, Shanghai, Singapore, Manila, and other cities where he has taught. He is also a popular visiting speaker, having given dozens of invited talks and seminars in recent years to faculty and students in the United States, China, Canada, Malaysia, India, and other countries.

Courtesy Steven McShane

Steve earned his PhD from Michigan State University, where he specialized in organizational behavior and labor relations. He also holds a Master's of Industrial Relations from the University of Toronto and an undergraduate degree from Queen's University in Canada. Steve is a past president of the Administrative Sciences Association of Canada (the Canadian equivalent of the Academy of Management) and served as director of graduate programs in Simon Fraser University's business faculty. He has conducted executive programs with Nokia, TÜV-SÜD, Wesfarmers Group, Main Roads WA, McGraw-Hill, ALCOA World Alumina Australia, and many other organizations.

Along with coauthoring *M:Organizational Behavior*, Fourth Edition, Steve is lead coauthor of *Organizational Behavior*, Eighth Edition (2018); *Canadian Organizational Behaviour*, Tenth Edition (2018); and *Organisational Behaviour: Asia Pacific*, Fifth Edition (2016). He is also coauthor of editions or translations of his organizational behavior books in China, India, Quebec, Taiwan, and Brazil. Steve has published several dozen articles and conference papers on workplace values, training transfer, organizational learning, exit–voice–loyalty, employee socialization, wrongful dismissal, media bias in business magazines, and other diverse topics.

Steve enjoys spending his leisure time hiking, swimming, body board surfing, canoeing, skiing, and traveling with his wife and two daughters.

Mary Ann Von Glinow

Dr. Von Glinow is a Knight Ridder Eminent Scholar Chair in International Management at Florida International University and is senior editor for the *Journal of International Business Studies (JIBS)*. She served as 2010 to 2012 president of the Academy of International Business (AIB) and the 1994–1995 president of the Academy of Management (AOM). Previously on the Marshall School faculty of the University of Southern California, she has an MBA and a PhD in management science from Ohio State University, and is a Fellow of the Academy of Management, the Academy of International Business, and the Pan-Pacific Business Association. She sits on 13 editorial review boards and numerous international panels and teaches in executive programs in Latin America, Asia, and the United States.

Courtesy Mary Ann Von Glinow

Dr. Von Glinow has authored over 100 journal articles and 13 books, most of which have been translated into Chinese, Hindi, and Spanish. Her book on organizational learning capability won a Gold Book Award from the Ministry of Economic Affairs in Taiwan in 2002. She is the 2005 recipient of the Academy of Management's Distinguished Service Award, one of the highest honors bestowed by the Academy.

Mary Ann has consulted widely and is on the board of directors of several organizations, including the advisory board to Volvo-Geely in China. She is actively involved in several animal welfare organizations and received the 1996 Humanitarian Award of the Year from Miami's Adopt-a-Pet.

Contents

nages

©Elnur/Shutterstock

©Jacob Lund/Shutterstock

What's New
in the Fourth Edition

M: Organizational Behavior, Fourth Edition, has been significantly revised, guided by useful feedback from reviewers and our active monitoring of evidence-based literature. All chapters have new examples and either new or revised factoids; most chapters have new conceptual content or literature foundation. The most substantial changes have occurred in Chapter 1 (introduction to OB), Chapter 4 (workplace emotions, attitudes, and stress), Chapter 6 (decision making and creativity), Chapter 8 (communication), and Chapter 10 (conflict and negotiation). The authors personally researched, selected, and wrote all of this content, thereby providing superior integration of knowledge and ensuring that the examples are relevant and recent. Here are the key changes we've made to this fourth edition, broken out by chapter:

Chapter 1: Introduction to the Field of Organizational Behavior

Technological change has been added in the section on contemporary developments facing organizations. The section on perspectives of organizational effectiveness has been streamlined. Most topics have updated content, particularly the text on the four contemporary developments, why study OB, and several aspects of organizational effectiveness.

Chapter 2: Individual Behavior, Personality, and Values

Several topics in this chapter have been updated, particularly coverage of the five-factor model of personality and work performance, values and individual behavior, and moral sensitivity.

Chapter 3: Perceiving Ourselves and Others in Organizations

This book pioneered the full model of self-concept and its relevance to organizational behavior. This edition further develops this important topic and provides new information on the opposing motives for distinctiveness and inclusion. The section on stereotyping also incorporates the concept of stereotype threat.

Chapter 4: Workplace Emotions, Attitudes, and Stress

This edition significantly revises and updates discussion on four key workplace stressors, with new writing about organizational constraints and interpersonal conflict as stressors. In addition, there is new content on attitude–behavior contingencies.

Chapter 5: Employee Motivation

New to this edition is the topic of intrinsic and extrinsic motivation, as well as the question of whether introducing extrinsic sources of motivation reduces intrinsic motivation. We also have reorganized and refined the writing on drives and needs, Maslow's needs hierarchy, and four-drive theory. The previous edition introduced the social and information processing characteristics of jobs. This edition further refines that emerging topic.

Chapter 6: Decision Making and Creativity

This chapter has been substantially revised and updated in several ways. Design thinking now receives more attention as a concept and practice to improve workplace creativity. The topic of problems with information processing when choosing alternatives also has been substantially updated. Additional updates have been made to solution-focused problems, problems with goals, implicit favorite bias, and satisficing (problems with maximization).

Chapter 7: Team Dynamics

This edition refines discussion introduced in the previous edition on the three characteristics that distinguish types of teams. It also offers more detail about social loafing, team mental models (as part of team development), and team development through team building.

Chapter 8: Communicating in Teams and Organizations

This edition substantially revises and updates the important topic of choosing the best communication medium. Specifically, this topic

1 | Introduction to the Field of Organizational Behavior

©Robert Kneschke/Shutterstock

Learning Objectives

After you read this chapter, you should be able to:

LO1-1 Define organizational behavior and organizations, and discuss the importance of this field of inquiry.

LO1-2 Debate the organizational opportunities and challenges of technological change, globalization, emerging employment relationships, and workforce diversity.

LO1-3 Discuss the anchors on which organizational behavior knowledge is based.

LO1-4 Compare and contrast the four perspectives of organizational effectiveness.

Apple and Amazon are the two most admired companies in the world, according to *Fortune* magazine's annual list. Yet neither of these firms was on anyone's radar screen two decades ago. Apple was on life support in the late 1990s, barely clinging to a few percentage points of market share in the computer industry. Amazon started selling books online in 1995, a few months after its founder, Jeff Bezos, took a course from the American Booksellers Association on how to start a bookstore![1]

The dramatic growth of Apple and Amazon illustrates the many workplace activities that contribute to success in today's turbulent economic environment. In every sector of the economy, organizations need skilled and motivated people who can realize their potential, work in teams, and maintain a healthy lifestyle. They need leaders with foresight and vision, who support innovative work practices and make decisions that consider the interests of multiple stakeholders. In other words, the best companies succeed through the concepts and practices that we discuss in this organizational behavior book.

Our purpose is to help you understand what goes on in organizations. We examine the factors that make companies effective, improve employee well-being, and drive successful collaboration among co-workers. We look at organizations from numerous and diverse perspectives, from the deepest foundations of employee thoughts and behavior (personality, self-concept, attitudes, etc.) to the complex interplay between the organization's structure and culture and its external environment. Along this journey, we emphasize why things happen and what you can do to predict and guide organizational events.

We begin this chapter by introducing you to the field of organizational behavior and why it is important to your career and to organizations. This is followed by an overview of four major societal developments facing organizations: technological change, globalization, emerging employment relationships, and increasing workforce diversity. We then describe four anchors that guide the development of organizational behavior knowledge. The latter part of this chapter describes the "ultimate dependent variable" in organizational behavior by presenting the four main perspectives of organizational effectiveness. The chapter closes with an integrative model of organizational behavior, which serves as a road map to guide you through the topics in this book.

> **organizational behavior (OB)** the study of what people think, feel, and do in and around organizations
>
> **organizations** groups of people who work interdependently toward some purpose

> **LO1-1** Define organizational behavior and organizations, and discuss the importance of this field of inquiry.

THE FIELD OF ORGANIZATIONAL BEHAVIOR

Organizational behavior (OB) is the study of what people think, feel, and do in and around organizations. It looks at employee behavior, decisions, perceptions, and emotional responses. It examines how individuals and teams in organizations relate to each other and to their counterparts in other organizations. OB also encompasses the study of how organizations interact with their external environments, particularly in the context of employee behavior and decisions. OB researchers systematically study these topics at multiple levels of analysis, namely, the individual, team (including interpersonal), and organization.[3]

The definition of organizational behavior begs the question: What are organizations? **Organizations** are groups of people who work interdependently toward some purpose.[4] Notice that organizations are not buildings or government-registered entities. In fact, many organizations exist with neither physical walls nor government documentation to confer their legal status. Organizations have existed for as long as people have worked together. Massive temples dating back to 3500 BC were constructed through the

The World's Most Admired Companies[2]

organized actions of multitudes of people. Craftspeople and merchants in ancient Rome formed guilds, complete with elected managers. More than 1,000 years ago, Chinese factories were producing 125,000 tons of iron each year.[5]

One key feature of all organizations throughout history is that they are collective entities.[6] They consist of human beings—typically, but not necessarily, employees—who interact with each other in an *organized* way. This organized relationship requires communication, coordination, and collaboration to achieve organizational objectives. As such, all organizational members have degrees of interdependence; they accomplish goals by sharing materials, information, or expertise with coworkers.

A second key feature of organizations is that their members have a collective sense of pur-

One key feature of all organizations is that they consist of human beings who interact with each other in an *organized* way.
©Image Source

pose. This collective purpose isn't always well defined or agreed on. Most companies have vision and mission statements, but they are sometimes out of date or don't describe what employees actually try to achieve. Still, imagine an organization without a collective sense of purpose. It would be an assemblage of

had changed the name of its MBA human relations course to "Organizational Behavior."

Although the field of OB is recent, experts in other fields have been studying organizations for many centuries. The Greek philosopher Plato (400 BC) wrote about the essence of

people without direction or unifying force. So, whether they are designing and marketing the latest communication technology at Apple or selling almost anything on the Internet at Amazon, people working in organizations do have some sense of collective purpose.

Historical Foundations of Organizational Behavior

Organizational behavior emerged as a distinct field sometime around the early 1940s.[8] During that decade, a few researchers began describing their research as organizational (rather than sociological or psychological). And by the late 1940s, Harvard

leadership, and the Chinese philosopher Confucius (500 BC) extolled the virtues of ethics and leadership. Economist Adam Smith (late 1700s) discussed the benefits of job specialization and division of labor. German sociologist Max Weber (early 1900s) wrote about rational organizations, the work ethic, and charismatic leadership. Around the same time, industrial engineer Frederick Winslow Taylor proposed systematic ways to organize work processes and motivate employees through goal setting and rewards.[9]

Political scientist Mary Parker Follett (1920s) offered new ways of thinking about constructive conflict, team dynamics, power, and leadership. Harvard professor Elton Mayo and his colleagues (1930s and 1940s) established the "human relations" school of management, which pioneered research on employee attitudes, formal team dynamics, informal groups, and supervisor leadership style. American executive and Harvard associate Chester Barnard (1930s) wrote insightful views regarding organizational communication, coordination, leadership and authority, organizations as open systems, and team dynamics.[10] This brief historical tour indicates that OB has been around for a long time; it just wasn't organized into a unified discipline until around World War II.

Why Study Organizational Behavior?

In all likelihood, you are reading this book as part of a required course in organizational behavior. Apart from degree or diploma requirements, why should you learn the ideas and practices discussed in this book? After all, who ever heard of a career path leading to a "vice president of OB" or a "chief OB officer"? Our answer to this question begins with survey findings that students who have been in the workforce for some time typically point to OB as one of their most valuable courses. Why? Because they have learned through experience that OB *does make a difference* to one's career success.[11] There are three main reasons why OB theories and practices are personally important to you (see Exhibit 1.1).

Frederick Winslow Taylor
©Paul Fearn/Alamy Stock Photo

Comprehend and Predict Workplace Events

Everyone has an inherent drive to make sense of what is going on around him or her.[12] This need is particularly strong in organizations because they are highly complex and ambiguous contexts that have a profound effect on our lives. The field of organizational behavior uses scientific research to discover systematic relationships, which give us a valuable foundation for comprehending organizational life.[13] This knowledge satisfies our curiosity about why events occur and reduces our anxiety about circumstances that would otherwise be unexpected and unexplained. Furthermore, OB knowledge improves our ability to predict and anticipate future events so we can get along with others, achieve our goals, and minimize unnecessary career risks.

Adopt More Accurate Personal Theories

A frequent misunderstanding is that OB is common sense. Of course, some OB knowledge is very similar to the theories you have developed through personal experience. But personal theories are usually not quite as precise as they need to be. Perhaps they explain and predict some situations, but not others. For example, one study found that when liberal arts students and chief executive officers were asked to choose the preferred organizational structure in various situations, their commonsense answers were typically wrong because they oversimplified well-known theory and evidence on that topic.[14] (We discuss organizational structures in Chapter 12.) Throughout this book you also will discover that OB research has debunked some ideas that people thought were "common sense." Overall, we believe the OB knowledge you will gain by reading this book will help you challenge and refine your personal theories, and give you more accurate and complete perspectives of organizational events.

Influence Organizational Events

Probably the greatest value of OB knowledge is that it helps us get things done in the workplace by influencing organizational events.[15] By definition, organizations are people who work together to accomplish things, so we need a toolkit of knowledge and skills to work successfully with others. Studies consistently observe that the most important knowledge and skills that employers desire in employees relate to the topics we discuss in this book, such as building teams, motivating coworkers, handling workplace conflicts, making decisions, and changing employee behavior. No matter what career path you choose, you'll find that

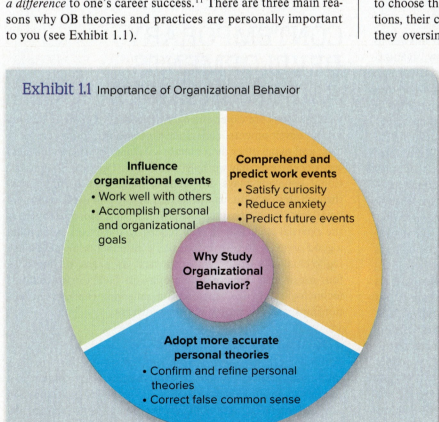

Exhibit 1.1 Importance of Organizational Behavior

Influence organizational events
- Work well with others
- Accomplish personal and organizational goals

Comprehend and predict work events
- Satisfy curiosity
- Reduce anxiety
- Predict future events

Why Study Organizational Behavior?

Adopt more accurate personal theories
- Confirm and refine personal theories
- Correct false common sense

OB concepts play an important role in performing your job and working more effectively within organizations.

Organizational Behavior Is for Everyone Organizational behavior is discussed by some writers as a topic for managers. Effective management does depend on OB concepts and practices, but this book pioneered the broader view that OB is valuable for everyone who works in and around organizations. Whether you are a software engineer, customer service representative, foreign exchange analyst, or chief executive officer, you need to understand and apply the many organizational behavior topics that are discussed in this book. In fact, OB knowledge is probably more valuable than ever before because employees increasingly need to be proactive, self-motivated, and able to work effectively with coworkers without management intervention. In the words of one forward-thinking OB writer more than four decades ago: Everyone is a manager.[16]

Probably the greatest value of OB knowledge is that it helps us get things done in the workplace by influencing organizational events.
©ColorBlind Images/Blend Images LLC

OB and the Bottom Line Up to this point, our answer to the question "Why study OB?" has focused on how organizational behavior knowledge benefits you as an individual. However, OB is also vital to the organization's survival and success.[17] For instance, the best 100 companies to work for in America (i.e., companies with the highest levels of employee satisfaction) enjoy significantly higher financial performance than other businesses within the same industry. Companies with higher levels of employee engagement have higher sales and profitability (see Chapter 5). OB practices also are associated with various indicators of hospital performance, such as lower patient mortality rates and higher patient satisfaction. Other studies have consistently found a positive relationship between the quality of leadership and the company's financial performance.

The bottom-line value of organizational behavior is supported by research into the best predictors of investment portfolio performance. These investigations suggest that leadership, performance-based rewards, employee development, employee attitudes, and other specific OB characteristics are important "positive screens" for selecting companies with the highest and most consistent long-term investment gains.[18] Overall, the organizational behavior concepts, theories, and practices presented throughout this book make a positive difference to you personally, to the organization, and ultimately to society.

LO1-2 Debate the organizational opportunities and challenges of technological change, globalization, emerging employment relationships, and workforce diversity.

CONTEMPORARY DEVELOPMENTS FACING ORGANIZATIONS

Organizations are experiencing unprecedented change. Technological developments, consumer expectations, global competition, and many other factors have substantially altered business strategy and everyday workplace activities. The field of organizational behavior plays a vital role in guiding organizations through this continuous turbulence. As we will explain in more detail later in this chapter, organizations are deeply affected by the external environment. Consequently, they need to maintain a good organization–environment fit by anticipating and adjusting to changes in society. Over the next few pages, we introduce four major environmental developments facing organizations: technological change, globalization, emerging employment relationships, and increasing workforce diversity.

Technological Change

Technological change has always been a disruptive force in organizations, as well as in society.[19] Waterwheels, cotton gins, steam engines, microprocessors (such as in automated systems and artificial intelligence), and many other innovations dramatically boost productivity, but also usually displace employees and render obsolete entire occupational groups. Other technologies, such as the telegraph, smartphone, and the Internet, have increased productivity but also altered work relationships and patterns of behavior with coworkers, clients, and suppliers. Still other technologies aim to improve health and well-being, such as the development of better medicines and medical equipment, new leisure apparatus, and environmentally safer materials.

Information technology is one of the most significant forms of technological change in recent times.[20] As we discuss in Chapter 8, communication patterns and power dynamics have substantially changed due to the introduction of email and other forms of digital messaging. Social media and other collaboration technologies are slowly replacing email, and will further reshape how people associate and coordinate with each other. Some OB experts argue that information technology gives employees a stronger voice through direct communication with executives and broader distribution of their opinions to coworkers and beyond.

Information technology also has created challenges, such as tethering people to their jobs for longer hours, reducing their attention spans at work, and increasing techno-stress. We discuss these concerns below and in Chapter 4 (workplace stress). At a macro-level, information technology has reconfigured entire organizations by integrating suppliers and other external entities into the transformation process. Eventually, technology may render organizations less of a place where people work and more of a process or network where people collaborate across space and time (see Chapter 12).

Globalization

Globalization refers to economic, social, and cultural connectivity with people in other parts of the world. Organizations globalize when they actively participate in other countries and cultures. Although businesses have traded goods across borders for centuries, the degree of globalization today is unprecedented because information technology and transportation systems allow a much more intense level of connectivity and interdependence around the planet.[22]

Globalization offers numerous benefits to organizations in terms of larger markets, lower costs, and greater access to knowledge and innovation. At the same time, there is considerable debate about whether globalization benefits developing nations and the extent to which it is responsible for increasing work intensification, reduced job security, and poor work–life balance in developed countries.[23]

The field of organizational behavior focuses on the effects of globalization on organizations and how to lead and work effectively in this emerging reality. Throughout this book, we will refer to the effects of globalization on teamwork, diversity, cultural values, organizational structure, leadership, and other themes. Globalization has brought more complexity and new ways of working to the workplace. It also requires additional knowledge and skills that we will discuss in this book, such as emotional intelligence, a global mindset, nonverbal communication, and conflict handling.

Emerging Employment Relationships

Technology, globalization, and several other developments have substantially altered the employment relationship in most countries. Before the digital age, most employees would finish work after eight or nine hours and could separate their personal time from their employment. Today, they are more likely to be connected to work on a 24/7 schedule. Globalization increases competitive pressure to work longer and creates a 24-hour schedule because coworkers, suppliers, and clients work in different time zones. Information technology enables employers and others to easily and quickly communicate with employees beyond their traditional workday.

Little wonder that one of the most important employment issues over the past decade has been **work–life balance**. Work–life balance occurs when people are able to minimize conflict between their work and nonwork demands.[24] Most employees lack this balance because they spend too many hours each week performing or thinking about their job, whether at the workplace, at home,

Social Media Technology Reshapes the Workplace[21]

21% of 2,027 employed American adults say they spend between 1 and 6 hours using social media tools or mobile applications to help get their job done.

46% of 9,908 information workers polled across 32 countries say that social media tools have somewhat or greatly increased their productivity.

58% of 1,000 American employees polled say they would prefer to work at a company that uses internal (enterprise) social media.

42% of 9,908 information workers polled across 32 countries say that social media tools have resulted in more workplace collaboration.

60% of 2,186 American hiring and human resource managers say they use social media sites to research job candidates (up from 52% the previous year and 11% in 2006).

(photo): ©pictafolio/E+/Getty Images

or on vacation. This focus on work leaves too little time to fulfill nonwork needs and obligations. Our discussion of work-related stress (Chapter 4) will examine work–life balance issues in more detail.

Another employment relationship trend is for employees to work away from the organization's traditional common work site.[25] One form of this *remote work* arrangement involves performing most job duties at client sites throughout the day. Repair technicians and management consultants regularly work at client sites, for example. Longer-term remote work occurs where employees are assigned to partner organizations. For instance, biotechnology firm Anteo Diagnostics dispatches its scientists for several weeks or months to partner companies around the world, where they jointly investigate the effectiveness of Anteo's patented nano glue products on the partner firm's point-of-care technology.

Telecommuting The best-known form of remote work is **telecommuting** (also called *teleworking*) whereby information technology enables employees to work from home one or more workdays per month rather than commute to the office. An estimated 37 percent of U.S. workers telecommute, with almost one-third of them working from home at least six days each month. The U.S. government reports that 23 percent of employees perform some or all of their work at home (but that includes taking work home after attending the office, not just telecommuting).[26]

Is telecommuting good for employees and organizations? This question continues to be debated because it produces

Most employees lack work–life balance because they spend too many hours each week performing or thinking about their job, whether at the workplace, at home, or on vacation.
©ALMAGAMI/Shutterstock

Exhibit 1.2 Potential Benefits and Risks of Telecommuting

Potential Benefits	Potential Risks
• Better employee work–life balance	• More social isolation
• Attractive benefit for job applicants	• Lower team cohesion
• Low employee turnover	• Weaker organizational culture
• Higher employee productivity	• More stressful due to home space and roles
• Reduced greenhouse gas emissions	
• Reduced corporate real estate and office costs	

---

several potential benefits and risks (see Exhibit 1.2).[27] One advantage is that telecommuters usually experience better work–life balance because they have more time and somewhat more control to juggle work with family obligations. For example, a study of 25,000 IBM employees found that female telecommuters with children were able to work 40 hours per week, whereas female employees with children who work solely at the office could manage only 30 hours before feeling work–life balance tension. Work–life balance is less likely to improve when telecommuters lack sufficient workspace and privacy at home and have increased family responsibilities on telecommuting days.

Job applicants—particularly millennials—identify telecommuting as an attractive job feature, and turnover is usually lower among telecommuting employees. Research also indicates that telecommuters have higher productivity than nontelecommuters, likely because they experience less stress and tend to transfer some former commuting time to work time. Telecommuting also improves productivity by enabling employees to work at times when the weather or natural disasters block access to the office.

Several companies report that telecommuting has reduced greenhouse gas emissions and office expenses. For instance, health insurer Aetna estimates that its telecommuting employees (31 percent of the workforce) annually avoid using two million gallons of gas, thereby reducing carbon dioxide emissions by more than 23,000 metric tons. With many employees working from home, Aetna also has been able to reduce its real estate and related costs by between 15 and 25 percent.[28]

Telecommuting also has several disadvantages.[29] Telecommuters frequently report more social isolation. They also receive less word-of-mouth information, which may have implications for promotional opportunities and workplace relations. Telecommuting also tends to weaken relationships among coworkers, resulting in lower team cohesion. Organizational culture is also potentially weaker when most employees work from home for a significant part of their workweek.

Telecommuting success depends on several characteristics of the employee, job, and organization.[30] Employees who work effectively from home typically have higher self-motivation, self-organization, need for autonomy, and information technology skills. Those who telecommute most of the time also fulfill their social needs more from sources outside the workplace. Jobs are better suited to telecommuting when the tasks do not require resources at the workplace, the work is performed independently from coworkers, and task performance is measurable.

Organizations improve telecommuting success by rewarding and promoting employees based on their performance rather than their presence in the office (face time). Effective companies also help telecommuters maintain sufficient cohesion with their team and psychological connectedness with the organization. This occurs by limiting the number of telecommuting days, having special meetings or events where all employees assemble at the workplace, and regularly using video communication and other technology that improves personal relatedness.

(currently 18 percent), 14 percent will be of Asian descent (currently 6 percent), and 13 percent will be African American (currently 14 percent).[32]

Diversity also includes differences in personalities, beliefs, values, and attitudes.[33] We can't directly see this **deep-level diversity**, but it is evident in a person's choices, words, and actions. Deep-level diversity is revealed when employees have different perceptions and attitudes about the same situation (see Chapter 10) and when they form like-minded informal social groups (see Chapter 7). Some deep-level diversity is associated with surface-level attributes. For example, studies report significant differences between men and women regarding their preference of

> ❝ Employees who work effectively from home typically have higher self-motivation, self-organization, need for autonomy, and information technology skills. ❞

connect

SELF-ASSESSMENT 1.1: Are You a Good Telecommuter?
Telecommuting is an increasingly popular workplace relationship, and it potentially offers benefits for both companies and telecommuters. However, some people are better suited than others to telecommuting and other forms of remote work. You can discover how well you adjust to telecommuting and remote work by locating this self-assessment in Connect if it is assigned by your instructor.

Increasing Workforce Diversity

Immigrants to the United States and many other countries have much more multicultural origins than a few decades ago, resulting in a much more diverse workforce in most organizations. In addition, globalization has increased the diversity of people employees interact with in partner organizations (suppliers, clients, etc.) located elsewhere in the world.

When discussing workforce diversity, we usually think about **surface-level diversity**—the observable demographic and other overt differences among members of a group, such as their race, ethnicity, gender, age, and physical capabilities.[31] Surface-level diversity in the United States and many other countries has increased substantially over the past few decades. For instance, people with non-Caucasian or Hispanic origin currently represent almost 40 percent of the American population. Within the next 50 years, an estimated one-quarter of Americans will be Hispanic

conflict-handling styles, ethical principles, and approaches to communicating with other people in various situations.[34]

An example of deep-level diversity is the variations in beliefs and expectations across generations.[35] Exhibit 1.3 illustrates the distribution of the American workforce by major generational cohorts: *Baby Boomers* (born from 1946 to 1964), *Generation Xers* (born from 1965 to 1980), and *Millennials* (also called *Generation Yers*, born between 1981 and 1997).

Generational deep-level diversity does exist to some extent, but it tends to be subtler than the popular press would suggest. Also, some generational differences are actually due to age, not cohort.[37] For instance, Millennials have a stronger motivation for personal development, advancement, and recognition, whereas Baby Boomers are more motivated by interesting and meaningful work. Research indicates that as Millennials age, their motivation for learning and advancement will wane and their motivation for interesting and meaningful work will increase.

Consequences of Diversity

Workforce diversity offers numerous advantages to organizations.[38] Teams with high informational diversity—members have different knowledge and skills—tend to be more creative and

Exhibit 1.3 America's Multigenerational Workforce[36]

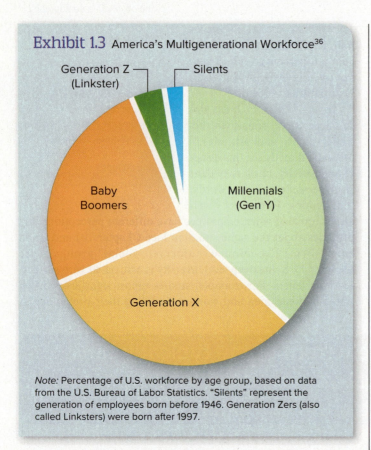

Note: Percentage of U.S. workforce by age group, based on data from the U.S. Bureau of Labor Statistics. "Silents" represent the generation of employees born before 1946. Generation Zers (also called Linksters) were born after 1997.

make better decisions in complex situations compared to teams with less informational diversity. A workforce with surface- and deep-level diversity is also more representative of most communities, so companies are better able to recognize and address community needs. These and other benefits may explain why companies that win diversity awards have higher financial returns, at least in the short run.[39]

Diversity also poses challenges in the workplace.[40] One problem is that employees with diverse backgrounds usually take longer to perform effectively together because they experience numerous communication problems and create "faultlines" in informal group dynamics (see Chapter 7). Some forms of diversity also increase the risk of dysfunctional conflict, which reduces information sharing and satisfaction with coworkers (see Chapter 10). Research suggests that these problems can offset the advantages of diversity in some situations.

But even with these challenges, companies need to make diversity a priority because surface-level diversity and some forms of deep-level diversity are moral and legal imperatives. Companies that offer an inclusive workplace are, in essence, fulfilling the ethical standard of fairness in their decisions regarding employment and the allocation of rewards. Inclusive workplace practices improve the quality of hiring and promotion, and increase employee satisfaction and loyalty. Companies that create an inclusive workplace also nurture a culture of respect, which, in turn, improves cooperation and coordination among employees.

OB THEORY TO PRACTICE

Diversity as Competitive Advantage at MasterCard

©Pau Barrena/Bloomberg/Getty Images

Supporting workforce diversity is the right thing to do as well as a source of competitive advantage at MasterCard Incorporated. "Our culture of inclusion has established us as a global company of empowered employees who use their diversity of thought, experience and background to advance innovation and MasterCard's contributions to society," says MasterCard president and CEO Ajay Banga (shown in this photo).

Banga personally chairs MasterCard's Global Diversity and Inclusion Council and meets several times each year with its eight Business Resource Groups. More than half of MasterCard's employees participate in these diversity-based groups, which serve as internal business consultants to guide the company on consumer preferences, cultural insights, and access to networks. "By valuing a culture of inclusion, we gain additional insights and perspectives that allow us to make the best decisions for our business and customers," explains Donna Johnson, MasterCard's chief diversity officer.[41]

LO1-3   Discuss the anchors on which organizational behavior knowledge is based.

ANCHORS OF ORGANIZATIONAL BEHAVIOR KNOWLEDGE

Technological change, globalization, emerging employment relationships, and increasing workforce diversity are just a few of the societal changes that make organizational behavior knowledge more useful than ever before. To understand these and other topics, the field of organizational behavior relies on a set of basic beliefs or knowledge structures (see Exhibit 1.4). These conceptual anchors represent the principles on which OB knowledge is developed and refined.[42]

The Systematic Research Anchor

A key feature of OB knowledge is that it should be based on systematic research, which typically involves forming research questions, systematically collecting data, and testing hypotheses against those data.[43] Systematic research investigation is the basis for **evidence-based management**, which involves making decisions and taking actions guided by research evidence. It makes perfect sense that management practice should be founded on the best available systematic knowledge. Yet many of us who study organizations using systematic methods are amazed at how often corporate leaders and other staff embrace fads, untested consulting models, and their own pet beliefs without bothering to find out if they actually work![44]

Why don't decision makers consistently apply evidence-based management? One reason is that they are bombarded with ideas from consultant reports, popular business books, newspaper articles, and other sources, which makes it difficult to figure out which ones are based on good evidence. A second reason is that good OB research is necessarily generic; it is rarely described in the context of a specific problem in a specific organization. Decision makers therefore have the difficult task of figuring out which theories are relevant to their unique situation.

A third reason why organizational leaders follow popular management fads that lack research evidence is because the sources of these fads are rewarded for marketing their ideas, not for testing to see if they actually work. Indeed, some management concepts have become popular (some have even found their way into OB textbooks!) because of heavy marketing, not because of any evidence that they are valid. A fourth reason is that human beings are affected by several perceptual errors and decision-making biases, as we will learn in Chapter 3 and Chapter 6. For instance, decision makers have a natural tendency to look for evidence that supports their pet beliefs and ignore evidence that opposes those beliefs.

OB experts have identified several ways to create a more evidence-based organization.[45] First, be skeptical of hype, which is apparent when so-called experts say the idea is "new," "revolutionary," and "proven." In reality, most management ideas are adaptations, evolutionary, and never proven (science can disprove but never prove; it can only find evidence to support a practice). Second, the company should embrace collective expertise rather than rely on charismatic stars and management gurus. Third, stories provide useful illustrations and possibly preliminary evidence of a useful practice, but they should never become the main foundation to support management action. Instead, rely on more systematic investigation with a larger sample. Finally, take a neutral stance toward popular trends and ideologies. Executives tend to get caught up in what their counterparts at other companies are doing without determining the validity of those trendy practices or their relevance to their own organizations.

A key feature of OB knowledge is that it should be based on systematic research, which becomes the foundation for evidence-based management.
©Wavebreakmedia Ltd PH26L/Alamy Stock Photo

Exhibit 1.4 Anchors of Organizational Behavior Knowledge

Systematic research anchor	Study organizations using systematic research methods
Multidisciplinary anchor	Import knowledge from other disciplines, not just create its own knowledge
Contingency anchor	Recognize that the effectiveness of an action may depend on the situation
Multiple levels of analysis anchor	Understand OB events from three levels of analysis: individual, team, organization

The Multidisciplinary Anchor

Another organizational behavior anchor is that the field should welcome theories and knowledge from other disciplines, not just from its own isolated research base. For instance, psychological research has aided our understanding of individual and interpersonal behavior. Sociologists have contributed to our knowledge of team dynamics, organizational socialization, organizational power, and other aspects of the social system. OB knowledge also has benefited from knowledge in emerging fields such as communications, marketing, and information systems.

This practice of borrowing theory from other disciplines is inevitable. Organizations have central roles in society, so they are studied in many social sciences. Furthermore, organizations consist of people who interact with each other, so there is an inherent intersection between OB and most disciplines that study human beings. However, by relying too much on theories developed in other fields, OB faces the risk of lagging rather than leading in knowledge production. In contrast, OB-bred theories allow researchers to concentrate on the quality and usefulness of the theory, and be the first to understand and apply that knowledge.[46]

The Contingency Anchor

People and their work environments are complex, and the field of organizational behavior recognizes this by stating that the effect of one variable on another variable often depends on the characteristics of the situation or people involved. In practice, this means that we can't count on having the same result in every situation when we apply an intervention. Instead, a particular action may have different consequences under different conditions.[47] For example, earlier in this chapter we said that the success of telecommuting depends on specific characteristics of the employee, job, and organization. Contingencies are identified in many OB theories, such as the best leadership style, the best conflict-handling style, and the best organizational structure. Of course, it would be so much simpler if we could rely on "one best way" theories, in which a particular concept or practice has the same results in every situation. OB experts do try to keep theories as simple as possible, but the contingency anchor is always on their mind.[48]

The Multiple Levels of Analysis Anchor

Organizational behavior recognizes that what goes on in organizations can be placed into three levels of analysis: individual, team (including interpersonal), and organization. In fact, advanced empirical research currently being conducted carefully identifies the appropriate level of analysis for each variable in the study and then measures at that level of analysis. For example, team norms and cohesion are measured as team variables, not as characteristics of individuals within each team.

Although OB research and writing peg each variable within one of these levels of analysis, most variables are understood best by thinking of them from all three levels of analysis.[49] Communication is located in this book as a team (interpersonal) process, for instance, but it also includes individual and organizational processes. Therefore, you should try to think about each OB topic at the individual, team, and organizational levels, not just at one of these levels.

LO1-4 Compare and contrast the four perspectives of organizational effectiveness.

PERSPECTIVES OF ORGANIZATIONAL EFFECTIVENESS

Almost all organizational behavior theories have the implicit or explicit objective of making organizations more effective.[50] In fact, **organizational effectiveness** is considered the "ultimate dependent variable" in organizational behavior.[51] This means that organizational effectiveness is the outcome that most OB theories are ultimately trying to achieve. Many theories use different labels—organizational performance, success, goodness, health, competitiveness, excellence—but they are basically presenting models and recommendations that help organizations to be more effective.

Many years ago, OB experts thought the best indicator of a company's effectiveness was how well it achieved its stated objectives. According to this definition, Delta Air Lines would be an effective organization if it met or exceeded its annual sales and profit targets. Today, we know that this goal perspective might not indicate organizational effectiveness at all. Any leadership team could set corporate goals that are easy to achieve, yet the company would be left in the dust by competitors' more aggressive objectives. Worse still, some goals might ultimately put the company out of business. For example, they may focus employees on reducing costs whereas success may require more focus on product or service quality.

The best yardstick of organizational effectiveness is a composite of four perspectives: open systems, organizational learning, high-performance work practices, and stakeholders.[52] Organizations are effective when they have a good fit with their external environment, are learning organizations, have efficient and adaptive internal subsystems (i.e., high-performance work practices), and satisfy the needs of key stakeholders. Over the next few pages, we examine each of these perspectives in more detail.

Open Systems Perspective

The **open systems** perspective of organizational effectiveness is one of the earliest and most-entrenched ways of thinking about organizations.[53] Indeed, the other major organizational effectiveness perspectives mainly provide more detail to specific sections of the open systems model. This perspective views organizations as complex organisms that "live" within an external environment, as Exhibit 1.5 illustrates. The word *open* describes this permeable relationship, whereas *closed systems* operate without dependence on or interaction with an external environment.

As open systems, organizations depend on the external environment for resources, including raw materials, job applicants, financial resources, information, and equipment. The external environment also consists of rules and expectations, such as laws and cultural norms, that place demands on how organizations should operate. Some resources (e.g., raw materials) are imported from the external environment, are transformed into product or services, and then become outputs exported to the external environment. Other resources (e.g., job applicants, equipment) become subsystems in the transformation process.

Inside the organization are numerous subsystems, such as departments, teams, informal groups, information systems, work processes, and technological processes.[54] These subsystems are dependent on each other as they transform inputs into outputs. Some outputs (e.g., products and services) may be valued by the external environment, whereas other outputs (e.g., employee layoffs, pollution) are undesirable by-products that may have adverse effects on the environment and the organization's relationship with that environment. Throughout this process, organizations receive feedback from the external environment regarding the value of their outputs, the availability of future inputs, and the appropriateness of the transformation process.

Organization–Environment Fit The open systems perspective states that organizations are effective when they maintain a good "fit" with their external environment.[55] Good fit exists when the organization's inputs, processes, and outputs are aligned with the external environment's needs, expectations, and resources. Organizations maintain a good environmental fit in three ways:

- **Adapt to the environment:** Effective organizations closely and continuously monitor the environment for emerging conditions that pose a threat or opportunity. Then they reconfigure their internal subsystems to align more closely with that shifting environment. There are many ways that companies are adaptive (called their *dynamic capability*), such as by changing the type or volume of products produced, shifting to different input resources that are more plentiful or reliable, and designing better production (transformation) processes.

- **Influence the environment:** Effective organizations don't merely respond to emerging conditions; they actively try to influence their

Exhibit 1.5 Open Systems Perspective of Organizations

The open systems perspective states that organizations are effective when they maintain a good "fit" with their external environment.
©Palto/Getty Images

energy. Another indicator is their *adaptability*. Organizations need to adapt to their external environment, and this usually includes a transformation process that adapts to new products and sometimes new ways of making those products. A third indicator of an effective transformation process is *innovativeness*. Innovation involves the discovery, design, and creation of products and work processes that are superior to what competitors can offer.

An important feature of an effective transformation process is how well the internal subsystems coordinate with each other.[58] Coordination is one of the most important OB concepts because organizations consist of people working together to achieve collective goals. As companies grow, they develop increasingly complex subsystems, which makes coordination more and more difficult. Complexity increases the risk that information gets lost, ideas and resources are hoarded, messages are misinterpreted, and rewards are distributed unfairly. Subsystems are interconnected, so small work practice changes in one subsystem may ripple through the organization and undermine the effectiveness of other subsystems. Consequently, organizations rely on

> ## An important feature of an effective transformation process is how well the internal subsystems coordinate with each other.

environment. For instance, businesses rely on marketing to increase demand for their products or services. Some firms gain exclusive rights to particular resources (e.g., sole provider of a popular brand) or restrict competitor access to valued resources. Still others lobby for legislation that strengthens their position in the marketplace or try to delay legislation that would disrupt their business activities.

- **Move to a more favorable environment:** Sometimes the current environment becomes so challenging that organizations cannot adapt or influence it enough to survive. For instance, the current environment might have extreme resource scarcity, too many competitors, too little demand for the firm's products, or onerous rules that make the transformation process too expensive. Under these circumstances, organizations often move to a more benevolent environment that can support their future. For example, Target closed its Canadian business after a few years because it underestimated the competition, stumbled on the transformation process (distribution and inventory challenges), and mismatched consumer expectations (location, pricing).[56]

Effective Transformation Process In addition to maintaining a good fit with the external environment, effective organizations have a transformation process that does well at converting inputs to outputs.[57] The most common indicator of effective internal subsystems is their *efficiency*. Efficient organizations produce more goods or services with less labor, materials, and

coordinating mechanisms to maintain an efficient, adaptive, and innovative transformation process (see Chapter 12).

Organizational Learning Perspective

The open systems perspective has traditionally focused on physical resources that enter the organization and are processed into physical goods (outputs). But whether their outputs are physical or cognitive, successful companies rely on knowledge as a key ingredient to success. This second perspective of organizational effectiveness, called **organizational learning**, states that the best organizations find ways to acquire, share, use, and store knowledge. Knowledge is a resource or asset, called **intellectual capital**, that exists in three forms: human capital, structural capital, and relationship capital.[59]

- **Human capital**: Human capital refers to the knowledge, skills, and abilities that employees carry around in their heads. It is a competitive advantage because employees are essential for the organization's survival and success, and their talents are difficult to find, to copy, and to replace with technology.[61] Human capital is also a huge risk for most organizations because it literally leaves the organization every day when employees go home![62]

- **Structural capital**: Even if every employee left the organization, some intellectual capital remains as structural capital. It includes the knowledge captured and retained in an organization's systems and structures, such as the documented work procedures, physical layout of production and office space, and the finished products (which can be reverse engineered to discover how they were made).[63]

- **Relationship capital**: Relationship capital is the value derived from an organization's relationships with customers, suppliers, and others who provide added mutual value for the organization. It includes the organization's goodwill, brand image, and combination of relationships that organizational members have with people outside the organization.[64]

An organization's intellectual capital develops and is maintained through the four organizational learning processes shown in Exhibit 1.6: acquiring, sharing, using, and storing knowledge.[65]

Acquiring Knowledge Acquiring knowledge refers to bringing in knowledge from the external environment as well as through discovery. It occurs daily when employees casually observe changes in the external environment as well as when they receive formal training from sources outside the organization. Knowledge acquisition also occurs through environmental

> ❝ An organization's ability to learn, and translate that learning into action rapidly, is the ultimate competitive advantage.[60] ❞
>
> —Jack Welch, former CEO of General Electric

Exhibit 1.6 Four Organizational Learning Processes

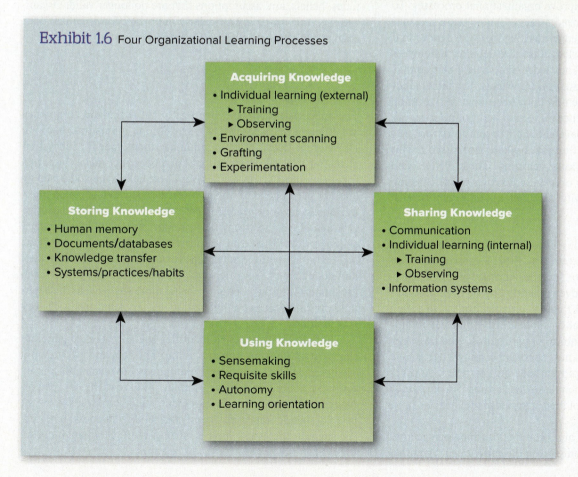

Acquiring Knowledge
- Individual learning (external)
  - ▸ Training
  - ▸ Observing
- Environment scanning
- Grafting
- Experimentation

Storing Knowledge
- Human memory
- Documents/databases
- Knowledge transfer
- Systems/practices/habits

Sharing Knowledge
- Communication
- Individual learning (internal)
  - ▸ Training
  - ▸ Observing
- Information systems

Using Knowledge
- Sensemaking
- Requisite skills
- Autonomy
- Learning orientation

scanning, such as actively monitoring consumer trends, proposed government legislation, and competitor activities. A third method is to hire skilled staff and buy complementary businesses (called *grafting*). Finally, knowledge acquisition occurs through experimentation—generating new ideas and products through creative discovery and testing.

Sharing Knowledge Sharing knowledge refers to distributing knowledge throughout the organization. This mainly occurs through formal and informal communication with coworkers, as well as through various forms of in-house learning (training, observation, etc.). Companies encourage informal communication through

Having a Hoot with Organizational Learning

Hootsuite relies on organizational learning practices to retain its leadership in social media technology. The leading provider of social media management and analytics acquires knowledge by actively hiring new employees and buying entire companies (grafting). "Maybe the only person we can find is already within a startup. We want to get that person over, so we have to buy the company," says Hootsuite CEO Ryan Holmes.

Hootsuite encourages experimentation through Hoot-Hackathons, intensive two-day events during which employees work together to build new products. The company encourages knowledge sharing through open-space offices and a supportive culture. It also holds a monthly "parliament"—a social gathering hosted by two departments. "The real point [of parliament] is that team members from different departments collaborate in the creative process, building ties that carry over to more serious stuff," says Holmes.[67]

©Chaay Tee/Shutterstock

their organizational structure, workspace design, corporate culture, and social activities.[66] Company intranets and digital information repositories also support knowledge sharing.

Using Knowledge Knowledge is a competitive advantage only when it is applied to improve organizational processes. To use knowledge, employees need a mental map (sense making) so they are aware the knowledge exists and know where to find it in the organization. Knowledge use also requires employees with sufficient prerequisite knowledge and skills. For example, financial analysts need foundation knowledge in mathematics and financial products to use new knowledge on asset valuation methods. Autonomy is another important condition for knowledge use; employees must have enough freedom to try out new ideas. Knowledge use also flourishes where workplace norms strongly support organizational learning. These beliefs and norms represent a **learning orientation**, which we discuss further on the topics of creativity (Chapter 6) and organizational culture (Chapter 13).[68]

Storing Knowledge Storing knowledge is the process of retaining knowledge for later retrieval. Stored knowledge, often called *organizational memory*, includes knowledge that employees recall as well as knowledge embedded in the organization's systems and structures.[69] Effective organizations also retain knowledge in human capital by motivating employees to stay with the company. Furthermore, organizations encourage employees to share what they know so valuable knowledge is held by coworkers when an employee does quit or retire. Another strategy is to actively document knowledge when it is created by debriefing teams on details of their knowledge of clients or product development.

One last point about the organizational learning perspective: effective organizations not only learn; they also unlearn routines and patterns of behavior that are no longer appropriate.[70] Unlearning removes knowledge that no longer adds value and, in fact, may undermine the organization's effectiveness. Some forms of unlearning involve replacing dysfunctional policies, procedures, and routines. Other forms of unlearning erase attitudes, beliefs, and assumptions that are no longer valid. Organizational unlearning is particularly important for organizational change, which we discuss in Chapter 14.

High-Performance Work Practices Perspective

The open systems perspective states that successful companies are efficient and adaptive at transforming inputs into outputs. However, it does not offer guidance about specific subsystem characteristics or organizational practices that make the transformation process more effective. These details are addressed by another perspective of organizational effectiveness, called **high-performance work practices (HPWPs)**. The HPWP perspective is founded on the belief that human capital—the knowledge, skills, and abilities that employees possess—is an important source of competitive advantage for organizations.[71] Motivated and skilled employees offer competitive advantage by transforming inputs to outputs better, by being more sensitive to the external environment, and by having better relations with key stakeholders.

The HPWP perspective identifies specific ways to generate the most value from human capital. The four most frequently identified HPWP practices are employee involvement, job autonomy, competency development, and rewards for performance and competency development.[72] Each of these four work practices alone improves organizational effectiveness, but studies suggest that they have a stronger effect when bundled together.[73]

The four most frequently identified HPWP practices are employee involvement, job autonomy, competency development, and rewards for performance and competency development.
©OPOLJA/Shutterstock

The first two factors—involving employees in decision making and giving them more autonomy over their work activities—strengthen employee motivation as well as improve decisions, organizational responsiveness, and commitment to change. In high-performance workplaces, employee involvement and job autonomy often take the form of self-directed teams (see Chapter 7). The third factor, employee competency development, refers to recruiting, selecting, and training so employees are equipped with the relevant knowledge and skills. The fourth high-performance work practice is linking performance and skill development to various financial and nonfinancial rewards valued by employees.

High-performance work practices improve an organization's effectiveness in three ways.[75] First, as we mentioned earlier,

High Performance Work Practices in Selected OECD and Partner Countries[74]

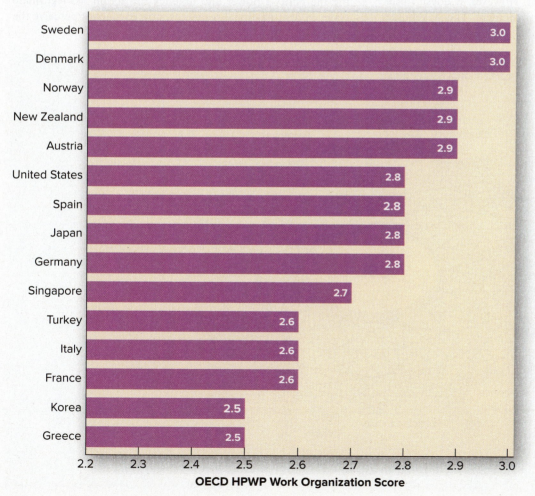

Country	Score
Sweden	3.0
Denmark	3.0
Norway	2.9
New Zealand	2.9
Austria	2.9
United States	2.8
Spain	2.8
Japan	2.8
Germany	2.8
Singapore	2.7
Turkey	2.6
Italy	2.6
France	2.6
Korea	2.5
Greece	2.5

OECD HPWP Work Organization Score

Average composite score on high-performance work practices reported by employees in selected countries. Higher scores indicate higher HPWP practices in that country. This scale represents "work organization" HPWP practices, which exclude rewards but include work flexibility/autonomy, planning one's own work, cooperating and sharing information with coworkers, and training others. Data were collected from more than 215,000 adults in OECD and partner countries with a minimum 4,000 respondents per country. This chart shows a selection of the 34 countries measured in the study.

stakeholders

individuals, groups, and other entities that affect, or are affected by, the organization's objectives and actions

these activities develop employee skills and knowledge (human capital), which directly improve individual behavior and performance. Second, companies with superior human capital tend to adapt better to rapidly changing environments. This adaptability occurs because employees are better at performing diverse tasks in unfamiliar situations when they are highly skilled and have more freedom to perform their work. A third explanation is that HPWP practices strengthen employee motivation and positive attitudes toward the employer. HPWPs represent the company's investment in its workforce, which motivates employees to reciprocate through greater effort in their jobs and assistance to coworkers.

The HPWP perspective is still developing, but it already reveals important information about specific organizational practices that improve an organization's effectiveness through its employees. Still, this perspective offers an incomplete picture of organizational effectiveness. The remaining gaps are filled by the stakeholder perspective of organizational effectiveness.

Stakeholder Perspective

The open systems perspective says that effective organizations adapt to the external environment. However, it doesn't offer much detail about the external environment. The stakeholder perspective offers more specific information and guidance by focusing on the organization's relationships with stakeholders. Stakeholders include organizations, groups, and other entities that affect, or are affected by, the company's objectives and actions.[76] The stakeholder perspective personalizes the open systems perspective; it identifies specific social entities in the external environment as well as employees and others within the organization (the internal environment). This perspective also recognizes that stakeholder relations are dynamic; they can be negotiated and influenced, not just taken as a fixed condition. In general, the stakeholder perspective states that organizations are more effective when they understand, manage, and satisfy stakeholder needs and expectations.[77]

There are many types of stakeholders, and they are continuously evolving. Consider the key stakeholders identified by CSL Limited in Exhibit 1.7. The global leader in blood-related products and vaccines pays attention to more than a dozen groups, and likely others that aren't included in this diagram. Understanding, managing, and satisfying the interests of stakeholders is challenging because they have conflicting interests and organizations lack sufficient resources to satisfy everyone. Therefore, organizational leaders need to decide how much priority to give to each group.[78] Research has identified several factors that influence the prioritization of stakeholders, including the entity's power and urgency for action, its legitimate claim to organizational resources, how executives perceive the

Exhibit 1.7 CSL Limited's Key Organizational Stakeholders

Source: CSL Limited

organization's environment, the organization's culture, and the personal values of the corporate board and CEO.

Values, Ethics, and Corporate Social Responsibility

The stakeholder perspective provides valuable details about features of the external environment that are missing from the open systems perspective. Equally important, the stakeholder perspective incorporates values, ethics, and corporate social responsibility into the organizational effectiveness equation. As mentioned, personal values influence how corporate boards and CEOs allocate organizational resources to stakeholders.[79] **Values** are relatively stable, evaluative beliefs that guide our preferences for outcomes or courses of action in a variety of situations.[80] Values help us know what is right or wrong, or good or bad, in the world. Chapter 2 explains how values anchor our thoughts and to some extent motivate our actions.

Although values exist within individuals, groups of people often hold similar values, so we tend to ascribe these *shared values* to the team, department, organization, profession, or entire society. For example, Chapter 13 discusses the importance and dynamics of organizational culture, which includes shared values across the company. Many firms strive to become values-driven organizations, whereby employee decisions and behavior are guided mainly by the collective values identified as critical to the organization's success.[81]

By focusing on values, the stakeholder perspective also highlights the importance of ethics and corporate social responsibility. In fact, the stakeholder perspective emerged out of earlier writing on those two topics. **Ethics** refers to the study of moral principles or values that determine whether actions are right or wrong and outcomes are good or bad. We rely on our ethical values to determine "the right thing to do." Ethical behavior is driven by the moral principles we use to make decisions. These moral principles represent fundamental values. One recent survey of 7,700 employed Millennials in 29 countries reported that 87 percent believe "the success of a business should be measured in terms of more than just its financial performance." However, only 58 percent of them believe that businesses "behave in an ethical manner."[82] Chapter 2 discusses the main influences on ethical decisions and behavior in the workplace.

Corporate social responsibility (CSR) consists of organizational activities intended to benefit society and the environment beyond the firm's immediate financial interests or legal obligations.[83] It is the view that companies have a contract with society, in which they must serve stakeholders beyond stockholders and customers. In some situations, the interests of the firm's stockholders should be secondary to those of other stakeholders.[84] As part of CSR, many companies have adopted the triple-bottom-line philosophy: They try to support or "earn positive returns" in the economic, social, and environmental spheres of sustainability. Firms that adopt the triple bottom line aim to survive and be profitable in the marketplace (economic), but they also intend to maintain or improve conditions for society (social) as well as the physical environment.[85]

Not everyone agrees that organizations need to cater to a wide variety of stakeholders. Many years ago, economist Milton Friedman pronounced that "there is one and only one social responsibility of business—to use its resources and engage in activities designed to increase its profits."[87] Friedman is highly respected for developing economic

> "Corporate social responsibility is the view that companies have a contract with society, in which they must serve stakeholders beyond stockholders and customers."

---

values relatively stable, evaluative beliefs that guide a person's preferences for outcomes or courses of action in a variety of situations

ethics the study of moral principles or values that determine whether actions are right or wrong and outcomes are good or bad

corporate social responsibility (CSR) organizational activities intended to benefit society and the environment beyond the firm's immediate financial interests or legal obligations

---

High Expectations for Corporate Social Responsibility[86]

89% of more than 2,000 executives surveyed say companies have a moral responsibility to address societal and environmental issues that go beyond legal requirements.

17% of 1,200 American consumers surveyed say they would not consider working for a company they believe is not socially responsible, even if they were well-qualified and the job pays well.
(photo: ©CostinT/Getty Images)

64% of 1,409 CEOs surveyed across 83 countries say that corporate social responsibility is core to their business (not just a stand-alone program).

80% of 18,150 adults surveyed globally say it is somewhat or very important for their own employer to be responsible to society and the environment.

theory, but few writers take this extreme view today. Almost all *Fortune* 500 companies publish sustainability reports, and the view among most executives is that corporate social responsibility is critically important to being competitive in today's marketplace. The emerging evidence is that companies with a positive CSR reputation tend to have better financial performance, more loyal employees (stronger organizational identification), and better relations with customers, job applicants, and other stakeholders.[88]

Connecting the Dots: An Integrative Model of Organizational Behavior

Open systems, organizational learning, high-performance work practices, and stakeholders represent the four perspectives of organizational effectiveness. Organizational effectiveness is the ultimate dependent variable in organizational behavior, so it is directly or indirectly predicted by all other OB variables. The

relationship between organizational effectiveness and other OB variables is shown in Exhibit 1.8. This diagram is an integrative road map for the field of organizational behavior, and for the structure of this book. It is a meta-model of the various OB topics and concepts, each of which has its own explanatory models. For instance, you will learn about employee motivation theories and practices in Chapter 5 and leadership theories and skills in Chapter 11. Exhibit 1.8 gives you a bird's-eye view of the book and its various topics, to see how they fit together.

As Exhibit 1.8 illustrates, individual inputs and processes influence individual outcomes, which in turn have a direct effect on the organization's effectiveness. For example, how well organizations transform inputs to outputs and satisfy key stakeholders is dependent on how well employees perform their jobs and make logical and creative decisions. Individual inputs, processes, and outcomes are identified in the two left-side boxes of our integrating OB model and are the center of attention in Part 2 of this book. After introducing a model of individual behavior and results, we will learn about personality and values—two of the most important individual characteristics—and later examine various individual processes, such as self-concept, perceptions, emotions, attitudes, motivation, and self-leadership.

Part 3 of this book directs our attention to team and interpersonal inputs, processes, and outcomes. These topics are found in the two boxes on the right side of Exhibit 1.8. The chapter on team dynamics (Chapter 7) offers an integrative model for that specific topic, which shows how team inputs (i.e., team composition, size, and other team characteristics) influence team processes (team development, cohesion, and others), which then affect team performance and other outcomes. Later chapters in Part 3 examine specific interpersonal and team processes listed in Exhibit 1.8, including communication, power and influence, conflict, and leadership.

Exhibit 1.8 illustrates that team processes and outcomes affect individual processes and outcomes. As an example, employee personal well-being is partly affected by the mutual support received from team members and other coworkers. The opposite is also true; individual processes affect team and interpersonal dynamics in organizations.

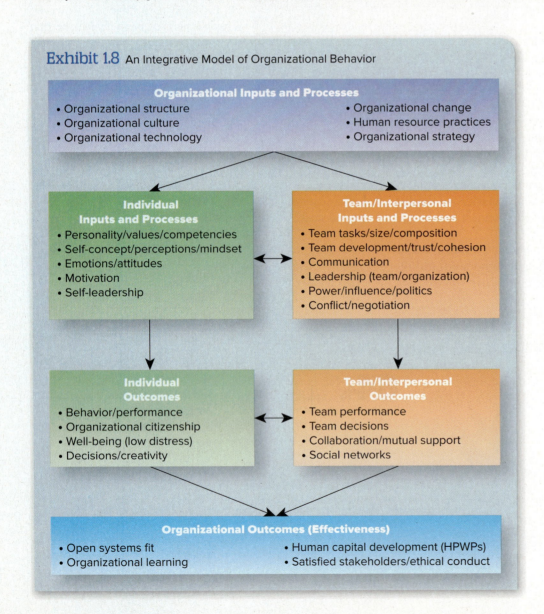

Exhibit 1.8 An Integrative Model of Organizational Behavior

Organizational Inputs and Processes
- Organizational structure
- Organizational culture
- Organizational technology
- Organizational change
- Human resource practices
- Organizational strategy

Individual Inputs and Processes
- Personality/values/competencies
- Self-concept/perceptions/mindset
- Emotions/attitudes
- Motivation
- Self-leadership

Team/Interpersonal Inputs and Processes
- Team tasks/size/composition
- Team development/trust/cohesion
- Communication
- Leadership (team/organization)
- Power/influence/politics
- Conflict/negotiation

Individual Outcomes
- Behavior/performance
- Organizational citizenship
- Well-being (low distress)
- Decisions/creativity

Team/Interpersonal Outcomes
- Team performance
- Team decisions
- Collaboration/mutual support
- Social networks

Organizational Outcomes (Effectiveness)
- Open systems fit
- Organizational learning
- Human capital development (HPWPs)
- Satisfied stakeholders/ethical conduct

For instance, we will learn that self-concept among individual team members influences the team's cohesion.

The top area of Exhibit 1.8 highlights the macro-level influence of organizational inputs and processes on both teams and individuals. These organizational-level variables are mainly discussed in Part 4, including organizational structure, organizational culture, and organizational change. However, we also will refer to human resource practices, information systems, and additional organizational-level variables throughout this book where they have a known effect on individual, interpersonal, and team dynamics.

THE JOURNEY BEGINS

This chapter gives you some background about the field of organizational behavior. But it's only the beginning of our journey. Throughout this book, we will challenge you to learn new ways of thinking about how people work in and around organizations. We begin this process in Chapter 2 by presenting a basic model of individual behavior, then introducing over the next few chapters various stable and mercurial characteristics of individuals that relate to elements of the individual behavior model. Next, this book moves to the team level of analysis. We examine a model of team effectiveness and specific features of high-performance teams. We also look at decision making and creativity, communication, power and influence, conflict, and leadership. Finally, we shift our focus to the organizational level of analysis, where the topics of organizational structure, organizational culture, and organizational change are examined in detail.

Study Checklist

Connect® Management is available for *M Organizational Behavior.* Additional resources include:

✓ Interactive Applications:
  - **Case Analysis:** Apply concepts within the context of a real-world situation.
  - **Drag and Drop:** Work through an interactive example to test your knowledge of the concepts.
  - **Video Case:** See management in action through interactive videos.

✓ **SmartBook**™—SmartBook is the first and only adaptive reading experience available today. Distinguishing what you know from what you don't, and honing in on concepts you are most likely to forget, SmartBook personalizes content for you in a continuously adapting reading experience. Reading is no longer a passive and linear experience, but an engaging and dynamic one where you are more likely to master and retain important concepts and go to class better prepared.

©Natthawat Jamnapa/123RF

Notes

1. F. Manjoo and J. Caplan, "Apple Nation," *Fast Company*, no. 147 (2010): 69–76; R. L. Brandt, *One Click: Jeff Bezos and the Rise of Amazon.com* (New York: Portfolio/Penguin, 2011); "World's Most Admired Companies," *Fortune* (Time, Inc., February 16, 2017), http://beta.fortune.com/worlds-most-admired-companies/ (accessed February 27, 2017).

2. "World's Most Admired Companies," *Fortune* (Time, Inc., February 16, 2017), http://fortune.com/worlds-most-admired-companies/ (accessed June 18, 2017).

3. M. Warner, "Organizational Behavior Revisited," *Human Relations* 47 (1994): 1151–66; R. Westwood and S. Clegg, "The Discourse of Organization Studies: Dissensus, Politics, and Paradigms," in *Debating Organization: Point-Counterpoint in Organization Studies*, ed. R. Westwood and S. Clegg (Malden, MA: Wiley-Blackwell, 2003), 1–42.

4. R. N. Stern and S. R. Barley, "Organizations as Social Systems: Organization Theory's Neglected Mandate," *Administrative Science Quarterly* 41 (1996): 146–62; D. Katz and R. L. Kahn, *The Social Psychology of Organizations* (New York: Wiley, 1966), chap. 2.

5. L. E. Greiner, "A Recent History of Organizational Behavior," in *Organizational Behavior*, ed. S. Kerr (Columbus, OH: Grid, 1979), 3–14; J. Micklethwait and A. Wooldridge, *The Company: A Short History of a Revolutionary Idea* (New York: Random House, 2003).

6. T. Lawson, "The Nature of the Firm and Peculiarities of the Corporation," *Cambridge Journal of Economics* 39, no. 1 (2015): 1–32.

7. B. Schlender, "The Three Faces of Steve," *Fortune* (November 9, 1998): 96–101.

8. "A Field Is Born," *Harvard Business Review* 86, no. 7/8 (2008): 164; P. R. Lawrence, "The Key Job Design Problem Is Still Taylorism," *Journal of Organizational Behavior* 31, no. 2/3 (2010): 412–21; L. W. Porter and B. Schneider, "What Was, What Is, and What May Be in OP/OB," *Annual Review of Organizational Psychology and Organizational Behavior* 1, no. 1 (2014): 1–21.

9. T. Takala, "Plato on Leadership," *Journal of Business Ethics* 17 (1998): 785–98; J. A. Fernandez, "The Gentleman's Code of Confucius: Leadership by Values," *Organizational Dynamics* 33, no. 1 (2004): 21–31; A. M. Blake and J. L. Moseley, "Frederick Winslow Taylor: One Hundred Years of Managerial Insight," *International Journal of Management* 28, no. 4 (2011): 346–53; J. W. Stutje, ed., *Charismatic Leadership and Social Movements: The Revolutionary Power of Ordinary Men and Women,* International Studies in Social History (New York: Berghahn Books, 2012).

10. C. D. Wrege, "Solving Mayo's Mystery: The First Complete Account of the Origin of the Hawthorne Studies—the Forgotten Contributions of C. E. Snow and H. Hibarger" (paper presented at the Academy of Management Proceedings, August 1976), 12–16; P. Graham, ed., *Mary Parker Follett: Prophet of Management* (Boston: Harvard Business School Press, 1995); J. H. Smith, "The Enduring Legacy of Elton Mayo," *Human Relations* 51, no. 3 (1998): 221–49; E. O'Connor, "Minding the Workers: The Meaning of 'Human' and 'Human Relations' in Elton Mayo," *Organization* 6, no. 2 (1999): 223–46.

11. The extent to which OB influences career success depends on course pedagogy as well as the practical value of the OB concepts covered in the course. In fact, OB scholars have an ongoing debate about the practical relevance of OB research. See, for example: J. P. Walsh et al., "On the Relationship between Research and Practice: Debate and Reflections," *Journal of Management Inquiry* 16, no. 2 (2007): 128–54; R. Gulati, "Tent Poles, Tribalism, and Boundary Spanning: The Rigor-Relevance Debate in Management Research," *Academy of Management Journal* 50, no. 4 (2007): 775–82; J. Pearce and L. Huang, "The Decreasing Value of Our Research to Management Education," *Academy of Management Learning & Education* 11, no. 2 (2012): 247–62; J. M. Bartunek and S. L. Rynes, "Academics and Practitioners Are Alike and Unlike: The Paradoxes of Academic–Practitioner Relationships," *Journal of Management* 40, no. 5 (2014): 1181–201; N. Butler, H. Delaney, and S. Spoelstra, "Problematizing 'Relevance' in the Business School: The Case of Leadership Studies," *British Journal of Management* 26, no. 4 (2015): 731–44.

12. P. R. Lawrence and N. Nohria, *Driven: How Human Nature Shapes Our Choices* (San Francisco: Jossey-Bass, 2002).

13. S. L. Rynes et al., "Behavioral Coursework in Business Education: Growing Evidence of a Legitimacy Crisis," *Academy of Management Learning & Education* 2, no. 3 (2003): 269–83; R. P. Singh and A. G. Schick, "Organizational Behavior: Where Does It Fit in Today's Management Curriculum?," *Journal of Education for Business* 82, no. 6 (2007): 349.

14. R. L. Priem and J. Rosenstein, "Is Organization Theory Obvious to Practitioners? A Test of One Established Theory," *Organization Science* 11, no. 5 (2000): 509–24. MBA students in the study performed much better than the other two groups.

15. R. S. Rubin and E. C. Dierdorff, "How Relevant Is the MBA? Assessing the Alignment of Required Curricula and Required Managerial Competencies," *Academy of Management Learning & Education* 8, no. 2 (2009): 208–24; Y. Baruch and O. Lavi-Steiner, "The Career Impact of Management Education from an Average-Ranked University: Human Capital Perspective," *Career Development International* 20, no. 3 (2015): 218–37.

16. M. S. Myers, *Every Employee a Manager* (New York: McGraw-Hill, 1970).

17. M. A. West et al., "Reducing Patient Mortality in Hospitals: The Role of Human Resource Management," *Journal of Organizational Behavior* 27, no. 7 (2006): 983–1002; A. Edmans, "The Link between Job Satisfaction and Firm Value, with Implications for Corporate Social Responsibility," *Academy of Management Perspectives* 26, no. 4 (2012): 1–19; A. M. Baluch, T. O. Salge, and E. P. Piening, "Untangling the Relationship between HRM and Hospital Performance: The Mediating Role of Attitudinal and Behavioural HR Outcomes," *The International Journal of Human Resource Management* 24, no. 16 (2013): 3038–61; I. S. Fulmer and R. E. Ployhart, "'Our Most Important Asset': A Multidisciplinary/Multilevel Review of Human Capital Valuation for Research and Practice," *Journal of Management* 40, no. 1 (2014): 161–92; D. C. Hambrick and T. J. Quigley, "Toward More Accurate Contextualization of the CEO Effect on Firm Performance," *Strategic Management Journal* 35, no. 4 (2014): 473–91.

18. J. T. Comeault and D. Wheeler, "Human Capital–Based Investment Criteria for Total Shareholder Returns," in *Pensions at Work: Socially Responsible Investment of Union-Based Pension Funds*, ed. J. Quarter, I. Carmichael, and S. Ryan (Toronto: University of Toronto Press, 2008); R. Barker et al., "Can Company-Fund Manager Meetings Convey Informational Benefits? Exploring the Rationalisation of Equity Investment Decision Making by UK Fund Managers," *Accounting, Organizations and Society* 37, no. 4 (2012): 207–22; S. Abhayawansa, M. Aleksanyan, and J. Bahtsevanoglou, "The Use of Intellectual Capital Information by Sell-Side Analysts in Company Valuation," *Accounting and Business Research* 45, no. 3 (2015): 279–306.

19. M. L. Tushman and P. Anderson, "Technological Discontinuities and Organizational Environments," *Administrative Science Quarterly* 31, no. 3 (1986): 439–65; I. McNeil, ed., *An Encyclopedia of the History of Technology* (New York: Routledge, 1990); H. C. Lucas, *The Search for Survival: Lessons from Disruptive Technologies* (Westport, CT: Praeger, 2012); E. Brynjolfsson and A. McAfee, *The Second Machine Age: Work, Progress, and Prosperity in a Time of Brilliant Technologies* (New York: Norton, 2014); M. A. Schilling, "Technology Shocks, Technological Collaboration, and Innovation Outcomes," *Organization Science* 26, no. 3 (2015): 668–86.

20. W. R. Scott, "Comparing Organizations: Empirical and Theoretical Issues," in *Studying Differences between Organizations: Comparative Approaches to Organizational Research, Research in the Sociology of Organizations*, vol. 26, ed. B. G. King et al. (Bingley, UK: Emerald Group Publishing Limited, 2009), 45–62; S. J. Miles and W. G. Mangold, "Employee Voice: Untapped Resource or Social Media Time Bomb?," *Business Horizons* 57, no. 3 (2014): 401–11; S. Brooks, "Does Personal Social Media Usage Affect Efficiency and Well-Being?," *Computers in Human Behavior* 46 (2015): 26–37; J. C. Pillet and K. D. A. Carillo, "Email-Free Collaboration: An Exploratory Study on the Formation of New Work Habits among Knowledge Workers," *International Journal of Information Management* 36, no. 1 (2016): 113–25.

21. Gagen MacDonald, *Internal Social Media–A Business Driver* (Chicago: Gagen MacDonald, 2012); Microsoft, *Microsoft Survey on Enterprise Social Use and Perceptions* (Seattle, WA: Microsoft, 2013); Spherion, *Emerging Workforce Study* (Atlanta: Spherion, 2015); CareerBuilder, "Number of Employers Using Social Media to Screen Candidates Has Increased 500 Percent over the Last Decade," news release (Chicago: CareerBuilder, April 28, 2016).

22. Y. H. Ferguson and R. W. Mansbach, *Globalization: The Return of Borders to a Borderless World* (Abingdon, UK: Routledge, 2012). The early history of globalization is discussed in K. Moore and D. C. Lewis, *The Origins of Globalization* (Hoboken, NJ: Taylor and Francis, 2009). Five views of globalization and the effects of technology on globalization are discussed in R. Kwon, "What Factors Matter for Trade at the Global Level? Testing Five Approaches to Globalization, 1820–2007," *International Journal of Comparative Sociology* 54, no. 5/6 (2013): 391–419.

23. The ongoing debate regarding the advantages and disadvantages of globalization is discussed in M. F. Guillén, "Is Globalization Civilizing, Destructive or Feeble? A Critique of Five Key Debates in the Social Science Literature," *Annual Review of Sociology* 27 (2001): 235–60; J. Bhagwati, *In Defense of Globalization* (New York: Oxford University Press, 2004); M. Wolf, *Why Globalization Works* (New Haven, CT: Yale University Press, 2004).

24. E. Greenblatt, "Work/Life Balance: Wisdom or Whining," *Organizational Dynamics* 31, no. 2 (2002): 177–93; W. G. Bennis and R. J. Thomas, *Geeks and Geezers* (Boston: Harvard Business School Press, 2002), 74–79.

25. T. L. Johns, "The Third Wave of Virtual Work," *Harvard Business Review* 91, no. 1 (2013): 66–73.

26. J. M. Jones, "In U.S., Telecommuting for Work Climbs to 37%," news release (Washington, DC: Gallup, August 19, 2015); U.S. Bureau of Labor Statistics, "American Time Use Survey—2014 Results," news release (Washington, DC: U.S. Department of Labor, June 24, 2015).

27. E. J. Hill et al., "Workplace Flexibility, Work Hours, and Work–Life Conflict: Finding an Extra Day or Two," *Journal of Family Psychology* 24, no. 3 (2010): 349–58; M. C. Noonan and J. L. Glass, "The Hard Truth about Telecommuting," *Monthly Labor Review* 135, no. 6 (2012): 38–45; B. H. Martin and R. MacDonnell, "Is Telework Effective for Organizations?," *Management Research Review* 35, no. 7 (2012): 602–16; T. D. Allen, T. D. Golden, and K. M. Shockley, "How Effective Is Telecommuting? Assessing the Status of Our Scientific Findings," *Psychological Science in the Public Interest* 16, no. 2 (2015): 40–68; N. Bloom et al., "Does Working from Home Work? Evidence from a Chinese Experiment," *The Quarterly Journal of Economics* 130, no. 1 (2015): 165–218; R. S. Gajendran, D. A. Harrison, and K. Delaney-Klinger, "Are Telecommuters Remotely Good Citizens? Unpacking Telecommuting's Effects on Performance Via I-Deals and Job Resources," *Personnel Psychology* 68, no. 2 (2015): 353–93.

28. D. Meinert, "Make Telecommuting Pay Off," *HR Magazine*, June 2011, 33; M. McQuigge, "A Panacea for Some, Working from Home Still a Tough Sell for Some Employers," *Canadian Press* (Toronto), June 26, 2013; Aetna, "Teleworking on the Rise, Saving Costs and the Environment," May 2015, https://news.aetna.com/2015/05/teleworking-rise-saving-costs-environment/ (accessed March 4, 2016).

29. C. A. Bartel, A. Wrzesniewski, and B. M. Wiesenfeld, "Knowing Where You Stand: Physical Isolation, Perceived Respect, and Organizational Identification among Virtual Employees," *Organization Science* 23, no. 3 (2011): 743–57; E. E. Kossek, R. J. Thompson, and B. A. Lautsch, "Balanced Workplace Flexibility: Avoiding the Traps," *California Management Review* 57, no. 4 (2015): 5–25.

30. T. A. O'Neill, L. A. Hambley, and G. S. Chatellier, "Cyberslacking, Engagement, and Personality in Distributed Work Environments," *Computers in Human Behavior* 40 (2014): 152–60; N. W. Van Yperen, E. F. Rietzschel, and K. M. M. De Jonge, "Blended Working: For Whom It May (Not) Work," *PLoS ONE* 9, no. 7 (2014): e102921; D. Karis, D. Wildman, and A. Mané, "Improving Remote Collaboration with Video Conferencing and Video Portals," *Human–Computer Interaction* 31, no. 1 (2016): 1–58.

31. D. A. Harrison et al., "Time, Teams, and Task Performance: Changing Effects of Surface- and Deep-Level Diversity on Group Functioning," *Academy of Management Journal* 45, no. 5 (2002): 1029–46; W. J. Casper, J. H. Wayne, and J. G. Manegold, "Who Will We Recruit? Targeting Deep- and Surface-Level Diversity with Human Resource Policy Advertising," *Human Resource Management* 52, no. 3 (2013): 311–32; J. E. Mathieu et al., "A Review and Integration of Team Composition Models: Moving toward a Dynamic and Temporal Framework," *Journal of Management* 40, no. 1 (2014): 130–60.

32. J. M. Ortman and C. E. Guarneri, *United States Population Projections: 2000 to 2050* (Washington, DC: U.S. Census Bureau, December 11, 2009); D'V. Cohn, *Future Immigration Will Change the Face of America by 2065*, (Washington, DC: Pew Research Center, October 5, 2015); U.S. Census Bureau, "Quickfacts" (Washington, DC: U.S. Census Bureau, 2016), https://www.census.gov/quickfacts (accessed June 18, 2017).

33. J. Qin, N. Muenjohn, and P. Chhetri, "A Review of Diversity Conceptualizations: Variety, Trends, and a Framework," *Human Resource Development Review* 13, no. 2 (2014): 133–57.

34. M. H. Davis, S. Capobianco, and L. A. Kraus, "Gender Differences in Responding to Conflict in the Workplace: Evidence from a Large Sample of Working Adults," *Sex Roles* 63, no. 7 (2010): 500–14; J. L. Locke, *Duels and Duets: Why Men and Women Talk So Differently* (New York: Cambridge University Press, 2011); R. Friesdorf, P. Conway, and B. Gawronski, "Gender Differences in Responses to Moral Dilemmas: A Process Dissociation Analysis," *Personality and Social Psychology Bulletin* 41, no. 5 (2015): 696–713.

35. E. Bolland and C. Lopes, *Generations and Work* (New York: Palgrave Macmillan, 2014); P. Taylor, *The Next America: Boomers, Millennials, and the Looming Generational Showdown* (New York: PublicAffairs, 2014); J. Bristow, *Baby Boomers and Generational Conflict* (London: Palgrave Macmillan, 2015).

36. U.S. Bureau of Labor Statistics, "Labor Force Statistics from the Current Population Survey," *Division of Labor Force Statistics* (Washington, D.C.: U.S. Bureau of Labor Statistics, February 8, 2016), https://www.bls.gov/cps/cpsaat03.htm (accessed June 18, 2017).

37. E. Parry and P. Urwin, "Generational Differences in Work Values: A Review of Theory and Evidence," *International Journal of Management Reviews* 13 (2011): 79–96; D. T. A. M. Kooij et al., "Age and Work-Related Motives: Results of a Meta-Analysis," *Journal of Organizational Behavior* 32, no. 2 (2011): 197–225.

38. M.-E. Roberge and R. van Dick, "Recognizing the Benefits of Diversity: When and How Does Diversity Increase Group Performance?," *Human Resource Management Review* 20, no. 4 (2010): 295–308; M. Singal, "The Business Case for Diversity Management in the Hospitality Industry," *International Journal of Hospitality Management* 40 (2014): 10–19; C.-M. Lu et al., "Effect of Diversity on Human Resource Management and Organizational Performance," *Journal of Business Research* 68, no. 4 (2015): 857–61; Y. Zhang and M.-Y. Huai, "Diverse Work Groups and Employee Performance: The Role of Communication Ties," *Small Group Research* 47, no. 1 (2016): 28–57.

39. D. Porras, D. Psihountas, and M. Griswold, "The Long-Term Performance of Diverse Firms," *International Journal of Diversity* 6, no. 1 (2006): 25–34; R. A. Weigand, "Organizational Diversity, Profits and Returns in U.S. Firms," *Problems & Perspectives in Management* 5, no. 3 (2007): 69–83.

40. T. Kochan et al., "The Effects of Diversity on Business Performance: Report of the Diversity Research Network," *Human Resource Management* 42 (2003): 3–21; S. T. Bell et al., "Getting Specific about Demographic Diversity Variable and Team Performance Relationships: A Meta-Analysis," *Journal of Management* 37, no. 3 (2011): 709–43; S. M. B. Thatcher and P. C. Patel, "Group Faultlines: A Review, Integration, and Guide to Future Research," *Journal of Management* 38, no. 4 (2012): 969–1009; C. Ozgen et al., "Does Cultural Diversity of Migrant Employees Affect Innovation?," *International Migration Review* 48 (2014): S377–S416.

41. *Mastercard Diversity and Inclusion* (Purchase, NY: MasterCard, July 24, 2014); "Top 10 Employers Have More Women, Minority Leaders," *Diversity Inc.*, April 19, 2016; "Diversity in the Workplace," *About MasterCard,* 2016, www.diversityinc.com/mastercard-worldwide-2015/ (accessed July 12, 2016).

42. Most of these anchors are mentioned in J. D. Thompson, "On Building an Administrative Science," *Administrative Science Quarterly* 1, no. 1 (1956): 102–11.

43. This anchor has a colorful history dating back to critiques of business schools in the 1950s. Soon after, systematic research became a mantra for many respected scholars. See, for example, J. D. Thompson, "On Building an Administrative Science," *Administrative Science Quarterly* 1, no. 1 (1956): 102–11.

44. J. Pfeffer and R. I. Sutton, *Hard Facts, Dangerous Half-Truths, and Total Nonsense* (Boston: Harvard Business School Press, 2006); D. M. Rousseau and S. McCarthy, "Educating Managers from an Evidence-Based Perspective," *Academy of Management Learning & Education* 6, no. 1 (2007): 84–101; R. B. Briner and D. M. Rousseau, "Evidence-Based I-O Psychology: Not There Yet," *Industrial and Organizational Psychology* 4, no. 1 (2011): 3–22.

45. J. Pfeffer and R. I. Sutton, *Hard Facts, Dangerous Half-Truths, and Total Nonsense* (Boston: Harvard Business School Press, 2006).

46. M. N. Zald, "More Fragmentation? Unfinished Business in Linking the Social Sciences and the Humanities," *Administrative Science Quarterly* 41 (1996): 251–61; C. Heath and S. B. Sitkin, "Big-B versus Big-O: What Is Organizational About Organizational Behavior?," *Journal of Organizational Behavior* 22 (2001): 43–58; C. Oswick, P. Fleming, and G. Hanlon, "From Borrowing to Blending: Rethinking the Processes of Organizational Theory Building," *Academy of Management Review* 36, no. 2 (2011): 318–37.

47. C. M. Christensen and M. E. Raynor, "Why Hard-Nosed Executives Should Care about Management Theory," *Harvard Business Review* (2003): 66–74; C. E. J. Härtel and J. M. O'Connor, "Contextualizing Research: Putting Context Back into Organizational Behavior Research," *Journal of Management & Organization* 20, no. 4 (2014): 417–22. For an excellent critique of the "one best way" approach in early management scholarship, see P. F. Drucker, "Management's New Paradigms," *Forbes* (1998): 152–77.

48. H. L. Tosi and J. W. Slocum Jr., "Contingency Theory: Some Suggested Directions," *Journal of Management* 10 (1984): 9–26.

49. D. M. Rousseau and R. J. House, "Meso Organizational Behavior: Avoiding Three Fundamental Biases," in *Trends in Organizational Behavior*, ed. C. L. Cooper and D. M. Rousseau (Chichester, UK: Wiley, 1994), 13–30.

50. S. A. Mohrman, C. B. Gibson, and A. M. Mohrman Jr., "Doing Research That Is Useful to Practice: A Model and Empirical Exploration," *Academy of Management Journal* 44 (2001): 357–75; J. P. Walsh et al., "On the Relationship between Research and Practice," *Journal of Management Inquiry* 16, no. 2 (June 2007): 128–54. Similarly, in 1961, Harvard business professor Fritz Roethlisberger proposed that the field of OB is concerned with human behavior "from the points of view of both (a) its determination . . . and (b) its improvement." See P. B. Vaill, "F. J. Roethlisberger and the Elusive Phenomena of Organizational Behavior," *Journal of Management Education* 31, no. 3 (2007): 321–38.

51. R. H. Hall, "Effectiveness Theory and Organizational Effectiveness," *Journal of Applied Behavioral Science* 16, no. 4 (1980): 536–45; K. Cameron, "Organizational Effectiveness: Its Demise and Re-Emergence through Positive Organizational Scholarship," in *Great Minds in Management*, ed. K. G. Smith and M. A. Hitt (New York: Oxford University Press, 2005), 304–30.

52. A. A. Amirkhanyan, H. J. Kim, and K. T. Lambright, "The Performance Puzzle: Understanding the Factors Influencing Alternative Dimensions and Views of Performance," *Journal of Public Administration Research and Theory* 24, no. 1 (2014): 1–34.

53. Chester Barnard gives one of the earliest descriptions of organizations as systems interacting with external environments and that are composed of subsystems. See C. Barnard, *The Functions of the Executive* (Cambridge, MA: Harvard University Press, 1938), esp. chap. 6. Also see F. E. Kast and J. E. Rosenzweig, "General Systems Theory: Applications for Organization and Management," *Academy of Management Journal* 15, no. 4 (1972): 447–65; P. M. Senge, *The Fifth Discipline: The Art and Practice of the Learning Organization* (New York: Doubleday Currency, 1990); G. Morgan, *Images of Organization*, 2nd ed. (Newbury Park, CA: Sage, 1996); A. de Geus, *The Living Company* (Boston: Harvard Business School Press, 1997).

54. D. P. Ashmos and G. P. Huber, "The Systems Paradigm in Organization Theory: Correcting the Record and Suggesting the Future," *Academy of Management Review* 12, no. 4 (1987): 607–21.

55. D. Katz and R. L. Kahn, *The Social Psychology of Organizations* (New York: Wiley, 1966), chap. 2; J. McCann, "Organizational Effectiveness: Changing Concepts for Changing Environments," *Human Resource Planning* 27, no. 1 (2004): 42–50; A. H. Van de Ven, M. Ganco, and C. R. Hinings, "Returning to the Frontier of Contingency Theory of Organizational and Institutional Designs," *Academy of Management Annals* 7, no. 1 (2013): 391–438.

56. D. Dahlhoff, "Why Target's Canadian Expansion Failed," *Harvard Business Review* (2015), https://hbr.org/2015/01/why-targets-canadian-expansion-failed; "Brian Cornell Addresses Questions About Exiting Canada," *A Bullseye View* (Minneapolis: Target, January 15, 2015), https://corporate.target.com/article/2015/01/qa-brian-cornell-target-exits-canada (accessed February 28, 2017).

57. C. Ostroff and N. Schmitt, "Configurations of Organizational Effectiveness and Efficiency," *Academy of Management Journal* 36, no. 6 (1993): 1345–61; R. Andrews and T. Entwistle, "Four Faces of Public Service Efficiency," *Public Management Review* 15, no. 2 (2013): 246–64; R. M. Walker, J. Chen, and D. Aravind, "Management Innovation and Firm Performance: An Integration of Research Findings," *European Management Journal* 33, no. 5 (2015): 407–22.

58. K. E. Weick, *The Social Psychology of Organizing* (Reading, MA: Addison-Wesley, 1979); S. Brusoni and A. Prencipe, "Managing Knowledge in Loosely Coupled Networks: Exploring the Links between Product and Knowledge Dynamics," *Journal of Management Studies* 38, no. 7 (2001): 1019–35.

59. T. A. Stewart, *Intellectual Capital: The New Wealth of Organizations* (New York: Currency/Doubleday, 1997); L.-C. Hsu and C.-H. Wang, "Clarifying the Effect of Intellectual Capital on Performance: The Mediating Role of Dynamic Capability," *British Journal of Management* (2011): 179–205; A. L. Mention and N. Bontis, "Intellectual Capital and Performance within the Banking Sector of Luxembourg and Belgium," *Journal of Intellectual Capital* 14, no. 2 (2013): 286–309; K. Asiaei and R. Jusoh, "A Multidimensional View of Intellectual Capital: The Impact on Organizational Performance," *Management Decision* 53, no. 3 (2015): 668–97.

60. R. Slater, *Jack Welch & the G.E. Way: Management Insights and Leadership Secrets of the Legendary CEO* (New York: McGraw-Hill, 1999).

61. J. Barney, "Firm Resources and Sustained Competitive Advantage," *Journal of Management* 17, no. 1 (1991): 99–120.

62. J. P. Hausknecht and J. A. Holwerda, "When Does Employee Turnover Matter? Dynamic Member Configurations, Productive Capacity, and Collective Performance," *Organization Science* 24, no. 1 (2013): 210–25.

63. P. Cleary, "An Empirical Investigation of the Impact of Management Accounting on Structural Capital and Business Performance," *Journal of Intellectual Capital* 16, no. 3 (2015): 566–86; L. M. Gogan, D. C. Duran, and A. Draghici, "Structural Capital—A Proposed Measurement Model," *Procedia Economics and Finance* 23 (2015): 1139–46.

64. Some organizational learning researchers use the label "social capital" instead of "relationship capital." Social capital is discussed later in this book as the goodwill and resulting resources shared among members in a social network. The two concepts may be identical (as those writers suggest). However, we continue to use "relationship capital" for intellectual capital because social capital typically refers to individual relationships whereas relationship capital also includes value not explicit in social capital, such as the organization's goodwill and brand value.

65. G. Huber, "Organizational Learning: The Contributing Processes and Literature," *Organizational Science* 2 (1991): 88–115; D. A. Garvin, *Learning in Action: A Guide to Putting the Learning Organization to Work* (Boston: Harvard Business School Press, 2000); H. Shipton, "Cohesion or Confusion? Towards a Typology for Organizational Learning Research," *International Journal of Management Reviews* 8, no. 4 (2006): 233–52; D. Jiménez-Jiménez and J. G. Cegarra-Navarro, "The Performance Effect of Organizational Learning and Market Orientation," *Industrial Marketing Management* 36, no. 6 (2007): 694–708. One recent study suggests that these organizational learning processes aren't always beneficial because they may be more costly or burdensome than the value they create. See S. S. Levine and M. J. Prietula, "How Knowledge Transfer Impacts Performance: A Multilevel Model of Benefits and Liabilities," *Organization Science* 23, no. 6 (2012): 1748–66.

66. B. van den Hooff and M. Huysman, "Managing Knowledge Sharing: Emergent and Engineering Approaches," *Information & Management* 46, no. 1 (2009): 1–8.

67. M. Rodgers, "Culture Club: Ambrosia Humphrey—Hootsuite," *Perch Communications Blog*, September 9, 2013, http://perch.co/blog/culture-club-ambrosia-humphrey-hootsuite/; R. Holmes, "Innovate or Die: 3 Ways to Stay Ahead of the Curve," *HootSuite Blog*, September 13, 2013, http://blog.hootsuite.com/innovate-or-die-hackathon/; Q. Casey, "Buying the Company to Acquire the Talent," *Vancouver Sun*, December 17, 2013.

68. Learning orientation differs somewhat from "learning goal orientation," as well from the educational psychology meaning of this phrase. See G. T. M. Hult, R. F. Hurley, and G. A. Knight, "Innovativeness: Its Antecedents and Impact on Business Performance," *Industrial Marketing Management* 33, no. 5 (2004): 429–38; J. C. Real, J. L. Roldán, and A. Leal, "From Entrepreneurial Orientation and Learning Orientation to Business Performance: Analysing the Mediating Role of Organizational Learning and the Moderating Effects of Organizational Size," *British Journal of Management* 25, no. 2 (2014): 186–208; K. Tajeddini, "Analyzing the Influence of Learning Orientation and Innovativeness on Performance of Public Organizations: The Case of Iran," *Journal of Management Development* 35, no. 2 (2016): 134–53.

69. M. N. Wexler, "Organizational Memory and Intellectual Capital," *Journal of Intellectual Capital* 3, no. 4 (2002): 393–414; M. Fiedler and I. Welpe, "How Do Organizations Remember? The Influence of Organizational Structure on Organizational Memory," *Organization Studies* 31, no. 4 (2010): 381–407.

70. M. E. McGill and J. W. Slocum Jr., "Unlearn the Organization," *Organizational Dynamics* 22, no. 2 (1993): 67–79; A. E. Akgün, G. S. Lynn, and J. C. Byrne, "Antecedents and Consequences of Unlearning in New Product Development Teams," *Journal of Product Innovation Management* 23 (2006): 73–88.

71. L. Sels et al., "Unravelling the HRM-Performance Link: Value-Creating and Cost-Increasing Effects of Small Business HRM," *Journal of Management Studies* 43, no. 2 (2006): 319–42; G. S. Benson, S. M. Young, and E. E. Lawler III, "High-Involvement Work Practices and Analysts' Forecasts of Corporate Earnings," *Human Resource Management* 45, no. 4 (2006): 519–37; J. Combs et al., "How Much Do High-Performance Work Practices Matter? A Meta-Analysis of Their Effects on Organizational Performance," *Personnel Psychology* 59, no. 3 (2006): 501–28; G. A. Fine and T. Hallett, "Group Cultures and the Everyday Life of Organizations: Interaction Orders and Meso-Analysis," *Organization Studies* (2014): 1–20.

72. E. E. Lawler III, S. A. Mohrman, and G. E. Ledford Jr., *Strategies for High Performance Organizations* (San Francisco: Jossey-Bass, 1998); P. Tharenou, A. M. Saks, and C. Moore, "A Review and Critique of Research on Training and Organizational-Level Outcomes," *Human Resource Management Review* 17, no. 3 (2007): 251–73; D. Y. Jeong and M. Choi, "The Impact of High-Performance Work Systems on Firm Performance: The Moderating Effects of the Human Resource Function's Influence," *Journal of Management & Organization* 22, no. 3 (May 2016).

73. M. Subramony, "A Meta-Analytic Investigation of the Relationship between HRM Bundles and Firm Performance," *Human Resource Management* 48, no. 5 (2009): 745–68.

74. OECD, *Skills Matter: Further Results from the Survey of Adult Skills*, OECD Skills Studies (Paris: OECD Publishing, June 2016). Also from Annex A, spreadsheet data file associated with tables in the OECD publication.

75. J. Camps and R. Luna-Arocas, "A Matter of Learning: How Human Resources Affect Organizational Performance," *British Journal of Management* 23, no. 1 (2012): 1–21; R. R. Kehoe and P. M. Wright, "The Impact of High-Performance Human Resource Practices on Employees' Attitudes and Behaviors," *Journal of Management* 39, no. 2 (2013): 366–91; B. Fabi, R. Lacoursière, and L. Raymond, "Impact of High-Performance Work Systems on Job Satisfaction, Organizational Commitment, and Intention to Quit in Canadian Organizations," *International Journal of Manpower* 36, no. 5 (2015): 772–90.

76. J. Tullberg, "Stakeholder Theory: Some Revisionist Suggestions," *The Journal of Socio-Economics* 42 (2013): 127–35.

77. R. E. Freeman, J. S. Harrison, and A. C. Wicks, *Managing for Stakeholders: Survival, Reputation, and Success* (New Haven, CT: Yale University Press, 2007); B. L. Parmar et al., "Stakeholder Theory: The State of the Art," *Academy of Management Annals* 4, no. 1 (2010): 403–45; S. Sachs and E. Rühli, *Stakeholders Matter: A New Paradigm for Strategy in Society* (Cambridge, UK: Cambridge University Press, 2011).

78. A. Santana, "Three Elements of Stakeholder Legitimacy," *Journal of Business Ethics* 105, no. 2 (2012): 257–65; D. Crilly and P. Sloan, "Autonomy or Control? Organizational Architecture and Corporate Attention to Stakeholders," *Organization Science* 25, no. 2 (2014): 339–55; M. Hall, Y. Millo, and E. Barman, "Who and What Really Counts? Stakeholder Prioritization and Accounting for Social Value," *Journal of Management Studies* 52, no. 7 (2015): 907–34; D. Weitzner and Y. Deutsch, "Understanding Motivation and Social Influence in Stakeholder Prioritization," *Organization Studies* 36, no. 10 (2015): 1337–60.

79. R. E. Freeman, A. C. Wicks, and B. Parmar, "Stakeholder Theory and 'the Corporate Objective Revisited,'" *Organization Science* 15, no. 3 (2004): 364–69; B. R. Agle et al., "Dialogue: Toward Superior Stakeholder Theory," *Business Ethics Quarterly* 18, no. 2 (2008): 153–90; R. B. Adams, A. N. Licht, and L. Sagiv, "Shareholders and Stakeholders: How Do Directors Decide?," *Strategic Management Journal* 32, no. 12 (2011): 1331–55.

80. B. M. Meglino and E. C. Ravlin, "Individual Values in Organizations: Concepts, Controversies, and Research," *Journal of Management* 24, no. 3 (1998): 351–89; A. Bardi and S. H. Schwartz, "Values and Behavior: Strength and Structure of Relations," *Personality and Social Psychology Bulletin* 29, no. 10 (2003): 1207–20; S. Hitlin and J. A. Pilavin, "Values: Reviving a Dormant Concept," *Annual Review of Sociology* 30 (2004): 359–93.

81. Some popular books that emphasize the importance of personal and organizational values include J. C. Collins and J. I. Porras, *Built to Last: Successful Habits of Visionary Companies* (London: Century, 1995); C. A. O'Reilly III and J. Pfeffer, *Hidden Value* (Cambridge, MA: Harvard Business School Press, 2000); J. Reiman, *The Story of Purpose: The Path to Creating a Brighter Brand, a Greater Company, and a Lasting Legacy* (Hoboken, NJ: Wiley, 2013); R. Barrett, *The Values-Driven Organization: Unleashing Human Potential for Performance and Profit* (New York: Routledge, 2014); R. E. Freeman and E. R. Auster, *Bridging the Values Gap: How Authentic Organizations Bring Values to Life* (Oakland, CA: Berrett-Koehler, 2015).

82. *The 2016 Deloitte Millennial Survey: Winning over the Next Generation of Leaders* (New York: Deloitte Touche Tohmatsu, January 2016).

83. M. van Marrewijk, "Concepts and Definitions of CSR and Corporate Sustainability: Between Agency and Communion," *Journal of Business Ethics* 44 (2003): 95–105; M. L. Barnett, "Stakeholder Influence Capacity and the Variability of Financial Returns to Corporate Social Responsibility," *Academy of Management Review* 32, no. 3 (2007): 794–816.

84. L. S. Paine, *Value Shift* (New York: McGraw-Hill, 2003); A. Mackey, T. B. Mackey, and J. B. Barney, "Corporate Social Responsibility and Firm Performance: Investor Preferences and Corporate Strategies," *Academy of Management Review* 32, no. 3 (2007): 817–35.

85. S. Zadek, *The Civil Corporation: The New Economy of Corporate Citizenship* (London: Earthscan, 2001); S. Hart and M. Milstein, "Creating Sustainable Value," *Academy of Management Executive* 17, no. 2 (2003): 56–69.

86. "Four in Ten (37%) Employees Rate Corporate Social Responsibility 'Very Important' When It Comes to Their Employer," news release (New York: Ipsos, June 25, 2013); J. Browne, R. Nuttall, and T. Stadlen, *Connect: How Companies Succeed by Engaging Radically with Society* (London: WH Allen, 2015); Aflac, *National Survey on Corporate Social Responsibility* (Columbus, GA: Aflac, November 12, 2016); PricewaterhouseCoopers, *19th Annual Global CEO Survey: Redefining Business Success in a Changing World* (New York: PwC, January 2016).

87. M. Friedman, *Capitalism and Freedom*, 40th Anniversary ed. (Chicago: University of Chicago Press, 2002), chap. 8; N. Vorster, "An Ethical Critique of Milton Friedman's Doctrine on Economics and Freedom," *Journal for the Study of Religions and Ideologies* 9, no. 26 (2010): 163–88.

88. A. B. Carroll and K. M. Shabana, "The Business Case for Corporate Social Responsibility: A Review of Concepts, Research and Practice," *International Journal of Management Reviews* 12, no. 1 (2010): 85–105; H. Aguinis and A. Glavas, "What We Know and Don't Know about Corporate Social Responsibility: A Review and Research Agenda," *Journal of Management* 38, no. 4 (2012): 932–68.

2 | Individual Behavior, Personality, and Values

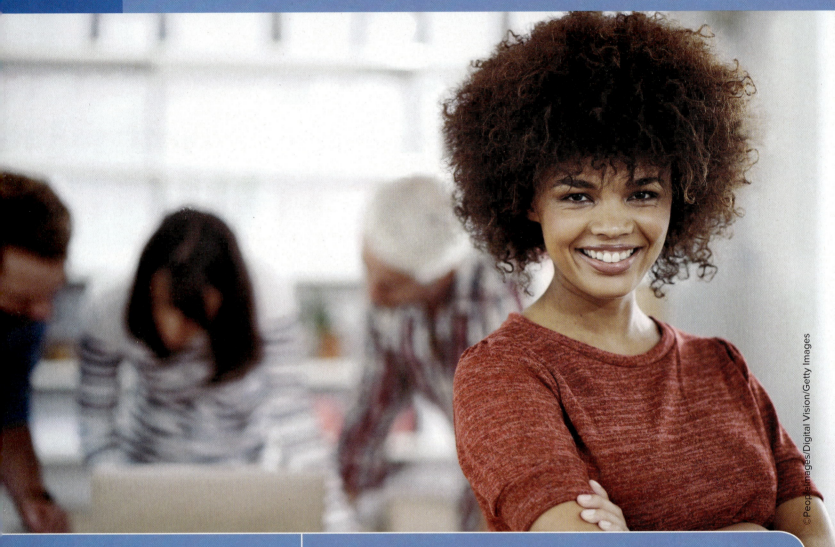

©PeopleImages/Digital Vision/Getty Images

Learning Objectives

After you read this chapter, you should be able to:

LO2-1 Describe the four factors that directly influence individual behavior and performance.

LO2-2 Summarize the five types of individual behavior in organizations.

LO2-3 Describe personality and discuss how the "Big Five" personality dimensions and four MBTI types relate to individual behavior in organizations.

LO2-4 Summarize Schwartz's model of individual values and discuss the conditions where values influence behavior.

LO2-5 Describe three ethical principles and discuss three factors that influence ethical behavior.

LO2-6 Describe five values commonly studied across cultures.

G etting hired at Bridgewater Associates—the world's largest hedge fund—is not a cakewalk. The process begins with applicants watching online videos depicting the culture and daily office life at the Westport, Connecticut, investment firm. Next, they spend two or three more hours completing four online assessments, including a popular measure of personality traits (MBTI). Applicants who pass the online selection process engage in a structured interview over the phone with consultants, who further assess the individual's character. Even after accepting Bridgewater's job offer, new recruits take a final two-hour personality test developed by the company. Bridgewater then uses the application data to produce the new hire's "baseball card"—a compact profile of his or her personality, abilities, culture fit, and performance. Bridgeport employees can view any coworker's profile on their phone or tablet using the firm's highly secure baseball card app.[1]

The hiring process at Bridgewater Associates is unusual. But what the hedge fund has in common with other organizations is its attempt to understand each job applicant's ability, motivation, personality, values, and other personal characteristics. These characteristics are central topics in this chapter. We begin by introducing the four direct drivers of individual behavior and performance that enable employees at Bridgewater Associates and other companies to provide peak performance. Next, we review the five types of individual behavior that represent the individual-level dependent variables found in most organizational behavior research. We then turn our attention to personality and values, which are the two relatively stable characteristics of individuals. Finally, this chapter presents the topics of ethical and cross-cultural values.

> **LO2-1** Describe the four factors that directly influence individual behavior and performance.

MARS MODEL OF INDIVIDUAL BEHAVIOR AND PERFORMANCE

For most of the past century, experts have investigated the direct predictors of individual behavior and performance.[2] One of the earliest formulas was *performance = person × situation*, where *person* includes individual characteristics and *situation* represents external influences on the individual's behavior. Another frequently mentioned formula is *performance = ability × motivation*.[3] Sometimes known as the "skill-and-will" model, this formula elaborates two specific characteristics within the person that influence individual performance. Some organizational studies use the *ability-motivation-opportunity (AMO)* model, which refers to the three variables but with a limited interpretation of the situation. Along with ability, motivation, and situation, researchers have more recently identified a fourth key direct predictor of individual behavior and performance: role perceptions (the individual's expected role obligations).[4]

Exhibit 2.1 illustrates these four variables—motivation, ability, role perceptions, and situational factors—which are represented by the acronym *MARS*.[5] All four factors are critical influences on an individual's voluntary behavior and performance; if any one of them is low in a given situation, the employee would perform the task poorly. For example, motivated salespeople with clear role perceptions and sufficient resources (situational factors) will not perform their jobs as well if they lack sales skills and related knowledge (ability). Motivation, ability, and role perceptions are clustered together in the model because they are located within the person. Situational factors are external to the individual but still affect his or her behavior and performance.[6] The four MARS variables are the direct predictors of employee performance, customer service, coworker collegiality, ethical behavior, and all other forms of voluntary behavior in the workplace. Let's look in more detail at each of the four factors in the MARS model.

Employee Motivation

Motivation represents the forces within a person that affect his or her direction, intensity, and persistence of voluntary behavior.[7] *Direction* refers to the path along which people steer their effort. In other words, motivation is goal-directed, not random. People have choices about what they are trying to achieve and at what level of quality, quantity, and so forth. They are motivated to arrive at work on time, finish a project a few hours early, or aim for many other targets.

The second element of motivation, called *intensity*, is the amount of effort allocated to the goal. Intensity is all about how much people push themselves to complete a task. Two employees might be motivated to finish their project a few hours earlier than expected (direction), but only one of them puts forth enough effort (intensity) to achieve this goal. The third element of motivation is *persistence*, which refers to the length of time that the individual continues to exert effort toward an objective. Employees sustain their effort until they reach their goal or give up beforehand.

To help remember these three elements of motivation, consider the metaphor of driving a car in which the thrust of the engine is your effort. Direction refers to where you steer the car, intensity is how much you put your foot down on the gas pedal, and persistence is for how long you drive toward your destination. Remember that motivation is a force that exists within individuals; it is not their actual behavior. Thus, direction, intensity, and persistence are cognitive (thoughts) and emotional conditions that directly cause us to move.

Ability

Employee abilities also make a difference in behavior and task performance. **Ability** includes both the natural aptitudes and the learned capabilities required to successfully complete a task. *Aptitudes* are the natural talents that help employees learn specific tasks more quickly and perform them better. For example, finger dexterity is an aptitude by which individuals learn more quickly and potentially achieve higher performance at picking up and handling small objects with their fingers. Employees with high finger dexterity are not necessarily better than others at first; rather, they usually learn the skill faster and eventually reach a higher level of performance. *Learned capabilities* are the physical and mental skills and knowledge you have acquired. They tend to wane over time when not in use. Aptitudes and

> I believe the real difference between success and failure in a corporation can be very often traced to the question of how well the organization brings out the great energies and talents of its people.[8]
>
> —Thomas J. Watson Jr.,
> IBM's second CEO

learned capabilities (skills and knowledge) are the main elements of a broader concept called *competencies*, which are characteristics of a person that result in superior performance.[9]

The challenge is to match a person's abilities with the job's requirements because a good match tends to increase employee performance and well-being. One matching strategy is to select applicants who already demonstrate the required competencies. For example, companies ask applicants to perform work samples, provide references for checking their past performance, and complete various selection tests. A second strategy is to train employees who lack specific knowledge or skills needed for the job.[10] The third person–job matching strategy is to redesign the job so that employees are given tasks only within their current abilities. For example, a complex task might be simplified—some aspects of the work are transferred to others—so a new employee performs only tasks that he or she is currently able to perform. As the employee becomes more competent at these tasks, other tasks are added back into the job.

Role Perceptions

Along with motivation and ability, employees require accurate **role perceptions** to perform their jobs well. Role perceptions refer to how clearly people understand the job duties (roles) assigned to or expected of them. These perceptions range from

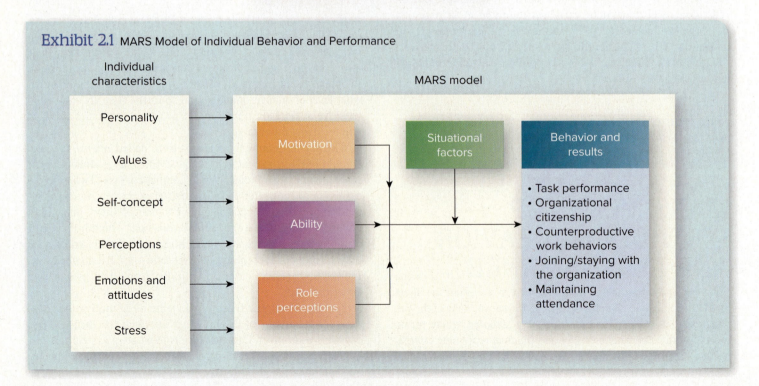

Exhibit 2.1 MARS Model of Individual Behavior and Performance

Individual characteristics

- Personality
- Values
- Self-concept
- Perceptions
- Emotions and attitudes
- Stress

MARS model

- Motivation
- Ability
- Role perceptions

Situational factors

Behavior and results
- Task performance
- Organizational citizenship
- Counterproductive work behaviors
- Joining/staying with the organization
- Maintaining attendance

Mind the MARS Gap on Motivation, Ability, Role Perceptions, and Situational Factors[11]

60% of more than 13,000 employees surveyed across 34 countries say the skills gap is a real problem for their employer.

50% of 2.2 million employees surveyed worldwide strongly agree that they know what is expected of them at work.

33% of 195,600 American employees surveyed are engaged at work (indicator of work motivation).

25% of 2,061 UK adults surveyed say they receive insufficient training and development in their existing role.

24% of more than 400,000 employees surveyed across 500 organizations worldwide say that lack of tools is their top source of decreased productivity (second highest to unproductive coworkers).

(photo): ©Maren Wischnewski/Alamy Stock Photo

employees versus meeting with clients. The third form of role perceptions involves understanding the preferred behaviors or procedures for accomplishing tasks. Role ambiguity exists when an employee knows two or three ways to perform a task but misunderstands which of these the company prefers.

Role perceptions are important because they represent how well employees know where to direct their effort.[13] Employees with role clarity perform work more accurately and efficiently, whereas those with role ambiguity waste considerable time and energy by performing the wrong tasks or the right tasks in the wrong way. Furthermore, role clarity is essential for coordination with coworkers and other stakeholders. For instance, performers at Cirque du Soleil depend on one another to perform precise behaviors at exact times, such as catching each other in midair. Role clarity ensures that these expectations are met and the troupe's performances are executed safely. Finally, role clarity motivates employees because they have a higher belief that their effort will produce the expected outcomes. In other words, people are more confident when they know what is expected of them.

> ❝ Lack of role clarity may be an increasing concern as organizations move away from precisely defined job descriptions to broader work responsibilities. ❞

role clarity to role ambiguity. Role ambiguity may be a serious problem in organizations. When 7,000 employees in a recent global survey were asked what would most improve their performance, "greater clarity about what the organization needs from me" was identified as the most important factor.[12]

Role clarity exists in three forms. First, employees have clear role perceptions when they understand the specific duties or consequences for which they are accountable. This may seem obvious, but people are occasionally evaluated on job duties they were never told were within their zone of responsibility. This lack of role clarity may be an increasing concern as organizations move away from precisely defined job descriptions to broader work responsibilities.

Second, role clarity exists when employees understand the priority of their various tasks and performance expectations. This is illustrated in the classic dilemma of quantity versus quality, such as how many customers to serve in an hour (quantity) versus how well each customer should be served (quality). Role clarity in the form of task priorities also exists in the dilemma of allocating personal time and resources, such as how much time managers should devote to coaching

Role clarity ensures that artists at Cirque du Soleil understand what is expected of them and of each other, thereby supporting the troupe's high quality and safe performance.
©Picture Perfect/REX/Shutterstock

Situational Factors

Individual behavior and performance also depend on the situation, which is any context beyond the employee's immediate control.[14] The situation has two main influences on individual behavior and performance.[15] One influence is that the work context constrains or facilitates behavior and performance. Employees who are motivated and skilled and know their role obligations will nevertheless perform poorly if they lack time, budget, physical work facilities, and other resources. The second influence is that the work environment provides cues to guide and motivate people. For example, companies install barriers and warning signs in dangerous areas. These workplace features are situational factors that cue employees to avoid the nearby hazards.

LO2-2 Summarize the five types of individual behavior in organizations.

TYPES OF INDIVIDUAL BEHAVIOR

The four elements of the MARS model—motivation, ability, role perceptions, and situational factors—affect all voluntary workplace behaviors and performance. There are many varieties of individual behavior, but most can be organized into the five categories described over the next few pages: task performance, organizational citizenship, counterproductive work behaviors, joining and staying with the organization, and maintaining work attendance (Exhibit 2.2).

Task Performance

Task performance refers to the individual's voluntary goal-directed behaviors that contribute to organizational objectives.[16] Most jobs require incumbents to complete several tasks. For example, foreign exchange traders at Morgan Stanley must be able to identify and execute profitable trades, work cooperatively with clients and coworkers, assist in training new staff, and work on special telecommunications equipment without error. All tasks involve various degrees of working with people, data, things, and ideas.[17] Foreign exchange traders mainly work with data (e.g., performing technical analysis of trends), people (e.g., sharing information with coworkers and clients), and ideas (interpreting charts and company reports).

There are three types of task performance: proficient, adaptive, and proactive.[18]

- *Proficient task performance* refers to performing the work efficiently and accurately. It involves accomplishing the assigned work at or above the expected standards of quality, quantity, and other indicators of effectiveness.

- *Adaptive task performance* refers to how well employees modify their thoughts and behavior to align with and support a new or changing environment. Essentially, adaptive task performance is about how well employees respond to change in the workplace and in their job duties.

- *Proactive task performance* refers to how well employees take the initiative to anticipate and introduce new work patterns that benefit the organization. Proactive behaviors bring about change in oneself, coworkers, and the workplace to achieve what is perceived to be a better future for the organization.

Employees are expected to perform their work proficiently. However, adaptive and proactive task performance are also important, particularly when the work is ambiguous or dynamic. These conditions exist when the client's expectations are unclear, resources to perform the work have uncertain availability, and the methods used to perform the work are rapidly evolving due to emerging technology.

Organizational Citizenship

Employee behavior extends beyond performing specific tasks. It also includes **organizational citizenship behaviors (OCBs)**, which are various forms of cooperation and helpfulness to others that support the organization's social and psychological context.[19] Some OCBs are directed toward individuals, such as assisting coworkers with their work problems, adjusting your work schedules to accommodate coworkers, showing

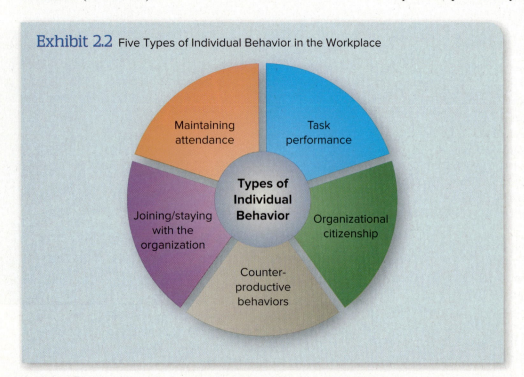

Exhibit 2.2 Five Types of Individual Behavior in the Workplace

Types of Individual Behavior
- Maintaining attendance
- Task performance
- Organizational citizenship
- Counterproductive behaviors
- Joining/staying with the organization

Organizational citizenship behaviors are various forms of cooperation and helpfulness to others that support the organization's social and psychological context.
©baranq/Shutterstock

task performance the individual's voluntary goal-directed behaviors that contribute to organizational objectives

organizational citizenship behaviors (OCBs) various forms of cooperation and helpfulness to others that support the organization's social and psychological context

counterproductive work behaviors (CWBs) voluntary behaviors that have the potential to directly or indirectly harm the organization

genuine courtesy toward coworkers, and sharing your work resources (supplies, technology, staff) with coworkers. Other OCBs represent cooperation and helpfulness toward the organization, such as supporting the company's public image, offering ideas beyond those required for your own job, attending voluntary functions that support the organization, and keeping up with new developments in the organization. Some OCBs are discretionary behaviors (employees don't have to perform them), but employees are expected to engage in some forms of organizational citizenship even if they aren't explicitly stated in job descriptions.[20]

counterproductive work behaviors (CWBs). CWBs are voluntary behaviors that have the potential to directly or indirectly harm the organization or its stakeholders.[23] This concept includes a wide array of behaviors, both intentional and unintentional, such as harassing coworkers, creating unnecessary conflict, deviating from preferred work methods (e.g., shortcuts that undermine work quality), being untruthful, stealing, sabotaging work, and wasting resources. CWBs are not minor concerns; research suggests that they can substantially undermine the organization's effectiveness.

Joining and Staying with the Organization

Organizations are people working together toward common goals, so another critical set of behaviors is joining and staying with the company. Employers face skill shortages when the economy is booming, but employing qualified people can be a problem even during recessions.

Equally important is ensuring that employees stay with the company.[24] Employee turnover removes valuable knowledge,

> **Employee turnover removes valuable knowledge, skills, and relationships with coworkers and external stakeholders, all of which take time for new staff to acquire.**

OCBs can have a significant effect on individual, team, and organizational effectiveness.[21] Employees who help others have higher task performance because they receive more support from coworkers. OCBs also increase team performance where members depend on one another. However, OCBs take time and energy away from performing tasks, which can undermine career success in companies that reward task performance. Also, employees with high organizational citizenship tend to have higher work–family conflict because of the amount of time required for these activities.[22]

Counterproductive Work Behaviors

Organizational behavior is interested in all workplace behaviors, including dysfunctional activities collectively known as

skills, and relationships with coworkers and external stakeholders, all of which take time for new staff to acquire. In later chapters, we identify other problems with employee turnover, such as its adverse effect on customer service, team development, and corporate culture strength. Employee turnover does offer some benefits, such as removing people with counterproductive work behaviors and opening up positions to new employees with fresh ideas. But overall, turnover tends to have a negative effect on organizational effectiveness.

Maintaining Work Attendance

Along with attracting and retaining employees, organizations need everyone to show up for work at scheduled times, whether in-person or through remote work arrangements. American

personality the relatively enduring pattern of thoughts, emotions, and behaviors that characterize a person, along with the psychological processes behind those characteristics

employees are absent from scheduled work an average of only five days per year. Yet, even low absenteeism can lead to increased workloads or overtime among coworkers, lower performance by temporary staff filling the vacant position, poorer coordination in the work process, poorer customer service, and potentially more workplace accidents.[25]

What are the main causes of absenteeism and lateness?[26] Employees often point to situational factors, such as bad weather, transit strike, personal illness, and family demands (e.g., sick children). Some absenteeism occurs because employees need to get away from workplace bullying, difficult customers, boring work, and other stressful conditions. Absenteeism is also higher in organizations with generous sick leave because this benefit minimizes the financial loss of taking time away from work.

Another factor in absenteeism is the person's values and personality. Finally, studies report that absenteeism is higher in teams with strong absence norms, meaning that team members tolerate and even expect coworkers to take time off.

Although most companies focus on minimizing absenteeism, a more serious behavior may be *presenteeism*—showing up for work when unwell, injured, preoccupied by personal problems, or faced with dangerous conditions getting to work.[27] These employees tend to be less productive and may reduce the productivity of coworkers. In addition, they may worsen their own health and increase health and safety risks for coworkers. Presenteeism is more common among employees with low job security, with no sick leave benefits, and whose absence would immediately affect many people. Personality traits also motivate some people to show up for work when others would gladly recover at home.[28] Personality is a widely cited predictor of most forms of individual behavior. It is also the most stable personal characteristic, so we introduce this topic next.

LO2-3 Describe personality and discuss how the "Big Five" personality dimensions and four MBTI types relate to individual behavior in organizations.

PERSONALITY IN ORGANIZATIONS

Personality is the relatively enduring pattern of thoughts, emotions, and behaviors that characterize a person, along with the psychological processes behind those characteristics.[30] In essence, personality is the bundle of characteristics that make us similar to or different from other people. We estimate an individual's personality by what he or she says and does, and we infer the person's internal states—including thoughts and emotions—from these observable behaviors.

People engage in a wide range of behaviors in their daily lives, yet close inspection of those actions reveals discernible patterns called *personality traits*.[31] Traits are broad concepts that allow us to label and understand individual differences. For example, some of your friends are probably quite talkative, whereas others tend to be quieter. Some people like to take risks, whereas others are risk-averse. Each trait implies that there is something within the person, rather than environmental influences alone, that predicts this behavioral tendency. In fact, studies report that an individual's personality traits measured in childhood predict many behaviors and outcomes in adulthood, including educational attainment, employment success, marital relationships, illegal activities, and health-risk behaviors.[32]

Although people have behavioral tendencies, they do not act the same way in all situations. Such consistency would be considered abnormal because it indicates a person's insensitivity to social norms, reward systems, and other external conditions.[33] People vary their behavior to suit the situation, even if the

Studies of identical twins reveal that heredity has a very large effect on personality.
©SuperStock

behavior is at odds with their personality. For example, talkative people remain relatively quiet in a library where "no talking" rules are explicit and strictly enforced. Even there, personality differences are apparent because talkative people tend to do more talking in libraries relative to other people talking in that setting.

Personality Determinants: Nature versus Nurture

Personality is shaped by both nature and nurture, although the relative importance of each continues to be debated and studied.[35] *Nature* refers to our genetic or hereditary origins—the genes that we inherit from our parents. Studies of identical twins reveal that heredity has a very large effect on personality; up to 50 percent of variation in behavior and 30 percent of temperament preferences can be attributed to a person's genetic characteristics. In other words, genetic code not only determines our eye color, skin tone, and physical shape; it also significantly affects our attitudes, decisions, and behavior.

Personality is also shaped by *nurture*—our socialization, life experiences, and other forms of interaction with the environment. Personality develops and changes mainly from childhood to young adulthood, typically stabilizing by around age 30. However, some personality changes continue to occur later in life. A few traits increase through to young adulthood, then decline in later years, whereas other traits tend to increase throughout most of our lifetime. Over a very long time, the type of work we perform also can influence our personality.[36]

The main explanation of why personality becomes more stable by adulthood is that we form a clearer and more rigid self-concept. This increasing clarity of "who we are" anchors our behavior with the help of our *executive function*. This is the part of the brain that monitors and regulates goal-directed behavior to keep it consistent with our self-concept. Our self-view becomes clearer and more stable with age, which increases the stability and consistency of our personality and behavior.[37] We discuss self-concept in more detail in Chapter 3. The main point here is that personality is not completely determined by heredity; life experiences, particularly early in life, also shape each individual's personality traits.

Five-Factor Model of Personality

Sociable, anxious, curious, dependable, suspicious, talkative, adventurous, and hundreds of other personality traits have been described over the years, so experts have tried to organize them into smaller clusters. The most researched and respected clustering of personality traits is the **five-factor (Big Five) model (FFM)**.[38] Several decades ago, personality experts identified more than 17,000 words that describe an individual's personality. These words were distilled down to five broad personality dimensions, each with a cluster of specific traits. Similar results were found in studies of different languages, suggesting that the five-factor model is fairly robust across cultures. These "Big Five" dimensions, represented by the handy acronym *CANOE*, are outlined in Exhibit 2.3 and described as follows:

- **Conscientiousness**. Characterizes people who are organized, dependable, goal-focused, thorough, disciplined, methodical, and industrious. People with low conscientiousness tend to be careless, disorganized, and less thorough.

- **Agreeableness**. Describes people who are trusting, helpful, good-natured, considerate, tolerant, selfless, generous, and flexible. People with low agreeableness tend to be uncooperative and intolerant of others' needs as well as more suspicious and self-focused.

five-factor (Big Five) model (FFM) the five broad dimensions representing most personality traits: conscientiousness, emotional stability, openness to experience, agreeableness, and extraversion

conscientiousness a personality dimension describing people who are organized, dependable, goal-focused, thorough, disciplined, methodical, and industrious

agreeableness a personality dimension describing people who are trusting, helpful, good-natured, considerate, tolerant, selfless, generous, and flexible

One regrets the loss even of one's worst habits. . . . They are such an essential part of one's personality.[34]

—Oscar Wilde, author (from *The Picture of Dorian Gray*)

neuroticism a personality dimension describing people who tend to be anxious, insecure, self-conscious, depressed, and temperamental

openness to experience a personality dimension describing people who are imaginative, creative, unconventional, curious, nonconforming, autonomous, and aesthetically perceptive

extraversion a personality dimension describing people who are outgoing, talkative, sociable, and assertive

- **Neuroticism.** Refers to people who tend to be anxious, insecure, self-conscious, depressed, and temperamental. In contrast, people with low neuroticism (high emotional stability) are poised, secure, and calm.

- **Openness to experience.** Characterizes people who are imaginative, creative, unconventional, curious, nonconforming, autonomous, and aesthetically perceptive. Those with low scores on this dimension tend to be more resistant to change, less open to new ideas, and more conventional and fixed in their ways.

- **Extraversion.** Describes people who are outgoing, talkative, energetic, sociable, and assertive. The opposite is *introversion*, which applies to those who are quiet, cautious, and less interactive with others. Extraverts get their energy from people and things around them, whereas introverts get their energy more from personal reflection on concepts and ideas. Introverts do not necessarily lack social skills. Instead, they are more inclined to direct their interests to ideas than to social events. Introverts feel more comfortable being alone than do extraverts.

SELF-ASSESSMENT 2.1: What is Your Big Five Personality?
Personality experts have organized the dozens of personality traits into five main dimensions, known as the five-factor or "Big Five" model. Each dimension consists of several specific personality traits that cluster together. Most scholarly research on personality relies on this model, but it is also useful in everyday life as a relatively easy categorization of personalities. You can discover your Big Five personality by locating this self-assessment in Connect if it is assigned by your instructor.

SELF-ASSESSMENT 2.2: Are You Introverted or Extraverted?
One of the most widely studied and discussed personality dimensions in the five-factor (Big Five) model of personality is introversion–extraversion. Introversion characterizes people who tend to be quiet, shy, and cautious. Extraversion characterizes people who tend to be outgoing, talkative, sociable, and assertive. You can discover your level of introversion or extraversion by locating this self-assessment in Connect if it is assigned by your instructor.

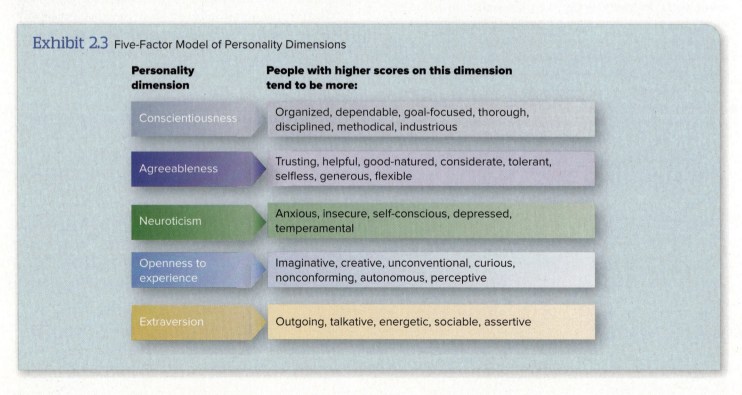

Exhibit 2.3 Five-Factor Model of Personality Dimensions

Personality dimension	People with higher scores on this dimension tend to be more:
Conscientiousness	Organized, dependable, goal-focused, thorough, disciplined, methodical, industrious
Agreeableness	Trusting, helpful, good-natured, considerate, tolerant, selfless, generous, flexible
Neuroticism	Anxious, insecure, self-conscious, depressed, temperamental
Openness to experience	Imaginative, creative, unconventional, curious, nonconforming, autonomous, perceptive
Extraversion	Outgoing, talkative, energetic, sociable, assertive

Five-Factor Model and Work Performance Personality mainly affects behavior and performance through motivation, specifically by influencing employees' direction and intensity of effort. Consequently, all of the five-factor model dimensions predict one or more types of employee behavior and performance to some extent. However, specific personality traits often predict employee performance better than the broad Big Five dimensions, which cluster several traits together. Also, the relationship between a personality dimension or trait and performance may be nonlinear. People with moderate extraversion perform better in sales jobs than those with high or low extraversion, for example.[39]

Exhibit 2.4 highlights which Big Five personality dimensions best predict five types of work behavior and performance.[40] Conscientiousness stands out as the best overall personality predictor of proficient task performance for most jobs. Conscientious employees set higher personal goals for themselves and are more persistent. People with higher conscientiousness also engage in more organizational citizenship and in less counterproductive work behavior.

Extraversion is the second best overall personality predictor of proficient task performance. It is also one of the better personality predictors of adaptive and proactive performance.

Assertiveness, a specific personality trait within the extraversion cluster, is a particularly strong predictor of adaptive and proactive performance. Assertive employees tend to have a "take charge" approach to situations, which is consistent with adapting to change and proactively initiating change. Extraversion is associated with influencing others and being comfortable in social settings, which (along with being assertive) explains why effective leaders and salespeople tend to be somewhat more extraverted than the general population.

Agreeableness is positively associated with organizational citizenship and negatively associated with counterproductive work behaviors.[41] The reason is that employees with high agreeableness are more cooperative, sensitive, flexible, and supportive. Agreeableness does not predict proficient or proactive task performance very well, mainly because it is associated with lower motivation to set goals and achieve results. However, agreeableness does predict one's performance as a team member as well as in customer service jobs.

Openness to experience is a weak predictor of proficient task performance, but it is one of the best personality predictors of adaptive and proactive performance. The main reason is that employees with higher openness scores have more curiosity,

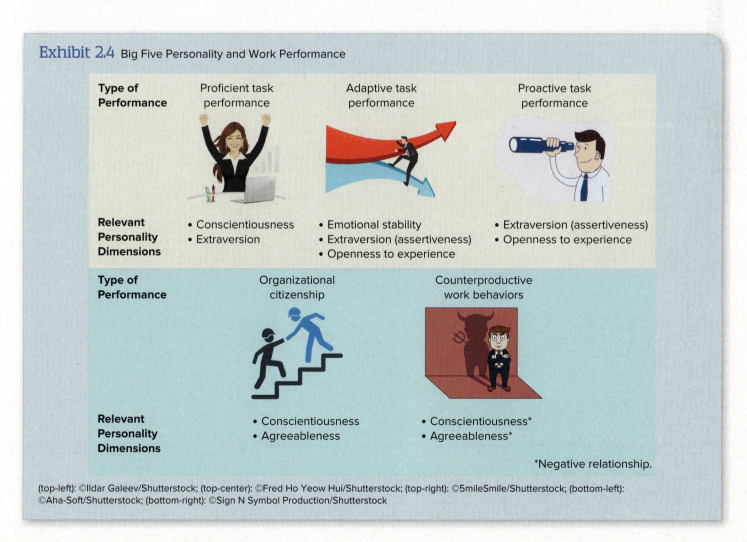

Exhibit 2.4 Big Five Personality and Work Performance

Type of Performance	Proficient task performance	Adaptive task performance	Proactive task performance
Relevant Personality Dimensions	• Conscientiousness • Extraversion	• Emotional stability • Extraversion (assertiveness) • Openness to experience	• Extraversion (assertiveness) • Openness to experience

Type of Performance	Organizational citizenship	Counterproductive work behaviors
Relevant Personality Dimensions	• Conscientiousness • Agreeableness	• Conscientiousness* • Agreeableness*

*Negative relationship.

(top-left): ©Ildar Galeev/Shutterstock; (top-center): ©Fred Ho Yeow Hui/Shutterstock; (top-right): ©5mileSmile/Shutterstock; (bottom-left): ©Aha-Soft/Shutterstock; (bottom-right): ©Sign N Symbol Production/Shutterstock

Myers-Briggs Type Indicator (MBTI) an instrument designed to measure the elements of Jungian personality theory, particularly preferences regarding perceiving and judging information

imagination, and tolerance of change.[42] These traits also explain why openness to change is associated with successful performance in creative work.

Emotional stability (low neuroticism) is one of the best personality predictors of adaptive performance.[43] The central explanation is that employees with higher emotional stability cope better with the ambiguity and uncertainty of change. In contrast, those with higher neuroticism view change as a threat, so they tend to avoid change and experience more stress when faced with workplace adjustments. These characteristics would suggest that emotional stability also predicts proactive performance, but the limited research has reported mixed results.

Jungian Personality Theory and the Myers-Briggs Type Indicator

The five-factor model of personality has the most research support, but it is not the most popular personality test in practice. That distinction goes to Jungian personality theory, which is measured through the **Myers-Briggs Type Indicator (MBTI)** (see Exhibit 2.5). Nearly a century ago, Swiss psychiatrist Carl Jung suggested that personality is mainly represented by the individual's preferences regarding perceiving and judging information.[44] Jung explained that the perceiving function—how people prefer to gather information—occurs through two competing orientations: *sensing (S)* and *intuition (N)*. Sensing involves perceiving information directly through the five senses; it relies on an organized structure to acquire factual and preferably quantitative details. In contrast, intuition relies more on insight and subjective experience to see relationships among variables. Sensing types focus on the here and now, whereas intuitive types focus more on future possibilities.

Jung also proposed that the judging function—how people prefer making decisions based on what they have perceived—should consist of two competing processes: *thinking (T)* and *feeling (F)*. People with a thinking orientation rely on rational cause–effect logic and systematic data collection to make decisions. Those with a strong feeling orientation give more weight to their emotional responses to the options presented, as well as to how those choices affect others. Jung noted that in addition to the four core processes of sensing, intuition, thinking, and feeling, people differ in their level of extraversion–introversion, which was introduced earlier as one of the Big Five personality traits.

The MBTI extends Jung's list of personality traits described above by also measuring Jung's broader

Exhibit 2.5 Jungian and Myers-Briggs Type Indicator Types[45]

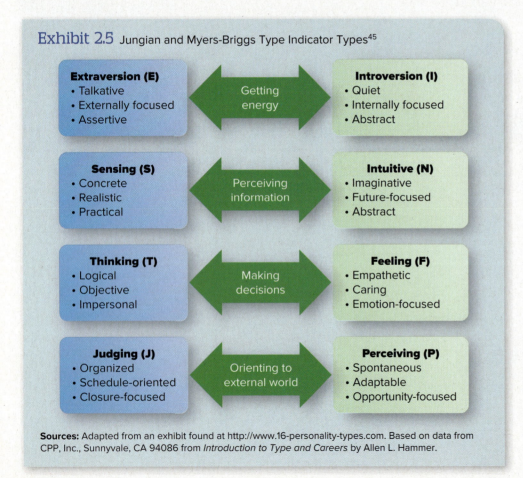

Extraversion (E) • Talkative • Externally focused • Assertive	Getting energy	**Introversion (I)** • Quiet • Internally focused • Abstract
Sensing (S) • Concrete • Realistic • Practical	Perceiving information	**Intuitive (N)** • Imaginative • Future-focused • Abstract
Thinking (T) • Logical • Objective • Impersonal	Making decisions	**Feeling (F)** • Empathetic • Caring • Emotion-focused
Judging (J) • Organized • Schedule-oriented • Closure-focused	Orienting to external world	**Perceiving (P)** • Spontaneous • Adaptable • Opportunity-focused

Sources: Adapted from an exhibit found at http://www.16-personality-types.com. Based on data from CPP, Inc., Sunnyvale, CA 94086 from *Introduction to Type and Careers* by Allen L. Hammer.

SELF-ASSESSMENT 2.4: Are You a Sensing or Intuitive Type?

Nearly a century ago, Swiss psychiatrist Carl Jung proposed that personality is primarily represented by the individual's preferences regarding perceiving and judging information. Jung explained that perceiving, which involves how people prefer to gather information or perceive the world around them, occurs through two competing orientations: sensing (S) and intuition (N). You can discover the extent to which you are a sensing or intuitive type by locating this self-assessment in Connect if it is assigned by your instructor.

categories of *perceiving* and *judging*, which represent a person's attitude toward the external world. People with a perceiving orientation are open, curious, and flexible. They prefer to keep their options open and to adapt spontaneously to events as they unfold. Judging types prefer order and structure and want to resolve problems quickly.

There are several reasons why the MBTI is popular, but it has a number of limitations. It is usually a poor predictor of job performance and should not be used for employment selection or promotion decisions.[46] There are also concerns about its measurement. MBTI can potentially identify employees who prefer face-to-face versus virtual teamwork, but the evidence so far suggests that it does not predict team development or leadership effectiveness.

The MBTI should not be used for employment selection or promotion decisions, but it can help in career counseling and executive coaching.
©Trinette Reed/Blend Images LLC; ©kyoshino/Getty Images

In spite of these limitations, the MBTI is the most widely studied measure of cognitive style in management research and is the most popular personality test for career counseling and executive coaching.[47] It is even being used by artificial intelligence engineers to adapt the behavior of robots to user preferences. MBTI takes a neutral or balanced approach by recognizing both the strengths and limitations of each personality type in different situations. In contrast, the five-factor model views people with higher scores as better than those with lower scores on each dimension. This may be a restrictive view of personality and makes the Big Five model more difficult to apply in coaching and development settings.[48]

LO2-4 Summarize Schwartz's model of individual values and discuss the conditions where values influence behavior.

VALUES IN THE WORKPLACE

Liam (not his real name) felt uncomfortable working in his previous project team at a consumer goods company. His coworkers were friendly and knowledgeable, but their views about customers and getting ahead in the company were irritating. Most of the other team members discussed new products as money makers without much thought to whether they actually satisfied customer needs. Conversations about getting ahead in the company focused on networking rather than achieving objectives. At one point, Liam felt so uncomfortable with the views of other team members that he began looking for a job at another company. Fortunately, he was transferred to a new project where most colleagues held values that were similar to his own.

Most of us have experienced situations similar to what Liam went through, where the values expressed by others clash with our own personal values. *Values*, a concept that we introduced in Chapter 1, are stable, evaluative beliefs that guide our preferences for outcomes or courses of action in a variety of situations.[49] They are the foundation of evaluations that something is right or wrong, good or bad, important or trivial. Values serve as a moral compass, advising and motivating what we ought to do in various situations. They also provide justification for past decisions and behavior.

People arrange values into a hierarchy of preferences, called a *value system*. Some individuals value new challenges more than they value conformity. Others value generosity more than frugality. Each person's unique value system is developed and

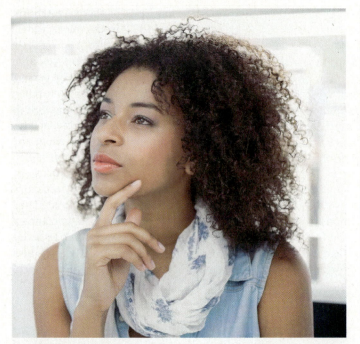
Values serve as a moral compass, advising and motivating what we ought to do in various situations.
©wavebreakmedia/Shutterstock

Values and personality traits are related to each other, but the two concepts differ in a few ways.[51] The most noticeable distinction is that values are evaluative; they tell us what we *ought* to do. Personality traits are descriptive; they are labels referring to what we naturally *tend* to do. A second distinction is that personality traits have minimal conflict with each other—you can have high agreeableness and high introversion, for example—whereas some values are opposed to other values. Someone who values excitement and challenge would have difficulty also valuing stability and moderation, for instance. Third, personality is somewhat more stable than values. The reason is that personality is influenced about equally by heredity and socialization, whereas values are influenced more by socialization than heredity.

Types of Values

Values come in many forms, and experts on this topic have devoted considerable attention to organizing them into clusters. By far, the most widely accepted model of personal values is the values circumplex developed and tested by social psychologist Shalom Schwartz and his colleagues.[52] This model clusters 57 values into 10 broad values categories that are organized into the circular model (circumplex) shown in Exhibit 2.6. The 10 categories include universalism, benevolence, tradition, conformity,

> ❝ Values and personality traits are related to each other, but the two concepts differ in a few ways. ❞

reinforced through socialization from parents, religious institutions, friends, personal experiences, and the society in which he or she lives. As such, a person's hierarchy of values is stable and long-lasting. For example, one study found that value systems of a sample of adolescents were remarkably similar 20 years later when they were adults.[50]

Values exist only within individuals—we call them *personal values*. However, groups of people might hold the same or similar values, so we tend to ascribe these *shared values* to the team, department, organization, profession, or entire society. The values shared by people throughout an organization (*organizational values*) receive fuller discussion in Chapter 13 because they are a key part of corporate culture. The values shared across a society (*cultural values*) receive attention in the last section of this chapter.

Exhibit 2.6 Schwartz's Values Circumplex

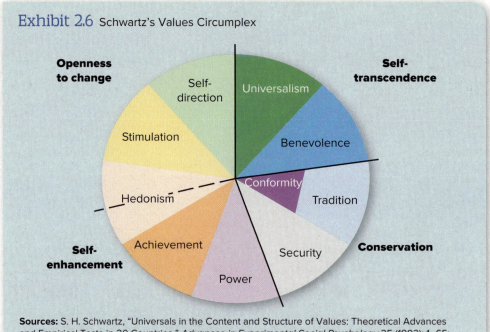

Sources: S. H. Schwartz, "Universals in the Content and Structure of Values: Theoretical Advances and Empirical Tests in 20 Countries," *Advances in Experimental Social Psychology* 25 (1992): 1–65; S. H. Schwartz and K. Boehnke, "Evaluating the Structure of Human Values with Confirmatory Factor Analysis," *Journal of Research in Personality* 38, no. 3 (2004): 230–55.

security, power, achievement, hedonism, stimulation, and self-direction. Each category is a cluster of more specific values (not shown). For example, conformity includes the specific values of politeness, honoring parents, self-discipline, and obedience.

These 10 broad values categories are further clustered into four quadrants. One quadrant, called *openness to change*, refers to the extent to which a person is motivated to pursue innovative ways. This quadrant includes the value categories of self-direction (creativity, independent thought), stimulation (excitement and challenge), and hedonism

> The more choices you have, the more your values matter.[54]
>
> —Michael Schrage
> (MIT Research Fellow and author)

our values hierarchy, then a job opportunity offering new experiences will appeal to us more than a job opportunity with more predictable and stable work.

Second, values indirectly motivate behavior by framing our perceptions of reality. Specifically, values influence whether we notice something as well as how we interpret it. Our decisions and actions are affected by how we perceive those situations. Third, we are motivated to act consistently with how we define ourselves and want to be viewed by others. If achievement is a key feature of our self-view and public image, then we try to ensure that our behavior is consistent with that value. The more clearly a behavior is aligned with a specific value that identifies us, the more motivated we are to engage in that behavior.

Personal values guide our decisions and behavior to some extent, but this connection isn't as strong as we might like to believe.[55] One reason for this "disconnect" between personal values and individual behavior is the situation. Personal values motivate us to engage in specific behavior, but the MARS model points out that the situation can prevent us from engaging in values-consistent behavior. For example, individuals with strong self-transcendent values are

(pursuit of pleasure, enjoyment, gratification of desires). The opposing quadrant is *conservation*, which is the extent to which a person is motivated to preserve the status quo. The conservation quadrant includes the value categories of conformity (adherence to social norms and expectations), security (safety and stability), and tradition (moderation and preservation of the status quo).

The third quadrant in Schwartz's circumplex model, called *self-enhancement*, refers to how much a person is motivated by self-interest. This quadrant includes the values categories of achievement (pursuit of personal success), power (dominance over others), and hedonism (a values category shared with openness to change). The opposite of self-enhancement is *self-transcendence*, which refers to motivation to promote the welfare of others and nature. Self-transcendence includes the value categories of benevolence (concern for others in one's life) and universalism (concern for the welfare of all people and nature).

Values and Individual Behavior

Personal values influence decisions and behavior in various ways.[53] First, values directly motivate our actions by shaping the relative attractiveness (*valence*) of the choices available. In other words, we experience more positive feelings toward alternatives that are aligned with our most important values. If stimulation is at the top of

Personal values guide our decisions and behavior to some extent, but this connection isn't as strong as we might like to believe.
©Borya Galperin/Shutterstock

motivated to engage in recycling and other environmentally friendly behaviors, but lack of recycling facilities prevents or severely limits this behavior. People also deviate from their personal values due to strong counter-motivational forces. For instance, employees caught in illegal business dealings sometimes attribute their unethical activities to pressure from management to achieve their performance at any cost.

Another reason why decisions and behavior are inconsistent with our personal values is that we don't actively think about them much of the time.[56] Values are abstract concepts, so their relevance is not obvious in many situations. Furthermore, many daily decisions and actions occur routinely, so we don't actively evaluate their consistency with our values. We do consciously consider our values in some situations, of course, such as realizing how much we value security when deciding whether to perform a risky task. However, many daily events do not trigger values awareness, so we act without the guidance of our personal values. We literally need to be reminded of our values so they guide our decisions and actions.

The effect of values awareness on behavior was apparent in a study in which students were given a math test and received a payment for each correct answer.[57] One group submitted their results to the experimenter for scoring, so they couldn't lie about their results. A second group could lie because they scored the test themselves and told the experimenter their test score. A third group was similar to the second (they scored their own test), but that test included the following statement, and students were required to sign their name to that statement: "I understand that this short survey falls under (the university's) honor system." The researchers estimated that some students cheated when they scored their own test without the "honor system" statement, whereas no one given the "honor system" form lied about the results. The university didn't actually have an official honor statement, but the message made students pay attention to their honesty. In short, people are more likely to apply their values (honesty, in this case) when they are explicitly reminded of those values and recognize their relevance to the situation.

Values Congruence

Values tell us what is right or wrong and what we ought to do. This evaluative characteristic affects how comfortable we are with specific organizations and individuals. The key concept here is *values congruence*, which refers to how similar a person's values hierarchy is to the values hierarchy of another entity, such as the employee's team or organization. This section of the chapter began by describing Liam's values incongruence with his project team, which affected his satisfaction, cohesion, and potentially performance in that team. Congruence with the organization's values tends to increase the employee's job satisfaction, loyalty, and organizational citizenship. It also tends to reduce stress and turnover. Furthermore, employees are more likely to make decisions that are compatible with organizational expectations when their personal values are congruent with the organization's shared value.[59]

Are organizations the most successful when every employee's personal values align with the company's values? Not at all! While a large degree of values congruence is necessary for the reasons just noted, organizations also benefit from some level of incongruence. Employees with diverse values offer different perspectives, which potentially lead to better decision making. Also, too much congruence can create a "corporate cult" that potentially undermines creativity, organizational flexibility, and business ethics.

LO2-5 Describe three ethical principles and discuss three factors that influence ethical behavior.

ETHICAL VALUES AND BEHAVIOR

When 195 business leaders across 15 countries were asked to identify the most important leader competencies, "high ethics and moral standards" was the top-rated item from the list of

74 characteristics. Similarly, when 1,000 CEOs and other top-level executives around the world were asked to list the most important attributes of effective leaders, the most frequently mentioned characteristic was *integrity*—the leader's ethical standards.[60] These surveys reveal the importance of ethics in the workplace. *Ethics* refers to the study of moral principles or values that determine whether actions are right or wrong and outcomes are good or bad (see Chapter 1). People rely on their ethical values to determine "the right thing to do."

Three Ethical Principles

To better understand business ethics, we need to consider three distinct types of ethical principles: utilitarianism, individual rights, and distributive justice.[61] Your personal values might sway you more toward one principle than the others, but all three should be actively considered when making decisions.

- *Utilitarianism.* This principle says the only moral obligation is to seek the greatest good for the greatest number of people. In other words, we should choose the option that provides the highest degree of satisfaction to those affected. One problem is that utilitarianism requires a cost–benefit analysis, yet many outcomes aren't measurable. Another problem is that utilitarianism could justify actions that other principles would consider immoral because those means produce the greatest good overall.

moral intensity the degree to which an issue demands the application of ethical principles

- *Individual rights.* This principle says that everyone has the same set of natural rights, such as freedom of speech, freedom of movement, right to physical security, and right to fair trial. The individual rights principle extends beyond legal rights to human rights that everyone is granted as a moral norm of society. One problem with this principle is that some individual rights may conflict with others. The shareholders' right to be informed about corporate activities may ultimately conflict with an executive's right to privacy, for example.

- *Distributive justice.* This principle says that the benefits and burdens of similar individuals should be the same; otherwise they should be proportional. For example, employees who contribute equally in their work should receive similar rewards, whereas those who make a lesser contribution should receive less. A variation of this principle says that

> ## It takes many good deeds to build a good reputation and only one bad one to lose it.
>
> —Attributed to Benjamin Franklin

Utilitarianism, individual rights, and distributive justice are three ethical principles that should be considered when making decisions.
©alphaspirit/Shutterstock

inequalities are acceptable when they benefit the least well off in society. The main problem with the distributive justice principle is that it is difficult to agree on who is "similar" and what factors are "relevant." We discuss distributive justice further in Chapter 5.

Moral Intensity, Moral Sensitivity, and Situational Influences

Along with ethical principles and their underlying values, three other factors influence ethical conduct in the workplace: the moral intensity of the issue, the individual's moral sensitivity, and situational factors.[62]

Moral Intensity Moral intensity is the degree to which an issue demands the application of ethical principles. Decisions with high moral intensity have strong ethical implications that usually affect many people, so the decision maker needs to carefully apply ethical principles to make the best choice. The moral intensity of a situation is higher when (a) the consequences of the decision could be very good or bad, (b) there is high agreement by others that the decision outcomes are good or bad, (c) there is a high probability that the good or bad outcomes will occur, and (d) many people will experience the consequences of the decision.[63]

Exhibit 2.7 Five Cross-Cultural Values

Value	Sample Countries	Representative Beliefs/Behaviors in "High" Cultures
Individualism	High: United States, Chile, Canada, South Africa Medium: Japan, Denmark Low: Taiwan, Venezuela	Defines self more by one's uniqueness; personal goals have priority; decisions have low consideration of effect on others; relationships are viewed as more instrumental and fluid.
Collectivism	High: Israel, Taiwan Medium: India, Denmark Low: United States, Germany, Japan	Defines self more by one's in-group membership; goals of self-sacrifice and harmony have priority; behavior regulated by in-group norms; in-group memberships are viewed as stable with a strong differentiation with out-groups.
Power distance	High: India, Malaysia Medium: United States, Japan Low: Denmark, Israel	Reluctant to disagree with or contradict the boss; managers are expected and preferred decision makers; perception of dependence on (versus interdependence with) the boss.
Uncertainty avoidance	High: Belgium, Greece Medium: United States, Norway Low: Denmark, Singapore	Prefer predictable situations; value stable employment, strict laws, and low conflict; dislike deviations from normal behavior.
Achievement orientation	High: Austria, Japan Medium: United States, Brazil Low: Sweden, Netherlands	Focus on outcomes (versus relationships); decisions based on contribution (equity versus equality); low empathy or showing emotions (versus strong empathy and caring).

Sources: Individualism and collectivism descriptions and results are from the meta-analysis reported in D. Oyserman, H. M. Coon, and M. Kemmelmeier, "Rethinking Individualism and Collectivism: Evaluation of Theoretical Assumptions and Meta-Analyses," *Psychological Bulletin* 128, no. 1 (2002): 3–72. The other information is from G. Hofstede, *Culture's Consequences*, 2nd ed. (Thousand Oaks, CA: Sage, 2001).

and South Africans generally exhibit high individualism, whereas Taiwan and Venezuela are countries with low individualism.[74] **Collectivism** is the extent to which we value our duty to groups to which we belong and to group harmony. Highly collectivist people define themselves by their group memberships, emphasize their personal connection to others in their in-groups, and value the goals and well-being of people within those groups.[75] Low collectivism countries include the United States, Japan, and Germany, whereas Israel and Taiwan have relatively high collectivism.

Contrary to popular belief, individualism is not the opposite of collectivism. In fact, the two concepts are typically uncorrelated.[76] For example, cultures that highly value duty to one's group do not necessarily give a low priority to personal freedom and uniqueness. Generally, people across all cultures define themselves by both their uniqueness and their relationship to others. It is an inherent characteristic of everyone's self-concept, which we discuss in the next chapter. Some cultures clearly emphasize either personal uniqueness or group obligations, but both have a place in a person's values and self-concept.

Also note that people in Japan have relatively low collectivism. This is contrary to many cross-cultural books, a few of which claim that Japan is one of the most collectivist countries on the planet! There are several explanations for the historical misinterpretation, ranging from problems defining and measuring collectivism to erroneous reporting of early cross-cultural research. Whatever the reasons, studies consistently report that people in Japan tend to have relatively low collectivism and moderate individualism (as indicated in Exhibit 2.7).[77]

Globalization may be an emerging reality, but values still differ to some extent across geographic regions.
©Rawpixel.com/Shutterstock

collectivism a cross-cultural value describing the degree to which people in a culture emphasize duty to groups to which they belong and to group harmony

power distance a cross-cultural value describing the degree to which people in a culture accept unequal distribution of power in a society

uncertainty avoidance a cross-cultural value describing the degree to which people in a culture tolerate ambiguity (low uncertainty avoidance) or feel threatened by ambiguity and uncertainty (high uncertainty avoidance)

achievement-nurturing orientation cross-cultural value describing the degree to which people in a culture emphasize competitive versus cooperative relations with other people

Power Distance

Power distance refers to the extent to which people accept unequal distribution of power in a society.[78] Those with high power distance value unequal power. Those in higher positions expect obedience to authority; those in lower positions are comfortable receiving commands from their superiors without consultation or debate. People with high power distance also prefer to resolve differences through formal procedures rather than direct informal discussion. In contrast, people with low power distance expect relatively equal power sharing. They view the relationship with their boss as one of interdependence, not dependence; that is, they believe their boss is also dependent on them, so they expect power sharing and consultation before decisions affecting them are made. People in India and Malaysia tend to have high power distance, whereas people in Denmark and Israel generally have low power distance. Americans collectively have medium-low power distance.

Uncertainty Avoidance

Uncertainty avoidance is the degree to which people tolerate ambiguity (low uncertainty avoidance) or feel threatened by ambiguity and uncertainty (high uncertainty avoidance). Employees with high uncertainty avoidance value structured situations in which rules of conduct and decision making are clearly documented. They usually prefer direct rather than indirect or ambiguous communications. Uncertainty avoidance tends to be high in Belgium and Greece and very high in Japan. It is generally low in Denmark and Singapore. Americans collectively have medium-low uncertainty avoidance.

Achievement-Nurturing Orientation

Achievement-nurturing orientation reflects a competitive versus cooperative view of relations with other people.[79] People with a high achievement orientation value assertiveness, competitiveness, and materialism. They appreciate people who are tough, and they favor the acquisition of money and material goods. In contrast, people in nurturing-oriented cultures emphasize relationships and the well-being of others. They focus on human interaction and caring rather than competition and personal success. People in Sweden, Norway, and the Netherlands have very low achievement orientation (i.e., they have a high nurturing orientation). In contrast, very high achievement orientation scores have been reported in Japan and Austria. The United States is located a little above the middle of the range on achievement-nurturing orientation.

Caveats about Cross-Cultural Knowledge

Cross-cultural organizational research has gained considerable attention over the past two decades, but we need to raise a few warning flags about cross-cultural knowledge. One problem is that too many studies have relied on small, convenient samples (such as students attending one university) to represent an entire culture.[81] The result is that many cross-cultural studies draw conclusions that might not generalize to the cultures they intended to represent. A second problem is that cross-cultural research and writing continue to rely on a major study conducted almost four decades ago of 116,000 IBM employees across dozens of countries. That study helped ignite subsequent cross-cultural research, but its findings are becoming out-of-date as values in some cultures have shifted over the years.[82]

A third concern is that cross-cultural studies often assume that each country has one culture.[83] In reality, the United States and many other countries have become culturally diverse. For example, a major review of past studies reported that, on average, African Americans have significantly higher individualism than European and Hispanic Americans, whereas Asian Americans have the lowest individualism among these demographic groups.[84]

Several studies also report cultural variations across geographic regions within the United States.[85] Collectivism is highest among Americans living in the southern states, California, and Hawaii; it is lowest in the Mountain, Northwest, and Great Plains states. Openness to experience is highest in the New England, Middle Atlantic, and Pacific regions; it is lowest in the Great Plains and midwestern and southeastern states.[86] Cultural differences within the United States are partly due to regional institutions, such as local governments, educational systems, and dominant religious groups.[87] For instance, research suggests that the number of rules and social controls (called *cultural tightness*) within each state explains differences in personality and values across the country.[88] Another reason for regional differences is that people with specific personality traits and personal values tend to migrate to places with particular geographic characteristics (mountains, ocean).[89] In summary, we need to recognize that cultural diversity often exists within countries, such as within the United States.

Study Checklist

Connect® Management is available for *M Organizational Behavior.* Additional resources include:

✓ Interactive Applications:
- **Decision Generator**
- **Drag and Drop:** Work through an interactive example to test your knowledge of the concepts.
- **Video Case:** See management in action through interactive videos.

✓ **SmartBook™**—SmartBook is the first and only adaptive reading experience available today. Distinguishing what you know from what you don't, and honing in on concepts you are most likely to forget, SmartBook personalizes content for you in a continuously adapting reading experience. Reading is no longer a passive and linear experience, but an engaging and dynamic one where you are more likely to master and retain important concepts and go to class better prepared.

©Natthawat Jamnapa/123RF

Notes

1. K. Roose, "Ray Dalio Is Building a Baseball Card Collection," *New York Magazine*, June 14, 2012; R. Feloni, "Here's Why the World's Largest Hedge Fund Makes Applicants Take 5 Personality Tests before Sitting through Hours of Intensive Interviews," *Business Insider*, August 16, 2016; R. Feloni, "These Are the Personality Tests You Take to Get a Job at the World's Largest Hedge Fund," *Business Insider*, August 27, 2016.

2. L. L. Thurstone, "Ability, Motivation, and Speed," *Psychometrika* 2, no. 4 (1937): 249–54; N. R. F. Maier, *Psychology in Industry*, 2nd ed. (Boston: Houghton Mifflin, 1955); V. H. Vroom, *Work and Motivation* (New York: Wiley, 1964); J. P. Campbell et al., *Managerial Behavior, Performance, and Effectiveness* (New York: McGraw-Hill, 1970).

3. R. S. Dalal, D. P. Bhave, and J. Fiset, "Within-Person Variability in Job Performance: A Theoretical Review and Research Agenda," *Journal of Management* 40, no. 5 (2014): 1396–436; S. Aryee et al., "Developing and Leveraging Human Capital Resource to Promote Service Quality: Testing a Theory of Performance," *Journal of Management* 42, no. 2 (2016): 480–99.

4. E. E. Lawler III and L. W. Porter, "Antecedent Attitudes of Effective Managerial Performance," *Organizational Behavior and Human Performance* 2 (1967): 122–42; O.-P. Kauppila, "So, What Am I Supposed to Do? A Multilevel Examination of Role Clarity," *Journal of Management Studies* 51, no. 5 (2014): 737–63.

5. Only a few sources have included all four factors. These include J. P. Campbell and R. D. Pritchard, "Motivation Theory in Industrial and Organizational Psychology," in *Handbook of Industrial and Organizational Psychology*, ed. M. D. Dunnette (Chicago: Rand McNally, 1976), 62–130; T. R. Mitchell, "Motivation: New Directions for Theory, Research, and Practice," *Academy of Management Review* 7, no. 1 (1982): 80–88; G. A. J. Churchill et al., "The Determinants of Salesperson Performance: A Meta-Analysis," *Journal of Marketing Research* 22, no. 2 (1985): 103–18; R. E. Plank and D. A. Reid, "The Mediating Role of Sales Behaviors: An Alternative Perspective of Sales Performance and Effectiveness," *Journal of Personal Selling & Sales Management* 14, no. 3 (1994): 43–56. The "MARS" acronym was coined by senior officers in the Singapore Armed Forces during a senior officer program taught by Steve McShane.

6. Technically, the model proposes that situational factors moderate the effects of the three within-person factors. For instance, the effect of employee motivation on behavior and performance depends on (is moderated by) the situation.

7. G. P. Latham and C. C. Pinder, "Work Motivation Theory and Research at the Dawn of the Twenty-First Century," *Annual Review of Psychology* 56 (2005): 485–516; G. P. Latham, *Work Motivation: History, Theory, Research, and Practice*, rev. ed. (Thousand Oaks, CA: Sage, 2012), 7.

8. T. J. Watson Jr., *A Business and Its Beliefs* (New York: McGraw-Hill, 2003), 4.

9. L. M. Spencer and S. M. Spencer, *Competence at Work: Models for Superior Performance* (New York: Wiley, 1993); D. Bartram, "The Great Eight Competencies: A Criterion-Centric Approach to Validation," *Journal of Applied Psychology* 90, no. 6 (2005): 1185–203; R. A. Roe, "Using Competences in Employee Development," in *Wiley Blackwell Handbook of the Psychology of Training, Development, and Performance Improvement*, ed. K. Kraiger et al. (Chichester: Wiley, 2014), 303–35.

10. P. Tharenou, A. M. Saks, and C. Moore, "A Review and Critique of Research on Training and Organizational-Level Outcomes," *Human Resource Management Review* 17, no. 3 (2007): 251–73; Y. Kim and R. E. Ployhart, "The Effects of Staffing and Training on Firm Productivity and Profit Growth before, during, and after the Great Recession," *Journal of Applied Psychology* 99, no. 3 (2014): 361–89; M. Choi and H. J. Yoon, "Training Investment and Organizational Outcomes: A Moderated Mediation Model of Employee Outcomes and Strategic Orientation of the HR Function," *The International Journal of Human Resource Management* 26, no. 20 (2015): 2632–51.

11. *The Interserve Society Report* (Reading, UK: Interserve, January 30, 2015); J. Harter, "Obsolete Annual Review: Gallup's Advice" (Washington, DC: Gallup, Inc., September 28, 2015); Randstad, "Prospects for Older Workers Shrink While the Skills Gap Widens," *Randstad Workmonitor* (Amsterdam, The Netherlands: Randstad Holding nv, June 2016); TINYpulse, *The Tinypulse 2015 Employee Engagement & Organizational Culture Report: The Era of Personal and Peer Accountability* (Seattle: TINYpulse, February 2016); Gallup Inc., *State of the American Workplace* (Washington, DC: Gallup, February 23, 2017).

12. BlessingWhite, *Employee Engagement Research Update* (Princeton, NJ: BlessingWhite, January 2013).

13. E. C. Dierdorff, R. S. Rubin, and D. G. Bachrach, "Role Expectations as Antecedents of Citizenship and the Moderating Effects of Work Context," *Journal of Management* 38, no. 2 (2012): 573–98; A. Newman, B. Allen, and Q. Miao, "I Can See Clearly Now: The Moderating Effects of Role Clarity on Subordinate Responses to Ethical Leadership," *Personnel Review* 44, no. 4 (2015): 611–28.

14. W. H. Cooper and M. J. Withey, "The Strong Situation Hypothesis," *Personality and Social Psychology Review* 13, no. 1 (2009): 62–72; N. A. Bowling et al., "Situational Strength as a Moderator of the Relationship between Job Satisfaction and Job Performance: A Meta-Analytic Examination," *Journal of Business and Psychology* 30, no. 1 (2015): 89–104; T. A. Judge and C. P. Zapata, "The Person–Situation Debate Revisited: Effect of Situation Strength and Trait Activation on the Validity of the Big Five Personality Traits in Predicting Job Performance," *Academy of Management Journal* 58, no. 4 (2015): 1149–79; J. F. Rauthmann and R. A. Sherman, "Situation Change: Stability and Change of Situation Variables between and within Persons," *Frontiers in Psychology* 6 (2016).

15. L. H. Peters and E. J. O'Connor, "Situational Constraints and Work Outcomes: The Influences of a Frequently Overlooked Construct," *Academy of Management Review* 5, no. 3 (1980): 391–97; G. Johns, "Commentary: In Praise of Context," *Journal of Organizational Behavior* 22 (2001): 31–42; C. E. J. Härtel and J. M. O'Connor, "Contextualizing Research: Putting Context Back into Organizational Behavior Research," *Journal of Management & Organization* 20, no. 4 (2014): 417–22.

16. R. D. Hackett, "Understanding and Predicting Work Performance in the Canadian Military," *Canadian Journal of Behavioural Science* 34, no. 2 (2002): 131–40; J. P. Campbell and B. M. Wiernik, "The Modeling and Assessment of Work Performance," *Annual Review of Organizational Psychology and Organizational Behavior* 2, no. 1 (2015): 47–74.

17. L. Tay, R. Su, and J. Rounds, "People-Things and Data-Ideas: Bipolar Dimensions?," *Journal of Counseling Psychology* 58, no. 3 (2011): 424–40.

18. M. A. Griffin, A. Neal, and S. K. Parker, "A New Model of Work Role Performance: Positive Behavior in Uncertain and Interdependent Contexts," *Academy of Management Journal* 50, no. 2 (2007): 327–47; S. K. Baard, T. A. Rench, and S. W. J. Kozlowski, "Performance Adaptation: A Theoretical Integration and Review," *Journal of Management* 40, no. 1 (2014): 48–99; D. K. Jundt, M. K. Shoss, and J. L. Huang, "Individual Adaptive Performance in Organizations: A Review," *Journal of Organizational Behavior* 36, no. S1 (2015): S53–S71.

19. D. W. Organ, "Organizational Citizenship Behavior: It's Construct Clean-up Time," *Human Performance* 10 (1997): 85–97; J. A. LePine, A. Erez, and D. E. Johnson, "The Nature and Dimensionality of Organizational Citizenship Behavior: A Critical Review and Meta-Analysis," *Journal of Applied Psychology* 87 (2002): 52–65; N. P. Podsakoff et al., "Consequences of Unit-Level Organizational Citizenship Behaviors: A Review and Recommendations for Future Research," *Journal of Organizational Behavior* 35, no. S1 (2014): S87–S119.

20. E. W. Morrison, "Role Definitions and Organizational Citizenship Behavior: The Importance of the Employee's Perspective," *Academy of Management Journal* 37, no. 6 (1994): 1543–67; N. Podsakoff et al., "Individual- and Organizational-Level Consequences of Organizational Citizenship Behaviors: A Meta-Analysis," *Journal of Applied Psychology* 94, no. 1 (2009): 122–41; E. C. Dierdorff, R. S. Rubin, and D. G. Bachrach, "Role Expectations as Antecedents of Citizenship and the Moderating Effects of Work Context," *Journal of Management* 38, no. 2 (2012): 573–98.

21. M. Ozer, "A Moderated Mediation Model of the Relationship between Organizational Citizenship Behaviors and Job Performance," *Journal of Applied Psychology* 96, no. 6 (2011): 1328–36; T. M. Nielsen et al., "Utility of OCB: Organizational Citizenship Behavior and Group Performance in a Resource Allocation Framework," *Journal of Management* 38, no. 2 (2012): 668–94.

22. A. C. Klotz and M. C. Bolino, "Citizenship and Counterproductive Work Behavior: A Moral Licensing View," *Academy of Management Review* 38, no. 2 (2013): 292-306; M. C. Bolino et al., "Exploring the Dark Side of Organizational Citizenship Behavior," *Journal of Organizational Behavior* 34, no. 4 (2013): 542-59.

23. M. Rotundo and P. Sackett, "The Relative Importance of Task, Citizenship, and Counterproductive Performance to Global Ratings of Job Performance: A Policy-Capturing Approach," *Journal of Applied Psychology* 87 (2002): 66-80; N. A. Bowling and M. L. Gruys, "Overlooked Issues in the Conceptualization and Measurement of Counterproductive Work Behavior," *Human Resource Management Review* 20, no. 1 (2010): 54-61; B. Marcus et al., "The Structure of Counterproductive Work Behavior: A Review, a Structural Meta-Analysis, and a Primary Study," *Journal of Management* 42, no. 1 (2016): 203-33.

24. T.-Y. Park and J. Shaw, "Turnover Rates and Organizational Performance: A Meta-Analysis," *Journal of Applied Psychology* 98, no. 2 (2013): 268-309; J. I. Hancock et al., "Meta-Analytic Review of Employee Turnover as a Predictor of Firm Performance," *Journal of Management* 39, no. 3 (2013): 573-603; J. G. Messersmith et al., "Turnover at the Top: Executive Team Departures and Firm Performance," *Organization Science* 25, no. 3 (2014): 776-93; B. C. Holtom and T. C. Burch, "A Model of Turnover-Based Disruption in Customer Services," *Human Resource Management Review* 26, no. 1 (2016): 25-36.

25. P. S. Goodman and R. S. Atkin, "Effects of Absenteeism on Individuals and Organizations," in *Absenteeism: New Approaches to Understanding, Measuring and Managing Employee Attendance*, ed. P. S. Goodman and R. S. Atkin (San Francisco: Jossey-Bass, 1984), 276-321; D. A. Harrison and J. J. Martocchio, "Time for Absenteeism: A 20-Year Review of Origins, Offshoots, and Outcomes," *Journal of Management* 24, no. 3 (1998): 305-50.

26. A. Väänänen et al., "The Role of Work Group in Individual Sickness Absence Behavior," *Journal of Health and Social Behavior* 49, no. 4 (2008): 452-67; W. Beemsterboer et al., "A Literature Review on Sick Leave Determinants (1984-2004)," *International Journal of Occupational Medicine and Environmental Health* 22, no. 2 (2009): 169-79; C. M. Berry, A. M. Lelchook, and M. A. Clark, "A Meta-Analysis of the Interrelationships between Employee Lateness, Absenteeism, and Turnover: Implications for Models of Withdrawal Behavior," *Journal of Organizational Behavior* 33, no. 5 (2012): 678-99; S. Störmer and R. Fahr, "Individual Determinants of Work Attendance: Evidence on the Role of Personality," *Applied Economics* 45, no. 19 (2012): 2863-75; M. Sliter, K. Sliter, and S. Jex, "The Employee as a Punching Bag: The Effect of Multiple Sources of Incivility on Employee Withdrawal Behavior and Sales Performance," *Journal of Organizational Behavior* 33, no. 1 (2012): 121-39; M. Biron and P. Bamberger, "Aversive Workplace Conditions and Absenteeism: Taking Referent Group Norms and Supervisor Support into Account," *Journal of Applied Psychology* 97, no. 4 (2012): 901-12.

27. G. Johns, "Presenteeism in the Workplace: A Review and Research Agenda," *Journal of Organizational Behavior* 31, no. 4 (2010): 519-42; R. K. Skagen and A. M. Collins, "The Consequences of Sickness Presenteeism on Health and Wellbeing over Time: A Systematic Review," *Social Science & Medicine* 161 (2016): 169-77.

28. G. Johns, "Attendance Dynamics at Work: The Antecedents and Correlates of Presenteeism, Absenteeism, and Productivity Loss," *Journal of Occupational Health Psychology* 16, no. 4 (2011): 483-500; D. Baker-McClearn et al., "Absence Management and Presenteeism: The Pressures on Employees to Attend Work and the Impact of Attendance on Performance," *Human Resource Management Journal* 20, no. 3 (2010): 311-28; R. Pohling et al., "Work-Related Factors of Presenteeism: The Mediating Role of Mental and Physical Health," *Journal of Occupational Health Psychology* 21, no. 2 (2016): 220-34.

29. M. B. Edmond, "How Sick Is Too Sick to Work? Presenteeism in Healthcare," *Medscape*, September 23, 2015; C. Chambers, *Superheroes Don't Take Sick Leave* (New Zealand: Association of Salaried Medical Specialists, November 2015); J. E. Szymczak et al., "Reasons Why Physicians and Advanced Practice Clinicians Work While Sick: A Mixed-Methods Analysis," *JAMA Pediatrics* 169, no. 9 (2015): 815-21; M. G. Sendén, K. Schenck-Gustafsson, and A. Fridner, "Gender Differences in Reasons for Sickness Presenteeism—A Study among GPs in a Swedish Health Care Organization," *Annals of Occupational and Environmental Medicine* 28, no. 50 (2016): 50.

30. Personality researchers agree on one point about the definition of personality: It is difficult to pin down. A definition necessarily captures one perspective of the topic more than others, and the concept of personality is itself very broad. The definition presented here is based on C. S. Carver and M. F. Scheier, *Perspectives on Personality*, 6th ed. (Boston: Allyn & Bacon, 2007); D. C. Funder, *The Personality Puzzle*, 4th ed. (New York: Norton, 2007).

31. D. P. McAdams and J. L. Pals, "A New Big Five: Fundamental Principles for an Integrative Science of Personality," *American Psychologist* 61, no. 3 (2006): 204-17.

32. B. W. Roberts and A. Caspi, "Personality Development and the Person-Situation Debate: It's Déjà Vu All over Again," *Psychological Inquiry* 12, no. 2 (2001): 104-109; N. A. Turiano et al., "Personality and Substance Use in Midlife: Conscientiousness as a Moderator and the Effects of Trait Change," *Journal of Research in Personality* 46, no. 3 (2012): 295-305; C. R. Gale et al., "Neuroticism and Extraversion in Youth Predict Mental Wellbeing and Life Satisfaction 40 Years Later," *Journal of Research in Personality* 47, no. 6 (2013): 687-97; M. Pluess and M. Bartley, "Childhood Conscientiousness Predicts the Social Gradient of Smoking in Adulthood: A Life Course Analysis," *Journal of Epidemiology and Community Health* 69, no. 4 (2015): 330-38; M. Blatný et al., "Personality Predictors of Successful Development: Toddler Temperament and Adolescent Personality Traits Predict Well-Being and Career Stability in Middle Adulthood," *PLoS ONE* 10, no. 4 (2015): e0126032.

33. W. Mischel, "Toward an Integrative Science of the Person," *Annual Review of Psychology* 55 (2004): 1-22; W. H. Cooper and M. J. Withey, "The Strong Situation Hypothesis," *Personality and Social Psychology Review* 13, no. 1 (2009): 62-72; T. A. Judge and C. P. Zapata, "The Person–Situation Debate Revisited," *Academy of Management Journal* 58, no. 4 (2015): 1149-79.

34. O. Wilde, *The Picture of Dorian Gray* (New York: Barnes & Noble, 2003), 340.

35. W. Bleidorn, "What Accounts for Personality Maturation in Early Adulthood?," *Current Directions in Psychological Science* 24, no. 3 (2015): 245-52; T. J. C. Polderman et al., "Meta-Analysis of the Heritability of Human Traits Based on Fifty Years of Twin Studies," *Nature Genetics* 47, no. 7 (2015): 702-709; L. Penke and M. Jokela, "The Evolutionary Genetics of Personality Revisited," *Current Opinion in Psychology* 7 (2016): 104-109.

36. B. W. Roberts, K. E. Walton, and W. Viechtbauer, "Patterns of Mean-Level Change in Personality Traits across the Life Course: A Meta-Analysis of Longitudinal Studies," *Psychological Bulletin* 132, no. 1 (2006): 1-25; A. Terracciano, P. T. Costa, and R. R. McCrae, "Personality Plasticity after Age 30," *Personality and Social Psychology Bulletin* 32, no. 8 (2006): 999-1009; R. Mõttus et al., "Within-Trait Heterogeneity in Age Group Differences in Personality Domains and Facets: Implications for the Development and Coherence of Personality Traits," *PLoS ONE* 10, no. 3 (2015): e0119667; C.-H. Wu, "Personality Change Via Work: A Job Demand-Control Model of Big-Five Personality Changes," *Journal of Vocational Behavior* 92 (2016): 157-66.

37. R. F. Baumeister, B. J. Schmeichel, and K. D. Vohs, "Self-Regulation and the Executive Function: The Self as Controlling Agent," in *Social Psychology: Handbook of Basic Principles*, ed. A. W. Kruglanski and E. T. Higgins (New York: Guilford, 2007), 516–39; K. Murdock, K. Oddi, and D. Bridgett, "Cognitive Correlates of Personality: Links between Executive Functioning and the Big Five Personality Traits," *Journal of Individual Differences* 34, no. 2 (2013): 97–104; P. Baggetta and P. A. Alexander, "Conceptualization and Operationalization of Executive Function," *Mind, Brain, and Education* 10, no. 1 (2016): 10–33.

38. J. M. Digman, "Personality Structure: Emergence of the Five-Factor Model," *Annual Review of Psychology* 41 (1990): 417–40; O. P. John and S. Srivastava, "The Big Five Trait Taxonomy: History, Measurement, and Theoretical Perspectives," in *Handbook of Personality: Theory and Research*, ed. L. A. Pervin and O. P. John (New York: Guilford Press, 1999), 102–38; R. R. McCrae, J. F. Gaines, and M. A. Wellington, "The Five-Factor Model in Fact and Fiction," in *Personality and Social Psychology*, 2nd ed., ed. H. A. Tennen and J. M. Suls, Handbook of Psychology, ed. I. B. Weiner, vol. 5 (New York: Wiley, 2012), 65–91.

39. H. Le et al., "Too Much of a Good Thing: Curvilinear Relationships between Personality Traits and Job Performance," *Journal of Applied Psychology* 96, no. 1 (2011): 113–33; A. M. Grant, "Rethinking the Extraverted Sales Ideal: The Ambivert Advantage," *Psychological Science* 24, no. 6 (2013): 1024–30; G. Blickle et al., "Extraversion and Job Performance: How Context Relevance and Bandwidth Specificity Create a Non-linear, Positive, and Asymptotic Relationship," *Journal of Vocational Behavior* 87 (2015): 80–88.

40. M. R. Barrick and M. K. Mount, "Yes, Personality Matters: Moving on to More Important Matters," *Human Performance* 18, no. 4 (2005): 359–72; P. R. Sackett and P. T. Walmsley, "Which Personality Attributes Are Most Important in the Workplace?," *Perspectives on Psychological Science* 9, no. 5 (2014): 538–51; L. M. Penney, E. David, and L. A. Witt, "A Review of Personality and Performance: Identifying Boundaries, Contingencies, and Future Research Directions," *Human Resource Management Review* 21, no. 4 (2011): 297–310; T. Judge et al., "Hierarchical Representations of the Five-Factor Model of Personality in Predicting Job Performance: Integrating Three Organizing Frameworks with Two Theoretical Perspectives," *Journal of Applied Psychology* 98, no. 6 (2013): 875–925; J. Huang et al., "Personality and Adaptive Performance at Work: A Meta-Analytic Investigation," *Journal of Applied Psychology* 99, no. 1 (2014): 162–79.

41. R. D. S. Chiaburu et al., "The Five-Factor Model of Personality Traits and Organizational Citizenship Behaviors: A Meta-Analysis," *Journal of Applied Psychology* 96, no. 6 (2011): 1140–66.

42. A. Neal et al., "Predicting the Form and Direction of Work Role Performance from the Big 5 Model of Personality Traits," *Journal of Organizational Behavior* 33, no. 2 (2012): 175–92.

43. J. L. Huang et al., "Personality and Adaptive Performance at Work," *Journal of Applied Psychology* 99, no. 1 (2014): 162–79.

44. C. G. Jung, *Psychological Types*, trans. H. G. Baynes (Princeton, NJ: Princeton University Press, 1971); I. B. Myers, *The Myers-Briggs Type Indicator* (Palo Alto, CA: Consulting Psychologists Press, 1987).

45. Adapted from an exhibit found at www.16-personality-types.com. Based on data from CPP, Inc., Sunnyvale, CA 94086 from *Introduction to Type and Careers* by Allen L. Hammer.

46. J. Michael, "Using the Myers-Briggs Type Indicator as a Tool for Leadership Development? Apply with Caution," *Journal of Leadership & Organizational Studies* 10 (2003): 68–81; R. M. Capraro and M. M. Capraro, "Myers-Briggs Type Indicator Score Reliability across Studies: A Meta-Analytic Reliability Generalization Study," *Educational and Psychological Measurement* 62 (2002): 590–602; B. S. Kuipers et al., "The Influence of Myers-Briggs Type Indicator Profiles on Team Development Processes," *Small Group Research* 40, no. 4 (2009): 436–64; F. W. Brown and M. D. Reilly, "The Myers-Briggs Type Indicator and Transformational Leadership," *Journal of Management Development* 28, no. 10 (2009): 916–32; A. Luse et al., "Personality and Cognitive Style as Predictors of Preference for Working in Virtual Teams," *Computers in Human Behavior* 29, no. 4 (2013): 1825–32.

47. R. B. Kennedy and D. A. Kennedy, "Using the Myers-Briggs Type Indicator in Career Counseling," *Journal of Employment Counseling* 41, no. 1 (2004): 38–44; K.-H. Lee, Y. Choi, and D. J. Stonier, "Evolutionary Algorithm for a Genetic Robot's Personality Based on the Myers-Briggs Type Indicator," *Robotics and Autonomous Systems* 60, no. 7 (2012): 941–61; S. J. Armstrong, E. Cools, and E. Sadler-Smith, "Role of Cognitive Styles in Business and Management: Reviewing 40 Years of Research," *International Journal of Management Reviews* 14, no. 3 (2012): 238–62.

48. J. B. Lloyd, "Unsubstantiated Beliefs and Values Flaw the Five-Factor Model of Personality," *Journal of Beliefs & Values* 36, no. 2 (2015): 156–64.

49. B. M. Meglino and E. C. Ravlin, "Individual Values in Organizations: Concepts, Controversies, and Research," *Journal of Management* 24, no. 3 (1998): 351–89; B. R. Agle and C. B. Caldwell, "Understanding Research on Values in Business," *Business and Society* 38, no. 3 (1999): 326–87; S. Hitlin and J. A. Pilavin, "Values: Reviving a Dormant Concept," *Annual Review of Sociology* 30 (2004): 359–93.

50. D. Lubinski, D. B. Schmidt, and C. P. Benbow, "A 20-Year Stability Analysis of the Study of Values for Intellectually Gifted Individuals from Adolescence to Adulthood," *Journal of Applied Psychology* 81 (1996): 443–51.

51. L. Parks and R. P. Guay, "Personality, Values, and Motivation," *Personality and Individual Differences* 47, no. 7 (2009): 675–84; L. Parks-Leduc, G. Feldman, and A. Bardi, "Personality Traits and Personal Values: A Meta-Analysis," *Personality and Social Psychology Review* 19, no. 1 (2015): 3–29.

52. S. H. Schwartz, "Universals in the Content and Structure of Values: Theoretical Advances and Empirical Tests in 20 Countries," *Advances in Experimental Social Psychology* 25 (1992): 1–65; D. Spini, "Measurement Equivalence of 10 Value Types from the Schwartz Value Survey across 21 Countries," *Journal of Cross-Cultural Psychology* 34, no. 1 (2003): 3–23; S. H. Schwartz and K. Boehnke, "Evaluating the Structure of Human Values with Confirmatory Factor Analysis," *Journal of Research in Personality* 38, no. 3 (2004): 230–55; S. H. Schwartz, "Studying Values: Personal Adventure, Future Directions," *Journal of Cross-Cultural Psychology* 42, no. 2 (2011): 307–19. Schwartz's model is currently being revised, but the new model is similar in overall design and still requires refinement. See S. H. Schwartz et al., "Refining the Theory of Basic Individual Values," *Journal of Personality and Social Psychology* 103, no. 4 (2012): 663–88.

53. N. T. Feather, "Values, Valences, and Choice: The Influence of Values on the Perceived Attractiveness and Choice of Alternatives," *Journal of Personality and Social Psychology* 68, no. 6 (1995): 1135–51; L. Sagiv, N. Sverdlik, and N. Schwarz, "To Compete or to Cooperate? Values' Impact on Perception and Action in Social Dilemma Games," *European Journal of Social Psychology* 41, no. 1 (2011): 64–77; S. H. Schwartz and T. Butenko, "Values and Behavior: Validating the Refined Value Theory in Russia," *European Journal of Social Psychology* 44, no. 7 (2014): 799–813.

54. M. Schrage, *Serious Play: How the World's Best Companies Simulate to Innovate* (Cambridge, MA: Harvard Business School Press, 1999), 98

55. G. R. Maio et al., "Addressing Discrepancies between Values and Behavior: The Motivating Effect of Reasons," *Journal of Experimental Social Psychology* 37, no. 2 (2001): 104–17; A. Bardi and S. H. Schwartz, "Values and Behavior: Strength and Structure of Relations," *Personality and Social Psychology Bulletin* 29, no. 10 (2003): 1207–20; L. Sagiv, N. Sverdlik, and N. Schwarz, "To Compete or to Cooperate? Values' Impact on Perception and Action in Social Dilemma Games," *European Journal of Social Psychology* 41, no. 1 (2011): 64–77; K. M. Sheldon and L. S. Krieger, "Walking the Talk: Value Importance, Value Enactment, and Well-Being," *Motivation and Emotion* 38 (2014): 609–19.

56. E. Dreezens et al., "The Missing Link: On Strengthening the Relationship between Values and Attitudes," *Basic and Applied Social Psychology* 30, no. 2 (2008): 142–52; S. Arieli, A. M. Grant, and L. Sagiv, "Convincing Yourself to Care About Others: An Intervention for Enhancing Benevolence Values," *Journal of Personality* 82, no. 1 (2014): 15–24.

57. N. Mazar, O. Amir, and D. Ariely, "The Dishonesty of Honest People: A Theory of Self-Concept Maintenance," *Journal of Marketing Research* 45 (2008): 633–44.

58. L. Colan, "The Authentic Workplace: Aligning Work and Personal Values," *Inc.*, November 30, 2016.

59. M. L. Verquer, T. A. Beehr, and S. H. Wagner, "A Meta-Analysis of Relations between Person–Organization Fit and Work Attitudes," *Journal of Vocational Behavior* 63 (2003): 473–89; J. W. Westerman and L. A. Cyr, "An Integrative Analysis of Person–Organization Fit Theories," *International Journal of Selection and Assessment* 12, no. 3 (2004): 252–61; J. R. Edwards and D. M. Cable, "The Value of Value Congruence," *Journal of Applied Psychology* 94, no. 3 (2009): 654–77; A. L. Kristof-Brown et al., "Collective Fit Perceptions: A Multilevel Investigation of Person–Group Fit with Individual-Level and Team-Level Outcomes," *Journal of Organizational Behavior* 35, no. 7 (2014): 969–89.

60. The Conference Board, *CEO Challenge 2014* (New York: The Conference Board, January 2014); S. Giles, "The Most Important Leadership Competencies, According to Leaders around the World," *Harvard Business Review Digital Articles* (March 2016): 2–6.

61. P. L. Schumann, "A Moral Principles Framework for Human Resource Management Ethics," *Human Resource Management Review* 11 (2001): 93–111; J. A. Boss, *Analyzing Moral Issues*, 6th ed. (New York: McGraw-Hill, 2013), chap. 1; A. Gustafson, "In Defense of a Utilitarian Business Ethic," *Business and Society Review* 118, no. 3 (2013): 325–60.

62. For analysis of these predictors of ethical conduct, see J. J. Kish-Gephart, D. A. Harrison, and L. K. Treviño, "Bad Apples, Bad Cases, and Bad Barrels: Meta-Analytic Evidence about Sources of Unethical Decisions at Work," *Journal of Applied Psychology* 95, no. 1 (2010): 1–32.

63. T. M. Jones, "Ethical Decision Making by Individuals in Organizations: An Issue-Contingent Model," *Academy of Management Review* 16 (1991): 366–95; T. Barnett, "Dimensions of Moral Intensity and Ethical Decision Making: An Empirical Study," *Journal of Applied Social Psychology* 31, no. 5 (2001): 1038–57; J. Tsalikis, B. Seaton, and P. Shepherd, "Relative Importance Measurement of the Moral Intensity Dimensions," *Journal of Business Ethics* 80, no. 3 (2008): 613–26; S. Valentine and D. Hollingworth, "Moral Intensity, Issue Importance, and Ethical Reasoning in Operations Situations," *Journal of Business Ethics* 108, no. 4 (2012): 509–23.

64. K. Weaver, J. Morse, and C. Mitcham, "Ethical Sensitivity in Professional Practice: Concept Analysis," *Journal of Advanced Nursing* 62, no. 5 (2008): 607–18; L. J. T. Pedersen, "See No Evil: Moral Sensitivity in the Formulation of Business Problems," *Business Ethics: A European Review* 18, no. 4 (2009): 335–48. According to one recent neuroscience study, the emotional aspect of moral sensitivity declines and the cognitive aspect increases between early childhood and young adulthood. See J. Decety, K. J. Michalska, and K. D. Kinzler, "The Contribution of Emotion and Cognition to Moral Sensitivity: A Neurodevelopmental Study," *Cerebral Cortex* 22, no. 1 (2012): 209–20.

65. D. You, Y. Maeda, and M. J. Bebeau, "Gender Differences in Moral Sensitivity: A Meta-Analysis," *Ethics & Behavior* 21, no. 4 (2011): 263–82; A. H. Chan and H. Cheung, "Cultural Dimensions, Ethical Sensitivity, and Corporate Governance," *Journal of Business Ethics* 110, no. 1 (2012): 45–59; J. R. Sparks, "A Social Cognitive Explanation of Situational and Individual Effects on Moral Sensitivity," *Journal of Applied Social Psychology* 45, no. 1 (2015): 45–54; S. J. Reynolds and J. A. Miller, "The Recognition of Moral Issues: Moral Awareness, Moral Sensitivity and Moral Attentiveness," *Current Opinion in Psychology* 6 (2015): 114–17.

66. J. Boegershausen, K. Aquino, and A. Reed II, "Moral Identity," *Current Opinion in Psychology* 6 (2015): 162–66.

67. N. Ruedy and M. Schweitzer, "In the Moment: The Effect of Mindfulness on Ethical Decision Making," *Journal of Business Ethics* 95, no. 1 (2010): 73–87.

68. M. H. Bazerman and F. Gino, "Behavioral Ethics: Toward a Deeper Understanding of Moral Judgment and Dishonesty," *Annual Review of Law and Social Science* 8, no. 1 (2012): 85–104; M. Knoll et al., "Examining the Moral Grey Zone: The Role of Moral Disengagement, Authenticity, and Situational Strength in Predicting Unethical Managerial Behavior," *Journal of Applied Social Psychology* 46, no. 1 (2016): 65–78.

69. Ethics & Compliance Initiative, *Global Business Ethics Survey: Measuring Risk and Promoting Workplace Integrity* (Arlington, VA: Ethics & Compliance Initiative, June 2016), 9.

70. H. Donker, D. Poff, and S. Zahir, "Corporate Values, Codes of Ethics, and Firm Performance: A Look at the Canadian Context," *Journal of Business Ethics* 82, no. 3 (2008): 527–37; G. Svensson et al., "Ethical Structures and Processes of Corporations Operating in Australia, Canada, and Sweden: A Longitudinal and Cross-Cultural Study," *Journal of Business Ethics* 86, no. 4 (2009): 485–506; L. Preuss, "Codes of Conduct in Organisational Context: From Cascade to Lattice-Work of Codes," *Journal of Business Ethics* 94, no. 4 (2010): 471–87.

71. G. Svensson et al., "Ethical Structures and Processes of Corporations Operating in Australia, Canada, and Sweden: A Longitudinal and Cross-Cultural Study," *Journal of Business Ethics* 86, no. 4 (2009): 485–506.

72. S. L. Grover, T. Nadisic, and D. L. Patient, "Bringing Together Different Perspectives on Ethical Leadership," *Journal of Change Management* 12, no. 4 (2012): 377–81; J. Jordan et al., "Someone to Look Up To: Executive–Follower Ethical Reasoning and Perceptions of Ethical Leadership," *Journal of Management* 39, no. 3 (2013): 660–83; J. Jaeger, "Compliance Culture Depends on Middle Management," *Compliance Week* (February 2014): 47–61.

73. "The TI Ethics Quick Test," *Corporate Governance* (Dallas: Texas Instruments, 2017), http://www.ti.com/corp/docs/company/citizen/ethics/quicktest.shtml (accessed June 16, 2017).

74. Individualism and collectivism information is from the meta-analysis by Oyserman et al., not the earlier findings by Hofstede. See D. Oyserman, H. M. Coon, and M. Kemmelmeier, "Rethinking Individualism and Collectivism: Evaluation of Theoretical Assumptions and Meta-Analyses," *Psychological Bulletin* 128, no. 1 (2002): 3–72. Consistent with Oyserman et al., a recent study found high rather than low individualism among Chileans. See A. Kolstad and S. Horpestad, "Self-Construal in Chile and Norway," *Journal of Cross-Cultural Psychology* 40, no. 2 (2009): 275–81.

75. F. S. Niles, "Individualism–Collectivism Revisited," *Cross-Cultural Research* 32 (1998): 315–41; C. P. Earley and C. B. Gibson, "Taking Stock in Our Progress on Individualism–Collectivism: 100 Years of Solidarity and Community," *Journal of Management* 24 (1998): 265–304; C. L. Jackson et al., "Psychological Collectivism: A Measurement Validation and Linkage to Group Member Performance," *Journal of Applied Psychology* 91, no. 4 (2006): 884–99.

76. D. Oyserman, H. M. Coon, and M. Kemmelmeier, "Rethinking Individualism and Collectivism: Evaluation of Theoretical Assumptions and Meta-Analyses," *Psychological Bulletin* 128, no. 1 (2002): 3–72. Also see F. Li and L. Aksoy, "Dimensionality of Individualism–Collectivism and Measurement Equivalence of Triandis and Gelfand's Scale," *Journal of Business and Psychology* 21, no. 3 (2007): 313–29. The "vertical–horizontal" distinction does not account for the lack of correlation between individualism and collectivism. See J. H. Vargas and M. Kemmelmeier, "Ethnicity and Contemporary American Culture: A Meta-Analytic Investigation of Horizontal–Vertical Individualism–Collectivism," *Journal of Cross-Cultural Psychology* 44, no. 2 (2013): 195–222.

77. M. Voronov and J. A. Singer, "The Myth of Individualism-Collectivism: A Critical Review," *Journal of Social Psychology* 142 (2002): 461–80; Y. Takano and S. Sogon, "Are Japanese More Collectivistic Than Americans?," *Journal of Cross-Cultural Psychology* 39, no. 3 (2008): 237–50; D. Dalsky, "Individuality in Japan and the United States: A Cross-Cultural Priming Experiment," *International Journal of Intercultural Relations* 34, no. 5 (2010): 429–35. Japan scored 46 on individualism in Hofstede's original study, placing it a little below the middle of the range and around the 60th percentile among the countries studied. Recent studies suggest that Japan has become even more individualistic in recent years. See Y. Ogihara et al., "Are Common Names Becoming Less Common? The Rise in Uniqueness and Individualism in Japan," *Frontiers in Psychology* 6 (2015): 1490.

78. G. Hofstede, *Culture's Consequences: Comparing Values, Behaviors, Institutions, and Organizations across Nations*, 2nd ed. (Thousand Oaks, CA: Sage, 2001).

79. G. Hofstede, *Culture's Consequences: Comparing Values, Behaviors, Institutions, and Organizations across Nations*, 2nd ed. (Thousand Oaks, CA: Sage, 2001). Hofstede used the terms *masculinity* and *femininity* for *achievement* and *nurturing orientation*, respectively. We (along with other writers) have adopted the latter two terms to minimize the sexist perspective of these concepts. Also, readers need to be aware that achievement orientation is assumed to be opposite of nurturing orientation, but this opposing relationship might be questioned.

80. T. Mickle and E. Pfanner, "Jim Beam's New Owner Mixes Global Cocktail," *The Wall Street Journal*, May 4, 2015, A1; K. Moritsugu, "Merging US, Japan Work Cultures a Challenge for Beam Suntory," Associated Press, January 15, 2016.

81. V. Taras, J. Rowney, and P. Steel, "Half a Century of Measuring Culture: Review of Approaches, Challenges, and Limitations Based on the Analysis of 121 Instruments for Quantifying Culture," *Journal of International Management* 15, no. 4 (2009): 357–73.

82. N. Jacob, "Cross-Cultural Investigations: Emerging Concepts," *Journal of Organizational Change Management* 18, no. 5 (2005): 514–28; V. Taras, B. L. Kirkman, and P. Steel, "Examining the Impact of Culture's Consequences: A Three-Decade, Multilevel, Meta-Analytic Review of Hofstede's Cultural Value Dimensions," *Journal of Applied Psychology* 95, no. 3 (2010): 405–39.

83. R. L. Tung and A. Verbeke, "Beyond Hofstede and GLOBE: Improving the Quality of Cross-Cultural Research," *Journal of International Business Studies* 41, no. 8 (2010): 1259–74.

84. D. Oyserman, H. M. Coon, and M. Kemmelmeier, "Rethinking Individualism and Collectivism: Evaluation of Theoretical Assumptions and Meta-Analyses," *Psychological Bulletin* 128, no. 1 (2002): 3–72. However, a recent meta-analysis found only minor differences across ethnic groups. See J. H. Vargas and M. Kemmelmeier, "Ethnicity and Contemporary American Culture: A Meta-Analytic Investigation of Horizontal–Vertical Individualism–Collectivism," *Journal of Cross-Cultural Psychology* 44, no. 2 (2013): 195–222.

85. J. A. Vandello and D. Cohen, "Patterns of Individualism and Collectivism across the United States," *Journal of Personality and Social Psychology* 77, no. 2 (1999): 279–92; B. MacNab, R. Worthley, and S. Jenner, "Regional Cultural Differences and Ethical Perspectives within the United States: Avoiding Pseudo-Emic Ethics Research," *Business and Society Review* 115, no. 1 (2010): 27–55; J. Lun, B. Mesquita, and B. Smith, "Self- and Other-Presentational Styles in the Southern and Northern United States: An Analysis of Personal Ads," *European Journal of Social Psychology* 41, no. 4 (2011): 435–45; P. J. Rentfrow et al., "Divided We Stand: Three Psychological Regions of the United States and Their Political, Economic, Social, and Health Correlates," *Journal of Personality and Social Psychology* 105, no. 6 (2013): 996–1012.

86. V. C. Plaut, H. Rose Markus, and M. E. Lachman, "Place Matters: Consensual Features and Regional Variation in American Well-Being and Self," *Journal of Personality and Social Psychology* 83, no. 1 (2002): 160–84; P. J. Rentfrow, "Statewide Differences in Personality: Toward a Psychological Geography of the United States," *American Psychologist* 65, no. 6 (2010): 548–58; K. H. Rogers and D. Wood, "Accuracy of United States Regional Personality Stereotypes," *Journal of Research in Personality* 44, no. 6 (2010): 704–13; J. Lieske, "The Changing Regional Subcultures of the American States and the Utility of a New Cultural Measure," *Political Research Quarterly* 63, no. 3 (2010): 538–52.

87. P. J. Rentfrow, "Statewide Differences in Personality: Toward a Psychological Geography of the United States," *American Psychologist* 65, no. 6 (2010): 548–58; J. Lieske, "The Changing Regional Subcultures of the American States and the Utility of a New Cultural Measure," *Political Research Quarterly* 63, no. 3 (2010): 538–52.

88. J. R. Harrington and M. J. Gelfand, "Tightness–Looseness across the 50 United States," *Proceedings of the National Academy of Sciences* 111, no. 22 (2014): 7990–95.

89. M. Motyl et al., "How Ideological Migration Geographically Segregates Groups," *Journal of Experimental Social Psychology* 51 (2014): 1–14; S. Oishi, T. Talhelm, and M. Lee, "Personality and Geography: Introverts Prefer Mountains," *Journal of Research in Personality* 58 (2015): 55–68.

self-serving bias the tendency to attribute our favorable outcomes to internal factors and our failures to external factors

fundamental attribution error the tendency to see the person rather than the situation as the main cause of that person's behavior

with others and to assign praise or blame to them.[57] Suppose a coworker didn't complete his or her task on a team project. You would approach this situation differently if you believed the coworker was lazy or lacked sufficient skill (an internal attribution) than if you believed the poor performance was due to lack of time or resources available to the coworker (an external attribution). Similarly, our respect for a leader depends on whether we believe his or her actions are due to personal characteristics or the situation. We also react differently to attributions of our own behavior and performance. Students who make internal attributions about their poor grades, for instance, are more likely to drop out of their programs than if they make external attributions about those grades.[58]

Attribution Errors The attribution process is susceptible to errors. One such error is **self-serving bias**—the tendency to attribute our failures to external causes more than internal causes,

while successes are due more to internal than external factors.[59] Simply put, we take credit for our successes and blame others or the situation for our mistakes. In annual reports, for example, executives mainly refer to their personal qualities as reasons for the company's successes and to competitors, unexpected legislation, and other external factors as reasons for the company's failures.[60] Self-serving bias occurs mainly because of the self-enhancement process described earlier in this chapter. By pointing to external causes of their own failures, and internal causes of their successes, people generate a more positive self-concept.

Another attribution error, **fundamental attribution error** (also called *correspondence bias*), is the tendency to overemphasize internal causes of another person's behavior and to discount or ignore external causes of his or her behavior.[61] We are more likely to attribute a coworker's late arrival for work to lack of motivation rather than to situational constraints (such as traffic congestion). This occurs because observers can't easily see the external factors that constrain another person's behavior. Also, people like to think that human beings (not the situation) are the prime sources of their behavior. Although fundamental attribution error does occur, recent reviews suggest it may be less common than previously thought.[62]

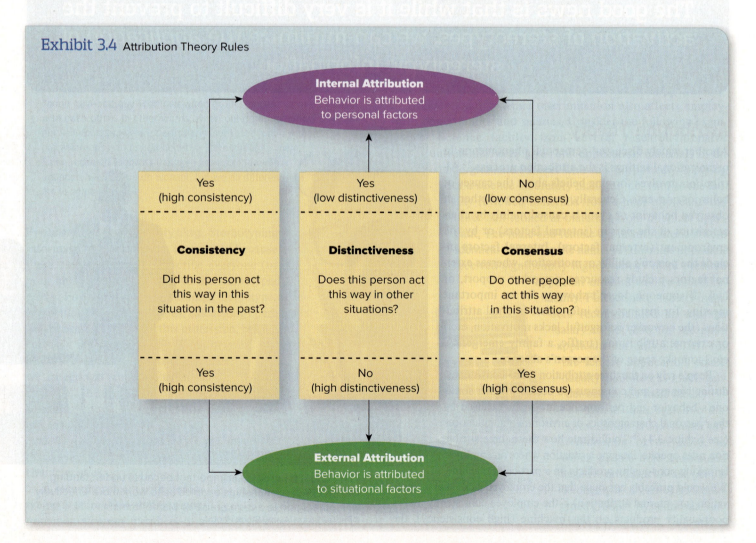

Exhibit 3.4 Attribution Theory Rules

Internal Attribution
Behavior is attributed to personal factors

Yes (high consistency)	Yes (low distinctiveness)	No (low consensus)
Consistency	**Distinctiveness**	**Consensus**
Did this person act this way in this situation in the past?	Does this person act this way in other situations?	Do other people act this way in this situation?
Yes (high consistency)	No (high distinctiveness)	Yes (high consensus)

External Attribution
Behavior is attributed to situational factors

Self-Fulfilling Prophecy

Self-fulfilling prophecy occurs when our expectations about another person cause that person to act in a way that is consistent with those expectations. In other words, our perceptions can influence reality. Exhibit 3.5 illustrates the four steps in the self-fulfilling prophecy process using the example of a supervisor and a subordinate.[63] The process begins when the supervisor forms expectations about the employee's future behavior and performance. These expectations are sometimes inaccurate because first impressions are usually formed from limited information. The supervisor's expectations influence his or her behavior toward employees. In particular, high-expectancy employees (those expected to do well) receive more emotional support through nonverbal cues (e.g., more smiling and eye contact), more frequent and valuable feedback and reinforcement, more challenging goals, better training, and more opportunities to demonstrate good performance.[64]

The third step in self-fulfilling prophecy includes two effects of the supervisor's behavior on the employee. First, through better training and more practice opportunities, a high-expectancy employee learns more skills and knowledge than a low-expectancy employee. Second, the high-expectancy employee becomes more self-confident, which results in higher motivation and willingness to set more challenging goals.[65] In the final step, high-expectancy employees have higher motivation and better skills, resulting in better performance, while the opposite is true of low-expectancy employees.

Self-fulfilling prophecy has been observed in many contexts. In one study, four Israeli Defense Force combat command course instructors were told that one-third of the incoming trainees had high command potential, one-third had normal potential, and the rest had unknown potential. The trainees had been randomly placed into these categories by the researchers, but the instructors were led to believe that the information they received was accurate. Consistent with self-fulfilling prophecy, high-expectancy soldiers performed significantly better by the end of the course than did trainees in the other groups. They also had more favorable attitudes toward the course and the instructor's leadership effectiveness. An analysis of dozens of leader intervention studies over the years found that self-fulfilling prophecy is one of the most powerful leadership effects on follower behavior and performance.[66]

Contingencies of Self-Fulfilling Prophecy The self-fulfilling prophecy effect is stronger in some situations than in others. It has a stronger effect at the beginning of a relationship, such as when employees are first hired. It is also stronger when several people (rather than just one person) hold the same expectations of the individual. In other words, we might be able to ignore one person's doubts about our potential but not the collective doubts of several people. The self-fulfilling prophecy effect is also stronger among people with a history of low achievement. These people tend to have lower self-esteem, so they are more easily influenced by others' opinions of them.[67]

The main lesson from the self-fulfilling prophecy literature is that leaders need to develop and maintain a positive, yet realistic, expectation toward all employees. This recommendation is consistent with the emerging philosophy of **positive organizational behavior**, which suggests that focusing on the positive rather than negative aspects of life will improve organizational success and individual well-being. Communicating hope and optimism is so important that it is identified as one of the critical success factors for physicians and surgeons. Training programs that make leaders aware of the power of positive expectations seem to have minimal effect, however. Instead, generating positive expectations and hope depends on a corporate culture of support and learning. Hiring

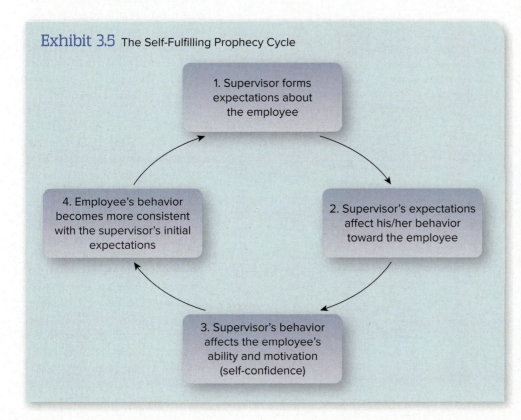

Exhibit 3.5 The Self-Fulfilling Prophecy Cycle

1. Supervisor forms expectations about the employee

2. Supervisor's expectations affect his/her behavior toward the employee

3. Supervisor's behavior affects the employee's ability and motivation (self-confidence)

4. Employee's behavior becomes more consistent with the supervisor's initial expectations

supervisors who are inherently optimistic toward their staff is another way of increasing the incidence of positive self-fulfilling prophecies.

Other Perceptual Effects

Self-fulfilling prophecy, attribution, and stereotyping are among the most common perceptual processes and biases in organizational settings, but there are many others. Four additional biases that have received attention in organizational settings are briefly described below.

Halo Effect The halo effect occurs when our general impression of a person, usually based on one prominent characteristic, distorts our perception of other characteristics of that person.[68] If a supervisor who values punctuality notices that an employee is sometimes late for work, the supervisor might form a negative overall opinion of the employee and evaluate that person's other traits unfavorably as well. The halo effect occurs most often when the manager lacks solid information—or isn't motivated to seek out the information—about the employee's performance on specific tasks. Instead, the manager relies on a general impression of the employee to fill in the missing information.

The halo effect occurs when our general impression of a person, usually based on one prominent characteristic, distorts our perception of other characteristics of that person.
(photo): ©YAY Media AS/Alamy

False-Consensus Effect The false-consensus effect (also called *similar-to-me effect*) occurs when people overestimate the extent to which others have similar beliefs or behaviors to our own.[69] Employees who are thinking of quitting their jobs overestimate the percentage of coworkers who also are thinking about quitting, for example. There are several explanations for false-consensus effect. One is that we are comforted believing that others are similar to us, particularly regarding less acceptable or divisive behavior. Put differently, we perceive "everyone does it" to create a more favorable view of behaviors that do not have a positive image (quitting our job, parking illegally, etc.).

A second explanation for false-consensus effect is that we interact more with people who have similar views and behaviors. This frequent interaction causes us to overestimate how common those views/behaviors are in the entire organization or society. Third, as noted earlier in this chapter, we are more likely to remember information that is consistent with our own views and selectively screen out information that is contrary to our beliefs. Fourth, our social identity process homogenizes people within groups, so we tend to think that everyone in that group has similar opinions and behavior, including the false-consensus attitude or behavior.

Primacy Effect The primacy effect is our tendency to rely on the first information we receive about people to quickly form an opinion of them.[70] It is the notion that first impressions are lasting impressions. This rapid perceptual organization and interpretation occurs because we need to make sense of the situation and, in particular, to trust others. The problem is that first impressions—particularly negative first impressions—are difficult to change. After categorizing someone, we tend to select subsequent information that supports our first impression and screen out information that opposes that impression.

First Impressions Count in Job Applications[71]

29% of chief financial officers say job applicants make the most mistakes in their résumé or cover letter (43% say most mistakes are made during the interview).

Some Résumé Gaffes
"Dear Sir or **Madman**."
"Assisted company executives with travel **arraignments**."
"I would like to work for a company that is **very lax** when it comes to **tardiness**."
"Instrumental for **ruining** entire operation for a Midwest chain store."
"My last employer **fried** me for no reason."
"Earned a diploma from a very **repudiated** college."
"Hope to hear from you, **shorty**."

36% of employers say they automatically dismiss a job applicant whose résumé is generic and doesn't seem personalized for the position.

58% of employers identified typos as the most common problems with résumés that led them to automatically dismiss a job applicant.

(photo): ©pathdoc/Shutterstock

43% of employers say they spend less than a minute looking at a résumé.

32% of employers say they automatically dismiss a job applicant whose résumé includes a large amount of wording from the job posting.

halo effect a perceptual error whereby our general impression of a person, usually based on one prominent characteristic, colors our perception of other characteristics of that person

false-consensus effect a perceptual error in which we overestimate the extent to which others have beliefs and characteristics similar to our own

primacy effect a perceptual error in which we quickly form an opinion of people based on the first information we receive about them

recency effect a perceptual error in which the most recent information dominates our perception of others

Johari Window a model of mutual understanding that encourages disclosure and feedback to increase our own open area and reduce the blind, hidden, and unknown areas

Recency Effect

The **recency effect** occurs when the most recent information dominates our perceptions.[72] This perceptual bias is most common when people (especially those with limited experience) make a decision involving complex information. For instance, auditors must digest large volumes of information in their judgments about financial documents, and the most recent information received prior to the decision tends to get weighted more heavily than information received at the beginning of the audit. Similarly, when supervisors evaluate the performance of employees over the previous year, the most recent performance information dominates the evaluation because it is the most easily recalled.

> **LO3-4** Discuss three ways to improve perceptions, with specific application to organizational situations.

IMPROVING PERCEPTIONS

We can't bypass the perceptual process, but we should try to minimize perceptual biases and distortions. Three potentially effective ways to improve perceptions include awareness of perceptual biases, self-awareness, and meaningful interaction.

Awareness of Perceptual Biases

One of the most obvious and widely practiced ways to reduce perceptual biases is by knowing that they exist. For example, diversity awareness training tries to minimize discrimination by making people aware of systemic discrimination as well as prejudices that occur through stereotyping. This training also attempts to dispel myths about people from various cultural and demographic groups. Awareness of perceptual biases can reduce these biases to some extent by making people more mindful of their thoughts and actions. However, awareness training has only a limited effect.[73] One problem is that teaching people to reject incorrect stereotypes has the unintended effect of reinforcing rather than reducing reliance on those stereotypes. Another problem is that diversity training is ineffective for people with deeply held prejudices against those groups.

Improving Self-Awareness

A more successful way to minimize perceptual biases is by increasing self-awareness.[74] We need to become more aware of our beliefs, values, and attitudes and, from that insight, gain a better understanding of biases in our own decisions and behavior.

This self-awareness tends to reduce perceptual biases by making people more open-minded and nonjudgmental toward others. Self-awareness is equally important in other ways. The emerging concept of authentic leadership emphasizes self-awareness as the first step in a person's ability to effectively lead others (see Chapter 11). Essentially, we need to understand our own values, strengths, and biases as a foundation for building a vision and leading others toward that vision.[75]

But how do we become more self-aware? One approach is to complete formal tests that indicate any implicit biases we might have toward others. The Implicit Association Test (IAT) is one such instrument. Although the accuracy of the IAT is being hotly debated by scholars, it attempts to detect subtle racial, age, gender, disability, and other forms of bias by associating positive and negative words with specific groups of people.[76] Many people are much more cautious about their stereotypes and prejudices after discovering that their test results show a personal bias against older people or individuals from different ethnic backgrounds.[77]

Another way to reduce perceptual biases through increased self-awareness is by applying the **Johari Window**.[78] Developed by Joseph Luft and Harry Ingram (hence the name "Johari"), this model of self-awareness and mutual understanding divides information about you into four "windows"—open, blind, hidden, and unknown—based on whether your own values, beliefs, and experiences are known to you and to others (see Exhibit 3.6). The *open area* includes information about you that is known both to you and to others. The *blind area* refers to information that is known to others but not to you. For example, your colleagues might notice that you are self-conscious and awkward when meeting the company's chief executive officer, but you are unaware of this fact. Information known to you but unknown to others is found in the *hidden area*. Finally, the *unknown area* includes your values, beliefs, and experiences that are buried so deeply that neither you nor others are aware of them.

The main objective of the Johari Window is to increase the size of the open area so that both you and your colleagues are aware of your perceptual limitations. This objective is partly accomplished by reducing the hidden area through *disclosure*—informing others of your beliefs, feelings, and experiences that may influence the work relationship. The open area also increases through *feedback* from others about your behavior. Feedback reduces your blind area because, according to recent studies, people near you are good sources of information about many (but not all) of your traits and behaviors.[79] Finally, the combination of disclosure and feedback occasionally produces revelations about you in the unknown area.

Meaningful Interaction

The Johari Window relies on direct conversations about ourselves and others, whereas *meaningful interaction* is a more indirect, yet potentially powerful, approach to improving self-awareness and mutual understanding.[80] Meaningful interaction is any activity in which people engage in valued (meaningful, not trivial) activities. The activities might be work related, such as when senior executives work alongside frontline staff. Or the activities might occur outside the workplace, such as when sales staff from several countries participate in outdoor challenges.

Meaningful interaction is founded on the **contact hypothesis**, which states that, under certain conditions, people who interact with each other will be less perceptually biased because they have a more personal understanding of the other person and their group.[81] Simply spending time with members of other groups can improve this understanding to some extent. However, meaningful interaction is strongest when people work closely and frequently with each other on a shared goal that requires mutual cooperation and reliance. Furthermore, everyone should have equal status in that context, should be engaged in a meaningful task, and should have positive experiences with each other in those interactions.

Meaningful interaction reduces dependence on stereotypes because we gain better knowledge about individuals and experience their unique attributes in action. Meaningful interaction also potentially improves empathy toward others. **Empathy** refers to understanding and being sensitive to the feelings, thoughts, and situations of others.[83] People empathize when they visualize themselves in the other person's place as if they are the other person. This perceptual experience is cognitive, emotional, and experiential. In other words, empathy occurs when we understand the other person's situation, feel his or her emotions in that context, and to some degree react to those thoughts and feelings as the other person does. Empathizing reduces attribution errors by improving our sensitivity to the external causes of another person's performance and behavior. However, trying to empathize with others without spending time with them might actually increase rather than reduce stereotyping and other perceptual biases.[84]

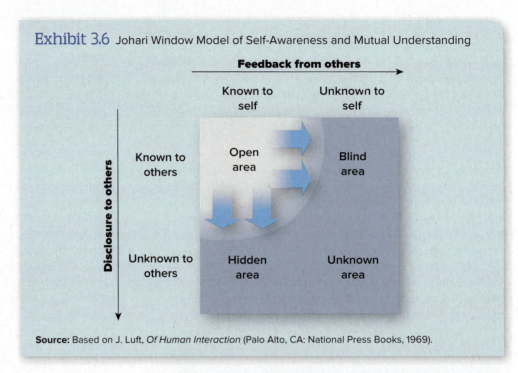

Exhibit 3.6 Johari Window Model of Self-Awareness and Mutual Understanding

Feedback from others

	Known to self	Unknown to self
Known to others	Open area	Blind area
Unknown to others	Hidden area	Unknown area

Disclosure to others

Source: Based on J. Luft, *Of Human Interaction* (Palo Alto, CA: National Press Books, 1969).

OB THEORY TO PRACTICE

Improving Executive Empathy on the Frontlines

Rick Forman developed a newfound appreciation for the work and personal lives of his employees when he recently worked in disguise as a checkout cashier, washroom cleaner, and distribution center forklift operator. The founder and CEO of Forman Mills, a New Jersey–based discount clothing chain, had several frustrating experiences with outdated equipment and misguided work processes, which he later changed. Heartfelt conversations with coworkers (who didn't know he was the CEO) also gave Forman a reality check about how his 2,900 employees live and work. "It made me realize what people are going through," says Forman. "You are actually talking to real people and you can empathize with their lives."[82]

©Andrey Burkov/Shutterstock

Mc Graw Hill Education connect®

SELF-ASSESSMENT 3.5: How Strong is Your Perspective Taking (Cognitive Empathy)?

Empathy refers to a person's understanding of and sensitivity to the feelings, thoughts, and situation of others. The "understanding" part of empathy is called perspective taking or cognitive empathy. It refers to a rational understanding of another person's circumstances. You can discover your level of cognitive empathy by locating this self-assessment in Connect if it is assigned by your instructor.

Mc Graw Hill Education connect®

SELF-ASSESSMENT 3.6: How Strong is Your Emotional Empathy?

Empathy refers to a person's understanding of and sensitivity to the feelings, thoughts, and situation of others. The "sensitivity" part of empathy is called emotional empathy. It refers to experiencing the feelings of the other person. You can discover your level of emotional empathy by locating this self-assessment in Connect if it is assigned by your instructor.

LO3-5 Outline the main features of a global mindset and justify its usefulness to employees and organizations.

GLOBAL MINDSET: DEVELOPING PERCEPTIONS ACROSS BORDERS

Global mindset has become an important characteristic of job applicants at companies with international operations. A **global mindset** refers to an individual's ability to perceive, know about, and process information across cultures. It includes (a) an awareness of, openness to, and respect for other views and practices in the world; (b) the capacity to empathize and act effectively across cultures; (c) the ability to process complex information about novel environments; and (d) the ability to comprehend and reconcile intercultural matters with multiple levels of thinking.[85]

Let's look at each of these features. First, global mindset occurs as people develop more of a global than local/parochial frame of reference about their business and its environment. They also have more knowledge and appreciation of many cultures and do not judge the competence of others by their national or ethnic origins. Second, global mindset includes understanding the mental models held by colleagues from other cultures as well as their emotional experiences in a given situation. Furthermore, this empathy translates into effective use of words and behaviors that are compatible with the local culture. Third, people with a strong global mindset are able to process and analyze large volumes of information in new and diverse situations. Finally, global mindset involves the capacity to quickly develop useful mental models of situations, particularly at both the local and global levels of analysis.

A global mindset offers tremendous value to organizations as well as to the employee's career opportunities.[86] People who develop a global mindset form better relationships across cultures by understanding and showing respect to distant colleagues and partners. They can sift through huge volumes of ambiguous and novel information transmitted in multinational relationships. They have a capacity to form networks and exchange resources more rapidly across borders. They also develop greater sensitivity and respond more quickly to emerging global opportunities.

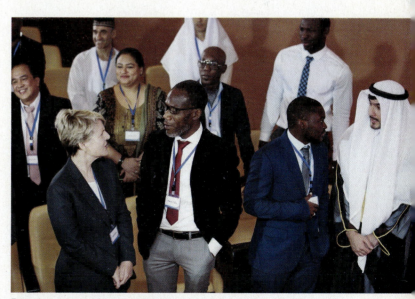

People who develop a global mindset form better relationships across cultures by understanding and showing respect to distant colleagues and partners.
©Rawpixel.com/Shutterstock

Developing a Global Mindset

Developing a global mindset involves improving one's perceptions, so the practices described earlier on awareness, self-awareness, and meaningful interaction are relevant. As with most perceptual capabilities, a global mindset begins with self-awareness—understanding one's own beliefs, values, and attitudes. Through self-awareness, people are more open-minded and nonjudgmental when receiving and processing complex information for decision making. In addition, companies develop a global mindset by giving employees opportunities to compare their own mental models with those of coworkers or partners from other regions of the world. For example, employees might participate in online forums about how well the product's design or marketing strategy is received in the United States versus India or Chile. When companies engage in regular discussions about global competitors, suppliers, and other stakeholders, they eventually move the employee's sphere of awareness more toward that global level.

A global mindset develops through better knowledge of people and cultures. Some of that knowledge is acquired through formal programs, such as expatriate and diversity training, but deeper absorption results from immersion in those cultures. Just as executives need to experience frontline jobs to better understand their customers and employees, employees also need to have meaningful interaction with colleagues from other cultures in those settings. The more people immerse themselves in the local environment (such as following local practices, eating local food, and using the local language), the more they tend to understand the perspectives and attitudes of their colleagues in those cultures.

OB THEORY TO PRACTICE

EY Employees Develop a Global Mindset through Immersion[87]

Jessica Grogan usually audits financial statements for clients in Buffalo, New York. But the EY (formerly called Ernst & Young) employee recently spent one week in Serra do Itajai National Park in Brazil with nine other EY colleagues from North and South America. Their tasks included providing strategic planning to a local eco-friendly hotel and an environmental consultancy company and helping scientists measure the diversity of birds in the park.

Grogan participated in one of EY's Corporate Responsibility Sabbaticals, which provide immersive volunteer experiences such as providing pro bono assistance for small businesses in developing countries. "The program helps our professionals grow into better leaders and teammates as they expand their global mindset by immersing themselves in a new culture alongside their colleagues," explains Deborah K. Holmes, EY's Americas director of corporate responsibility.

Jessica Grogan agrees that her experiences in Brazil were transformational. "I think the best thing I brought back was the global mindset I developed," she says. Of particular value was the opportunity to work with EY colleagues and clients from different backgrounds. "Just to get that diversity of thought, diversity of ideas and being able to bring it back, was the most rewarding part."

Study Checklist

Connect® Management is available for *M Organizational Behavior.* Additional resources include:

✓ Interactive Applications:
  - **Decision Generator**
  - **Sequencing**
  - **Video Case:** See management in action through interactive videos.

✓ **SmartBook™**—SmartBook is the first and only adaptive reading experience available today. Distinguishing what you know from what you don't, and honing in on concepts you are most likely to forget, SmartBook personalizes content for you in a continuously adapting reading experience. Reading is no longer a passive and linear experience, but an engaging and dynamic one where you are more likely to master and retain important concepts and go to class better prepared.

©Natthawat Jamnapa/123RF

Notes

1. W. Danielson, "A Preview of the Front-Line Leader with Chris Van Gorder," podcast in *The Entrepreneur's Library* (November 3, 2014), 23:44:00; I. MacDonald, "Leading the Way: Scripps Health CEO Takes Hands-on Approach to Frontline Staff Engagement," *FierceHealthcare*, April 9, 2015; C. Van Gorder, *The Front-Line Leader: Building a High-Performance Organization from the Ground Up* (San Francisco: Jossey-Bass, 2015); C. Van Gorder, "Seven Simple Strategies for Frontline Leaders," *USCPrice* (Los Angeles: University of Southern California, February 3, 2015), http://exechealthadmin.usc.edu/blog/seven-simple-strategies-for-frontline-leaders (accessed January 14, 2017).

2. D. Cooper and S. M. B. Thatcher, "Identification in Organizations: The Role of Self-Concept Orientations and Identification Motives," *Academy of Management Review* 35, no. 4 (2010): 516–38; J. Schaubroeck, Y. J. Kim, and A. C. Peng, "The Self-Concept in Organizational Psychology: Clarifying and Differentiating the Constructs," in *International Review of Industrial and Organizational Psychology*, vol. 12, ed. G. P. Hodgkinson and J. K. Ford (New York: Wiley, 2012): 1–38.

3. V. L. Vignoles, S. J. Schwartz, and K. Luyckx, "Introduction: Toward an Integrative View of Identity," in *Handbook of Identity Theory and Research*, ed. J. S. Schwartz, K. Luyckx, and L. V. Vignoles (New York: Springer New York, 2011), 1–27; L. Gaertner et al., "A Motivational Hierarchy within: Primacy of the Individual Self, Relational Self, or Collective Self?," *Journal of Experimental Social Psychology* 48, no. 5 (2012).

4. O. W. Holmes, *The Autocrat of the Breakfast-Table* (Boston: Phillips, Sampson, 1858), 58–59. This quotation, which Steve McShane slightly rewrote to remove sexist language, has a long and convoluted history. Pioneering psychology professor William James is almost always cited as the source, yet there is no evidence that he wrote this statement or anything similar. The first attribution of this quotation to William James may have been a 1958 *RAND Memoranda* publication (p. 925), and later in *Reader's Digest* (1962). Even if James did publish something similar, it is a highly condensed version of the humorous discussion of "six persons" that Oliver Wendell Holmes Sr. published decades before James began his career. Most likely, a RAND Corporation editor crafted this quotation from vague memory of Holmes's story and misattributed William James as the author because one of Holmes's characters in the story was "James." We cite Holmes as the source because he wrote the story from which this quotation is derived.

5. E. J. Koch and J. A. Shepperd, "Is Self-Complexity Linked to Better Coping? A Review of the Literature," *Journal of Personality* 72, no. 4 (2004): 727–60; A. R. McConnell, "The Multiple Self-Aspects Framework: Self-Concept Representation and Its Implications," *Personality and Social Psychology Review* 15, no. 1 (2011): 3–27; L. F. Emery, C. Walsh, and E. B. Slotter, "Knowing Who You Are and Adding to It: Reduced Self-Concept Clarity Predicts Reduced Self-Expansion," *Social Psychological and Personality Science* 6, no. 3 (2015): 259–66.

6. C. M. Brown et al., "Between Two Selves: Comparing Global and Local Predictors of Speed of Switching between Self-Aspects," *Self and Identity* 15, no. 1 (2016): 72–89.

7. J. D. Campbell et al., "Self-Concept Clarity: Measurement, Personality Correlates, and Cultural Boundaries," *Journal of Personality and Social Psychology* 70, no. 1 (1996): 141–56.

8. J. Lodi-Smith and B. W. Roberts, "Getting to Know Me: Social Role Experiences and Age Differences in Self-Concept Clarity during Adulthood," *Journal of Personality* 78, no. 5 (2010): 1383–410.

9. E. J. Koch and J. A. Shepperd, "Is Self-Complexity Linked to Better Coping? A Review of the Literature," *Journal of Personality* 72, no. 4 (2004): 727–60; T. D. Ritchie et al., "Self-Concept Clarity Mediates the Relation between Stress and Subjective Well-Being," *Self and Identity* 10, no. 4 (2010): 493–508.

10. A. T. Brook, J. Garcia, and M. A. Fleming, "The Effects of Multiple Identities on Psychological Well-Being," *Personality and Social Psychology Bulletin* 34, no. 12 (2008): 1588–600; A. T. Church et al., "Relating Self-Concept Consistency to Hedonic and Eudaimonic Well-Being in Eight Cultures," *Journal of Cross-Cultural Psychology* 45, no. 5 (2014): 695–712.

11. J. D. Campbell, "Self-Esteem and Clarity of the Self-Concept," *Journal of Personality and Social Psychology* 59, no. 3 (1990).

12. S. Hannah et al., "The Psychological and Neurological Bases of Leader Self-Complexity and Effects on Adaptive Decision-Making," *Journal of Applied Psychology* 98, no. 3 (2013): 393–411; S. J. Creary, B. B. Caza, and L. M. Roberts, "Out of the Box? How Managing a Subordinate's Multiple Identities Affects the Quality of a Manager-Subordinate Relationship," *Academy of Management Review* 40, no. 4 (2015): 538–62.

13. C. Peus et al., "Authentic Leadership: An Empirical Test of Its Antecedents, Consequences, and Mediating Mechanisms," *Journal of Business Ethics* 107, no. 3 (2012): 331–48; F. O. Walumbwa, M. A. Maidique, and C. Atamanik, "Decision-Making in a Crisis: What Every Leader Needs to Know," *Organizational Dynamics* 43, no. 4 (2014): 284–93; B. Mittal, "Self-Concept Clarity: Exploring Its Role in Consumer Behavior," *Journal of Economic Psychology* 46 (2015): 98–110.

14. C. L. Guenther and M. D. Alicke, "Deconstructing the Better-Than-Average Effect," *Journal of Personality and Social Psychology* 99, no. 5 (2010): 755–70; S. Loughnan et al., "Universal Biases in Self-Perception: Better and More Human Than Average," *British Journal of Social Psychology* 49 (2010): 627–36; H. C. Boucher, "Understanding Western–East Asian Differences and Similarities in Self-Enhancement," *Social and Personality Psychology Compass* 4, no. 5 (2010): 304–17; A. Gregg, C. Sedikides, and J. Gebauer, "Dynamics of Identity: Between Self-Enhancement and Self-Assessment," in *Handbook of Identity Theory and Research*, ed. S. J. Schwartz, K. Luyckx, and V. L. Vignoles (New York: Springer, 2011), 305–27.

15. D. Dunning, C. Heath, and J. M. Suls, "Flawed Self-Assessment: Implications for Health, Education, and the Workplace," *Psychological Science in the Public Interest* 5, no. 3 (2004): 69–106; D. A. Moore, "Not So above Average after All: When People Believe They Are Worse Than Average and Its Implications for Theories of Bias in Social Comparison," *Organizational Behavior and Human Decision Processes* 102, no. 1 (2007): 42–58.

16. D. Gosselin et al., "Comparative Optimism among Drivers: An Intergenerational Portrait," *Accident Analysis & Prevention* 42, no. 2 (2010): 734–40; P. M. Picone, G. Battista Dagnino, and A. Minà, "The Origin of Failure: A Multidisciplinary Appraisal of the Hubris Hypothesis and Proposed Research Agenda," *Academy of Management Perspectives* 28, no. 4 (2014): 447–68; G. Chen, C. Crossland, and S. Luo, "Making the Same Mistake All over Again: CEO Overconfidence and Corporate Resistance to Corrective Feedback," *Strategic Management Journal* 36, no. 10 (2015): 1513–35.

17. K. P. Cross, "Not Can, but *Will* College Teaching Be Improved?," *New Directions for Higher Education*, no. 17 (1977): 1–15; U.S. Merit Systems Protection Board, *Accomplishing Our Mission: Results of the 2005 Merit Principles Survey* (Washington, DC: U.S. Merit Systems Protection Board, December 6, 2007); J. Montier, *Behavioral Investing* (Chicester, UK: Wiley, 2007), 82–83; V. G. Perry, "Is Ignorance Bliss? Consumer Accuracy in Judgments about Credit Ratings," *Journal of Consumer Affairs* 42, no. 2 (2008): 189–205; J. M. Twenge, W. K. Campbell, and B. Gentile, "Generational Increases in Agentic Self-Evaluations among American College Students, 1966–2009," *Self and Identity* 11, no. 4 (2011): 409–27; A. Sundström, "The Validity of Self-Reported Driver Competence: Relations between Measures of Perceived Driver Competence and Actual Driving Skill," *Transportation Research Part F: Traffic Psychology and Behaviour* 14, no. 2 (2011): 155–63.

18. This quotation has been cited since the 1930s, yet we were unable to find it in any of Dewey's writing. The earliest known reference to this quotation is Dale Carnegie's famous self-help book, where the statement is attributed to Dewey. See D. Carnegie, *How to Win Friends and Influence People*, 1st ed. (New York: Simon & Schuster, 1936), 43–44 (p. 19 in later editions).

19. W. B. Swann Jr., P. J. Rentfrow, and J. S. Guinn, "Self-Verification: The Search for Coherence," in *Handbook of Self and Identity*, ed. M. R. Leary and J. Tagney (New York: Guilford, 2002), 367–83; D. M. Cable and V. S. Kay, "Striving for Self-Verification during Organizational Entry," *Academy of Management Journal* 55, no. 2 (2012): 360–80.

20. F. Anseel and F. Lievens, "Certainty as a Moderator of Feedback Reactions? A Test of the Strength of the Self-Verification Motive," *Journal of Occupational & Organizational Psychology* 79, no. 4 (2006): 533–51; T. Kwang and W. B. Swann, "Do People Embrace Praise Even When They Feel Unworthy? A Review of Critical Tests of Self-Enhancement versus Self-Verification," *Personality and Social Psychology Review* 14, no. 3 (2010): 263–80.

21. M. R. Leary, "Motivational and Emotional Aspects of the Self," *Annual Review of Psychology* 58, no. 1 (2007): 317–44; A. Meister, K. A. Jehn, and S. M. B. Thatcher, "Feeling Misidentified: The Consequences of Internal Identity Asymmetries for Individuals at Work," *Academy of Management Review* 39, no. 4 (2014): 488–512.

22. We have described three components of core self-evaluation. The remaining component is the personality trait emotional stability, which was described in Chapter 2. However, personality is a behavior tendency, whereas core self-evaluation includes only "evaluation focused" variables. There is also recent concern about whether locus of control is part of self-evaluation. See R. E. Johnson, C. C. Rosen, and P. E. Levy, "Getting to the Core of Core Self-Evaluation: A Review and Recommendations," *Journal of Organizational Behavior* 29 (2008): 391–413; C.-H. Chang et al., "Core Self-Evaluations: A Review and Evaluation of the Literature," *Journal of Management* 38, no. 1 (2012): 81–128; R. E. Johnson et al., "Getting to the Core of Locus of Control: Is It an Evaluation of the Self or the Environment?," *Journal of Applied Psychology* 100, no. 5 (2015): 1568–78.

23. E. Dockterman, "Google Invests $50 Million to Close the Tech Gender Gap," *Time*, June 21, 2014, 16; M. della Cava, "Google, Pixar Team Up to Teach Kids Joy of Coding," *USA Today*, December 7, 2015, B4; C. Preece, "Is a Lack of Self-Belief Pushing Girls Away from STEM?," *IT Pro*, February 9, 2016; A.T. Kearney and Your Life, *Tough Choices: The Real Reasons A-Level Students Are Steering Clear of Science and Maths* (London: A.T. Kearney, February 2016).

24. W. B. Swann Jr., C. Chang-Schneider, and K. L. McClarty, "Do People's Self-Views Matter?: Self-Concept and Self-Esteem in Everyday Life," *American Psychologist* 62, no. 2 (2007): 84–94; J. L. Pierce, D. G. Gardner, and C. Crowley, "Organization-Based Self-Esteem and Well-Being: Empirical Examination of a Spillover Effect," *European Journal of Work and Organizational Psychology* 25, no. 2 (2016): 181–99.

25. A. Bandura, *Self-Efficacy: The Exercise of Control* (New York: W. H. Freeman, 1997). Evidence suggests that self-efficacy predicts performance. However, one recent study suggests that past performance predicts self-efficacy and that self-efficacy has a modest effect on future performance. See T. Sitzmann and G. Yeo, "A Meta-Analytic Investigation of the Within-Person Self-Efficacy Domain: Is Self-Efficacy a Product of Past Performance or a Driver of Future Performance?," *Personnel Psychology* 66, no. 3 (2013): 531–68.

26. G. Chen, S. M. Gully, and D. Eden, "Validation of a New General Self-Efficacy Scale," *Organizational Research Methods* 4, no. 1 (2001): 62–83.

27. J. B. Rotter, "Generalized Expectancies for Internal versus External Control of Reinforcement," *Psychological Monographs* 80, no. 1 (1966): 1–28.

28. T. W. H. Ng, K. L. Sorensen, and L. T. Eby, "Locus of Control at Work: A Meta-Analysis," *Journal of Organizational Behavior* 27 (2006): 1057–87; Q. Wang, N. A. Bowling, and K. J. Eschleman, "A Meta-Analytic Examination of Work and General Locus of Control," *Journal of Applied Psychology* 95, no. 4 (2010): 761–68.

29. G. J. Leonardelli, C. L. Pickett, and M. B. Brewer, "Optimal Distinctiveness Theory: A Framework for Social Identity, Social Cognition, and Intergroup Relations," in *Advances in Experimental Social Psychology*, ed. M. P. Zanna and J. M. Olson (San Diego, CA: Academic Press, 2010), 63–113; M. Ormiston, "Explaining the Link between Objective and Perceived Differences in Groups: The Role of the Belonging and Distinctiveness Motives," *Journal of Applied Psychology* 101, no. 2 (2016): 222–36.

30. We describe relational self-concept as a form of social identity because such connections are inherently social and the dyads are typically members of a collective entity. For example, an employee has a relationship identity with his/her boss, but this is connected to a social identity with the team or department. However, recent discussion suggests that relational self-concept also may be part of personal identity or a separate form of self-concept. See B. E. Ashforth, B. S. Schinoff, and K. M. Rogers, "'I Identify with Her,' 'I Identify with Him': Unpacking the Dynamics of Personal Identification in Organizations," *Academy of Management Review* 41, no. 1 (2016): 28–60.

31. M. A. Hogg and D. J. Terry, "Social Identity and Self-Categorization Processes in Organizational Contexts," *Academy of Management Review* 25 (2000): 121–40; C. Sedikides and A. P. Gregg, "Portraits of the Self," in *The Sage Handbook of Social Psychology*, ed. M. A. Hogg and J. Cooper (London: Sage, 2003), 110–38; S. A. Haslam and N. Ellemers, "Identity Processes in Organizations," in *Handbook of Identity Theory and Research*, ed. J. S. Schwartz, K. Luyckx, and L. V. Vignoles (New York: Springer New York, 2011), 715–44.

32. M. R. Edwards, "Organizational Identification: A Conceptual and Operational Review," *International Journal of Management Reviews* 7, no. 4 (2005): 207–30; E. S. Lee, T. Y. Park, and B. Koo, "Identifying Organizational Identification as a Basis for Attitudes and Behaviors: A Meta-Analytic Review," *Psychological Bulletin* 141, no. 5 (2015): 1049–80.

33. M. B. Brewer, "The Social Self: On Being the Same and Different at the Same Time," *Personality and Social Psychology Bulletin* 17, no. 5 (1991): 475–82; R. Imhoff and H.-P. Erb, "What Motivates Nonconformity? Uniqueness Seeking Blocks Majority Influence," *Personality and Social Psychology Bulletin* 35, no. 3 (2009): 309–20; K. R. Morrison and S. C. Wheeler, "Nonconformity Defines the Self: The Role of Minority Opinion Status in Self-Concept Clarity," *Personality and Social Psychology Bulletin* 36, no. 3 (2010): 297–308; M. G. Mayhew, J. Gardner, and N. M. Ashkanasy, "Measuring Individuals' Need for Identification: Scale Development and Validation," *Personality and Individual Differences* 49, no. 5 (2010): 356–61.

34. See, for example, W. B. Swann Jr., R. E. Johnson, and J. K. Bosson, "Identity Negotiation at Work," *Research in Organizational Behavior* 29 (2009): 81–109; J. L. Herman and S. J. Zaccaro, "The Complex Self-Concept of the Global Leader," in *Advances in Global Leadership*, vol. 8, ed. J. S. Oslanld, M. Li, and Y. Wang (Bingley, UK: Emerald Group Publishing Limited, 2014), 93–111; A. M. Grant, J. M. Berg, and D. M. Cable, "Job Titles as Identity Badges: How Self-Reflective Titles Can Reduce Emotional Exhaustion," *Academy of Management Journal* 57, no. 4 (2014): 1201–25; L. Ramarajan, "Past, Present and Future Research on Multiple Identities: Toward an Intrapersonal Network Approach," *The Academy of Management Annals* 8, no. 1 (2014): 589–659.

35. E. I. Knudsen, "Fundamental Components of Attention," *Annual Review of Neuroscience* 30, no. 1 (2007): 57–78. For an evolutionary psychology perspective of selective attention and organization, see L. Cosmides and J. Tooby, "Evolutionary Psychology: New Perspectives on Cognition and Motivation," *Annual Review of Psychology* 64, no. 1 (2013): 201–29.

36. A. Bechara and A. R. Damasio, "The Somatic Marker Hypothesis: A Neural Theory of Economic Decision," *Games and Economic Behavior* 52, no. 2 (2005): 336-72; T. S. Saunders and M. J. Buehner, "The Gut Chooses Faster Than the Mind: A Latency Advantage of Affective over Cognitive Decisions," *Quarterly Journal of Experimental Psychology* 66, no. 2 (2012): 381-88; A. Aite et al., "Impact of Emotional Context Congruency on Decision Making under Ambiguity," *Emotion* 13, no. 2 (2013): 177-82.

37. Plato, *The Republic*, trans. D. Lee (Harmondsworth, UK: Penguin, 1955).

38. D. J. Simons and C. F. Chabris, "Gorillas in Our Midst: Sustained Inattentional Blindness for Dynamic Events," *Perception* 28 (1999): 1059-74.

39. R. S. Nickerson, "Confirmation Bias: A Ubiquitous Phenomenon in Many Guises," *Review of General Psychology* 2, no. 2 (1998): 175-220; A. Gilbey and S. Hill, "Confirmation Bias in General Aviation Lost Procedures," *Applied Cognitive Psychology* 26, no. 5 (2012): 785-95; A. M. Scherer, P. D. Windschitl, and A. R. Smith, "Hope to Be Right: Biased Information Seeking Following Arbitrary and Informed Predictions," *Journal of Experimental Social Psychology* 49, no. 1 (2013): 106-12.

40. C. Wastell et al., "Identifying Hypothesis Confirmation Behaviors in a Simulated Murder Investigation: Implications for Practice," *Journal of Investigative Psychology and Offender Profiling* 9, no. 2 (2012): 184-98; D. K. Rossmo, "Case Rethinking: A Protocol for Reviewing Criminal Investigations," *Police Practice and Research* 17, no. 3 (2016): 212-28.

41. Earl Derr Biggars, the author of the Charlie Chan novels, is sometimes cited as the source of this quotation. However, this statement is found only in the 1935 film *Charlie Chan in Egypt*, which is based on Biggars' character. It does not appear in any Charlie Chan novels.

42. C. N. Macrae and G. V. Bodenhausen, "Social Cognition: Thinking Categorically about Others," *Annual Review of Psychology* 51 (2000): 93-120; K. A. Quinn and H. E. S. Rosenthal, "Categorizing Others and the Self: How Social Memory Structures Guide Social Perception and Behavior," *Learning and Motivation* 43, no. 4 (2012): 247-58; L. T. Phillips, M. Weisbuch, and N. Ambady, "People Perception: Social Vision of Groups and Consequences for Organizing and Interacting," *Research in Organizational Behavior* 34 (2014): 101-27.

43. S. Avugos et al., "The 'Hot Hand' Reconsidered: A Meta-Analytic Approach," *Psychology of Sport and Exercise* 14, no. 1 (2013): 21-27. For a discussion of cognitive closure and perception, see A. Roets et al., "The Motivated Gatekeeper of Our Minds: New Directions in Need for Closure Theory and Research," in *Advances in Experimental Social Psychology*, ed. M. O. James and P. Z. Mark (San Diego, CA: Academic Press, 2015), 221-83.

44. J. Willis and A. Todorov, "First Impressions: Making Up Your Mind after a 100-ms Exposure to a Face," *Psychological Science* 17, no. 7 (2006): 592-98; A. Todorov, M. Pakrashi, and N. N. Oosterhof, "Evaluating Faces on Trustworthiness after Minimal Time Exposure," *Social Cognition* 27, no. 6 (2009): 813-33. For related research on thin slices, see D. Kahneman, *Thinking Fast and Slow* (New York: Farrar, Strauss and Giroux, 2011); M. L. Slepian, K. R. Bogart, and N. Ambady, "Thin-Slice Judgments in the Clinical Context," *Annual Review of Clinical Psychology* 10, no. 1 (2014): 131-53.

45. P. M. Senge, *The Fifth Discipline: The Art and Practice of the Learning Organization* (New York: Doubleday Currency, 1990), chap. 10; T. J. Chermack, "Mental Models in Decision Making and Implications for Human Resource Development," *Advances in Developing Human Resources* 5, no. 4 (2003): 408-22; P. N. Johnson-Laird, "Mental Models and Deductive Reasoning," in *Reasoning: Studies of Human Inference and Its Foundations*, ed. J. E. Adler and L. J. Rips (Cambridge: Cambridge University Press, 2008); S. Ross and N. Allen, "Examining the Convergent Validity of Shared Mental Model Measures," *Behavior Research Methods* 44, no. 4 (2012): 1052-62.

46. G. W. Allport, *The Nature of Prejudice* (Reading, MA: Addison-Wesley, 1954); J. C. Brigham, "Ethnic Stereotypes," *Psychological Bulletin* 76, no. 1 (1971): 15-38; D. J. Schneider, *The Psychology of Stereotyping* (New York: Guilford, 2004); S. Kanahara, "A Review of the Definitions of Stereotype and a Proposal for a Progressional Model," *Individual Differences Research* 4, no. 5 (2006): 306-21.

47. L. Jussim, J. T. Crawford, and R. S. Rubinstein, "Stereotype (in)Accuracy in Perceptions of Groups and Individuals," *Current Directions in Psychological Science* 24, no. 6 (2015): 490-97.

48. C. N. Macrae, A. B. Milne, and G. V. Bodenhausen, "Stereotypes as Energy-Saving Devices: A Peek inside the Cognitive Toolbox," *Journal of Personality and Social Psychology* 66 (1994): 37-47; J. W. Sherman et al., "Stereotype Efficiency Reconsidered: Encoding Flexibility under Cognitive Load," *Journal of Personality and Social Psychology* 75 (1998): 589-606; C. N. Macrae and G. V. Bodenhausen, "Social Cognition: Thinking Categorically About Others," *Annual Review of Psychology* 51 (2000): 93-120; A.-K. Newheiser and J. F. Dovidio, "Individual Differences and Intergroup Bias: Divergent Dynamics Associated with Prejudice and Stereotyping," *Personality and Individual Differences* 53, no. 1 (2012): 70-74.

49. J. C. Turner and S. A. Haslam, "Social Identity, Organizations, and Leadership," in *Groups at Work: Theory and Research*, ed. M. E. Turner (Mahwah, NJ: Erlbaum, 2001), 25-65; J. Jetten, R. Spears, and T. Postmes, "Intergroup Distinctiveness and Differentiation: A Meta-Analytic Integration," *Journal of Personality and Social Psychology* 86, no. 6 (2004): 862-79; M. A. Hogg et al., "The Social Identity Perspective: Intergroup Relations, Self-Conception, and Small Groups," *Small Group Research* 35, no. 3 (2004): 246-76; K. Hugenberg and D. F. Sacco, "Social Categorization and Stereotyping: How Social Categorization Biases Person Perception and Face Memory," *Social and Personality Psychology Compass* 2, no. 2 (2008): 1052-72.

50. N. Halevy, G. Bornstein, and L. Sagiv, "'In-Group Love' and 'Out-Group Hate' as Motives for Individual Participation in Intergroup Conflict: A New Game Paradigm," *Psychological Science* 19, no. 4 (2008): 405-11; T. Yamagishi and N. Mifune, "Social Exchange and Solidarity: In-Group Love or Out-Group Hate?," *Evolution and Human Behavior* 30, no. 4 (2009): 229-37; N. Halevy, O. Weisel, and G. Bornstein, "'In-Group Love' and 'Out-Group Hate' in Repeated Interaction between Groups," *Journal of Behavioral Decision Making* 25, no. 2 (2012): 188-95; M. Parker and R. Janoff-Bulman, "Lessons from Morality-Based Social Identity: The Power of Outgroup 'Hate,' Not Just Ingroup 'Love,'" *Social Justice Research* 26, no. 1 (2013): 81-96.

51. T. Schmader and W. M. Hall, "Stereotype Threat in School and at Work: Putting Science into Practice," *Policy Insights from the Behavioral and Brain Sciences* 1, no. 1 (2014): 30-37; C. R. Pennington et al., "Twenty Years of Stereotype Threat Research: A Review of Psychological Mediators," *PLoS ONE* 11, no. 1 (2016): e0146487.

52. C. A. Moss-Racusin et al., "Science Faculty's Subtle Gender Biases Favor Male Students," *Proceedings of the National Academy of Sciences* 109, no. 41 (2012): 16474-79.

53. S. T. Fiske, "Stereotyping, Prejudice, and Discrimination," in *Handbook of Social Psychology*, ed. D. T. Gilbert, S. T. Fiske, and G. Lindzey (New York: McGraw-Hill, 1998): 357-411; M. Hewstone, M. Rubin, and H. Willis, "Intergroup Bias," *Annual Review of Psychology* 53 (2002): 575-604; C. Stangor, "The Study of

Stereotyping, Prejudice, and Discrimination within Social Psychology: A Quick History of Theory and Research," in *Handbook of Prejudice, Stereotyping, and Discrimination*, ed. T. D. Nelson (New York: Psychology Press, 2016), 1-22.

54. J. A. Bargh and T. L. Chartrand, "The Unbearable Automaticity of Being," *American Psychologist* 54, no. 7 (1999): 462-79; S. T. Fiske, "What We Know Now about Bias and Intergroup Conflict, the Problem of the Century," *Current Directions in Psychological Science* 11, no. 4 (2002): 123-28; R. Krieglmeyer and J. W. Sherman, "Disentangling Stereotype Activation and Stereotype Application in the Stereotype Misperception Task," *Journal of Personality and Social Psychology* 103, no. 2 (2012): 205-24. On the limitations of some stereotype training, see B. Gawronski et al., "When 'Just Say No' Is Not Enough: Affirmation versus Negation Training and the Reduction of Automatic Stereotype Activation," *Journal of Experimental Social Psychology* 44 (2008): 370-77.

55. H. H. Kelley, *Attribution in Social Interaction* (Morristown, NJ: General Learning Press, 1971); B. F. Malle, "Attribution Theories: How People Make Sense of Behavior," in *Theories of Social Psychology*, ed. D. Chadee (Chichester, UK: Blackwell, 2011), 72-95. This "internal-external" or "person-situation" perspective of the attribution process differs somewhat from the original "intentional-unintentional" perspective, which says that we try to understand the deliberate or accidental/involuntary reasons why people engage in behaviors, as well as the reasons for behavior. Some writers suggest the original perspective is more useful. See B. F. Malle, "Time to Give Up the Dogmas of Attribution: An Alternative Theory of Behavior Explanation," in *Advances in Experimental Social Psychology*, vol. 44, ed. K. M. Olson and M. P. Zanna (San Diego: Elsevier Academic, 2011), 297-352.

56. H. H. Kelley, "The Processes of Causal Attribution," *American Psychologist* 28 (1973): 107-28.

57. D. Lange and N. T. Washburn, "Understanding Attributions of Corporate Social Irresponsibility," *Academy of Management Review* 37, no. 2 (2012): 300-26. Recent reviews explain that attribution is an incomplete theory for understanding how people determine causation and assign blame. See S. A. Sloman and D. Lagnado, "Causality in Thought," *Annual Review of Psychology* 66, no. 1 (2015): 223-47; M. D. Alicke et al., "Causal Conceptions in Social Explanation and Moral Evaluation: A Historical Tour," *Perspectives on Psychological Science* 10, no. 6 (2015): 790-812.

58. J. M. Crant and T. S. Bateman, "Assignment of Credit and Blame for Performance Outcomes," *Academy of Management Journal* 36 (1993): 7-27; B. Weiner, "Intrapersonal and Interpersonal Theories of Motivation from an Attributional Perspective," *Educational Psychology Review* 12 (2000): 1-14; N. Bacon and P. Blyton, "Worker Responses to Teamworking: Exploring Employee Attributions of Managerial Motives," *International Journal of Human Resource Management* 16, no. 2 (2005): 238-55.

59. D. T. Miller and M. Ross, "Self-Serving Biases in the Attribution of Causality: Fact or Fiction?," *Psychological Bulletin* 82, no. 2 (1975): 213-25; J. Shepperd, W. Malone, and K. Sweeny, "Exploring Causes of the Self-Serving Bias," *Social and Personality Psychology Compass* 2, no. 2 (2008): 895-908.

60. E. W. K. Tsang, "Self-Serving Attributions in Corporate Annual Reports: A Replicated Study," *Journal of Management Studies* 39, no. 1 (2002): 51-65; N. J. Roese and J. M. Olson, "Better, Stronger, Faster: Self-Serving Judgment, Affect Regulation, and the Optimal Vigilance Hypothesis," *Perspectives on Psychological Science* 2, no. 2 (2007): 124-41; R. Hooghiemstra, "East-West Differences in Attributions for Company Performance: A Content Analysis of Japanese and U.S. Corporate Annual Reports," *Journal of Cross-Cultural Psychology* 39, no. 5 (2008): 618-29.

61. D. T. Gilbert and P. S. Malone, "The Correspondence Bias," *Psychological Bulletin* 117, no. 1 (1995): 21-38.

62. B. F. Malle, "The Actor-Observer Asymmetry in Attribution: A (Surprising) Meta-Analysis," *Psychological Bulletin* 132, no. 6 (2006): 895-919; C. W. Bauman and L. J. Skitka, "Making Attributions for Behaviors: The Prevalence of Correspondence Bias in the General Population," *Basic and Applied Social Psychology* 32, no. 3 (2010): 269-77.

63. Similar models are presented in D. Eden, "Self-Fulfilling Prophecy as a Management Tool: Harnessing Pygmalion," *Academy of Management Review* 9 (1984): 64-73; R. H. G. Field and D. A. Van Seters, "Management by Expectations (MBE): The Power of Positive Prophecy," *Journal of General Management* 14 (1988): 19-33; D. O. Trouilloud et al., "The Influence of Teacher Expectations on Student Achievement in Physical Education Classes: Pygmalion Revisited," *European Journal of Social Psychology* 32 (2002): 591-607.

64. P. Whiteley, T. Sy, and S. K. Johnson, "Leaders' Conceptions of Followers: Implications for Naturally Occurring Pygmalion Effects," *Leadership Quarterly* 23, no. 5 (2012): 822-34; J. Weaver, J. F. Moses, and M. Snyder, "Self-Fulfilling Prophecies in Ability Settings," *Journal of Social Psychology* 156, no. 2 (2016): 179-89.

65. D. Eden, "Interpersonal Expectations in Organizations," in *Interpersonal Expectations: Theory, Research, and Applications*, ed. P. D. Blanck (Cambridge: Cambridge University Press, 1993), 154-78.

66. D. Eden, "Pygmalion Goes to Boot Camp: Expectancy, Leadership, and Trainee Performance," *Journal of Applied Psychology* 67 (1982): 194-99; B. J. Avolio et al., "A Meta-Analytic Review of Leadership Impact Research: Experimental and Quasi-Experimental Studies," *The Leadership Quarterly* 20, no. 5 (2009): 764-84; P. Whiteley, T. Sy, and S. K. Johnson, "Leaders' Conceptions of Followers: Implications for Naturally Occurring Pygmalion Effects," *Leadership Quarterly* 23, no. 5 (2012): 822-34.

67. S. Madon, L. Jussim, and J. Eccles, "In Search of the Powerful Self-Fulfilling Prophecy," *Journal of Personality and Social Psychology* 72, no. 4 (1997): 791-809; A. E. Smith, L. Jussim, and J. Eccles, "Do Self-Fulfilling Prophecies Accumulate, Dissipate, or Remain Stable over Time?," *Journal of Personality and Social Psychology* 77, no. 3 (1999): 548-65; S. Madon et al., "Self-Fulfilling Prophecies: The Synergistic Accumulative Effect of Parents' Beliefs on Children's Drinking Behavior," *Psychological Science* 15, no. 12 (2005): 837-45.

68. W. H. Cooper, "Ubiquitous Halo," *Psychological Bulletin* 90 (1981): 218-44; P. Rosenzweig, *The Halo Effect . . . and the Eight Other Business Delusions That Deceive Managers* (New York: Free Press, 2007); J. W. Keeley et al., "Investigating Halo and Ceiling Effects in Student Evaluations of Instruction," *Educational and Psychological Measurement* 73, no. 3 (2013): 440-57.

69. B. Mullen et al., "The False Consensus Effect: A Meta-Analysis of 115 Hypothesis Tests," *Journal of Experimental Social Psychology* 21, no. 3 (1985): 262-83; F. J. Flynn and S. S. Wiltermuth, "Who's with Me? False Consensus, Brokerage, and Ethical Decision Making in Organizations," *Academy of Management Journal* 53, no. 5 (2010): 1074-89; B. Roth and A. Voskort, "Stereotypes and False Consensus: How Financial Professionals Predict Risk Preferences," *Journal of Economic Behavior & Organization* 107, Part B (2014): 553-65.

70. E. A. Lind, L. Kray, and L. Thompson, "Primacy Effects in Justice Judgments: Testing Predictions from Fairness Heuristic Theory," *Organizational Behavior and Human Decision Processes* 85 (2001): 189-210; T. Mann and M. Ferguson, "Can We Undo Our First Impressions? The Role of Reinterpretation in Reversing

Implicit Evaluations," *Journal of Personality & Social Psychology* 108, no. 6 (2015): 823–49; B. C. Holtz, "From First Impression to Fairness Perception: Investigating the Impact of Initial Trustworthiness Beliefs," *Personnel Psychology* 68, no. 3 (2015): 499–546.

71. Careerbuilder, "Careerbuilder Releases Study of Common and Not-So-Common Resume Mistakes That Can Cost You the Job," news release (Chicago: Careerbuilder, September 11, 2013); Accountemps, "Survey: Job Interview Trips up More Candidates Than Any Other Step in Hiring Process," news release (Menlo Park, CA: Accountemps, April 2, 2014); Careerbuilder, "Careerbuilder's Annual Survey Reveals the Most Outrageous Resume Mistakes Employers Have Found," news release (Chicago: Careerbuilder, September 22, 2016); "Top 25 Worst Resume Objective Statements," *Robert Half Blog*, May 17, 2017, https://www.roberthalf.com/blog/top-25-worst-resume-objective-statements.

72. D. D. Steiner and J. S. Rain, "Immediate and Delayed Primacy and Recency Effects in Performance Evaluation," *Journal of Applied Psychology* 74 (1989): 136–42; K. T. Trotman, "Order Effects and Recency: Where Do We Go from Here?," *Accounting & Finance* 40 (2000): 169–82; W. Green, "Impact of the Timing of an Inherited Explanation on Auditors' Analytical Procedures Judgements," *Accounting and Finance* 44 (2004): 369–92.

73. D. E. Hogan and M. Mallott, "Changing Racial Prejudice through Diversity Education," *Journal of College Student Development* 46, no. 2 (2005): 115–25; B. Gawronski et al., "When 'Just Say No' Is Not Enough: Affirmation versus Negation Training and the Reduction of Automatic Stereotype Activation," *Journal of Experimental Social Psychology* 44 (2008): 370–77; M. M. Duguid and M. C. Thomas-Hunt, "Condoning Stereotyping? How Awareness of Stereotyping Prevalence Impacts Expression of Stereotypes," *Journal of Applied Psychology* 100, no. 2 (2015): 343–59; F. Dobbin and A. Kalev, "Why Diversity Programs Fail," *Harvard Business Review* 94, no. 7/8 (2016): 52–60.

74. T. W. Costello and S. S. Zalkind, *Psychology in Administration: A Research Orientation* (Englewood Cliffs, NJ: Prentice Hall, 1963), 45–46; J. M. Kouzes and B. Z. Posner, *The Leadership Challenge*, 4th ed. (San Francisco: Jossey-Bass, 2007), chap. 3.

75. W. L. Gardner et al., "'Can You See the Real Me?' A Self-Based Model of Authentic Leader and Follower Development," *Leadership Quarterly* 16 (2005): 343–72; C. Peus et al., "Authentic Leadership: An Empirical Test of Its Antecedents, Consequences, and Mediating Mechanisms," *Journal of Business Ethics* 107, no. 3 (2012): 331–48.

76. A. G. Greenwald et al., "Understanding and Using the Implicit Association Test: III. Meta-Analysis of Predictive Validity," *Journal of Personality and Social Psychology* 97, no. 1 (2009): 17–41; M. C. Wilson and K. Scior, "Attitudes Towards Individuals with Disabilities as Measured by the Implicit Association Test: A Literature Review," *Research in Developmental Disabilities* 35, no. 2 (2014): 294–321; B. A. Nosek et al., "Understanding and Using the Brief Implicit Association Test: Recommended Scoring Procedures," *PLoS ONE* 9, no. 12 (2014): e110938; B. Schiller et al., "Clocking the Social Mind by Identifying Mental Processes in the IAT with Electrical Neuroimaging," *Proceedings of the National Academy of Sciences* 113, no. 10 (2016): 2786–91.

77. J. T. Jost et al., "The Existence of Implicit Bias Is Beyond Reasonable Doubt: A Refutation of Ideological and Methodological Objections and Executive Summary of Ten Studies That No Manager Should Ignore," *Research in Organizational Behavior* 29 (2009): 39–69. The science-as-male implicit stereotype is discussed in F. L. Smyth and B. A. Nosek, "On the Gender-Science Stereotypes Held by Scientists: Explicit Accord with Gender-Ratios, Implicit Accord with Scientific Identity," *Frontiers in Psychology* 6 (2015).

78. J. Luft, *Of Human Interaction* (Palo Alto, CA: National Press, 1969). For a variation of this model, see J. Hall, "Communication Revisited," *California Management Review* 15 (1973): 56–67. For recent discussion of the Johari blind spot, see A.-M. B. Gallrein et al., "You Spy with Your Little Eye: People Are 'Blind' to Some of the Ways in Which They Are Consensually Seen by Others," *Journal of Research in Personality* 47, no. 5 (2013): 464–71; A.-M. B. Gallrein et al., "I Still Cannot See It—A Replication of Blind Spots in Self-Perception," *Journal of Research in Personality* 60 (2016): 1–7.

79. S. Vazire and M. R. Mehl, "Knowing Me, Knowing You: The Accuracy and Unique Predictive Validity of Self-Ratings and Other-Ratings of Daily Behavior," *Journal of Personality and Social Psychology* 95, no. 5 (2008): 1202–16; D. Leising, A.-M. B. Gallrein, and M. Dufner, "Judging the Behavior of People We Know: Objective Assessment, Confirmation of Preexisting Views, or Both?," *Personality and Social Psychology Bulletin* 40, no. 2 (2014): 153–63.

80. T. F. Pettigrew and L. R. Tropp, "A Meta-Analytic Test of Intergroup Contact Theory," *Journal of Personality and Social Psychology* 90, no. 5 (2006): 751–83; Y. Amichai-Hamburger, B. S. Hasler, and T. Shani-Sherman, "Structured and Unstructured Intergroup Contact in the Digital Age," *Computers in Human Behavior* 52 (2015): 515–22.

81. The contact hypothesis was first introduced in G. W. Allport, *The Nature of Prejudice* (Reading, MA: Addison-Wesley, 1954), chap. 16.

82. J. M. Von Bergen, "'Undercover' Opens Forman Mills Boss' Eyes," *Philadelphia Inquirer*, January 20, 2015, C01; J. M. Von Bergen, "Forman Mills CEO Rick Forman Capitalized on 'Undercover Boss': TV Makeover Was the Real Thing," *Philadelphia Inquirer*, May 22, 2015, A19.

83. R. Elliott et al., "Empathy," *Psychotherapy* 48, no. 1 (2011): 43–49; J. Zaki, "Empathy: A Motivated Account," *Psychological Bulletin* 140, no. 6 (2014): 1608–47; E. Teding van Berkhout and J. Malouff, "The Efficacy of Empathy Training: A Meta-Analysis of Randomized Controlled Trials," *Journal of Counseling Psychology* 63, no. 1 (2016): 32–41.

84. M. Tarrant, R. Calitri, and D. Weston, "Social Identification Structures the Effects of Perspective Taking," *Psychological Science* 23, no. 9 (2012): 973–78; J. L. Skorinko and S. A. Sinclair, "Perspective Taking Can Increase Stereotyping: The Role of Apparent Stereotype Confirmation," *Journal of Experimental Social Psychology* 49, no. 1 (2013): 10–18.

85. There is no consensus on the meaning of global mindset. The elements identified in this book are common among most of the recent writing on this subject. See, for example, S. J. Black, "The Mindset of Global Leaders: Inquisitiveness and Duality," in *Advances in Global Leadership*, vol. 4, ed. W. H. Mobley and E. Weldon (Bingley, UK: Emerald Group Publishing Limited, 2005), 181–200; O. Levy et al., "What We Talk about When We Talk about 'Global Mindset': Managerial Cognition in Multinational Corporations," *Journal of International Business Studies* 38, no. 2 (2007): 231–58; S. Beechler and D. Baltzley, "Creating a Global Mindset," *Chief Learning Officer* 7, no. 6 (2008): 40–45; M. Javidan and D. Bowen, "The 'Global Mindset' of Managers: What It Is, Why It Matters, and How to Develop It," *Organizational Dynamics* 42, no. 2 (2013): 145–55.

86. A. K. Gupta and V. Govindarajan, "Cultivating a Global Mindset," *Academy of Management Executive* 16, no. 1 (2002): 116–26.

87. M. Glynn, "Putting Business Skills to Work—in a Brazilian Rainforest," *Buffalo News*, August 9, 2015; S. McCabe, "2016 EY-Earthwatch Ambassadors Program Donates 3,000 Hours of Research to Brazil, Mexico," *Accounting Today*, July 8, 2016.

Several contingencies at each stage in the cognitive model of attitudes weaken the ability to predict behavior from beliefs, feelings, and behavioral intentions.
©Peshkova/Shutterstock

individual's attitude. This is potentially true, but several contingencies at each stage in the model usually weaken that relationship. Let's begin with the beliefs–feelings link. People with the same beliefs might form quite different feelings toward the attitude object because they have different valences for those beliefs. Two employees who report to the same boss have the same belief that their boss makes them work hard. Yet one employee dislikes the boss because s/he has a negative valence toward hard work whereas the other employee has a positive valence toward hard work, and so has a positive evaluation of the boss.

The effect of feelings on behavioral intentions also depends on contingencies. Two employees might equally dislike their boss, but it isn't easy to predict their behavioral intentions from those feelings. One employee is motivated to complain to the union or upper management while the other employee is motivated to find a job elsewhere. People with the same feelings toward the attitude object often develop different behavioral intentions because of

their unique experiences, personal values, self-concept, and other individual differences. Later in this chapter we describe the four main responses to dissatisfaction and other negative attitudes.

Finally, the model indicates that behavioral intentions are the best predictors of a person's behavior. However, the strength of this link also depends on other factors, such as the person's ability, situational factors, and possibly role ambiguity (see the MARS model in Chapter 2). For example, two people might intend to quit because they dislike their boss, but only one does so because the other employee can't find another job.

How Emotions Influence Attitudes and Behavior

The cognitive model describes to some extent how employees form and change their attitudes, but emotions also have a central role in this process.[14] As the right side of Exhibit 4.2 illustrates, emotions are usually initiated by perceptions of the world around us. Our brain tags incoming sensory information with emotional markers based on a quick and imprecise evaluation of whether that information supports or threatens our innate drives. These markers are not calculated feelings; they are automatic and nonconscious emotional responses based on very thin slices of sensory information.[15] The experienced emotions then influence our feelings about the attitude object. For example, Google employees experience positive emotions from the high-quality free meals, fun-oriented and friendly work spaces, ongoing learning opportunities, and supportive coworkers, all of which generate positive attitudes toward the company.

To explain this process in more detail, consider once again your attitude toward mergers. You might experience worry, nervousness, or relief upon learning that your company intends to merge with a competitor. The fuzzy dots on the right side of Exhibit 4.2 depict the numerous emotional episodes you experience upon hearing the merger announcement, subsequently thinking about the merger, discussing the merger with coworkers, and so on. These emotions are transmitted to your brain's cognitive centers, where they are logically analyzed along with other information about the attitude object.[16] Thus, while you are consciously evaluating whether the merger is good or bad, your emotions are already sending core affect (good–bad) signals, which sway your conscious evaluation. In fact, we often deliberately "listen in" on our emotions to help us consciously decide whether to support or oppose something.[17]

> While you are consciously evaluating whether something is good or bad, your emotions are already sending core affect (good–bad) signals, which sway your conscious evaluation.

The influence of both cognitive reasoning and emotions on attitudes is most apparent when they disagree with each other. People occasionally experience this mental tug-of-war, sensing that something isn't right even though they can't think of any logical reason to be concerned. This conflicting experience indicates that the person's logical analysis of the situation (left side of Exhibit 4.2) generates feelings that differ from the emotional reaction (right side of Exhibit 4.2).[18] Should we pay attention to our emotional response or our logical analysis? This question is not easy to answer, but some studies indicate that while executives tend to make quick decisions based on their gut feelings (emotional response), the best decisions tend to occur when executives spend time logically evaluating the situation.[19] Therefore, we should pay attention to both the cognitive and emotional sides of the attitude model and hope they agree with each other most of the time!

Generating Positive Emotions at Work Google and many other companies seem to be well aware of the dual cognitive–emotional attitude process because they try to inject more positive experiences in the workplace.[20] Some critics might argue that the organization's main focus should be to create positive emotions through the job itself as well as natural everyday occurrences such as polite customers and supportive coworkers. Still, many people perform work that is difficult to enjoy much of the time. Employees perform tasks that are repetitive or they necessarily interact with unfriendly customers. Research has found that humor and fun at work—whether natural or contrived—can potentially counteract some of the negative emotions from the work itself.[21] Overall, corporate leaders need to keep in mind that emotions shape employee attitudes and, as we will discuss later, attitudes influence various forms of work-related behavior.

One last comment about Exhibit 4.2: Notice the arrow from the emotional episodes to behavior. It indicates that emotions directly influence a person's behavior without conscious thought. This occurs when we jump suddenly if someone sneaks up on us. It also occurs in everyday situations because even low-intensity emotions automatically change our facial expressions. These actions are not carefully thought out. They are automatic emotional responses that are learned or hardwired by heredity for particular situations.[23]

Cognitive Dissonance

Imagine that you have just signed a contract for new electronic whiteboards to be installed throughout the company's meeting rooms. The deal was expensive but, after consulting several staff, you felt that the technology would be valuable in this electronic age. Yet, you felt a twinge of regret soon after signing the contract.

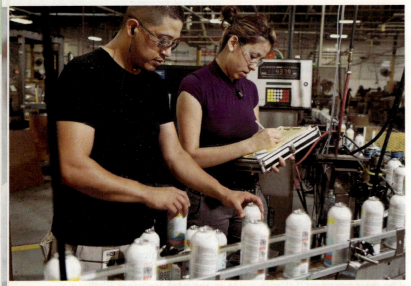

Job satisfaction has less effect on performance where employees' work effort is paced by technology or interdependence with coworkers in the production process.
©DreamPictures/Shannon Faulk/Getty Images

Why does job satisfaction affect employee performance only to some extent? One reason is that general attitudes (such as job satisfaction) don't predict specific behaviors very well. As the EVLN model explained, reduced performance (a form of neglect) is only one of four possible responses to dissatisfaction. A second reason is that some employees have little control over their performance because their work effort is paced by technology or interdependence with

"We really believe that if you put the employees first, they really and truly will take better care of the customer than anybody else."[63]

—Kip Tindell, chair and cofounder of The Container Store

coworkers in the production process. An assembly-line worker, for instance, installs a fixed number of windshields each hour with about the same quality of installation whether he or she has high or low job satisfaction.

A third consideration is that job performance might cause job satisfaction, rather than vice versa.[61] Higher performers tend to have higher satisfaction because they receive more rewards and recognition than do low-performing employees. The connection between job satisfaction and performance isn't stronger because many organizations do not reward good performance very well.

Job Satisfaction and Customer Satisfaction

Wegmans Food Markets in Rochester, New York, has an unusual motto: *Employees first, customers second.* Why doesn't Wegmans have customers at the top of the stakeholder list? Their rationale is that customer satisfaction is a natural outcome of employee satisfaction. Put differently, it is difficult to keep customers happy if employee morale is low. Virgin founder Sir Richard Branson made this point many years ago: "It just seems common sense to me that if you start with a happy, well-motivated workforce, you're much more likely to have happy customers."[62]

Research supports these beliefs. In fact, evidence suggests that job satisfaction has a stronger effect on customer service than on overall performance. The effect of job satisfaction on customer service and company profits is detailed in the **service profit chain model**, diagrammed in Exhibit 4.5. This model shows that

Exhibit 4.5 Service Profit Chain Model

Organizational practices → Employee satisfaction and commitment → Employee retention / Employee motivation and behavior → Service quality → Customer satisfaction/perceived value → Customer loyalty and referrals → Company profitability and growth

Sources: This model is based on J. I. Heskett, W. E. Sasser, and L. A. Schlesinger, *The Service Profit Chain* (New York: Free Press, 1997); A. J. Rucci, S. P. Kirn, and R. T. Quinn, "The Employee-Customer-Profit Chain at Sears," *Harvard Business Review* 76 (1998): 83–97; S. P. Brown and S. K. Lam, "A Meta-Analysis of Relationships Linking Employee Satisfaction to Customer Responses," *Journal of Retailing* 84, no. 3 (2008): 243–55.

job satisfaction has a positive effect on customer service, which eventually benefits shareholder financial returns.

The service profit chain model process begins with workplace practices that increase or decrease job satisfaction. The resulting level of satisfaction then influences whether employees stay (employee retention) as well as their motivation and behavior on the job. Retention, motivation, and behavior affect service quality, which influences the customer's satisfaction, perceived value of the service, and tendency to recommend the service to others (referrals). These customer activities influence the company's profitability and growth. The service profit chain model has considerable research support. However, the benefits of job satisfaction take considerable time to flow through to the organization's bottom line.[64]

There are two key explanations why satisfied employees tend to produce happier and more loyal customers.[65] One explanation is that job satisfaction tends to put employees in a more positive mood, and people in a good mood more naturally and frequently display friendliness and positive emotions. When employees have good feelings, their behavior "rubs off" on most (but not all) customers, so customers feel happier and consequently form a positive evaluation of the service experience (i.e., higher service quality). The effect is also mutual—happy customers make employees happier—which can lead to a virtuous cycle of positive emotions in the service experience.

The second explanation is that satisfied employees are less likely to quit their jobs, so they have more work experience (i.e., better knowledge and skills) to serve clients. Lower turnover also enables customers to have the same employees serve them, so there is more consistent service. Some evidence indicates that customers build their loyalty to specific employees, not to the organization, so keeping employee turnover low tends to build customer loyalty.

Job Satisfaction and Business Ethics

Job satisfaction is important not only because of its effect on employee behavior. Job satisfaction is also an ethical issue that influences the organization's reputation in the community. People spend a large portion of their time working in organizations, and many societies now expect companies to provide work environments that are safe and enjoyable. Indeed, employees in several countries closely monitor ratings of the best companies to work for, an indication that employee satisfaction is a virtue worth considerable goodwill to employers. The importance of this is apparent when an organization has low job satisfaction. The company typically tries to hide this fact, and when morale problems become public, corporate leaders are usually quick to take steps to improve the situation.

ORGANIZATIONAL COMMITMENT

Organizational commitment represents the other half (with job satisfaction) of what some experts call "overall job attitude." **Affective organizational commitment** is the employee's emotional attachment to, involvement in, and identification with an organization. Affective commitment is a psychological bond whereby one chooses to be dedicated to and responsible for the organization.[66]

Affective commitment differs from **continuance commitment**, which is a calculative attachment to the organization. This calculation takes two forms.[67] One form occurs where an employee has no alternative employment opportunities (e.g., "I dislike working here, but there are no other jobs available."). This condition exists where unemployment is high, employees lack the skills sought by other employers, or the employee's skills are so specialized that there is limited demand for them nearby. The other form of continuance commitment occurs where leaving the company would be a significant financial sacrifice (e.g., "I hate this place but can't afford to quit!"). This perceived sacrifice condition occurs when the company offers high pay, benefits, and other forms of economic exchange in the employment relationship, or where quitting forfeits a large deferred financial bonus.

Consequences of Affective and Continuance Commitment

Affective commitment can be a significant competitive advantage.[68] Employees with a strong psychological connection with the organization are less likely to quit their jobs and be absent from work. They also have higher work motivation and organizational citizenship, as well as somewhat higher job performance. Organizational commitment also improves customer satisfaction because long-tenure employees have better knowledge of work practices and because clients like to do business with the same employees. One problem is that employees with very high affective commitment tend to have high conformity, which results in lower creativity. Another problem is that these employees are motivated to defend the organization, even if it involves illegal activity. However, most companies suffer from too little rather than too much affective commitment.

In contrast to the benefits of affective commitment, employees with high levels of continuance commitment tend to have *lower* performance and are *less* likely to engage in organizational citizenship behaviors. Furthermore, unionized employees with high continuance commitment are more likely to use formal grievances, whereas employees with high affective commitment engage in more cooperative problem solving when employee–employer relations sour.[69] Although some level of financial connection may be necessary, employers should not rely on

service profit chain model a theory explaining how employees' job satisfaction influences company profitability indirectly through service quality, customer loyalty, and related factors

affective organizational commitment an individual's emotional attachment to, involvement in, and identification with an organization

continuance commitment an individual's calculative attachment to an organization

- *Shared values.* The definition of affective commitment refers to a person's identification with the organization, and that identification is highest when employees believe their values are congruent with the organization's dominant values. Employees also experience more positive emotions when their personal values are aligned with corporate values and actions, which increases their motivation to stay with the organization.[72]

continuance commitment instead of affective commitment. Employers still need to win employees' hearts (affective commitment) beyond tying them financially to the organization (continuance commitment).

Building Organizational Commitment

There are almost as many ways to build and maintain affective commitment as there are topics in this book, but the most frequently mentioned strategies are

- *Justice and support.* Affective commitment is higher in organizations that fulfill their obligations to employees and abide by humanitarian values such as fairness, courtesy, forgiveness, and moral integrity. These values relate to the concept of organizational justice, which we discuss in the next chapter. Similarly, organizations that support employee well-being tend to cultivate higher levels of loyalty in return.[71]

- *Trust.* **Trust** refers to positive expectations one person has toward another person in situations involving risk.[73] Trust means putting faith in the other person or group. It is also a reciprocal activity: To receive trust, you must demonstrate trust. Employees identify with and feel obliged to work for an organization only when they trust its leaders. This explains why layoffs are one of the greatest blows to affective commitment. By reducing job security, companies reduce the trust employees have in their employer and the employment relationship.[74]

- *Organizational comprehension.* Organizational comprehension refers to how well employees understand the organization, including its strategic direction, social dynamics, and physical layout.[75] This awareness is a necessary prerequisite to affective commitment because it is difficult to identify with or feel loyal to something that you don't know very well. Furthermore, lack of information produces uncertainty, and the resulting stress can distance employees from that source of uncertainty (i.e., the organization). The practical implication here is to ensure that employees

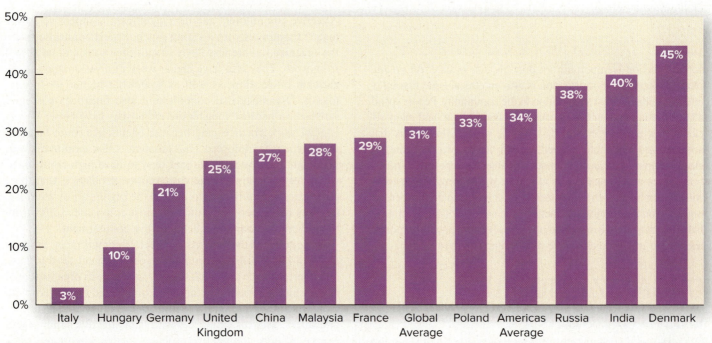

Affective Commitment around the Planet[70]

Percentage of employees surveyed in selected countries who say they feel "totally committed" to their employer. Almost 230,000 people in 31 countries across all regions were surveyed for Kelly Services.
©Image Credit

develop a reasonably clear and complete mental model of the organization. This occurs by giving staff information and opportunities to keep up to date about organizational events, interact with coworkers, discover what goes on in different parts of the organization, and learn about the organization's history and future plans.[76]

- *Employee involvement.* Employee involvement increases affective commitment by strengthening the employee's psychological ownership and social identity with the organization.[77] Employees feel part of the organization when they participate in decisions that guide the organization's future (see Chapter 6). Employee involvement also builds loyalty because it demonstrates the company's trust in its employees.

Organizational commitment and job satisfaction represent two of the most often studied and discussed attitudes in the workplace. Each is linked to emotional episodes and cognitive judgments about the workplace and relationship with the company. Emotions also play an important role in another concept that is on everyone's mind these days: stress. The final section of this chapter provides an overview of work-related stress and how it can be managed.

LO4-4 Describe the stress experience and review four major stressors.

WORK-RELATED STRESS AND ITS MANAGEMENT

When asked if they often feel stressed, most employees these days say, "Yes!" Not only do most people understand the concept; they claim to have plenty of personal experience with it. **Stress** is most often described as an adaptive response to a situation that is perceived as challenging or threatening to the person's well-being.[78] It is a physiological and psychological condition that prepares us to adapt to hostile or noxious environmental conditions. Our heart rate increases, muscles tighten, breathing speeds up, and perspiration increases. Our body also moves more blood to the brain, releases adrenaline and other hormones, fuels the system by releasing more glucose and fatty acids, activates systems that sharpen our senses, and conserves

> Organizational comprehension is a necessary prerequisite to affective commitment because it is difficult to identify with or feel loyal to something that you don't know very well.

resources by shutting down our immune system. One school of thought suggests that stress is a negative evaluation of the external environment. However, critics of this *cognitive appraisal* perspective point out that stress is more accurately described as an emotional experience, which may occur before or after a conscious evaluation of the situation.[79]

Whether stress is a complex emotion or a cognitive evaluation of the environment, it has become a pervasive experience in the daily lives of most people. Stress is typically described as a negative experience. This is known as *distress*—the degree of physiological, psychological, and behavioral deviation from healthy functioning. However, some level and form of stress—called *eustress*—is a necessary part of life because it activates and motivates people to achieve goals, change their environments, and succeed in life's challenges.[80] Our focus is on the causes and management of distress because it has become a chronic problem in many societies.

General Adaptation Syndrome

The word *stress* was first used more than 500 years ago to describe the human response to harsh environmental conditions. However, it wasn't until the 1930s that researcher Hans Selye (often described as the "father" of stress research) first

trust positive expectations one person has toward another person in situations involving risk

stress an adaptive response to a situation that is perceived as challenging or threatening to the person's well-being

Stressed Out, Burnt Out[81]

52% of more than 1,000 American workers surveyed say they are stressed at work on a day-to-day basis.

31% of 1,000 German workers surveyed report that they felt stressed at work the previous day.

58% of 400 Canadian workers surveyed say they are stressed at work on a day-to-day basis.

42% of 6,700 Americans surveyed say they have purposely changed jobs due to a stressful work environment.

66% of more than 900 Americans surveyed say their company/office does "nothing" to help alleviate stress in the workplace.

(source): ©donskarpo/Getty Images

general adaptation syndrome a model of the stress experience, consisting of three stages: alarm reaction, resistance, and exhaustion

stressors any environmental conditions that place a physical or emotional demand on the person

documented the stress experience, called the **general adaptation syndrome**. Selye determined that people have a fairly consistent and automatic physiological response to stressful situations, which helps them cope with environmental demands.[82]

The general adaptation syndrome consists of the three stages shown in Exhibit 4.6. The *alarm reaction* stage occurs when a threat or challenge activates the physiological stress responses that were noted above. The individual's energy level and coping effectiveness decrease in response to the initial shock. The second stage, *resistance*, activates various biochemical, psychological, and behavioral mechanisms that give the individual more energy and engage coping mechanisms to overcome or remove the source of stress. To focus energy on the source of the stress, the body reduces resources to the immune system during this stage. This explains why people are more likely to catch a cold or some other illness when they experience prolonged stress. People have a limited resistance capacity, and if the source of stress persists, the

individual will eventually move into the third stage, *exhaustion*. Most of us are able to remove the source of stress or remove ourselves from that source before becoming too exhausted. However, people who frequently reach exhaustion have increased risk of long-term physiological and psychological damage.[83]

Consequences of Distress

Stress takes its toll on the human body.[84] Many people experience tension headaches, muscle pain, and related problems mainly due to muscle contractions from the stress response. High stress levels also contribute to cardiovascular disease, including heart attacks and strokes, and may be associated with some forms of cancer. One major review estimated that more than 100,000 deaths annually and as much as 8 percent of health care costs in the United States are due to the consequences of work-related stress. Stress also produces various psychological consequences such as job dissatisfaction, moodiness, depression, and lower organizational commitment. Furthermore, various behavioral outcomes have been linked to high or persistent stress, including lower job performance, poor decision making, and increased workplace accidents and aggressive behavior. Most people react to stress through "fight or flight," so, as a form of flight, increased absenteeism is another outcome of stress.[85]

Stressors: The Causes of Stress

Before identifying ways to manage work-related stress, we must first understand its causes, known as stressors. **Stressors** include any environmental conditions that place a physical or emotional demand on a person.[86] There are numerous stressors in the workplace and in life in general. Four of the most common work-related stressors are organizational constraints, interpersonal conflict, work overload, and low task control.[87]

Organizational Constraints

Stress research has identified organizational constraints as one of the most pervasive causes of workplace stress.[88] This stressor includes lack of equipment, supplies, budget funding, coworker support, information, and other resources necessary to complete the required work. Most employees experience stress because these constraints interfere with task performance, which indirectly

Exhibit 4.6 General Adaptation Syndrome

Stage 1 — Alarm reaction | Stage 2 — Resistance | Stage 3 — Exhaustion

Ability to cope: High / Normal state / Low

Time

Source: Adapted from H. Selye, *The Stress of Life* (New York: McGraw-Hill, 1956).

threatens their rewards, status, and job security. Organizational constraints refer to situational factors, which is one of the four direct predictors of individual behavior and performance (see the MARS model in Chapter 2). It is the only direct influence on individual performance that is beyond the employee's immediate control. This lack of control is a powerful stressor because it threatens the individual's fundamental drive to influence his or her external environment.

Interpersonal Conflict Employees usually agree on the organization's overall objectives, but they frequently disagree with each other regarding how to achieve those goals as well as how the work and resources should be distributed along that journey. Therefore, conflict is a way of life in organizations. As we will learn in Chapter 10, dysfunctional conflict can easily flair up and, left unchecked, escalate to a level that produces considerable stress and counterproductive work behaviors. Most interpersonal conflict is caused by structural sources such as ambiguous rules, lack of resources, and conflicting goals between employees or departments. However, a fast-growing form of interpersonal conflict is *psychological harassment*, which

ranges from threats and bullying to subtle yet persistent forms of incivility.[89] *Sexual harassment* is also a major stressor that falls within the interpersonal conflict category. This occurs when a person's employment or job performance is conditional on unwanted sexual relations and/or the person experiences sexual conduct from others (such as posting pornographic material) that unreasonably interferes with work performance or creates an intimidating, hostile, or offensive working environment.[90]

Work Overload Work overload is one of the most common workplace stressors. Employees are under pressure to complete more work with more effort than they can provide within the allotted time.[91] Work overload is evident when employees consume more of their personal time to get the job done. Technology and globalization also contribute to work overload because they tether employees to work for more hours of the day. People increasingly work with coworkers in distant time zones, and their communication habits of being constantly "on" make it difficult to separate work from personal life. Some employees amplify their work overload by adopting an "ideal worker norm" in which they expect themselves and others to work longer hours. For many, toiling away far beyond the normal workweek is a badge of honor, a symbol of their superhuman capacity to perform above others. For example, 39 percent of millennial employees in one recent large-scale survey admitted that they work long hours and have a 24/7 schedule so they look like a "work martyr" to their boss.[92]

Low Task Control Workplace stress is higher when employees lack control over how and when they perform their tasks as well as lack control over the pace of work activity. Work is potentially more stressful when it is paced by a machine, it involves monitoring equipment, or the work schedule is controlled by someone else. Low task control is a stressor because employees face high workloads without the ability to adjust the pace of the load to their own energy, attention

Work overload is a common workplace stressor because employees are under pressure to complete more work with more effort than they can provide within the allotted time.
©Antonio Guillem/Shutterstock

span, and other resources. Furthermore, the degree to which low task control is a stressor increases with the burden of responsibility the employee must carry.[93] Assembly-line workers have low task control, but their stress can be fairly low if their level of responsibility is also low. In contrast, sports coaches are under immense pressure to win games (high responsibility), yet they have little control over what happens on the playing field (low task control).

Individual Differences in Stress

People exposed to the same stressor experience different levels of stress. One contributing factor is the employee's physical health. Regular exercise and a healthy lifestyle produce a larger store of energy to cope with stress. A second individual difference is the coping strategy employees use to ward off a particular stressor.[94] People sometimes figure out ways to remove the stressor or to minimize its presence. Seeking support from others, reframing the stressor in a more positive light, blaming others for the stressor, and denying the stressor's existence are some other coping mechanisms. Specific coping strategies work better for specific stressors, and some are better across all stressors.[95] Thus, someone who uses a less effective coping mechanism in a particular situation would experience more stress in response to that situation. People have a tendency to rely on one or two coping strategies, and those who rely on generally poor coping strategies (such as denying the stressor exists) are going to experience more stress.

Personality is the third and possibly the most important reason why people experience different levels of stress when faced with the same stressor.[96] Individuals with low neuroticism (high emotional stability) usually experience lower stress levels because, by definition, they are less prone to anxiety, depression, and other negative emotions. Extraverts also tend to experience lower stress than do introverts, likely because extraversion includes a degree of positive thinking and extraverts interact with others, which helps buffer the effect of stressors. Those with a positive self-concept—high self-esteem, self-efficacy, and internal locus of control (see Chapter 3)—feel more confident and in control when faced with a stressor. In other words, they tend to have a stronger sense of optimism.[97] Stress also tends to be higher among those who suffer from *workaholism*. Workaholics have an uncontrollable work motivation, constantly think about work, and have low work enjoyment.[98]

LO4-5 Identify five ways to manage workplace stress.

Managing Work-Related Stress

Many people deny the existence of their stress until it has more serious outcomes. This avoidance strategy creates a vicious cycle because the failure to cope with stress becomes another stressor on top of the one that created the stress in the first place. To prevent this vicious cycle, employers and employees need to apply one or more of the stress management strategies described next: remove the stressor, withdraw from the stressor, change stress perceptions, control stress consequences, and receive social support.[99]

Remove the Stressor There are many ways to remove the stressor, but some of the more common actions involve assigning employees to jobs that match their skills and preferences, reducing excessive workplace noise, having a complaint system that takes corrective action against harassment, and giving employees more control over the work process. Another important way that companies can remove stressors is through work–life balance initiatives. For example, personal leave benefits, such as maternity and paternity leave, temporarily offer employees paid nonwork time to manage special circumstances. Telecommuting potentially improves work–life balance by reducing or eliminating commuting time and increasing flexibility to perform nonwork obligations (such as picking up the kids from school).[101] Flexible work arrangements also enable employees to rearrange their time allocated to work and nonwork demands.

Withdraw from the Stressor Removing the stressor may be the ideal solution, but it is often not feasible. An alternative strategy is to permanently or temporarily remove employees from the stressor. Permanent withdrawal occurs when employees are transferred to jobs that are more compatible with their abilities and values. Temporarily withdrawing from stressors is the most frequent way that employees manage stress. Vacations and holidays are important opportunities for employees to recover from stress and reenergize for future challenges.[102] Many firms also provide innovative ways for employees to withdraw from stressful work throughout the day such as game rooms, ice cream cart breaks, nap rooms, and cafeterias that include live piano recitals.

Change Stress Perceptions How much stress employees experience depends on how they perceive the stressor.[104] Consequently, another way to manage stress is to help employees improve their self-concept so job challenges are

How Americans Cope with Work-Related Stress[100]

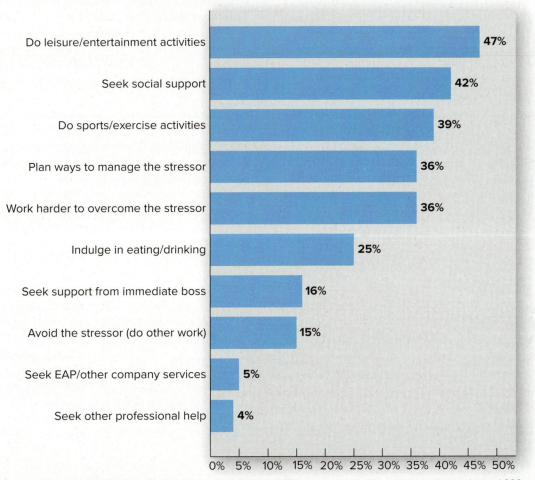

Coping Method	Percentage
Do leisure/entertainment activities	47%
Seek social support	42%
Do sports/exercise activities	39%
Plan ways to manage the stressor	36%
Work harder to overcome the stressor	36%
Indulge in eating/drinking	25%
Seek support from immediate boss	16%
Avoid the stressor (do other work)	15%
Seek EAP/other company services	5%
Seek other professional help	4%

This survey was conducted by Willis Towers Watson in 2013 from 5,070 Americans working at companies employing 1,000 or more people. Leisure/entertainment examples include shopping, reading, listening to music, watching movies/TV, and playing games. Social support sources include friends, family, and coworkers. Indulgence activities include eating less healthy food and drinking more alcohol. An "EAP" is an employee assistance program. Other professional help includes family doctor and psychologist.
©Image Credit

OB THEORY TO PRACTICE

Stress-Busting Power Naps at HubSpot

HubSpot has all the features that attract Millennial employees: games room, fully stocked kitchen, camping-themed meditation room, and a hammock-equipped nap room in a beach-like setting. A nap room? Yes, the Boston-based marketing-software company encourages employees not just to take a break from their busy workday, but to recharge the brain cells by nodding off for half an hour. "Getting 20 or 30 minutes to pay back some of the sleep I lost the night before can make me so much more effective," says a HubSpot executive. One recent survey estimated that 5 percent of large American firms have private spaces or pods designed for employees to take a nap.[103]

©David L. Ryan/The Boston Globe via Getty Images

not perceived as threatening. Personal goal setting and self-reinforcement also can reduce the stress that people experience when they enter new work settings. In addition, research suggests that some (but not all) forms of humor can improve optimism and create positive emotions by taking some psychological weight off a stressful situation.[105]

Control Stress Consequences Keeping physically fit and maintaining a healthy lifestyle are effective stress management strategies because they control stress consequences. Good physical fitness reduces the adverse physiological consequences of stress by helping employees moderate their breathing and heart rate, muscle tension, and stomach acidity. The key variable here is physical fitness, not exercise. Exercise leads to physical fitness, but research suggests that exercise does not reduce stress symptoms among people who are not yet physically fit.[106] Various forms of meditation reduce anxiety and other symptoms of stress, but their effect on blood pressure and other physiological symptoms is minimal.[107] Wellness programs also can assist in controlling the consequences of stress. These programs inform employees about better nutrition and fitness, regular sleep, and other good health habits. Many large companies offer *employee assistance programs (EAPs)*—counseling services that help employees resolve marital, financial, or work-related troubles.

Receive Social Support Social support occurs when coworkers, supervisors, family members, friends, and others provide emotional and/or informational support to buffer an individual's stress experience. For instance, employees whose managers are good at empathizing experienced fewer stress symptoms than do employees whose managers were less empathetic. Social support potentially (but not always) improves the person's optimism and self-confidence because support makes people feel valued and worthy. Social support also provides information to help the person interpret, comprehend, and possibly remove the stressor. For instance, to reduce a new employee's stress, coworkers could describe ways to handle difficult customers. Seeking social support is called a "tend and befriend" response to stress, and research suggests that women often take this route rather than the "fight-or-flight" response mentioned earlier.[108]

SELF-ASSESSMENT 4.6: How Do You Cope with Stressful Situations?
People cope with stress in several ways. The best coping strategy usually depends on the source of stress and other circumstances. However, people also have a natural preference for some types of coping strategies more than others. You can discover your preferences among four coping strategies by locating this self-assessment in Connect if it is assigned by your instructor.

Study Checklist

Connect® Management is available for *M Organizational Behavior.* Additional resources include:

✓ Interactive Applications:
- **Case Analysis:** Apply concepts within the context of a real-world situation.
- **Drag and Drop:** Work through an interactive example to test your knowledge of the concepts.
- **Video Case:** See management in action through interactive videos.

✓ **SmartBook**™—SmartBook is the first and only adaptive reading experience available today. Distinguishing what you know from what you don't, and honing in on concepts you are most likely to forget, SmartBook personalizes content for you in a continuously adapting reading experience. Reading is no longer a passive and linear experience, but an engaging and dynamic one where you are more likely to master and retain important concepts and go to class better prepared.

©Natthawat Jamnapa/123RF

Notes

1. J. D'Onfro, "An inside Look at Google's Best Employee Perks," *Inc.*, September 21, 2015; R. Gillett, "Why Google Is the Best Company to Work for in America," *Business Insider*, April 29, 2016; A. Hartmans, "What It's Really Like to Work at Google, the Best Company to Work for in the US," *Business Insider*, August 26, 2016; "Google Inc.," *Great Place to Work* (San Francisco: Great Place to Work® Institute, 2017), http://reviews.greatplacetowork.com/google-inc (accessed June 23, 2017).

2. Emotions are also cognitive processes. However, we use the narrow definition of *cognition* as a well-used label referring only to reasoning processes. Also, this and other chapters emphasize that emotional and cognitive processes are intertwined.

3. For discussion of emotions in marketing, economics, and sociology, see M. Hubert, "Does Neuroeconomics Give New Impetus to Economic and Consumer Research?," *Journal of Economic Psychology* 31, no. 5 (2010): 812–17; D. D. Franks, "Introduction," in *Neurosociology: The Nexus between Neuroscience and Social Psychology* (New York: Springer, 2010), 1–20; N. Martins, "Can Neuroscience Inform Economics? Rationality, Emotions and Preference Formation," *Cambridge Journal of Economics* 35, no. 2 (2011): 251–67; H. Plassmann, T. Z. Ramsøy, and M. Milosavljevic, "Branding the Brain: A Critical Review and Outlook," *Journal of Consumer Psychology* 22, no. 1 (2012): 18–36.

4. Although definitions of *emotion* vary, the definition stated here seems to be the most widely accepted. See, for example, N. H. Frijda, "Varieties of Affect: Emotions and Episodes, Moods, and Sentiments," in *The Nature of Emotion: Fundamental Questions*, ed. P. Ekman and R. J. Davidson (New York: Oxford University Press, 1994), 59–67; H. M. Weiss, "Conceptual and Empirical Foundations for the Study of Affect at Work," in *Emotions in the Workplace,* ed. R. G. Lord, R. J. Klimoski, and R. Kanfer (San Francisco: Jossey-Bass, 2002), 20–63; G. Van Kleef, H. van den Berg, and M. Heerdink, "The Persuasive Power of Emotions: Effects of Emotional Expressions on Attitude Formation and Change," *Journal of Applied Psychology* 100, no. 4 (2015): 1124–42.

5. R. Reisenzein, M. Studtmann, and G. Horstmann, "Coherence between Emotion and Facial Expression: Evidence from Laboratory Experiments," *Emotion Review* 5, no. 1 (2013): 16–23.

6. R. B. Zajonc, "Emotions," in *Handbook of Social Psychology*, ed. D. T. Gilbert, S. T. Fiske, and L. Gardner (New York: Oxford University Press, 1998), 591–634; P. Winkielman, "Bob Zajonc and the Unconscious Emotion," *Emotion Review* 2, no. 4 (2010): 353–62.

7. V. van Gogh, T. van Gogh, and I. Stone, *Dear Theo: The Autobiography* (New York: Doubleday, 1937; repr., 1995), 441. This quotation originally appeared in a letter sent by Vincent van Gogh to his brother Théo in 1889.

8. R. J. Larson, E. Diener, and R. E. Lucas, "Emotion: Models, Measures, and Differences," in *Emotions in the Workplace*, ed. R. G. Lord, R. J. Klimoski, and R. Kanfer (San Francisco: Jossey-Bass, 2002), 64–113; L. F. Barrett et al., "The Experience of Emotion," *Annual Review of Psychology* 58, no. 1 (2007): 373–403; M. Yik, J. A. Russell, and J. H. Steiger, "A 12-Point Circumplex Structure of Core Affect," *Emotion* 11, no. 4 (2011): 705–31.

9. R. F. Baumeister, E. Bratslavsky, and C. Finkenauer, "Bad Is Stronger Than Good," *Review of General Psychology* 5, no. 4 (2001): 323–70; A. Vaish, T. Grossmann, and A. Woodward, "Not All Emotions Are Created Equal: The Negativity Bias in Social-Emotional Development," *Psychological Bulletin* 134, no. 3 (2008): 383–403; R. H. Fazio et al., "Positive versus Negative Valence: Asymmetries in Attitude Formation and Generalization as Fundamental Individual Differences," in *Advances in Experimental Social Psychology*, vol. 51, ed. J. M. Olson and M. P. Zanna (Waltham, MA: Academic Press, 2015), 97–146; K. Bebbington et al., "The Sky Is Falling: Evidence of a Negativity Bias in the Social Transmission of Information," *Evolution and Human Behavior* 38, no. 1 (2017): 92–101.

10. A. P. Brief, *Attitudes in and around Organizations* (Thousand Oaks, CA: Sage, 1998); A. H. Eagly and S. Chaiken, "The Advantages of an Inclusive Definition of Attitude," *Social Cognition* 25, no. 5 (2007): 582–602; G. Bohner and N. Dickel, "Attitudes and Attitude Change," *Annual Review of Psychology* 62, no. 1 (2011): 391–417. The definition of *attitudes* is still being debated. This book adopts the three-component model (beliefs, feelings, behavioral intentions), whereas some writers describe attitude as relating only to the "feelings" component; however, they invariably include beliefs and intentions in their discussion of attitude. For definitions and various models of attitudes, see I. Ajzen, "Nature and Operation of Attitudes," *Annual Review of Psychology* 52 (2001): 27–58; D. Albarracin et al., "Attitudes: Introduction and Scope," in *The Handbook of Attitudes*, ed. D. Albarracín, B. T. Johnson, and M. P. Zanna (Mahwah, NJ: Erlbaum, 2005), 3–20; W. A. Cunningham and P. D. Zelazo, "Attitudes and Evaluations: A Social Cognitive Neuroscience Perspective," *TRENDS in Cognitive Sciences* 11, no. 3 (2007): 97–104; R. S. Dalal, "Job Attitudes: Cognition and Affect," in *Industrial and Organizational Psychology*, ed. I. B. Weiner, N. W. Schmitt, and S. Highhouse, Handbook of Psychology, *2nd ed., ed. I. B. Weiner, vol. 12 (New York: Wiley, 2012), 341–66.

11. Neuroscience has a slightly more complicated distinction in that conscious awareness is "feeling a feeling," whereas "feeling" is a nonconscious sensing of the body state created by emotion, which itself is a nonconscious neural reaction to a stimulus. However, this distinction is not significant for scholars focused on human behavior rather than brain activity, and the labels collide with popular understanding of "feeling." See A. R. Damasio, *The Feeling of What Happens: Body and Emotion in the Making of Consciousness* (New York: Harcourt Brace, 1999); F. Hansen, "Distinguishing between Feelings and Emotions in Understanding Communication Effects," *Journal of Business Research* 58, no. 10 (2005): 1426–36; T. Bosse, C. M. Jonker, and J. Treur, "Formalisation of Damasio's Theory of Emotion, Feeling and Core Consciousness," *Consciousness and Cognition* 17, no. 1 (2008): 94–113.

12. W. A. Cunningham and P. D. Zelazo, "Attitudes and Evaluations: A Social Cognitive Neuroscience Perspective," *TRENDS in Cognitive Sciences* 11, no. 3 (2007): 97–104; M. D. Lieberman, "Social Cognitive Neuroscience: A Review of Core Processes," *Annual Review of Psychology* 58, no. 1 (2007): 259–89; M. Fenton-O'Creevy et al., "Thinking, Feeling and Deciding: The Influence of Emotions on the Decision Making and Performance of Traders," *Journal of Organizational Behavior* 32 (2011): 1044–61. The dual emotion–cognition processes are likely the same as the implicit–explicit attitude processes reported by several scholars, as well as tacit knowledge structures. See W. J. Becker and R. Cropanzano, "Organizational Neuroscience: The Promise and Prospects of an Emerging Discipline," *Journal of Organizational Behavior* 31, no. 7 (2010): 1055–59; D. Kahneman, *Thinking Fast and Slow* (New York: Farrar, Straus and Giroux, 2011).

13. S. Orbell, "Intention-Behavior Relations: A Self-Regulation Perspective," in *Contemporary Perspectives on the Psychology of Attitudes*, ed. G. Haddock and G. R. Maio (East Sussex, UK: Psychology Press, 2004), 145–68.

14. H. M. Weiss and R. Cropanzano, "Affective Events Theory: A Theoretical Discussion of the Structure, Causes and Consequences of Affective Experiences at Work," *Research in Organizational Behavior* 18 (1996): 1–74; A. Bechara et al., "Deciding Advantageously before Knowing the Advantageous Strategy," *Science* 275, no. 5304 (1997): 1293–95; B. Russell and J. Eisenberg, "The Role of Cognition and Attitude in Driving Behavior: Elaborating on Affective Events Theory," in *Experiencing and Managing Emotions in the Workplace*, ed. N. M. Ashkanasy, C. E. J. Hartel, and W. J. Zerbe (Bingley, UK: Emerald Group, 2012), 203–24.

15. J. A. Bargh and M. J. Ferguson, "Beyond Behaviorism: On the Automaticity of Higher Mental Processes," *Psychological Bulletin* 126, no. 6 (2000): 925–45; P. Winkielman and K. C. Berridge, "Unconscious Emotion," *Current Directions in Psychological Science* 13, no. 3 (2004): 120–23; A. Moors, "Automaticity: Componential, Causal, and Mechanistic Explanations," *Annual Review of Psychology* 67, no. 1 (2016): 263–87.

16. A. R. Damasio, *Descartes' Error: Emotion, Reason, and the Human Brain* (New York: Putnam Sons, 1994); P. Ekman, "Basic Emotions," in *Handbook of Cognition and Emotion*, ed. T. Dalgleish and M. Power (San Francisco: Jossey-Bass, 1999), 45–60; A. R. Damasio, *The Feeling of What Happens: Body and Emotion in the*

48. Randstad, *Randstad Workmonitor 4th Quarter 2016* (Amsterdam: Randstad Holding nv, December 2016). Survey data were collected from 33 countries with a minimum of 400 interviews per country of adults working 24 hours or more per week. Respondents were asked: "How satisfied are you in general about working with your current employer?" This exhibit shows results from selected countries across the full range of results.

49. L. Saad, *Job Security Slips in U.S. Worker Satisfaction Rankings* (Princeton, NJ: Gallup, Inc., August 27, 2009); *Employee Engagement Report 2011* (Princeton, NJ: BlessingWhite, 2011). A recent Kelly Services Workforce Index survey reported that 66 percent of the 170,000 respondents in 30 countries plan to look for a job with another organization within the next year. See Kelly Global Workforce Index, *Acquisition and Retention in the War for Talent* (Troy, MI: Kelly Services, April 2012).

50. The problems with measuring attitudes and values across cultures are discussed in L. Saari and T. A. Judge, "Employee Attitudes and Job Satisfaction," *Human Resource Management* 43, no. 4 (2004): 395–407; A. K. Uskul et al., "How Successful You Have Been in Life Depends on the Response Scale Used: The Role of Cultural Mindsets in Pragmatic Inferences Drawn from Question Format," *Social Cognition* 31, no. 2 (2013): 222–36.

51. For a review of the various job satisfaction outcome theories, see R. S. Dalal, "Job Attitudes: Cognition and Affect," in *Industrial and Organizational Psychology*, ed. I. B. Weiner, N. W. Schmitt, and S. Highhouse, Handbook of Psychology, 2nd ed., ed. I. B. Weiner, vol. 12 (New York: John Wiley & Sons, 2012), 341–66.

52. D. Farrell, "Exit, Voice, Loyalty, and Neglect as Responses to Job Dissatisfaction: A Multidimensional Scaling Study," *Academy of Management Journal* 26, no. 4 (1983): 596–607; M. J. Withey and W. H. Cooper, "Predicting Exit, Voice, Loyalty, and Neglect," *Administrative Science Quarterly*, no. 34 (1989): 521–39; A. B. Whitford and S.-Y. Lee, "Exit, Voice, and Loyalty with Multiple Exit Options: Evidence from the US Federal Workforce," *Journal of Public Administration Research and Theory* 25, no. 2 (2015): 373–98. For a critique and explanation of historical errors in the EVLN model, see S. L. McShane, "Reconstructing the Meaning and Dimensionality of Voice in the Exit-Voice-Loyalty-Neglect Model," paper presented at the Voice and Loyalty Symposium, Annual Conference of the Administrative Sciences Association of Canada, Organizational Behaviour Division, Halifax, 2008.

53. T. R. Mitchell, B. C. Holtom, and T. W. Lee, "How to Keep Your Best Employees: Developing an Effective Retention Policy," *Academy of Management Executive* 15 (2001): 96–108; K. Morrell, J. Loan-Clarke, and A. Wilkinson, "The Role of Shocks in Employee Turnover," *British Journal of Management* 15 (2004): 335–49; M. Zhang, D. D. Fried, and R. W. Griffeth, "A Review of Job Embeddedness: Conceptual, Measurement Issues, and Directions for Future Research," *Human Resource Management Review* 22, no. 3 (2012): 220–31.

54. E. W. Morrison, "Employee Voice and Silence," *Annual Review of Organizational Psychology and Organizational Behavior* 1, no. 1 (2014): 173–97; M. R. Bashshur and B. Oc, "When Voice Matters: A Multilevel Review of the Impact of Voice in Organizations," *Journal of Management* 41, no. 5 (2015): 1530–54; P. K. Mowbray, A. Wilkinson, and H. H. M. Tse, "An Integrative Review of Employee Voice: Identifying a Common Conceptualization and Research Agenda," *International Journal of Management Reviews* 17, no. 3 (2015): 382–400.

55. A. O. Hirschman, *Exit, Voice, and Loyalty: Responses to Decline in Firms, Organizations, and States* (Cambridge, MA: Harvard University Press, 1970); E. A. Hoffmann, "Exit and Voice: Organizational Loyalty and Dispute Resolution Strategies," *Social Forces* 84, no. 4 (2006): 2313–30.

56. J. D. Hibbard, N. Kumar, and L. W. Stern, "Examining the Impact of Destructive Acts in Marketing Channel Relationships," *Journal of Marketing Research* 38 (2001): 45–61; J. Zhou and J. M. George, "When Job Dissatisfaction Leads to Creativity: Encouraging the Expression of Voice," *Academy of Management Journal* 44 (2001): 682–96.

57. M. J. Withey and I. R. Gellatly, "Situational and Dispositional Determinants of Exit, Voice, Loyalty and Neglect," *Proceedings of the Administrative Sciences Association of Canada, Organizational Behaviour Division*, 1998; D. C. Thomas and K. Au, "The Effect of Cultural Differences on Behavioral Responses to Low Job Satisfaction," *Journal of International Business Studies* 33, no. 2 (2002): 309–26; S. F. Premeaux and A. G. Bedeian, "Breaking the Silence: The Moderating Effects of Self-Monitoring in Predicting Speaking Up in the Workplace," *Journal of Management Studies* 40, no. 6 (2003): 1537–62; D. J. Travis, R. J. Gomez, and M. E. Mor Barak, "Speaking Up and Stepping Back: Examining the Link between Employee Voice and Job Neglect," *Children and Youth Services Review* 33, no. 10 (2011): 1831–41.

58. V. Venkataramani and S. Tangirala, "When and Why Do Central Employees Speak Up? An Examination of Mediating and Moderating Variables," *Journal of Applied Psychology* 95, no. 3 (2010): 582–91.

59. H. Wallop, "A Contented and Profitable Workforce?," *Daily Telegraph* (London), April 22, 2015, 15.

60. T. A. Judge et al., "The Job Satisfaction-Job Performance Relationship: A Qualitative and Quantitative Review," *Psychological Bulletin* 127, no. 3 (2001): 376–407; C. D. Fisher, "Why Do Lay People Believe That Satisfaction and Performance Are Correlated? Possible Sources of a Commonsense Theory," *Journal of Organizational Behavior* 24, no. 6 (2003): 753–77; L. Saari and T. A. Judge, "Employee Attitudes and Job Satisfaction," *Human Resource Management* 43, no. 4 (2004): 395–407. Other studies report stronger correlations with job performance when both the belief and feeling components of job satisfaction are consistent with each other and when overall job attitude (satisfaction and commitment combined) is being measured. See D. J. Schleicher, J. D. Watt, and G. J. Greguras, "Reexamining the Job Satisfaction-Performance Relationship: The Complexity of Attitudes," *Journal of Applied Psychology* 89, no. 1 (2004): 165–77; D. A. Harrison, D. A. Newman, and P. L. Roth, "How Important Are Job Attitudes? Meta-Analytic Comparisons of Integrative Behavioral Outcomes and Time Sequences," *Academy of Management Journal* 49, no. 2 (2006): 305–25. The positive relationship between job satisfaction and employee performance is also consistent with emerging research on the outcomes of positive organizational behavior. For example, see J. R. Sunil, "Enhancing Employee Performance through Positive Organizational Behavior," *Journal of Applied Social Psychology* 38, no. 6 (2008): 1580–600.

61. However, panel studies suggest that satisfaction has a stronger effect on performance than the other way around. For a summary, see C. D. Fisher, "Happiness at Work," *International Journal of Management Reviews* 12, no. 4 (2010): 384–412.

62. "The Greatest Briton in Management and Leadership," *Personnel Today* (2003): 20.

63. L. Wirthman, "Container Store Moves Ahead with Superb Communications among Employees," *Denver Post*, April 21, 2013.

64. J. I. Heskett, W. E. Sasser, and L. A. Schlesinger, *The Service Profit Chain* (New York: Free Press, 1997); S. P. Brown and S. K. Lam, "A Meta-Analysis of Relationships Linking Employee Satisfaction to Customer Responses," *Journal of Retailing* 84, no. 3 (2008): 243–55; T. J. Gerpott and M. Paukert, "The Relationship between Employee Satisfaction and Customer Satisfaction: A Meta-Analysis (*Der Zusammenhang Zwischen Mitarbeiter-Und Kundenzufriedenheit: Eine Metaanalyse*),"

Zeitschrift für Personalforschung 25, no. 1 (2011): 28-54; H. Evanschitzky, F. V. Wangenheim, and N. V. Wünderlich, "Perils of Managing the Service Profit Chain: The Role of Time Lags and Feedback Loops," *Journal of Retailing* 88, no. 3 (2012): 356-66; Y. Hong et al., "Missing Link in the Service Profit Chain: A Meta-Analytic Review of the Antecedents, Consequences, and Moderators of Service Climate," *Journal of Applied Psychology* 98, no. 2 (2013): 237-67.

65. W.-C. Tsai and Y.-M. Huang, "Mechanisms Linking Employee Affective Delivery and Customer Behavioral Intentions," *Journal of Applied Psychology* 87, no. 5 (2002): 1001-08; P. Guenzi and O. Pelloni, "The Impact of Interpersonal Relationships on Customer Satisfaction and Loyalty to the Service Provider," *International Journal of Service Industry Management* 15, no. 3/4 (2004): 365-84; S. J. Bell, S. Auh, and K. Smalley, "Customer Relationship Dynamics: Service Quality and Customer Loyalty in the Context of Varying Levels of Customer Expertise and Switching Costs," *Journal of the Academy of Marketing Science* 33, no. 2 (2005): 169-83; P. B. Barger and A. A. Grandey, "Service with a Smile and Encounter Satisfaction: Emotional Contagion and Appraisal Mechanisms," *Academy of Management Journal* 49, no. 6 (2006): 1229-38. On the reciprocal effect, see E. Kim and D. J. Yoon, "Why Does Service with a Smile Make Employees Happy? A Social Interaction Model," *Journal of Applied Psychology* 97, no. 5 (2012): 1059-67.

66. R. T. Mowday, L. W. Porter, and R. M. Steers, *Employee Organization Linkages: The Psychology of Commitment, Absenteeism, and Turnover* (New York: Academic Press, 1982); J. P. Meyer, "Organizational Commitment," *International Review of Industrial and Organizational Psychology* 12 (1997): 175-228. The definition and dimensions of organizational commitment continue to be debated. Some writers even propose that *affective commitment* refers only to one's psychological attachment to and involvement in the organization, whereas *identification* with the organization is a distinct concept further along a continuum of bonds. See O. N. Solinger, W. van Olffen, and R. A. Roe, "Beyond the Three-Component Model of Organizational Commitment," *Journal of Applied Psychology* 93, no. 1 (2008): 70-83; H. J. Klein, J. C. Molloy, and C. T. Brinsfield, "Reconceptualizing Workplace Commitment to Redress a Stretched Construct: Revisiting Assumptions and Removing Confounds," *Academy of Management Review* 37, no. 1 (2012): 130-51.

67. M. Taing et al., "The Multidimensional Nature of Continuance Commitment: Commitment Owing to Economic Exchanges versus Lack of Employment Alternatives," *Journal of Business and Psychology* 26, no. 3 (2011): 269-84; C. Vandenberghe and A. Panaccio, "Perceived Sacrifice and Few Alternatives Commitments: The Motivational Underpinnings of Continuance Commitment's Subdimensions," *Journal of Vocational Behavior* 81, no. 1 (2012): 59-72.

68. J. P. Meyer et al., "Affective, Continuance, and Normative Commitment to the Organization: A Meta-Analysis of Antecedents, Correlates, and Consequences," *Journal of Vocational Behavior* 61 (2002): 20-52; M. Riketta, "Attitudinal Organizational Commitment and Job Performance: A Meta-Analysis," *Journal of Organizational Behavior* 23 (2002): 257-66; J. P. Meyer and E. R. Maltin, "Employee Commitment and Well-Being: A Critical Review, Theoretical Framework and Research Agenda," *Journal of Vocational Behavior* 77, no. 2 (2010): 323-37.

69. J. P. Meyer et al., "Organizational Commitment and Job Performance: It's the Nature of the Commitment That Counts," *Journal of Applied Psychology* 74 (1989): 152-56; A. A. Luchak and I. R. Gellatly, "What Kind of Commitment Does a Final-Earnings Pension Plan Elicit?," *Relations Industrielles* 56 (2001): 394-417; Z. X. Chen and A. M. Francesco, "The Relationship between the Three Components of Commitment and Employee Performance in China," *Journal of Vocational Behavior* 62, no. 3 (2003): 490-510; H. Gill et al., "Affective and Continuance Commitment and Their Relations with Deviant Workplace Behaviors in Korea," *Asia Pacific Journal of Management* 28, no. 3 (2011): 595-607. The negative effect on performance might depend on the type of continuance commitment. See M. Taing et al., "The Multidimensional Nature of Continuance Commitment: Commitment Owing to Economic Exchanges versus Lack of Employment Alternatives," *Journal of Business and Psychology* 26, no. 3 (2011): 269-84.

70. Kelly Services, Kelly Global Workforce Index, *Engaging Active and Passive Job Seekers* (Troy, MI: Kelly Services, May 2014); Kelly Services, Kelly Global Workforce Index, *A World at Work* (Troy, MI: Kelly Services, September 2014).

71. J. E. Finegan, "The Impact of Person and Organizational Values on Organizational Commitment," *Journal of Occupational and Organizational Psychology* 73 (2000): 149-69; A. Panaccio and C. Vandenberghe, "Perceived Organizational Support, Organizational Commitment and Psychological Well-Being: A Longitudinal Study," *Journal of Vocational Behavior* 75, no. 2 (2009): 224-36.

72. A. L. Kristof-Brown, R. D. Zimmerman, and E. C. Johnson, "Consequences of Individuals' Fit at Work: A Meta-Analysis of Person-Job, Person-Organization, Person-Group, and Person-Supervisor Fit," *Personnel Psychology* 58, no. 2 (2005): 281-342; J. R. Edwards, "Chapter 4: Person-Environment Fit in Organizations: An Assessment of Theoretical Progress," *The Academy of Management Annals* 2 (2008): 167-230; M. E. Bergman et al., "An Event-Based Perspective on the Development of Commitment," *Human Resource Management Review* 23, no. 2 (2013): 148-60.

73. D. M. Rousseau et al., "Not So Different after All: A Cross-Discipline View of Trust," *Academy of Management Review* 23 (1998): 393-404.

74. D. K. Datta et al., "Causes and Effects of Employee Downsizing: A Review and Synthesis," *Journal of Management* 36, no. 1 (2010): 281-348.

75. Similar concepts on information acquisition are found in socialization and organizational change research. See, for example, P. Bordia et al., "Uncertainty during Organizational Change: Types, Consequences, and Management Strategies," *Journal of Business and Psychology* 18, no. 4 (2004): 507-32; H. D. Cooper-Thomas and N. Anderson, "Organizational Socialization: A Field Study into Socialization Success and Rate," *International Journal of Selection and Assessment* 13, no. 2 (2005): 116-28; T. N. Bauer, "Newcomer Adjustment during Organizational Socialization: A Meta-Analytic Review of Antecedents, Outcomes, and Methods," *Journal of Applied Psychology* 92, no. 3 (2007): 707-21.

76. T. S. Heffner and J. R. Rentsch, "Organizational Commitment and Social Interaction: A Multiple Constituencies Approach," *Journal of Vocational Behavior* 59 (2001): 471-90.

77. J. L. Pierce, T. Kostova, and K. T. Dirks, "Toward a Theory of Psychological Ownership in Organizations," *Academy of Management Review* 26, no. 2 (2001): 298-310; M. Mayhew et al., "A Study of the Antecedents and Consequences of Psychological Ownership in Organizational Settings," *The Journal of Social Psychology* 147, no. 5 (2007): 477-500; T.-S. Han, H.-H. Chiang, and A. Chang, "Employee Participation in Decision Making, Psychological Ownership and Knowledge Sharing: Mediating Role of Organizational Commitment in Taiwanese High-Tech Organizations," *The International Journal of Human Resource Management* 21, no. 12 (2010): 2218-33.

78. J. C. Quick et al., *Preventive Stress Management in Organizations* (Washington, DC: American Psychological Association, 1997), 3-4; R. S. DeFrank and J. M. Ivancevich, "Stress on the Job: An Executive Update," *Academy of Management Executive* 12 (1998): 55-66; A. L. Dougall and A. Baum, "Stress, Coping, and

Immune Function," in *Handbook of Psychology*, ed. M. Gallagher and R. J. Nelson (Hoboken, NJ: Wiley, 2003), 441–55. There are at least three schools of thought regarding the meaning of stress, and some reviews of the stress literature describe these schools without pointing to any one as the preferred definition. One reviewer concluded that the stress concept is so broad that it should be considered an umbrella concept, capturing a broad array of phenomena and providing a simple term for the public to use. See T. A. Day, "Defining Stress as a Prelude to Mapping Its Neurocircuitry: No Help from Allostasis," *Progress in Neuro-Psychopharmacology and Biological Psychiatry* 29, no. 8 (2005): 1195–200; R. Cropanzano and A. Li, "Organizational Politics and Workplace Stress," in *Handbook of Organizational Politics*, ed. E. Vigoda-Gadot and A. Drory (Cheltenham, UK: Edward Elgar, 2006), 139–60; R. L. Woolfolk, P. M. Lehrer, and L. A. Allen, "Conceptual Issues Underlying Stress Management," in *Principles and Practice of Stress Management*, ed. P. M. Lehrer, R. L. Woolfolk, and W. E. Sime (New York: Guilford Press, 2007), 3–15.

79. J. E. Finegan, "The Impact of Person and Organizational Values on Organizational Commitment," *Journal of Occupational and Organizational Psychology* 73 (2000): 149–69; A. L. Dougall and A. Baum, "Stress, Coping, and Immune Function," in *Handbook of Psychology,* ed. M. Gallagher and R. J. Nelson (Hoboken, NJ: Wiley, 2003), 441–55; R. S. Lazarus, *Stress and Emotion: A New Synthesis* (New York: Springer, 2006); L. W. Hunter and S. M. B. Thatcher, "Feeling the Heat: Effects of Stress, Commitment, and Job Experience on Job Performance," *Academy of Management Journal* 50, no. 4 (2007): 953–68.

80. M. G. González-Morales and P. Neves, "When Stressors Make You Work: Mechanisms Linking Challenge Stressors to Performance," *Work & Stress* 29, no. 3 (2015): 213–29; M. B. Hargrove, W. S. Becker, and D. F. Hargrove, "The HRD Eustress Model: Generating Positive Stress with Challenging Work," *Human Resource Development Review* 14, no. 3 (2015): 279–98.

81. Monster Worldwide, "Dangerously Stressful Work Environments Force Workers to Seek New Employment," news release (Weston, MA: Monster Worldwide, April 16, 2014); M. Nink, "The High Cost of Worker Burnout in Germany," *Gallup Business Journal*, March 17, 2016; Accountemps, "The Heat Is On: Six in 10 Employees Report Increased Work Stress," news release (Menlo Park, CA: PRNewswire, February 2, 2017); Accountemps, "The Heat Is On: Seven in 10 Canadian Employees Report Increased Work Stress," news release (Toronto: Robert Half, February 2, 2017).

82. H. Selye, "A Syndrome Produced by Diverse Nocuous Agents," *Nature* 138, no. 1 (1936): 32; H. Selye, *Stress without Distress* (Philadelphia: J. B. Lippincott, 1974). For the history of the word *stress*, see R. M. K. Keil, "Coping and Stress: A Conceptual Analysis," *Journal of Advanced Nursing* 45, no. 6 (2004): 659–65.

83. S. E. Taylor, R. L. Repetti, and T. Seeman, "Health Psychology: What Is an Unhealthy Environment and How Does It Get under the Skin?," *Annual Review of Psychology* 48 (1997): 411–47.

84. A. Rosengren et al., "Association of Psychosocial Risk Factors with Risk of Acute Myocardial Infarction in 11119 Cases and 13648 Controls from 52 Countries (the Interheart Study): Case-Control Study," *The Lancet* 364, no. 9438 (2004): 953–62; D. C. Ganster and C. C. Rosen, "Work Stress and Employee Health: A Multidisciplinary Review," *Journal of Management* 39, no. 5 (2013): 1085–122; J. Goh, J. Pfeffer, and S. A. Zenios, "The Relationship between Workplace Stressors and Mortality and Health Costs in the United States," *Management Science* 62, no. 2 (2016): 608–28.

85. R. C. Kessler, "The Effects of Stressful Life Events on Depression," *Annual Review of Psychology* 48 (1997): 191–214; M. S. Hershcovis et al., "Predicting Workplace Aggression: A Meta-Analysis," *Journal of Applied Psychology* 92, no. 1 (2007): 228–38.

86. K. Danna and R. W. Griffin, "Health and Well-Being in the Workplace: A Review and Synthesis of the Literature," *Journal of Management* 25, no. 3 (1999): 357–84.

87. C. C. Rosen et al., "Occupational Stressors and Job Performance: An Updated Review and Recommendations," in *New Developments in Theoretical and Conceptual Approaches to Job Stress*, ed. P. L. Perrewé and D. C. Ganster, Research in Occupational Stress and Well-Being, ed. P. Perrewé, J. Halbesleben, and C. Rose, vol. 8 (Bingley, UK: Emerald Group Publishing Limited, 2010), 1–60; A. E. Nixon et al., "Can Work Make You Sick? A Meta-Analysis of the Relationships between Job Stressors and Physical Symptoms," *Work & Stress* 25, no. 1 (2011): 1–22.

88. A. E. Nixon et al., "Can Work Make You Sick? A Meta-Analysis of the Relationships between Job Stressors and Physical Symptoms," *Work & Stress* 25, no. 1 (2011): 1–22; S. Pindek and P. E. Spector, "Organizational Constraints: A Meta-Analysis of a Major Stressor," *Work & Stress* 30, no. 1 (2016): 7–25.

89. C. M. Pearson and C. L. Porath, "On the Nature, Consequences and Remedies of Workplace Incivility: No Time for 'Nice'? Think Again," *Academy of Management Executive* 19, no. 1 (2005): 7–18; D. C. Yamada, "Workplace Bullying and American Employment Law: A Ten-Year Progress Report and Assessment," *Comparative Labor Law and Policy Journal* 32, no. 1 (2010): 251–84.

90. P. McDonald, "Workplace Sexual Harassment 30 Years On: A Review of the Literature," *International Journal of Management Reviews* 14, no. 1 (2012): 1–17.

91. N. A. Bowling et al., "A Meta-Analytic Examination of the Potential Correlates and Consequences of Workload," *Work & Stress* 29, no. 2 (2015): 95–113.

92. R. Drago, D. Black, and M. Wooden, *The Persistence of Long Work Hours*, Melbourne Institute Working Paper Series, Melbourne Institute of Applied Economic and Social Research, University of Melbourne, August 2005; L. Golden, "A Brief History of Long Work Time and the Contemporary Sources of Overwork," *Journal of Business Ethics* 84, no. S2 (2009): 217–27; M. Tarafdar, E. B. Pullins, and T. S. Ragu-Nathan, "Technostress: Negative Effect on Performance and Possible Mitigations," *Information Systems Journal* 25, no. 2 (2015): 103–32; E. Reid, "Embracing, Passing, Revealing, and the Ideal Worker Image: How People Navigate Expected and Experienced Professional Identities," *Organization Science* 26, no. 4 (2015): 997–1017; Project: Time Off, *The Work Martyr's Cautionary Tale: How the Millennial Experience Will Define America's Vacation Culture* (Washington, DC: Project: Time Off, August 17, 2016).

93. R. Karasek and T. Theorell, *Healthy Work: Stress, Productivity, and the Reconstruction of Working Life* (New York: Basic Books, 1990); N. Turner, N. Chmiel, and M. Walls, "Railing for Safety: Job Demands, Job Control, and Safety Citizenship Role Definition," *Journal of Occupational Health Psychology* 10, no. 4 (2005): 504–12.

94. R. S. Lazarus, *Stress and Emotion: A New Synthesis* (New York: Springer Publishing, 2006), chap. 5.

95. M. Zuckerman and M. Gagne, "The COPE Revised: Proposing a 5-Factor Model of Coping Strategies," *Journal of Research in Personality* 37 (2003): 169–204; S. Folkman and J. T. Moskowitz, "Coping: Pitfalls and Promise," *Annual Review of Psychology* 55 (2004): 745–74; C. A. Thompson et al., "On the Importance of Coping: A Model and New Directions for Research on Work and Family," *Research in Occupational Stress and Well-Being* 6 (2007): 73–113.

96. S. E. Taylor et al., "Psychological Resources, Positive Illusions, and Health," *American Psychologist* 55, no. 1 (2000): 99–109; F. Luthans and C. M. Youssef, "Emerging Positive Organizational Behavior," *Journal of Management* 33, no. 3 (2007): 321–49; P. Steel, J. Schmidt, and J. Shultz, "Refining the Relationship between Personality and Subjective Well-Being," *Psychological Bulletin* 134, no. 1 (2008): 138–61; G. Alarcon, K. J. Eschleman, and N. A. Bowling, "Relationships between Personality Variables and Burnout: A Meta-Analysis," *Work & Stress* 23, no. 3 (2009): 244–63; R. Kotov et al., "Linking 'Big' Personality Traits to Anxiety, Depressive, and Substance Use Disorders: A Meta-Analysis," *Psychological Bulletin* 136, no. 5 (2010): 768–821.

97. G. A. Bonanno, "Loss, Trauma, and Human Resilience: Have We Underestimated the Human Capacity to Thrive after Extremely Aversive Events?," *American Psychologist* 59, no. 1 (2004): 20–28; F. Luthans, C. M. Youssef, and B. J. Avolio, *Psychological Capital: Developing the Human Competitive Edge* (New York: Oxford University Press, 2007).

98. M. A. Clark et al., "All Work and No Play? A Meta-Analytic Examination of the Correlates and Outcomes of Workaholism," *Journal of Management* 42, no. 7 (2016): 1836–73; C. S. Andreassen et al., "The Relationships between Workaholism and Symptoms of Psychiatric Disorders: A Large-Scale Cross-Sectional Study," *PLoS ONE* 11, no. 5 (2016): e0152978.

99. This list is based on various reviews, but stress management interventions have been organized in several ways. See, for example, J. H. Ruotsalainen et al., "Preventing Occupational Stress in Healthcare Workers," *Cochrane Database of Systematic Reviews*, no. 4 (2015); L. E. Tetrick and C. J. Winslow, "Workplace Stress Management Interventions and Health Promotion," *Annual Review of Organizational Psychology and Organizational Behavior* 2, no. 1 (2015): 583–603.

100. Towers Watson, *The Business Value of a Healthy Workforce: United States, 2013/2014 Staying@Work Survey Report* (New York: Towers Watson, January 2014).

101. B. H. Martin and R. MacDonnell, "Is Telework Effective for Organizations?," *Management Research Review* 35, no. 7 (2012): 602–16; G. B. Cooke, J. Chowhan, and T. Cooper, "Dialing It In: A Missed Opportunity Regarding the Strategic Use of Telework?," *Relations Industrielles* 69, no. 3 (2014): 550–74; T. D. Allen, T. D. Golden, and K. M. Shockley, "How Effective Is Telecommuting? Assessing the Status of Our Scientific Findings," *Psychological Science in the Public Interest* 16, no. 2 (2015): 40–68.

102. C. Fritz et al., "Happy, Healthy, and Productive: The Role of Detachment from Work during Nonwork Time," *Journal of Applied Psychology* 95, no. 5 (2010): 977–83.

103. L. Evans, "Why You Should Let Your Employees Nap at Work," *Entrepreneur*, August 24, 2014; K. Martinez-Carter, "Asleep on the Job: Grabbing Forty Winks at Work," *BBC News*, January 9, 2014; S. Castellanos, "Five Top Nap Rooms at Boston-Area Tech Companies," *Boston Business Journal*, June 23, 2015; L. Moran, "Home Sweet Home, Hubspot Renews Lease for Global Headquarters in Cambridge," news release (Cambridge, MA: HubSpot, December 18, 2015).

104. M. Tuckey et al., "Hindrances Are Not Threats: Advancing the Multidimensionality of Work Stress," *Journal of Occupational Health Psychology* 20, no. 2 (2015): 131–47.

105. M. H. Abel, "Humor, Stress, and Coping Strategies," *Humor: International Journal of Humor Research* 15, no. 4 (2002): 365–81; N. A. Kuiper et al., "Humor Is Not Always the Best Medicine: Specific Components of Sense of Humor and Psychological Well-Being," *Humor: International Journal of Humor Research* 17, no. 1/2 (2004): 135–68; E. J. Romero and K. W. Cruthirds, "The Use of Humor in the Workplace," *Academy of Management Perspectives* 20, no. 2 (2006): 58–69; M. McCreaddie and S. Wiggins, "The Purpose and Function of Humor in Health, Health Care and Nursing: A Narrative Review," *Journal of Advanced Nursing* 61, no. 6 (2008): 584–95.

106. O. Kettunen et al., "Greater Levels of Cardiorespiratory and Muscular Fitness Are Associated with Low Stress and High Mental Resources in Normal but Not Overweight Men," *BMC Public Health* 16, no. 1 (2016): 788; M. Gerber et al., "Fitness Moderates the Relationship between Stress and Cardiovascular Risk Factors," *Medicine & Science in Sports & Exercise* 48, no. 11 (2016): 2075–81.

107. H. O. Dickinson et al., "Relaxation Therapies for the Management of Primary Hypertension in Adults," *Cochrane Database of Systematic Reviews*, no. 1 (2008).

108. C. Viswesvaran, J. I. Sanchez, and J. Fisher, "The Role of Social Support in the Process of Work Stress: A Meta-Analysis," *Journal of Vocational Behavior* 54, no. 2 (1999): 314–34; S. E. Taylor et al., "Biobehavioral Responses to Stress in Females: Tend-and-Befriend, Not Fight-or-Flight,"*Psychological Review* 107, no. 3 (2000): 411–29; T. A. Beehr, N. A. Bowling, and M. M. Bennett, "Occupational Stress and Failures of Social Support: When Helping Hurts," *Journal of Occupational Health Psychology* 15, no. 1 (2010): 45–59; B. A. Scott et al., "A Daily Investigation of the Role of Manager Empathy on Employee Well-Being," *Organizational Behavior and Human Decision Processes* 113, no. 2 (2010): 127–40; S. Y. Shin and S. G. Lee, "Effects of Hospital Workers? Friendship Networks on Job Stress," *PLoS ONE* 11, no. 2 (2016): e0149428.

others, etc.) and resulting emotions energize you to act, and your self-concept, social norms, and past experience direct that energy toward goal-directed behavior.

Exhibit 5.1 provides a useful template for understanding how drives and emotions are the prime sources of employee motivation and how individual characteristics (self-concept, experience, values) influence goal-directed behavior. You will see pieces of this theory when we discuss four-drive theory, expectancy theory, equity theory, and other concepts in this chapter. The remainder of this section describes theories that try to explain the dynamics of drives and needs.

Four-Drive Theory

How drives, needs, and emotions influence motivation is most effectively explained in **four-drive theory**. This theory states that emotions are the source of human motivation and that these emotions are generated through four drives identified from earlier psychological, sociological, and anthropological research. These drives are[15]

- *Drive to acquire.* This is the drive to seek out, take, control, and retain objects and personal experiences. It produces the need for achievement, competence, status, and self-esteem.[16] The drive to acquire also motivates competition.

- *Drive to bond.* This drive produces the need for belonging and affiliation. It explains why our self-concept is partly defined by associations with social groups (see Chapter 3). The drive to bond motivates people to cooperate and, consequently, is essential for organizations and societies.

Four-drive theory states that emotions are the source of human motivation and that these emotions are generated through the drive to acquire, bond, comprehend, and defend.
©Don Hammond/DesignPics

- *Drive to comprehend.* People are inherently curious and need to make sense of their environment and themselves.[17] They are motivated to discover answers to unknown as well as conflicting ideas.

- *Drive to defend.* This is the drive to protect ourselves physically, psychologically, and socially. Probably the first drive to develop, it creates a fight-or-flight response when we are confronted with threats to our physical safety, our possessions, our self-concept, our values, and the well-being of others.

All drives are hardwired in our brains (innate) and exist in all human beings (universal). They are also independent of one another; there is no hierarchy of drives. Four-drive theory states that only the drive to defend is reactive—it is triggered by threat. The other three drives are proactive—they are regularly activated by our perceptions to seek fulfillment.

How Drives Influence Motivation and Behavior Recall from Chapter 3 that the stimuli received through our senses are quickly and nonconsciously tagged with emotional markers.[18] Four-drive theory proposes that the four drives determine which emotions are tagged to incoming stimuli. Most of the time, we aren't aware of our emotional experiences because they are subtle and fleeting. However, emotions do become conscious experiences when they are sufficiently strong or when they significantly conflict with one another.

We began this chapter's discussion about drives by explaining how our self-concept, social norms, and past experience direct the motivational force of our emotions to decisions and behavior. Four-drive theory specifically recognizes this process, except that self-concept is replaced with personal values (see Exhibit 5.2). In other words, the theory states that a person's "mental skill set" develops behavioral intentions that are acceptable to society, consistent with their own moral compass, and have a high probability of achieving the goal of fulfilling those felt needs.[19]

Practical Implications of Four-Drive Theory The main recommendation from four-drive theory is that jobs and workplaces should provide a balanced opportunity to fulfill the four drives.[20] There are really two recommendations here. The first is that the best workplaces help employees fulfill all four drives. Employees continually seek fulfillment of their innate drives, so successful companies provide sufficient rewards, learning opportunities, social interaction, and so forth for all employees.

The second recommendation is that fulfillment of the four drives must be kept in balance; that is, organizations should avoid too much or too little opportunity to fulfill each drive. The reason for this advice is that the four drives counterbalance each other. The drive to bond, which motivates mutual support and cohesion, counterbalances the drive to acquire, which motivates competitiveness. Therefore, an organization that fuels the drive to acquire without the drive to bond may eventually suffer from organizational politics and dysfunctional conflict. The drive to comprehend, which motivates investigation of the unknown, counterbalances the drive to defend, which motivates people to avoid the unknown. Change and novelty in the workplace will feed the drive to comprehend, but too much of it will trigger the drive to defend as employees become territorial and resistant to change.

Exhibit 5.2 Four-Drive Theory of Motivation

Drive to acquire

Social norms

Personal values

Past experience

Drive to bond

Mental skill set channels emotional forces created by drives

Goal-directed choice and effort

Drive to comprehend

Drive to defend

Source: Based on information in P. R. Lawrence and N. Nohria, *Driven: How Human Nature Shapes Our Choices* (San Francisco: Jossey-Bass, 2002).

Maslow's Needs Hierarchy Theory

Four-drive theory is one of the few theories to incorporate recent neuroscience discoveries about the role of drives and emotions in human motivation. Mention needs and drives to most people, however, and they will probably refer to **Maslow's needs hierarchy theory**, which was developed by psychologist Abraham Maslow in the 1940s. Maslow condensed and organized the dozens of previously studied drives (which he called primary needs) into five basic categories, organized in a hierarchy from lowest to highest (see Exhibit 5.3): *physiological* (need for food, air, water, shelter, etc.), *safety* (need for security and stability), *belongingness/love* (need for interaction with and affection from others), *esteem* (need for self-esteem and social esteem/status), and *self-actualization* (need for self-fulfillment, realization of one's potential). Along with these five categories, Maslow identified the need to know and the need for aesthetic beauty as two innate drives that do not fit within the hierarchy.[21]

Maslow proposed that human beings are motivated by several of these primary needs (drives) at the same time, but the strongest source of motivation is the lowest unsatisfied need. As the person satisfies a lower-level need, the next higher need in the hierarchy becomes the strongest motivator and remains so even if never satisfied. The exception to this need fulfillment process is self-actualization. People have an ongoing need for self-actualization; it is never really fulfilled. Thus, while the bottom four groups are *deficiency needs* because they become activated when unfulfilled, self-actualization is known as a *growth need* because it continues to develop even when temporarily satiated.

In spite of its popularity, Maslow's needs hierarchy theory has been dismissed by most motivation experts.[22] Maslow assumed that everyone has the needs hierarchy that he depicted, whereas evidence suggests that each of us has a unique needs hierarchy. Some people place social status at the top of their personal hierarchy; others view personal development and growth above social relations or status. The reason why needs hierarchies differ from one person to the next is that employee needs are strongly influenced by self-concept, personal values, and personality.[23] People have different hierarchies of values (see Chapter 2), so they also have parallel differences in their needs hierarchies. If your most important values lean toward stimulation and self-direction, you probably pay more attention to self-actualization needs.[24]

Maslow's theory has become a historical footnote on employee motivation, but Maslow transformed how we think about human motivation.[25] First, Maslow emphasized that needs should be studied together (holistically) because human behavior is typically initiated by more than

Exhibit 5.3 Maslow's Needs Hierarchy

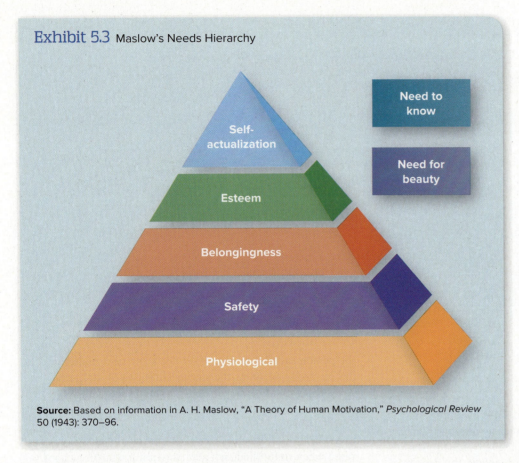

Source: Based on information in A. H. Maslow, "A Theory of Human Motivation," *Psychological Review* 50 (1943): 370–96.

one need at the same time. Previously, motivation experts had studied separately each of the dozens of needs and their underlying drives.[26] Second, Maslow recognized that motivation can be shaped by human thoughts (including self-concept, social norms, past experience), whereas earlier motivation experts focused mainly on how instincts motivated behavior.[27] Third, Maslow popularized the concept of *self-actualization*, suggesting that people are naturally motivated to reach their potential.[28] This positive view of motivation contrasted with previous motivation theories, which focused on need deficiencies such as hunger. By emphasizing motivation through growth and personal development rather than deficiencies, Maslow is considered a pioneer in *positive organizational behavior* (see Chapter 3).

Intrinsic and Extrinsic Motivation

By extolling the importance of self-actualization, Maslow launched an entirely new way of thinking about human motivation. People experience self-actualization by applying their skills and knowledge, observing how their talents achieve meaningful results, and experiencing personal growth through learning. These are the conditions for *intrinsic motivation*,

> **Intrinsic motivation occurs when people seek need fulfillment from doing the activity itself, not as a means to some other outcome.**

which refers to motivation controlled by the individual and experienced from the activity itself.[29] Intrinsic motivation occurs when people seek need fulfillment from doing the activity itself, not as a means to some other outcome. They enjoy applying their talents toward a meaningful task and experiencing progress or success in that task.

Behavior is intrinsically motivated when it is anchored in the innate drives for competence and autonomy.[30] People feel competent when applying their skills and observing positive, meaningful outcomes from those talents. People feel autonomous when their motivation is self-initiated rather than controlled from an external source. Intrinsic motivation contrasts with *extrinsic motivation*, which occurs when people are motivated to receive something that is beyond their personal control for instrumental reasons. In other words, they direct their effort toward a reward controlled by others that indirectly fulfills a need.

Extrinsic sources of motivation exist throughout organizations, such as pay incentives, recognition awards, and frequent reminders from the boss about work deadlines. These are extrinsic motivators because the outcomes (bonus, award, happy boss) are controlled by others and are not need fulfillment in themselves. The recognition award is a means to satisfy status needs, for example. However, extrinsic motivation also occurs when employees create their own internal pressure to act in association with external factors. For instance, we often experience an extrinsic motivation to complete our part of a team project because we worry how team members will react if we complete the work poorly or behind schedule.

Does Extrinsic Motivation Undermine Intrinsic Motivation?
There are two contrasting hypotheses about how extrinsic and intrinsic motivation work together.[31] The additive view suggests that someone performing an intrinsically motivating job becomes even more motivated by also receiving an extrinsic source of motivation for that work. The extrinsic motivator energizes the employee more than the intrinsic motivator alone. The contrasting hypothesis is that introducing extrinsic sources of motivation will reduce intrinsic motivation. For example, employees who were energized

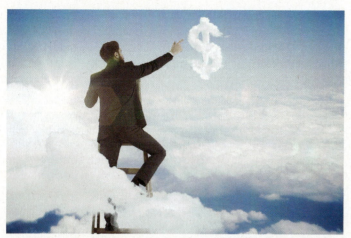

Pay incentives, recognition awards, and frequent reminders from the boss about work deadlines are extrinsic motivators because the outcomes are controlled by others and are not need fulfillment in themselves.
©Peshkova/Shutterstock

from the work itself will experience less of that intrinsic motivation when they receive extrinsic rewards such as a performance bonus. The explanation is that introducing extrinsic motivators diminishes the employee's feeling of autonomy, which is a key source of intrinsic motivation.

Which hypothesis is correct? So far, the research evidence is mixed.[32] Extrinsic motivators may reduce existing intrinsic motivation to some extent and under some conditions, but the effect is often minimal. Extrinsic rewards do not undermine intrinsic motivation when they are unexpected, such as a surprise bonus; when they have low value relative to the intrinsic motivator; and when they are not contingent on specific behavior (such as receiving a fixed salary). But when employees are engaged in intrinsically motivating work, employers should be careful about the potential unintended effect of undermining that motivation with performance bonuses and other sources of extrinsic motivation.[33]

Learned Needs Theory

Earlier in this chapter, we explained that needs are shaped, amplified, or suppressed through self-concept, social norms, and past experience. Maslow observed that individual differences influence need strength. Psychologist David McClelland further investigated the idea that need strength can be altered through social influences. McClelland examined three "learned" needs: achievement, affiliation, and power.[34]

- *Need for Achievement.* People with a high **need for achievement (nAch)** choose moderately challenging tasks, desire unambiguous feedback and recognition for their success, and prefer working alone rather than in teams. Except as a source of feedback, money is a weak motivator for people with high nAch, whereas it can be a strong motivator for those with low nAch.[35] Successful entrepreneurs tend to have high nAch, possibly because they establish challenging goals for themselves and thrive on competition.[36]

- *Need for Affiliation.* People with a high **need for affiliation (nAff)** seek approval from others, want to conform to others' wishes and expectations, and avoid conflict and confrontation. High-nAff employees generally work well in jobs where the main task is cultivating long-term relations. However, they tend to be less effective at allocating scarce resources and making other decisions that potentially generate conflict. Leaders and others in decision-making positions require a relatively low need for affiliation so their choices and actions are not biased by a personal need for approval.[37]

- *Need for Power.* People with a high **need for power (nPow)** want to exercise control over others, are highly involved in team decisions, rely on persuasion, and are concerned about maintaining their leadership position. Individuals who enjoy their power for its own sake, use it to advance personal interests, and wear their power as a status symbol have *personalized power*. Others mainly have a high need for *socialized power* because they desire power as a means to help others.[38] McClelland argues that effective leaders should have a high need for socialized rather than personalized power. They must have a high degree of altruism and social responsibility and be concerned about the consequences of their own actions on others.

McClelland developed training programs to test the idea that needs can be learned (amplified or suppressed) through reinforcement, learning, and social conditions. For example, one program increased achievement motivation by having participants write achievement-oriented stories, practice achievement-oriented behaviors in business games, and meet frequently with a reference group with other trainees to maintain their newfound achievement motivation.[39] Essentially, McClelland's program changed how people

need for achievement (nAch) a learned need in which people want to accomplish reasonably challenging goals and desire unambiguous feedback and recognition for their success

need for affiliation (nAff) a learned need in which people seek approval from others, conform to their wishes and expectations, and avoid conflict and confrontation

need for power (nPow) a learned need in which people want to control their environment, including people and material resources, to benefit either themselves (personalized power) or others (socialized power) viewed themselves (their self-concept), which amplified their need for achievement, affiliation, or power.

LO5-3 Discuss the expectancy theory model, including its practical implications.

EXPECTANCY THEORY OF MOTIVATION

The theories described so far mainly explain what motivates us—the prime movers of employee motivation—but they don't tell us what we are motivated to do. Four-drive theory recognizes that social norms, personal values, and past experience direct our effort, but it doesn't offer any detail about what goals we choose or where our effort is directed under various circumstances.

Expectancy theory offers more detail by predicting the goal-directed behavior where employees are most likely to direct their effort. Essentially, the theory states that work effort is aimed toward behaviors that people believe will produce the most favorable outcomes. It assumes that people are rational decision makers who choose where to direct their effort based on the probability of outcomes occurring and the positive or negative valences (expected satisfaction) of those outcomes (see Chapter 6).[40] This calculation, illustrated in Exhibit 5.4, states that an individual's effort level depends on three factors: effort-to-performance (E-to-P) expectancy, performance-to-outcome (P-to-O) expectancy, and outcome valences. Employee motivation is influenced by all three components of the expectancy theory model. If any component weakens, motivation weakens.

- *E-to-P expectancy.* This is the individual's perception that his or her effort will result in a particular level of performance. In some situations, employees may believe that they can unquestionably accomplish the task (a probability of 1.0). In other situations, they expect that even their highest level of effort will not result in the desired performance level (a probability of 0.0). In most cases, the E-to-P expectancy falls somewhere between these two extremes.

- *P-to-O expectancy.* This is the perceived probability that a specific behavior or performance level will lead to a particular outcome. In extreme cases, employees may believe that accomplishing a particular task (performance) will definitely result in a particular outcome (a probability of 1.0), or they may believe that successful performance will have no effect on this outcome (a probability of 0.0). More often, the P-to-O expectancy falls somewhere between these two extremes.

- *Outcome valences.* A *valence* is the anticipated satisfaction or dissatisfaction that an individual feels toward an outcome.[41] It ranges from negative to positive. (The actual range doesn't matter; it may be from −1 to +1 or from −100 to +100.) Outcomes have a positive valence when they are consistent with our values and satisfy our needs; they have a negative valence when they oppose our values and inhibit need fulfillment.

Applying Expectancy Theory

One of the appealing characteristics of expectancy theory is that it provides clear guidelines for increasing employee motivation, at least extrinsic motivation.[42] Several practical applications of expectancy theory are described below.

Increasing E-to-P Expectancies

E-to-P expectancies are influenced by the individual's belief that he or she can successfully complete the task. Some companies increase this can-do attitude by assuring employees that they have the necessary skills and knowledge, clear role perceptions, and necessary resources to reach the desired levels of performance. An important part of this process involves matching employee abilities to job requirements and clearly communicating the tasks required for the job. Similarly, E-to-P expectancies are learned, so behavior modeling and supportive feedback typically strengthen the individual's belief that he or she is able to perform the task.

Increasing P-to-O Expectancies

The most obvious ways to improve P-to-O expectancies are to measure

Exhibit 5.4 Expectancy Theory of Motivation

E-to-P expectancy	P-to-O expectancy	Valence
Probability that a specific effort level will result in a specific performance level	Probability that a specific performance level will result in specific outcomes	Anticipated satisfaction from the outcome

Effort → Performance → Outcome 1 +/−, Outcome 2 +/−, Outcome 3 +/−

Performance-to-Outcome Expectancy: The Missing Link[43]

56% of 8,254 employees surveyed in the United States, Canada, and five European countries say that they have a good understanding of how people are compensated at all levels of their company (36% say they don't have a good understanding).

44% of 31,000 employees surveyed in 29 countries say they see a clear link between performance and pay in their organization.

37% of American employees surveyed see NO link at all between their performance and their pay.

34% of U.S. federal government employees surveyed say that differences in performance are recognized in a meaningful way in their work unit.

44% of more than 4,000 employees in the United States and Canada say their manager differentiates between high and low performers.

©alxpin/Getty Images

employee performance accurately and distribute more valued rewards to those with higher job performance. P-to-O expectancies are perceptions, so employees also need to believe that higher performance will result in higher rewards. Furthermore, they need to know how that connection occurs, so leaders should use examples, anecdotes, and public ceremonies to illustrate when behavior has been rewarded.

Increasing Outcome Valences One size does not fit all when motivating and rewarding people. The valence of a reward varies from one person to the next because they have different needs. One solution is to individualize rewards by allowing employees to choose the rewards of greatest value to them. When this isn't possible, companies should ensure that everyone values the reward (i.e., positive valence). Finally, we need to watch out for countervalent outcomes. For example, if a company offers individual performance bonuses, it should beware of team norms that discourage employees from working above a minimum standard. These norms and associated peer pressure are countervalent outcomes to the bonus.

Overall, expectancy theory is a useful model that explains how people rationally figure out the best direction, intensity, and persistence of effort. It has been tested in a variety of situations and predicts employee motivation in different cultures.[44] One limitation with expectancy theory, however, is that it mainly explains extrinsic motivation; the model's features do not fit easily with intrinsic motivation. Another concern is that the theory ignores emotions as a source of motivation. The valence element of expectancy theory captures some of this emotional process, but only peripherally.[45] A third issue is that expectancy theory outlines how expectancies (probability of outcomes) affect motivation, but it doesn't explain how employees develop these expectancies.

Two theories that provide this explanation are organizational behavior modification and social cognitive theory, which we describe next.

OB THEORY TO PRACTICE

Putting Expectancy Theory into Practice

Increasing E → P expectancies

▶ Select people with the required skills and knowledge.

▶ Provide required training and clarify job requirements.

▶ Provide sufficient time and resources.

▶ Assign simpler or fewer tasks until employees can master them.

▶ Provide examples of similar employees who have successfully performed the task.

▶ Provide coaching to employees who lack self-confidence.

Increasing P → O expectancies

▶ Measure job performance accurately.

▶ Clearly explain the outcomes that will result from successful performance.

▶ Describe how the employee's rewards were based on past performance.

▶ Provide examples of other employees whose good performance has resulted in higher rewards.

Increasing outcome valences

▶ Distribute rewards that employees value.

▶ Individualize rewards.

▶ Minimize the presence of countervalent outcomes.

ORGANIZATIONAL BEHAVIOR MODIFICATION AND SOCIAL COGNITIVE THEORY

Expectancy theory states that motivation is determined by employee beliefs about expected performance and outcomes. But how do employees learn these expectancy beliefs? For example, how do they form the impression that a particular work activity is more likely to produce a promotion whereas other activities have little effect on promotions? Two theories—organizational behavior modification (OB Mod) and social cognitive theory—answer this question by explaining how people *learn* what to expect from their actions. As such, OB Mod and social cognitive theory supplement expectancy theory by explaining how people learn the expectancies that affect motivation.

Organizational Behavior Modification

For most of the first half of the 1900s, the dominant paradigm about managing individual behavior was *behaviorism*, which argues that a good theory should rely exclusively on behavior and the environment and ignore nonobservable cognitions and emotions.[46] Although behaviorists don't deny the existence of human thoughts and attitudes, they are unobservable and, therefore, irrelevant to scientific study. A variation of this paradigm, called **organizational behavior modification (OB Mod)**, eventually entered organizational studies of motivation and learning.[47]

A-B-Cs of OB Mod The core elements of OB Mod are depicted in the A-B-C model shown in Exhibit 5.5. Essentially, OB Mod attempts to change behavior (B) by managing its antecedents (A) and consequences (C).[48] *Consequences* are events following a particular behavior that influence its future occurrence. Consequences include receiving words of thanks from coworkers after assisting them, receiving preferred work schedules after being with the company longer than the average employee, and finding useful information on your smartphone after checking for new messages. Consequences also include no outcome at all, such as when no one says anything to you about how well you have been serving customers.

Antecedents are events preceding the behavior, informing employees that a particular action will produce specific consequences. An antecedent could be a sound from your smartphone signaling that a text message has arrived. Or it could be your supervisor's request to complete a specific task by tomorrow. Notice that antecedents do not cause behavior. The sound from your smartphone doesn't cause you to open the text message. Rather, the sound (antecedent) is a cue signaling that if you look at your phone messages (behavior), you will find a new message with potentially useful information (consequence).

Contingencies and Schedules of Reinforcement OB Mod identifies four types of consequences, called the *contingencies of reinforcement*.[49] *Positive reinforcement* occurs when the introduction of a consequence increases or maintains the frequency or future probability of a specific behavior. Receiving praise from coworkers is an example of positive reinforcement because the praise usually maintains or increases your likelihood of helping them in future. *Punishment* occurs when a consequence decreases the frequency or future probability of a specific behavior occurring. Most of us would consider being demoted or criticized by our coworkers as forms of punishment. A third type of consequence is *extinction*. The extinction consequence occurs when the target behavior decreases because no consequence follows it. For instance, research suggests that performance tends

Exhibit 5.5 A-B-Cs of Organizational Behavior Modification

| **Antecedents**
What happens before the behavior | → | **Behavior**
What the person says or does | → | **Consequences**
What happens after the behavior |

Example

| Your phone makes a distinctive sound | → | You check your phone for a new message | → | You learn useful information from the new message on your phone |

Source: Adapted from T. K. Connellan, *How to Improve Human Performance* (New York: Harper & Row, 1978), 50; F. Luthans and R. Kreitner, *Organizational Behavior Modification and Beyond* (Glenview, IL: Scott, Foresman, 1985), 85–88.

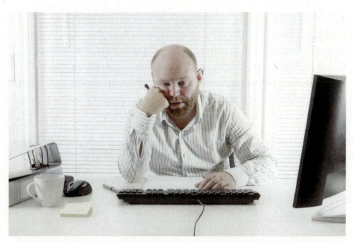

The extinction consequence occurs when the target behavior decreases because no consequence follows it.
©Kjetil Kolbjornsrud/Shutterstock

for learning new tasks is *continuous reinforcement*—providing positive reinforcement after every occurrence of the desired behavior. Aside from learning, the best schedule for motivating people is a *variable ratio schedule* in which employee behavior is reinforced after a variable number of times. Salespeople experience variable ratio reinforcement because they make a successful sale (the reinforcer) after a varying number of client calls. The variable ratio schedule makes behavior highly resistant to extinction because the reinforcer is never expected at a particular time or after a fixed number of accomplishments.

organizational behavior modification (OB Mod) a theory that explains employee behavior in terms of the antecedent conditions and consequences of that behavior

social cognitive theory a theory that explains how learning and motivation occur by observing and modeling others as well as by anticipating the consequences of our behavior

> ## Aside from learning, the best schedule for motivating people is a *variable ratio schedule* in which employee behavior is reinforced after a variable number of times.

to decline when managers stop congratulating employees for their good work.[50]

The fourth consequence in OB Mod, called *negative reinforcement*, is often confused with punishment. It's actually the opposite; negative reinforcement occurs when the removal or avoidance of a consequence increases or maintains the frequency or future probability of a specific behavior. It is usually the removal of punishment. For example, managers apply negative reinforcement when they *stop* criticizing employees whose substandard performance has improved.

Which of these four consequences works best? In most situations, positive reinforcement should follow desired behaviors and extinction (do nothing) should follow undesirable behaviors. Positive reinforcement is preferred because it leverages the power of *positive organizational behavior*; focusing on the positive rather than negative aspects of life will improve organizational success and individual well-being (see Chapter 3). In contrast, punishment and negative reinforcement generate negative emotions and attitudes toward the punisher (e.g., supervisor) and organization. However, punishment (dismissal, suspension, demotion, etc.) may be necessary for extreme behaviors, such as deliberately hurting a coworker or stealing inventory. Indeed, research suggests that, under some conditions, punishment maintains a sense of fairness among those who are affected by or aware of the employee's indiscretion.[51]

Along with the four consequences, OB Mod considers the frequency and timing of these reinforcers (called the *schedules of reinforcement*).[52] The most effective reinforcement schedule

Social Cognitive Theory

Organizational behavior modification states that behavior is learned only through personal interaction with the environment.[53] This view is no longer accepted; instead, experts recognize that people also learn and are motivated by observing others and inferring possible consequences of their actions. This contemporary view is explained by **social cognitive theory**, which states that much learning occurs by observing and modeling others as well as by anticipating the consequences of our behavior.[54] There are several pieces to social cognitive theory, but the three most relevant to employee motivation are learning behavior consequences, behavior modeling, and self-regulation.

Learning Behavior Consequences People learn the consequences of behavior by observing or hearing about what happened to other people, not just by directly experiencing the consequences.[55] Hearing that a coworker was fired for being rude to a client increases your belief that rude behavior will result in being fired. In the language of expectancy theory, learning behavior consequences changes a person's perceived P-to-O probability. Furthermore, people logically anticipate consequences in related situations. For instance, the story about the fired employee might also strengthen your P-to-O expectancy that being rude toward coworkers and suppliers (not just clients) will get you fired.

Behavior Modeling Along with observing others, people learn by imitating and practicing their behaviors.[56] Direct

self-reinforcement reinforcement that occurs when an employee has control over a reinforcer but doesn't "take" it until completing a self-set goal

goal setting the process of motivating employees and clarifying their role perceptions by establishing performance objectives

sensory experience helps us acquire tacit knowledge and skills, such as the subtle person–machine interaction while driving a vehicle. Behavior modeling also increases self-efficacy (see Chapter 3) because people gain more self-confidence after observing others and performing the task successfully themselves. Self-efficacy particularly improves when observers are similar to the model in age, experience, gender, and related features.

Self-Regulation An important feature of social cognitive theory is that human beings set goals and engage in other forms of intentional, purposive action. They establish their own short- and long-term objectives, choose their own standards of achievement, work out a plan of action, consider backup alternatives, and have the forethought to anticipate the consequences of their goal-directed behavior. Furthermore, people self-regulate by engaging in **self-reinforcement**; they reward and punish themselves for exceeding or falling short of their self-set goals.[57] For example, you might have a goal of completing the rest of this chapter, after which you reward yourself by having a snack. Raiding the refrigerator is a form of self-induced positive reinforcement for completing this reading assignment.

OB Mod and social cognitive theory explain how people learn probabilities of successful performance (E-to-P

Social cognitive theory states that people self-regulate through self-reinforcement; they reward and punish themselves for exceeding or falling short of their self-set goals.
©Tim Teebken/Photodisc/Getty Images

expectancies) as well as probabilities of various outcomes from that performance (P-to-O expectancies). As such, these theories explain motivation through their relationship with expectancy theory of motivation, described earlier. Elements of these theories also help us understand other motivation processes. For instance, self-regulation is the cornerstone of motivation through goal setting and feedback, which we discuss next.

LO5-5 Describe the characteristics of effective goal setting and feedback.

GOAL SETTING AND FEEDBACK

The City of Toronto's call center—311 Toronto—is a busy place. The center operates 24 hours per day, 7 days per week, and answers 1.5 million nonemergency calls in 180 languages each year. One of the center's objectives is to answer 80 percent of those calls within 75 seconds. It currently exceeds that goal (82 percent of calls are answered within 75 seconds) with an average talk time of 279 seconds. The 311 center also has a target of resolving 70 percent of calls at the first point of contact (i.e., not forwarding the caller elsewhere or calling back later), and exceeds this goal by addressing 73.7 percent of calls during the first contact.[58] Contact centers often have large digital displays that give employees visual feedback in the form of statistics associated with these key performance indicators.

The 311 Toronto operations and most other customer contact centers rely on goal setting to motivate employees and clarify their role perceptions. **Goal setting** potentially improves employee performance in two ways: (1) by amplifying the intensity and persistence of effort and (2) by giving employees clearer role perceptions so their effort is channeled toward behaviors that will improve work performance. Goal setting is more complex than simply telling someone to "do your best." It requires

Most customer contact centers rely on goal setting to motivate employees and clarify their role perceptions.
©MBI/Alamy Stock Photo

OB THEORY TO PRACTICE

The SMARTER Approach to Goal Setting

S *pecific.* Goals lead to better performance when they are specific. Specific goals state what needs to be accomplished; how it should be accomplished; and where, when, and with whom it should be accomplished. Specific goals clarify performance expectations, so employees can direct their effort more efficiently and reliably.

M *easurable.* Goals need to be measurable because motivation occurs when people have some indication of their progress and achievement of those goals. This measurement ideally includes how much (quantity), how well (quality), and at what cost the goal was achieved. Be aware, however, that some types of employee performance are difficult to measure, and they risk being neglected in companies preoccupied with quantifiable outcomes.[61]

A *chievable.* One of the trickiest aspects of goal setting is developing goals that are sufficiently but not overly challenging.[62] Easy goals result in performance that is well below the employee's potential. Yet, goals that are too challenging also may lead to reduced effort if employees believe there is a low probability of accomplishing them (i.e., low E-to-P expectancy). Recent studies also have found that very difficult goals increase the probability that employees will engage in unethical behavior to achieve them.[63]

R *elevant.* Goals need to be relevant to the individual's job and within his or her control. For example, a goal to reduce waste materials would have little value if employees don't have much control over waste in the production process.

T *ime-framed.* Goals need a due date. They should specify when the objective should be completed or when it will be assessed for comparison against a standard.

E *xciting.* Goals tend to be more effective when employees are committed to them, not just compliant. Challenging goals tend to be more exciting for most (but not all) employees because they are more likely to fulfill a person's growth needs when the goal is achieved. Goal commitment also increases when employees are involved in goal setting.[64]

R *eviewed.* The motivational value of goal setting depends on employees receiving feedback about reaching those goals.[65] Effective feedback requires measurement, which we discussed earlier in this list, but it also includes reflecting or discussing with others your goal progress and accomplishment. Reviewing goal progress and achievement helps employees redirect their effort. It is also a potential source of recognition that fulfills growth needs.

several specific characteristics.[59] One popular acronym—SMARTER—captures these characteristics fairly well:[60] Effective goals are specific, measurable, achievable, relevant to the employee's job, set within a time frame, exciting to create employee commitment, and reviewed both during and after the goal has been accomplished.

Characteristics of Effective Feedback

Feedback—information that lets us know whether we have achieved the goal or are properly directing our effort toward it—is a critical partner with goal setting. Feedback contributes to motivation and performance by clarifying role perceptions, improving employee skills and knowledge, and strengthening self-efficacy.[66] Effective feedback has many of the same characteristics as effective goal setting. It should be *specific* and *relevant*, that is, the information should refer to specific metrics (e.g., sales increased by 5 percent last month) and to the individual's behavior or outcomes within his or her control. Feedback also should be *timely*; the information should be available soon after the behavior or results occur so that employees see a clear association between their actions and the consequences. Feedback also should be *credible*. Employees are more likely to accept this information from trustworthy and believable sources.

One other important characteristic of effective feedback is that it should be *sufficiently frequent.* How frequent is "sufficiently"? The answer depends on at least two things. One consideration is the employee's knowledge and experience with the task. Employees working on new tasks should receive more frequent feedback because they require more behavior guidance and reinforcement. Employees who perform familiar tasks can receive less frequent feedback. The second factor is how long it takes to complete the task (i.e., its cycle time). Less frequent feedback usually occurs in jobs with a long cycle time (e.g., executives and scientists) because indicators of goal progress and accomplishment in these jobs are less frequent than in jobs with a short cycle time (e.g., grocery store cashiers).

Feedback through Strengths-Based Coaching Forty years ago, Peter Drucker observed that leaders are more effective when they focus on strengths rather than weaknesses. "The effective executive builds on strengths—their own strengths, the strengths of superiors, colleagues, subordinates; and on the strength of the situation," wrote the late management guru.[68] Maximizing employees' potential by focusing on their strengths rather than weaknesses is the essence of **strengths-based coaching** (also

connect

SELF-ASSESSMENT 5.3: What Is Your Goal Orientation?
Everyone sets goals for themselves, but people differ in the nature of those goals. Some view goals as challenges that assist learning. Others see goals as demonstrations of one's competence. Still others view goals as threatening one's image if they are not achieved. You can discover your dominant goal orientation by locating this self-assessment in Connect if it is assigned by your instructor.

Constructive, Timely Feedback at Adobe

Adobe Systems Incorporated realized that annual performance reviews didn't offer meaningful feedback, so the San Jose, California, software company replaced them with "Check-Ins." With agreed performance expectations, the manager and employee have timely, constructive, and sufficiently frequent check-in sessions. "We want people to be getting feedback on their performance against those expectations in real time (not just once a year)," says Donna Morris, Adobe's senior vice president of People & Places.

Check-ins are constructive future-focused discussions about the employee's personal development, but they sometimes include difficult conversations about poor performance. "Because you're in the moment and you're talking about things that are appropriate right then and there, [a check-in] gives you an opportunity to have a much more honest, more candid conversation," observes Eric Cox, Adobe's senior director of Global Strategy and Operations.[67]

many callers are waiting and the average time they have been waiting.

Some companies set up *multisource (360-degree) feedback*, which, as the name implies, is information about an employee's performance collected from a full circle of people, including subordinates, peers, supervisors, and customers. Multisource feedback tends to provide more complete and accurate information than feedback from a supervisor alone.[73] However, the process can be expensive and time-consuming, and the feedback tends to be ambiguous, conflicting, and inflated rather than accurate because coworkers try to minimize interpersonal conflict.

The preferred feedback source depends on the purpose of the information. Feedback from nonsocial sources, such as computer printouts or feedback directly from the job, is better when employees need to learn about goal progress and accomplishment. This is because information from nonsocial sources is considered more accurate than information from social sources. Negative feedback from nonsocial sources is also less damaging to self-esteem. In contrast, social sources tend to delay negative

> ## "Success is achieved by developing our strengths, not by eliminating our weaknesses."[72]
> — Marilyn vos Savant, author and magazine columnist

known as *appreciative coaching*).[69] In strengths-based coaching, employees describe areas of work where they excel or demonstrate potential. The coach guides this discussion by asking exploratory questions that help employees discover ways to build on these strengths. Situational barriers, as well as strategies to overcome those barriers, are identified to further support the employee's potential.

Strengths-based coaching is more motivating than traditional performance reviews because employees seek out feedback about their strengths, whereas they either become defensive about negative feedback or allow that information to weaken their self-efficacy.[70] Strengths-based coaching also recognizes that poor performance on some tasks is due more to motivation than ability. People can learn new skills throughout their working lives, but their weaker performance on some tasks is often due to lower motivation associated with their personality, interests, and preferences. These individual differences become quite stable fairly early in a person's career.[71]

Sources of Feedback

Feedback can originate from nonsocial or social sources. Nonsocial sources provide feedback without someone communicating that information. Corporate intranets allow many executives to receive feedback instantaneously on their computer, usually in the form of graphic output on an executive dashboard. Employees at contact centers view electronic displays showing how

information, leave some of it out, and distort the bad news in a positive way.[74] Employees should receive some positive feedback from social sources. It feels better to have coworkers say that you are performing the job well than to discover this from data on an impersonal computer screen.

Feedback from nonsocial sources is considered more accurate than information from social sources, which is better when employees need to learn about goal progress and accomplishment.
©Dan Bannister/Blend Images LLC

Evaluating Goal Setting and Feedback

Goal setting (in partnership with feedback) is generally a highly effective practice for employee motivation and performance.[75] Putting goal setting into practice can be challenging, however.[76] It tends to focus employees on a narrow subset of measurable performance indicators while ignoring aspects of job performance that are difficult to measure. There is also evidence that very difficult goals motivate some people to engage in unethical behavior to achieve those goals. Difficult goals are also stressful, which can undermine overall job performance.

Yet another problem is that goal setting tends to interfere with the learning process in new, complex jobs. Therefore, setting performance goals is effective in established jobs but should be avoided where an intense learning process is occurring. A final issue is that when goal achievement is tied to financial rewards, many employees are motivated to set easy goals (while making the boss think they are difficult) so that they have a higher probability of receiving the bonus or pay increase. As a former Ford Motor Company CEO once quipped: "At Ford, we hire very smart people. They quickly learn how to make relatively easy goals look difficult!"[77]

> **LO5-6** Summarize equity theory and describe ways to improve procedural justice.

ORGANIZATIONAL JUSTICE

Treating employees fairly is both morally correct and good for employee motivation, loyalty, and well-being. Yet feelings of injustice are regular occurrences in the workplace. To minimize these incidents, we need to first understand that there are two forms of organizational justice: distributive justice and procedural justice.[78] **Distributive justice** refers to perceived fairness in the outcomes we receive compared to our contributions and the outcomes and contributions of others. **Procedural justice** refers to fairness of the procedures used to decide the distribution of resources.

At its most basic level, the employment relationship is about employees exchanging their time, skills, and behavior for pay, fulfilling work, skill development opportunities, and so forth. What is considered "fair" in this exchange relationship varies with each person and situation.[79] An *equality principle* operates when we believe that everyone in the group should receive the same outcomes, such as when everyone gets subsidized meals in the company cafeteria. The *need principle* is applied when we believe that those with the greatest need should receive more outcomes than others with less need. This occurs, for instance, when employees get paid time off to recover from illness. The *equity principle* infers that people should be paid in proportion to their contribution. The equity principle is the most common distributive justice rule in organizational settings, so let's look at it in more detail.

Equity Theory

Feelings of equity are explained by **equity theory**, which says that employees determine feelings of equity by comparing their own outcome/input ratio to the outcome/input ratio of some

distributive justice perceived fairness in the individual's ratio of outcomes to contributions relative to a comparison of other's ratio of outcomes to contributions

procedural justice perceived fairness of the procedures used to decide the distribution of resources

equity theory a theory explaining how people develop perceptions of fairness in the distribution and exchange of resources

Not Paid What (They Believe) They're Worth[80]

53% of 31,000 employees surveyed globally say they are being paid fairly compared with others who fill similar positions in other companies.

44% of 7,700 executives and managers surveyed in several countries (5,136 in the United States) say that employees at their companies are paid fairly.

20% of 71,000 employees surveyed (most in the United States) say that they are paid fairly.

36% of 1,000 Australian advertising professionals surveyed say their bosses are NOT overpaid (26% say they ARE overpaid).

26% of 14,000 New Zealand public servants surveyed agree that their pay is fair compared to similar jobs in the wider labor market (53% disagree; 21% neither agree nor disagree).

©Don Farrall/Getty Images

other person.[81] As Exhibit 5.6 illustrates, the outcome/input ratio is the value of the outcomes you receive divided by the value of the inputs you provide in the exchange relationship. Inputs include such things as skill, effort, reputation, performance, experience, and hours worked. Outcomes are what employees receive from the organization such as pay, promotions, recognition, interesting jobs, and opportunities to improve one's skills and knowledge.

Equity theory states that we compare our outcome/input ratio with that of a comparison other.[82] The comparison other might be another person or group of people in other jobs (e.g., comparing your pay with your boss's pay) or another organization. Some research suggests that employees frequently collect information on several referents to form a "generalized" comparison other.[83] For the most part, however, the comparison other varies from one person to the next and is not easily identifiable.

The comparison of our own outcome/input ratio with the ratio of someone else results in perceptions of equity, underreward inequity, or overreward inequity. In the equity condition, people believe that their outcome/input ratio is similar to the ratio of the comparison other. In the underreward inequity situation, people believe their outcome/input ratio is lower than the comparison other's ratio. In the overreward inequity condition, people believe their ratio of outcomes/inputs is higher than the comparison other's ratio.

Inequity and Employee Motivation How do perceptions of equity or inequity affect employee motivation? The answer is illustrated in Exhibit 5.7. When people believe they are under- or overrewarded, they experience negative emotions (called *inequity tension*).[84] As we have pointed out throughout this chapter, emotions are the engines of motivation. In the case of inequity, people are motivated to reduce the emotional tension. Most people have a strong emotional response when they believe a situation is unfair, and this emotion nags at them until they take steps to correct the perceived inequity.

There are several ways to try to reduce the inequity tension.[85] Let's consider each of these in the context of underreward inequity. One action is to reduce our inputs so the outcome/input ratio is similar to that of the higher-paid coworker. Some employees do this by working more slowly, offering fewer suggestions, and engaging in less organizational citizenship behavior. A second action is to increase our outcomes. Some people who think they are underpaid ask for a pay raise. Others make unauthorized use of company resources. A third behavioral response is to increase the comparison other's inputs. We might subtly ask the better-paid coworker to do a larger share of the work, for instance. A fourth action is to reduce the comparison other's outcomes. This might occur by ensuring that the coworker gets less desirable jobs or working conditions. Another action, although uncommon, is to ask the company to reduce the coworker's pay so it is the same as yours.

A fifth action is perceptual rather than behavioral. It involves changing our beliefs about the situation. For example, we might believe that the coworker really is doing more (e.g., working longer hours) for that higher pay. Alternatively, we might change our perceptions of the value of some outcomes. We might initially believe it is unfair that a coworker gets more work-related travel than we do, but later we conclude that this travel is more inconvenient than desirable. A sixth action to reduce the inequity tension is to change the comparison other. Rather than

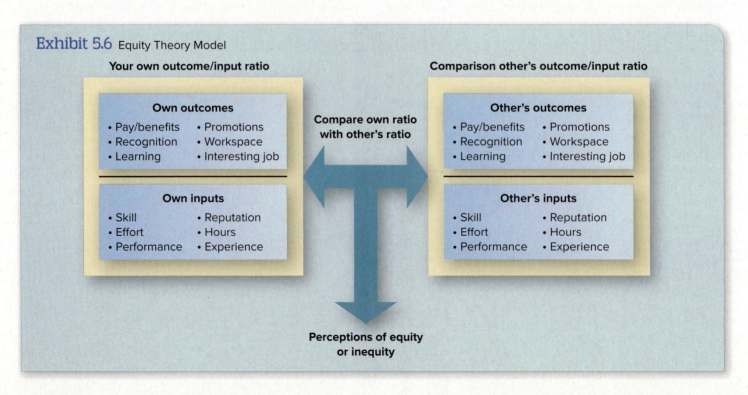

Exhibit 5.6 Equity Theory Model

Your own outcome/input ratio

Own outcomes
- Pay/benefits
- Recognition
- Learning
- Promotions
- Workspace
- Interesting job

Own inputs
- Skill
- Effort
- Performance
- Reputation
- Hours
- Experience

Compare own ratio with other's ratio

Comparison other's outcome/input ratio

Other's outcomes
- Pay/benefits
- Recognition
- Learning
- Promotions
- Workspace
- Interesting job

Other's inputs
- Skill
- Effort
- Performance
- Reputation
- Hours
- Experience

Perceptions of equity or inequity

Exhibit 5.7 Motivational Effects of Inequity Perceptions

Perceived inequity → Inequity tension (negative emotions) → Motivation to reduce tension →

Actions that reduce inequity tension
- Change our inputs
- Change our outcomes
- Change other's inputs
- Change other's outcomes
- Change our perceptions
- Change comparison other
- Leave the field

> **"I was underpaid for the first half of my life. I don't mind being overpaid for the second half."**[86]
> —Pierre Burton, journalist and popular history author

compare ourself with the higher-paid coworker, we might increasingly compare ourself with a friend or neighbor who works in a similar job. Finally, if the inequity tension is strong enough and can't be reduced through other actions, we might leave the field. This occurs by moving to another department, joining another company, or keeping away from the work site where the overpaid coworker is located.

People who feel overreward inequity would reverse these actions. Some overrewarded employees reduce their feelings of inequity by working harder; others encourage the underrewarded coworker to work at a more leisurely pace. A common reaction, however, is that the overrewarded employee changes his or her perceptions to justify the more favorable outcomes, such as believing the assigned work is more difficult or his or her skills are more valuable than the lower-paid coworker's skills.

Evaluating Equity Theory Equity theory is widely studied and quite successful at predicting various situations involving feelings of workplace injustice.[87] However, it isn't so easy to put into practice because the equity theory model doesn't identify the comparison other and doesn't indicate which inputs or outcomes are most valuable to each employee. The best solution here is for leaders to know their employees well enough to minimize the risk of inequity feelings. Open communication is also key, enabling employees to let decision makers know when they believe decisions are unfair. A second problem is that equity theory accounts for only some of our feelings of fairness or justice in the workplace. Experts now say that procedural justice is at least as important as distributive justice.

Procedural Justice

At the beginning of this section we defined two main forms of organizational justice: distributive and procedural. *Procedural justice* refers to fairness of the procedures used to decide the distribution of resources.[88] In other words, people evaluate fairness of the distribution of resources (distributive justice) as well as fairness of the conditions determining that distribution and its possible alteration (procedural justice).

There are several ways to improve procedural justice.[89] A good way to start is by giving employees "voice" in the process; encourage them to present their facts and perspectives on the issue. Voice also provides a "value-expressive" function; employees tend to feel better after having an opportunity to speak their mind. Procedural justice is also higher when the decision

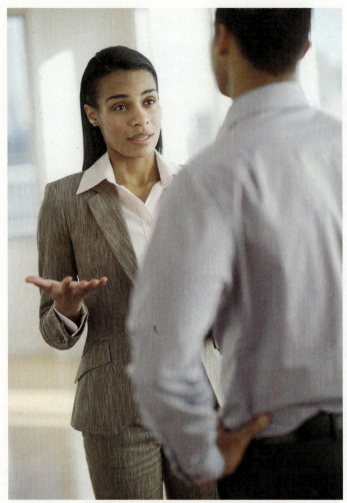

A key element of procedural justice is to give employees "voice" in the process so they can present their facts and perspectives on the issue.
©Tetra Images/Corbis

maker is perceived as unbiased, relies on complete and accurate information, applies existing policies consistently, and has listened to all sides of the dispute. If employees still feel unfairness in the allocation of resources, these feelings may dissipate if the company has an appeal process in which the decision is reviewed by a higher level of management.

Finally, people usually feel less injustice when they are given a full explanation of the decision and they are treated with respect throughout the complaint process. If employees believe a decision is unfair, refusing to explain how the decision was made could fuel their feelings of inequity. For instance, one study found that nonwhite nurses who experienced racism tended to file grievances only after experiencing disrespectful treatment in their attempt to resolve the racist situation. Another study reported that employees with repetitive strain injuries were more likely to file workers' compensation claims after experiencing disrespectful behavior from management. A third study noted that employees have stronger feelings of injustice

when the manager has a reputation of treating people unfairly most of the time.[90]

Consequences of Procedural Injustice Procedural justice has a strong influence on a person's emotions and motivation. Employees tend to experience anger toward the source of the injustice, which generates various response behaviors that scholars categorize as either withdrawal or aggression.[91] Notice how these actions are similar to the fight-or-flight responses described earlier in the chapter regarding situations that activate our drive to defend. Research suggests that being treated unfairly threatens our self-esteem and social status, particularly when others see that we have been unjustly treated. Employees retaliate to restore their self-esteem and reinstate their status and power in the relationship with the perpetrator of the injustice. Employees also engage in these counterproductive behaviors to educate the decision maker, thereby trying to minimize the likelihood of future injustices.[92]

> **LO5-7** List the advantages and disadvantages of job specialization and explain how to improve employee motivation through job design.

JOB DESIGN

How do you build a better job? That question has challenged organizational behavior experts, psychologists, engineers, and economists for a few centuries. Some jobs have very few tasks and usually require very little skill. Other jobs are immensely complex and require years of experience and learning to master them. From one extreme to the other, jobs have different effects on work efficiency and employee motivation. The ideal, at least from the organization's perspective, is to find the right combination so that work is performed efficiently but employees are engaged and satisfied.[93] This objective requires careful **job design**—the process of assigning tasks to a job, including the interdependency of those tasks with other jobs. A *job* is a set of tasks performed by one person. To understand this issue more fully, let's begin by describing early job design efforts aimed at increasing work efficiency through job specialization.

Job Design and Work Efficiency

By any measure, supermarket cashiers have highly repetitive work. One consulting firm estimated that cashiers should be able to scan each item in an average of 4.6 seconds. A British tabloid recently reported that cashiers at five supermarket chains in that country actually took between 1.75 and 3.25 seconds to scan each item from a standardized list of 20 products. Along with scanning, cashiers process the payment, move the divider stick, and (in some stores) bag the checked groceries.[94]

Supermarket cashiers perform jobs with a high degree of **job specialization**. Job specialization occurs when the work required to serve a customer—or provide any other product or

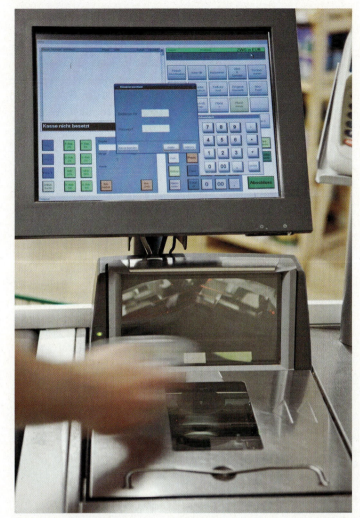

Supermarket cashier jobs have high job specialization; the cycle time is about 4 seconds to scan each grocery item before they repeat the activity with the next item.
©Antenna/Getty Images

changing over to a different type of activity. Even when people can change tasks quickly, their mental attention lingers on the previous type of work, which slows down performance on the new task.[95] A second reason for increased work efficiency is that employees can become proficient more quickly in specialized jobs. There are fewer physical and mental skills to learn and therefore less time required to train and develop people for high performance. Third, shorter work cycles give employees more frequent practice with the task, so jobs are mastered more quickly. Fourth, specialization tends to increase work efficiency by allowing employees with specific aptitudes or skills to be matched more precisely to the jobs for which they are best suited.[96]

The benefits of job specialization were noted more than 2,300 years ago by the Chinese philosopher Mencius and the Greek philosopher Plato. Scottish economist Adam Smith wrote 250 years ago about the advantages of job specialization. Smith described a small factory where 10 pin makers collectively produced as many as 48,000 pins per day because they performed specialized tasks. One person straightened the metal, another cut it, another sharpened one end of the cut piece, yet another added a white tip to the other end, and so forth. In contrast, Smith explained that if these 10 people worked alone producing complete pins, they would collectively manufacture no more than 200 pins per day.[97]

Scientific Management

One of the strongest advocates of job specialization was Frederick Winslow Taylor, an American industrial engineer who introduced the principles of **scientific management** in the early 1900s.[98] Scientific management consists of a toolkit of activities. Some of these interventions—employee selection, training, goal setting, and work incentives—are common today but were rare until Taylor popularized them. However, scientific management is mainly associated with high levels of job specialization and standardization of tasks to achieve maximum efficiency.

According to Taylor, the most effective companies have detailed procedures and work practices developed by engineers, enforced by supervisors, and executed by employees. Even the supervisor's tasks should be divided: One person manages operational efficiency, another manages inspection, and another is the disciplinarian. Taylor and other industrial engineers demonstrated that scientific management significantly improves work efficiency. No doubt, some of the increased productivity can be credited to training, goal setting, and work incentives, but job specialization quickly became popular in its own right.

service—is subdivided into separate jobs assigned to different people. For instance, supermarkets have separate jobs for checking out customers, stocking shelves, preparing fresh foods, and so forth. Except in the smallest family grocery stores, one person would not perform all of these tasks as part of one job. Each resulting job includes a narrow subset of tasks, usually completed in a short cycle time. *Cycle time* is the time required to complete the task before starting over with another item or client. Supermarket cashiers have a cycle time of about 4 seconds to scan each item before they repeat the activity with the next item. They also have a cycle time for serving each customer, which works out to somewhere between 20 and 40 times per hour in busy stores.

Why would companies divide work into such tiny bits? The simple answer is that job specialization potentially improves work efficiency. One reason for this higher efficiency is that employees have less variety of tasks to juggle (such as checking out customers versus stocking shelves), so there is less time lost

Problems with Job Specialization

Frederick Winslow Taylor and his contemporaries focused on how job specialization reduces labor "waste" by improving the mechanical efficiency of work (i.e., skills matching, faster learning, less switchover time). Yet they didn't seem to notice how this extreme job specialization adversely affects employee attitudes and motivation. Some jobs—such as scanning grocery items—can be so specialized that they soon become tedious, trivial, and socially isolating. Specialized jobs with very short cycle times often produce higher levels of employee turnover and absenteeism. Companies sometimes have to pay higher wages to attract job applicants to this dissatisfying, narrowly defined work.[99]

Job specialization affects output quality, but in two opposing ways. Job incumbents of specialized jobs potentially produce higher-quality results because, as we mentioned earlier, they master their work faster than do employees in jobs with many and varied tasks. This higher proficiency explains why specialist lawyers tend to provide better quality service than do generalist lawyers.[100] But many jobs (such as supermarket cashiers) are specialized to the point that they are highly repetitive and tedious. In these repetitive jobs, the positive effect of higher proficiency is easily offset by the negative effect of lower attentiveness and motivation caused by the tedious work patterns.

Job specialization also undermines work quality. By performing a small part of the overall work, employees have difficulty striving for better quality or even noticing flaws with that overall output. As one observer of an automobile assembly line reports: "Often [employees] did not know how their jobs related to the total picture. Not knowing, there was no incentive to strive for quality—what did quality even mean as it related to a bracket whose function you did not understand?"[101]

Job Design and Work Motivation

Frederick Winslow Taylor may have overlooked the motivational effect of job characteristics, but it is now the central focus of many job design initiatives. The motivational potential of the job itself is the focus of the **job characteristics model**, shown in Exhibit 5.8. The job characteristics model identifies five core job dimensions that produce three psychological states.

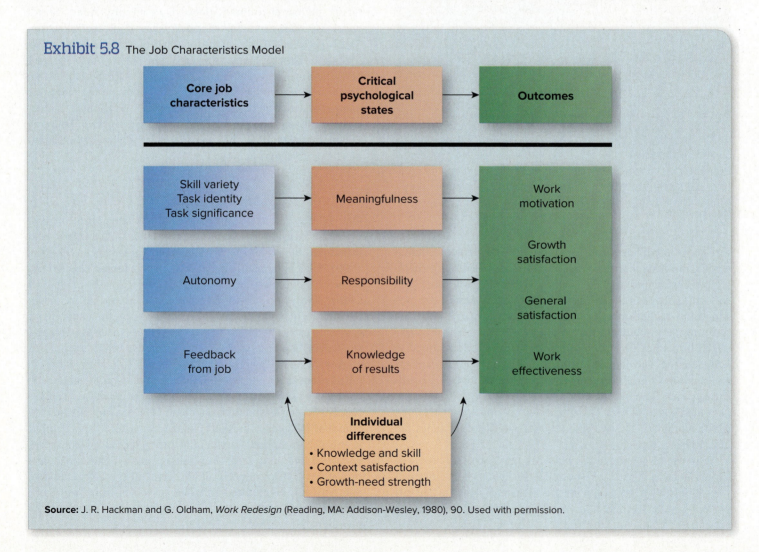

Exhibit 5.8 The Job Characteristics Model

Source: J. R. Hackman and G. Oldham, *Work Redesign* (Reading, MA: Addison-Wesley, 1980), 90. Used with permission.

Employees who experience these psychological states tend to have higher levels of internal work motivation (motivation from the work itself), job satisfaction (particularly satisfaction with the work itself), and work effectiveness.[102]

Core Job Characteristics The job characteristics model identifies five core job characteristics. Under the right conditions, employees are more motivated and satisfied when jobs have higher levels of these characteristics:

- *Skill variety.* **Skill variety** refers to the use of different skills and talents to complete a variety of work activities. For example, sales clerks who

normally only serve customers might be assigned the additional duties of stocking inventory and changing storefront displays.

- *Task identity.* **Task identity** is the degree to which a job requires completion of a whole or identifiable piece of work, such as assembling an entire broadband modem rather than just soldering in the circuitry.

- *Task significance.* **Task significance** is the degree to which the job affects the organization and/or larger society. It is an observable characteristic of the job (you can see how it benefits others) as well as a perceptual awareness. For example, some companies ask customers to speak to employees about the importance of the products or services to them.

- *Autonomy.* Jobs with high levels of autonomy provide freedom, independence, and discretion in scheduling the work and determining the procedures to be used to complete the work. In autonomous jobs, employees make their own decisions rather than rely on detailed instructions from supervisors or procedure manuals. Autonomy is considered the core motivational element of job design.[103] As we learned in Chapter 4, autonomy is also an important mechanism to reduce stress in some situations.

- *Job feedback.* Job feedback is the degree to which employees can tell how well they are doing from direct sensory information from the job itself. Airline pilots can tell how well they land their aircraft, and road crews can see how well they have prepared the roadbed and laid the asphalt.

Critical Psychological States The five core job characteristics affect employee motivation and satisfaction through three critical psychological states, shown in Exhibit 5.8. Skill variety, task identity, and task significance directly contribute to the job's *experienced meaningfulness*—the belief that one's work is worthwhile or important. Autonomy directly contributes to feelings of *experienced responsibility*—a sense of being personally accountable for the work outcomes. The third critical psychological state is *knowledge of results*—an awareness of the work outcomes based on information from the job itself.

Individual Differences Job design doesn't increase work motivation for everyone in every situation. Employees must have the required skills and knowledge to master the more challenging work. Otherwise, job design tends to increase stress and reduce job performance. The original model also states that employees will be motivated by the five core job characteristics only when they are satisfied with their work context (e.g., working conditions, job security) and have a high *growth need strength*. Growth need strength refers to an individual's need for personal growth and development, such as work that offers challenges, cognitive stimulation, learning, and independent thought and action.[105] However, research findings have been mixed, suggesting that employees might be motivated by job design no

OB THEORY TO PRACTICE

Increasing Task Significance through Higher Purpose

Accounting professionals serve a vital role in society, yet they don't perceive this task significance in many of their daily work activities because the benefits are long term and involve many coworkers.

To increase task significance awareness, KPMG showed its staff a video documenting the professional services firm's historic contributions to society. Employees also were invited to share stories about how their jobs as auditors have had a positive impact on others. KPMG was overwhelmed with 42,000 submissions, some of which were depicted in posters around the organization.

In less than one year, this "higher purpose" awareness initiative had substantially reduced employee turnover intentions, particularly when the employee's manager spent time discussing KPMG's impact on society. KPMG's ranking on the list of Best 100 Companies to Work For in America jumped 17 places the year after the task significance campaign was launched.[104]

What do you do at KPMG?

WE HELP NATIONS HEAL.

After the tragic events of 9/11, KPMG teams worked around the clock to monitor the cleanup, helping the city track $9 billion in expenses and laying the foundation for recovery.

KPMG. We're here for a purpose.

KPMG

Inspire confidence. Empower change.

Source: KPMG

task interdependence
the extent to which team members must share materials, information, or expertise in order to perform their jobs

job enlargement the practice of adding more tasks to an existing job

job enrichment the practice of giving employees more responsibility for scheduling, coordinating, and planning their own work

matter how they feel about their job context or how high or low they score on growth needs.[106]

Social and Information Processing Job Characteristics

The job characteristics model overlooks two clusters of job features: social characteristics and information processing demands.[107] One social characteristic is the extent to which the job requires employees to interact with other people (coworkers, clients, government representatives, etc.). This required social interaction is associated with emotional labor, discussed in Chapter 4, as well as with **task interdependence**, which is the extent to which employees need to share materials, information, or expertise with each other (see Chapter 7). A second social characteristic of the job is feedback from others. The job characteristics model identifies feedback from the job itself as a source of motivation. Feedback from clients, co-workers, and other social sources is also important, particularly for rapid learning and when the feedback is favorable.

The other cluster of job characteristics missing from the job characteristics model relates to the information processing demands of the job.[108] One information processing demand is how predictable the job duties are from one day to the next (called *task variability*). Employees in jobs with high task variability have nonroutine work patterns; they perform different types of tasks from one day to the next and don't know which tasks are required until that time. The second information processing demand, called *task analyzability*, refers to how much the job can be performed using known procedures and rules. Jobs with high task analyzability have a ready-made "cookbook" to guide people in those jobs through most decisions and actions, whereas jobs with low task analyzability require employee creativity and judgment to determine the best course of action. Task variability and task analyzability are important job characteristics to consider when designing organizational structures, so we discuss both of them in Chapter 12.

Job Design Practices That Motivate

Three main strategies can increase the motivational potential of jobs: job rotation, job enlargement, and job enrichment.

Job Rotation Many grocery stores reduce the tedium of checkout work by moving cashiers to other jobs during the work shift. This job rotation adds some skill variety into the workday, and many companies have found that it improves employee motivation and satisfaction to some extent. A second benefit of job rotation is that it minimizes health risks from repetitive strain and heavy lifting because employees use different muscles and physical positions in the various jobs. A third benefit is that job rotation supports multiskilling; employees learn several jobs, which makes it easier for the company to fill temporary vacancies.

Job Enlargement **Job enlargement** adds tasks to an existing job. This might involve combining two or more complete jobs into one or just adding one or two more tasks to an existing job. Either way, skill variety increases because there are more tasks to perform.

Job Enrichment **Job enrichment** occurs when employees are given more responsibility for scheduling, coordinating, and planning their own work.[109] For example, employees have more enriched jobs when they are responsible for a variety of tasks and have enough autonomy to plan their work and choose when to perform each task. Job enrichment potentially increases job satisfaction and work motivation, and reduces absenteeism and turnover. Productivity is also higher when task identity and job feedback are improved. Product and service quality tend to improve because job enrichment increases the jobholder's felt responsibility and sense of ownership over the product or service.[110]

One way to increase job enrichment is by combining highly interdependent tasks into one job. This *natural grouping* approach occurs in the video journalist job because it naturally groups tasks together to complete an entire product (i.e., a news story). By forming natural work units, jobholders have stronger feelings of responsibility for an identifiable body of work. They feel a sense of ownership and, therefore, tend to increase job quality. Forming natural work units increases task identity and task significance because employees perform a complete product or service and can more readily see how their work affects others.

A second job enrichment strategy, called *establishing client relationships*, involves putting employees in direct contact with their clients rather than using another job group or the supervisor as the liaison between the employee and the customer. Establishing client relationships increases task significance because employees see a line-of-sight connection between their work and consequences for customers. By being directly responsible for specific clients, employees also have more information and can make better decisions affecting those clients.[111]

> Forming natural work units increases task identity and task significance because employees perform a complete product or service and can more readily see how their work affects others.

Study Checklist

Connect® Management is available for *M Organizational Behavior.* Additional resources include:

✓ Interactive Applications:
- **Decision Generator**
- **Drag and Drop:** Work through an interactive example to test your knowledge of the concepts.
- **Video Case:** See management in action through interactive videos.

✓ **SmartBook™**—SmartBook is the first and only adaptive reading experience available today. Distinguishing what you know from what you don't, and honing in on concepts you are most likely to forget, SmartBook personalizes content for you in a continuously adapting reading experience. Reading is no longer a passive and linear experience, but an engaging and dynamic one where you are more likely to master and retain important concepts and go to class better prepared.

©Natthawat Jamnapa/123RF

Notes

1. I. Tiznado et al., "Incentive Schemes for Bus Drivers: The Case of the Public Transit System in Santiago, Chile," *Research in Transportation Economics* 48 (2014): 77-83; R. M. Johnson, D. H. Reiley, and J. C. Muñoz, "'The War for the Fare': How Driver Compensation Affects Bus System Performance," *Economic Inquiry* 53, no. 3 (2015): 1401-19.

2. C. C. Pinder, *Work Motivation in Organizational Behavior* (Upper Saddle River, NJ: Prentice Hall, 1998); R. M. Steers, R. T. Mowday, and D. L. Shapiro, "The Future of Work Motivation Theory," *Academy of Management Review* 29 (2004): 379-87.

3. W. H. Macey and B. Schneider, "The Meaning of Employee Engagement," *Industrial and Organizational Psychology* 1 (2008): 3-30; A. M. Saks and J. A. Gruman, "What Do We Really Know about Employee Engagement?," *Human Resource Development Quarterly* 25, no. 2 (2014): 155-82.

4. D. Macleod and N. Clarke, *Engaging for Success: Enhancing Performance through Employee Engagement* (London: UK Government, Department for Business Innovation and Skills, July 2009); P. M. Bal and A. H. De Lange, "From Flexibility Human Resource Management to Employee Engagement and Perceived Job Performance across the Lifespan: A Multisample Study," *Journal of Occupational and Organizational Psychology* 88 (2015): 126-54.

5. S. Crabtree, "Worldwide, 13% of Employees Are Engaged at Work," news release (Washington, DC: Gallup, Inc., October 8, 2013); A. Adkins, "Employee Engagement in U.S. Stagnant in 2015," news release (Washington, DC: Gallup, Inc., January 13, 2016); Aon Hewitt, *2017 Trends in Global Employee Engagement* (Chicago: Aon Hewitt, April 10, 2017).

6. Several sources attempt to identify and organize the drivers of employee engagement. See, for example, D. Robinson, S. Perryman, and S. Hayday, *The Drivers of Employee Engagement* (Brighton, UK: Institute for Employment Studies, 2004); W. H. Macey et al., *Employee Engagement: Tools for Analysis, Practice, and Competitive Advantage* (Malden, MA: Wiley-Blackwell, 2009); D. Macleod and N. Clarke, *Engaging for Success: Enhancing Performance through Employee Engagement* (London: UK Government, Department for Business Innovation and Skills, July 2009); M. Stairs and M. Galpin, "Positive Engagement: From Employee Engagement to Workplace Happiness," in *Oxford Handbook of Positive Psychology of Work,* ed. P. A. Linley, S. Harrington, and N. Garcea (New York: Oxford University Press, 2010), 155-72.

7. C. Shaw, "DHL Express Recognises Excelling Employees," *Times of Swaziland,* June 28, 2013; K. Allen, "The Art of Engagement" (Bonn, Germany: Deutsche Post DHL, August 12, 2013), http://www.dpdhl.com/en/logistics_around_us/from_our_divisions/ken_allen_the_art_of_engagement.html (accessed August 21, 2013); "Employee Engagement Crucial for Business Success," *How We Made It in Africa,* February 20, 2015; "Engaged Employees Are Better Performers," *The Citizen* (Gauteng, South Africa), February 24, 2015.

8. The confusing array of definitions about drives and needs has been the subject of criticism for a half century. See, for example, R. S. Peters, "Motives and Motivation," *Philosophy* 31 (1956): 117-30; H. Cantril, "Sentio, Ergo Sum: 'Motivation' Reconsidered," *Journal of Psychology* 65, no. 1 (1967): 91-107; G. R. Salancik and J. Pfeffer, "An Examination of Need-Satisfaction Models of Job Attitudes," *Administrative Science Quarterly* 22, no. 3 (1977): 427-56.

9. D. W. Pfaff, *Drive: Neurobiological and Molecular Mechanisms of Sexual Motivation* (Cambridge, MA: MIT Press, 1999); A. Blasi, "Emotions and Moral Motivation," *Journal for the Theory of Social Behaviour* 29, no. 1 (1999): 1-19; T. V. Sewards and M. A. Sewards, "Fear and Power-Dominance Drive Motivation: Neural Representations and Pathways Mediating Sensory and Mnemonic Inputs, and Outputs to Premotor Structures," *Neuroscience and Biobehavioral Reviews* 26 (2002): 553-79; K. C. Berridge, "Motivation Concepts in Behavioral Neuroscience," *Physiology & Behavior* 81, no. 2 (2004): 179-209. We distinguish drives from emotions, but future research may find that the two concepts are not so different as is stated here. Woodworth is credited with either coining or popularizing the term *drives* in the context of human motivation. His classic book is certainly the first source to discuss the concept in detail. See R. S. Woodworth, *Dynamic Psychology* (New York: Columbia University Press, 1918).

10. G. Loewenstein, "The Psychology of Curiosity: A Review and Reinterpretation," *Psychological Bulletin* 116, no. 1 (1994): 75-98; A. E. Kelley, "Neurochemical Networks Encoding Emotion and Motivation: An Evolutionary Perspective," in *Who Needs Emotions? The Brain Meets the Robot,* ed. J. M. Fellous and M. A. Arbib (New York: Oxford University Press, 2005), 29-78; M. R. Leary, "Motivational and Emotional Aspects of the Self," *Annual Review of Psychology* 58, no. 1 (2007): 317-44; L. A. Leotti, S. S. Iyengar, and K. N. Ochsner, "Born to Choose: The Origins and Value of the Need for Control," *Trends in Cognitive Sciences* 14, no. 10 (2010): 457-63.

11. K. Passyn and M. Sujan, "Self-Accountability Emotions and Fear Appeals: Motivating Behavior," *Journal of Consumer Research* 32, no. 4 (2006): 583–89; S. G. Barsade and D. E. Gibson, "Why Does Affect Matter in Organizations?," *Academy of Management Perspectives* 21, no. 2 (2007): 36–59.

12. V. Lombardi Jr., What *It Takes to Be #1: Vince Lombardi on Leadership* (New York: McGraw-Hill, 2001), 39.

13. A. R. Damasio, *The Feeling of What Happens: Body and Emotion in the Making of Consciousness* (New York: Harcourt Brace, 1999), 286.

14. S. Hitlin, "Values as the Core of Personal Identity: Drawing Links between Two Theories of Self," *Social Psychology Quarterly* 66, no. 2 (2003): 118–37; B. Monin, D. A. Pizarro, and J. S. Beer, "Deciding versus Reacting: Conceptions of Moral Judgment and the Reason-Affect Debate," *Review of General Psychology* 11, no. 2 (2007): 99–111; D. D. Knoch and E. E. Fehr, "Resisting the Power of Temptations. The Right Prefrontal Cortex and Self-Control," *Annals of the New York Academy of Sciences* 1104, no. 1 (2007): 123.

15. P. R. Lawrence and N. Nohria, *Driven: How Human Nature Shapes Our Choices* (San Francisco: Jossey-Bass, 2002); N. Nohria, B. Groysberg, and L. E. Lee, "Employee Motivation: A Powerful New Model," *Harvard Business Review* (2008): 78–84. On the application of four-drive theory to leadership, see P. R. Lawrence, *Driven to Lead* (San Francisco: Jossey-Bass, 2010).

16. The drive to acquire is likely associated with research on getting ahead, desire for competence, the selfish gene, and desire for social distinction. See R. H. Frank, *Choosing the Right Pond: Human Behavior and the Quest for Status* (New York: Oxford University Press, 1985); L. Gaertner et al., "The 'I,' the 'We,' and the 'When': A Meta-Analysis of Motivational Primacy in Self-Definition," *Journal of Personality and Social Psychology* 83, no. 3 (2002): 574–91; J. Hogan and B. Holland, "Using Theory to Evaluate Personality and Job-Performance Relations: A Socioanalytic Perspective," *Journal of Applied Psychology* 88, no. 1 (2003): 100–12; R. Dawkins, *The Selfish Gene,* 30th anniversary ed. (Oxford, UK: Oxford University Press, 2006); M. R. Leary, "Motivational and Emotional Aspects of the Self," *Annual Review of Psychology* 58, no. 1 (2007): 317–44; B. S. Frey, "Awards as Compensation," *European Management Journal* 4 (2007): 6–14.

17. J. Litman, "Curiosity and the Pleasures of Learning: Wanting and Liking New Information," *Cognition and Emotion* 19, no. 6 (2005): 793–814; T. G. Reio Jr. et al., "The Measurement and Conceptualization of Curiosity," *Journal of Genetic Psychology* 167, no. 2 (2006): 117–35.

18. A. R. Damasio, *Descartes' Error: Emotion, Reason, and the Human Brain* (New York: Putnam Sons, 1994); A. Bechara et al., "Deciding Advantageously before Knowing the Advantageous Strategy," Science 275, no. 5304 (1997): 1293–95; J. E. LeDoux, "Emotion Circuits in the Brain," *Annual Review of Neuroscience* 23 (2000): 155–84; P. Winkielman and K. C. Berridge, "Unconscious Emotion," *Current Directions in Psychological Science* 13, no. 3 (2004): 120–23; M. Reimann and A. Bechara, "The Somatic Marker Framework as a Neurological Theory of Decision-Making: Review, Conceptual Comparisons, and Future Neuroeconomics Research," *Journal of Economic Psychology* 31, no. 5 (2010): 767–76.

19. P. R. Lawrence and N. Nohria, *Driven: How Human Nature Shapes Our Choices* (San Francisco: Jossey-Bass, 2002), 145–47; R. F. Baumeister, E. J. Masicampo, and K. D. Vohs, "Do Conscious Thoughts Cause Behavior?," *Annual Review of Psychology* 62, no. 1 (2011): 331–61.

20. P. R. Lawrence and N. Nohria, *Driven: How Human Nature Shapes Our Choices* (San Francisco: Jossey-Bass, 2002), chap. 11.

21. A. H. Maslow, "A Theory of Human Motivation," *Psychological Review* 50 (1943): 370–96; A. H. Maslow, *Motivation and Personality* (New York: Harper & Row, 1954).

22. D. T. Hall and K. E. Nougaim, "An Examination of Maslow's Need Hierarchy in an Organizational Setting," *Organizational Behavior and Human Performance* 3, no. 1 (1968): 12; M. A. Wahba and L. G. Bridwell, "Maslow Reconsidered: A Review of Research on the Need Hierarchy Theory," *Organizational Behavior and Human Performance* 15 (1976): 212–40; E. L. Betz, "Two Tests of Maslow's Theory of Need Fulfillment," *Journal of Vocational Behavior* 24, no. 2 (1984): 204–20; P. A. Corning, "Biological Adaptation in Human Societies: A 'Basic Needs' Approach," *Journal of Bioeconomics* 2, no. 1 (2000): 41–86. For a recent proposed revision of the model, see D. T. Kenrick et al., "Renovating the Pyramid of Needs: Contemporary Extensions Built upon Ancient Foundations," *Perspectives on Psychological Science* 5, no. 3 (2010): 292–314.

23. L. Parks and R. P. Guay, "Personality, Values, and Motivation," *Personality and Individual Differences* 47, no. 7 (2009): 675–84.

24. B. A. Agle and C. B. Caldwell, "Understanding Research on Values in Business," *Business and Society* 38 (1999): 326–87; B. Verplanken and R. W. Holland, "Motivated Decision Making: Effects of Activation and Self-Centrality of Values on Choices and Behavior," *Journal of Personality and Social Psychology* 82, no. 3 (2002): 434–47; S. Hitlin and J. A. Pilavin, "Values: Reviving a Dormant Concept," *Annual Review of Sociology* 30 (2004): 359–93.

25. K. Dye, A. J. Mills, and T. G. Weatherbee, "Maslow: Man Interrupted—Reading Management Theory in Context," *Management Decision* 43, no. 10 (2005): 1375–95.

26. A. H. Maslow, "A Preface to Motivation Theory," *Psychosomatic Medicine* 5 (1943): 85–92.

27. S. Kesebir, J. Graham, and S. Oishi, "A Theory of Human Needs Should Be Human-Centered, Not Animal-Centered," *Perspectives on Psychological Science* 5, no. 3 (2010): 315–19.

28. A. H. Maslow, *Maslow on Management* (New York: Wiley, 1998).

29. M. Gagné and E. L. Deci, "Self-Determination Theory and Work Motivation," *Journal of Organizational Behavior* 26, no. 4 (2005): 331–62; C. P. Cerasoli, J. M. Nicklin, and M. T. Ford, "Intrinsic Motivation and Extrinsic Incentives Jointly Predict Performance: A 40-Year Meta-Analysis," *Psychological Bulletin* 140, no. 4 (2014): 980–1008.

30. M. Gagné and D. Bhave, "Autonomy in the Workplace: An Essential Ingredient to Employee Engagement and Well-Being in Every Culture," in *Human Autonomy in Cross-Cultural Context*, ed. V. I. Chirkov, R. M. Ryan, and K. M. Sheldon, Cross-Cultural Advancements in Positive Psychology (Dordrecht, Netherlands: Springer Netherlands, 2011), 163–87; E. L. Deci and M. R. Ryan, "The Importance of Universal Psychological Needs for Understanding Motivation in the Workplace," in *The Oxford Handbook of Work Engagement, Motivation, and Self-Determination Theory*, ed. M. Gagne (New York: Oxford University Press, 2014), 13–32.

31. A. Kohn, *Punished by Rewards* (Boston: Houghton Mifflin, 1993); C. C. Pinder, *Work Motivation in Organizational Behavior*, 2nd ed. (New York: Psychology Press, 2008), chap. 3.

32. C. P. Cerasoli, J. M. Nicklin, and M. T. Ford, "Intrinsic Motivation and Extrinsic Incentives Jointly Predict Performance: A 40-Year Meta-Analysis," *Psychological Bulletin* 140, no. 4 (2014): 980–1008; Y. Garbers and U. Konradt, "The Effect of Financial Incentives on Performance: A Quantitative Review of Individual and Team-Based Financial Incentives," *Journal of Occupational and Organizational Psychology* 87, no. 1 (2014): 102–37. Earlier meta-analyses are discussed in C. C. Pinder, *Work Motivation in Organizational Behavior* (Upper Saddle River, NJ: Prentice Hall, 1998), 86–91.

33. J. Schroeder and A. Fishbach, "How to Motivate Yourself and Others? Intended and Unintended Consequences," *Research in Organizational Behavior* 35 (2015): 123–41.

34. D. C. McClelland, *The Achieving Society* (New York: Van Nostrand Reinhold, 1961); D. C. McClelland and D. H. Burnham, "Power Is the Great Motivator," *Harvard Business Review* 73 (1995): 126–39; D. Vredenburgh and Y. Brender, "The Hierarchical Abuse of Power in Work Organizations," *Journal of Business Ethics* 17 (1998): 1337–47; S. Shane, E. A. Locke, and C. J. Collins, "Entrepreneurial Motivation," *Human Resource Management Review* 13, no. 2 (2003): 257–79.

35. D. C. McClelland, *The Achieving Society* (New York: Van Nostrand Reinhold, 1961).

36. M. Frese and M. M. Gielnik, "The Psychology of Entrepreneurship," *Annual Review of Organizational Psychology and Organizational Behavior* 1, no. 1 (2014): 413–38.

37. W. H. Decker, T. J. Calo, and C. H. Weer, "Affiliation Motivation and Interest in Entrepreneurial Careers," *Journal of Managerial Psychology* 27, no. 3 (2012): 302–20; G. A. Yukl, *Leadership in Organizations*, 8th ed. (Upper Saddle River, NJ: Pearson Education, 2013), chap. 6; S. Leroy et al., "Synchrony Preference: Why Some People Go with the Flow and Some Don't," *Personnel Psychology* 68, no. 4 (2015): 759–809.

38. J. C. Magee and C. A. Langner, "How Personalized and Socialized Power Motivation Facilitate Antisocial and Prosocial Decision-Making," *Journal of Research in Personality* 42, no. 6 (2008): 1547–59; D. Rus, D. van Knippenberg, and B. Wisse, "Leader Self-Definition and Leader Self-Serving Behavior," *Leadership Quarterly* 21, no. 3 (2010): 509–29; C. Case and J. Maner, "Divide and Conquer: When and Why Leaders Undermine the Cohesive Fabric of Their Group," *Journal of Personality and Social Psychology* 107, no. 6 (2014): 1033–50.

39. D. Miron and D. C. McClelland, "The Impact of Achievement Motivation Training on Small Business," *California Management Review* 21 (1979): 13–28.

40. Expectancy theory of motivation in work settings originated in V. H. Vroom, *Work and Motivation* (New York: Wiley, 1964). The version of expectancy theory presented here was developed by Edward Lawler. Lawler's model provides a clearer presentation of the model's three components. P-to-O expectancy is similar to "instrumentality" in Vroom's original expectancy theory model. The difference is that instrumentality is a correlation whereas P-to-O expectancy is a probability. See J. P. Campbell et al., *Managerial Behavior, Performance, and Effectiveness* (New York: McGraw-Hill, 1970); E. E. Lawler III, *Motivation in Work Organizations* (Monterey, CA: Brooks-Cole, 1973); D. A. Nadler and E. E. Lawler, "Motivation: A Diagnostic Approach," in *Perspectives on Behavior in Organizations*, ed. J. R. Hackman, E. E. Lawler III, and L. W. Porter (New York: McGraw-Hill, 1983), 67–78.

41. M. Zeelenberg et al., "Emotional Reactions to the Outcomes of Decisions: The Role of Counterfactual Thought in the Experience of Regret and Disappointment," *Organizational Behavior and Human Decision Processes* 75, no. 2 (1998): 117–41; B. A. Mellers, "Choice and the Relative Pleasure of Consequences," *Psychological Bulletin* 126, no. 6 (2000): 910–24; R. P. Bagozzi, U. M. Dholakia, and S. Basuroy, "How Effortful Decisions Get Enacted: The Motivating Role of Decision Processes, Desires, and Anticipated Emotions," *Journal of Behavioral Decision Making* 16, no. 4 (2003): 273–95. The neuropsychology of valences and its associated "expected utility" is discussed in A. Bechara and A. R. Damasio, "The Somatic Marker Hypothesis: A Neural Theory of Economic Decision," *Games and Economic Behavior* 52, no. 2 (2005): 336–72.

42. D. A. Nadler and E. E. Lawler, "Motivation: A Diagnostic Approach," in *Perspectives on Behavior in Organizations,* ed. J. R. Hackman, E. E. Lawler III, and L. W. Porter (New York: McGraw-Hill, 1983), 70–73.

43. A. Fisher, "Expecting a Fat Year-End Bonus? Don't Get Your Hopes Up," *Fortune*, December 5, 2012; U.S. Office of Personnel Management, *Federal Employee Viewpoint Survey* (Washington, DC: Office of Personnel Management, September 2016); Willis Towers Watson, *Under Pressure to Remain Relevant, Employers Look to Modernize the Employee Value Proposition* (London: Willis Towers Watson, September 9, 2016); Willis Towers Watson, "U.S. Employees Give Performance Management Programs Mediocre Grades," news release (Arlington, VA: Willis Towers Watson, December 6, 2016); Glassdoor, *Global Salary Transparency Survey: Employee Perceptions of Talking Pay* (Mill Valley, CA: Glassdoor, April 2016).

44. For recent applications of expectancy in diverse settings, see R. L. Purvis, T. J. Zagenczyk, and G. E. McCray, "What's in It for Me? Using Expectancy Theory and Climate to Explain Stakeholder Participation, Its Direction and Intensity," *International Journal of Project Management* 33, no. 1 (2015): 3–14; E. Shweiki et al., "Applying Expectancy Theory to Residency Training: Proposing Opportunities to Understand Resident Motivation and Enhance Residency Training," *Advances in Medical Education and Practice* 6 (2015): 339–46; K. N. Bauer et al., "Re-Examination of Motivation in Learning Contexts: Meta-Analytically Investigating the Role Type of Motivation Plays in the Prediction of Key Training Outcomes," *Journal of Business and Psychology* 31, no. 1 (2016): 33–50.

45. This limitation was recently acknowledged by Victor Vroom, who had introduced expectancy theory in his 1964 book. See G. P. Latham, *Work Motivation: History, Theory, Research, and Practice* (Thousand Oaks, CA: Sage, 2007), 47–48.

46. J. B. Watson, *Behavior: An Introduction to Comparative Psychology* (New York: Henry Holt, 1914).

47. B. F. Skinner, *About Behaviorism* (New York: Knopf, 1974); J. Komaki, T. Coombs, and S. Schepman, "Motivational Implications of Reinforcement Theory," in *Motivation and Leadership at Work*, ed. R. M. Steers, L. W. Porter, and G. A. Bigley (New York: McGraw-Hill, 1996), 34–52; R. G. Miltenberger, *Behavior Modification: Principles and Procedures* (Pacific Grove, CA: Brooks/Cole, 1997).

48. T. K. Connellan, *How to Improve Human Performance* (New York: Harper & Row, 1978), 48–57; F. Luthans and R. Kreitner, *Organizational Behavior Modification and Beyond* (Glenview, IL: Scott, Foresman, 1985), 85–88.

49. B. F. Skinner, *Science and Human Behavior* (New York: Free Press, 1965); R. G. Miltenberger, *Behavior Modification: Principles and Procedures* (Pacific Grove, CA: Brooks/Cole, 1997), chaps. 4–6.

50. T. R. Hinkin and C. A. Schriesheim, "'If You Don't Hear from Me You Know You Are Doing Fine,'" *Cornell Hotel & Restaurant Administration Quarterly* 45, no. 4 (2004): 362–72.

51. L. K. Trevino, "The Social Effects of Punishment in Organizations: A Justice Perspective," *Academy of Management Review* 17 (1992): 647–76; L. E. Atwater et al., "Recipient and Observer Reactions to Discipline: Are Managers Experiencing Wishful Thinking?," *Journal of Organizational Behavior* 22, no. 3 (2001): 249–70.

52. G. P. Latham and V. L. Huber, "Schedules of Reinforcement: Lessons from the Past and Issues for the Future," *Journal of Organizational Behavior Management* 13 (1992): 125–49; B. A. Williams, "Challenges to Timing-Based Theories of Operant Behavior," *Behavioural Processes* 62 (2003): 115–23.

53. J. A. Bargh and M. J. Ferguson, "Beyond Behaviorism: On the Automaticity of Higher Mental Processes," *Psychological Bulletin* 126, no. 6 (2000): 925–45. Some writers argue that behaviorists long ago accepted the relevance of cognitive processes in behavior modification. See I. Kirsch et al., "The Role of Cognition in Classical and Operant Conditioning," *Journal of Clinical Psychology* 60, no. 4 (2004): 369–92.

54. A. Bandura, *Social Foundations of Thought and Action: A Social Cognitive Theory* (Englewood Cliffs, NJ: Prentice Hall, 1986); A. Bandura, "Social Cognitive Theory of Self-Regulation," *Organizational Behavior and Human Decision Processes* 50, no. 2 (1991): 248–87; A. Bandura, "Social Cognitive Theory: An Agentic Perspective," *Annual Review of Psychology* 52, no. 1 (2001): 1–26.

55. M. E. Schnake, "Vicarious Punishment in a Work Setting," *Journal of Applied Psychology* 71 (1986): 343–45; L. K. Trevino, "The Social Effects of Punishment in Organizations: A Justice Perspective," *Academy of Management Review* 17 (1992): 647–76; J. Malouff et al., "Effects of Vicarious Punishment: A Meta-Analysis," *Journal of General Psychology* 136, no. 3 (2009): 271–86.

56. A. Pescuric and W. C. Byham, "The New Look of Behavior Modeling," *Training & Development* 50 (1996): 24–30.

57. A. Bandura, "Self-Reinforcement: Theoretical and Methodological Considerations," *Behaviorism* 4 (1976): 135–55; C. A. Frayne and J. M. Geringer, "Self-Management Training for Improving Job Performance: A Field Experiment Involving Salespeople," *Journal of Applied Psychology* 85, no. 3 (2000): 361–72; J. B. Vancouver and D. V. Day, "Industrial and Organisation Research on Self-Regulation: From Constructs to Applications," *Applied Psychology: An International Journal* 54, no. 2 (2005): 155–85.

58. City of Toronto, *Budget 2016: Internal and Financial Services: 311 Toronto* (Toronto: City of Toronto, 2016); City of Toronto, "Performance Reports: 311 Toronto" (Toronto: City of Toronto, 2017), http://www1.toronto.ca (accessed March 15, 2017).

59. E. A. Locke and G. P. Latham, *A Theory of Goal Setting and Task Performance* (Englewood Cliffs, NJ: Prentice Hall, 1990); G. P. Latham, "Goal Setting: A Five-Step Approach to Behavior Change," *Organizational Dynamics* 32, no. 3 (2003): 309–18.

60. There are several variations of the SMARTER goal-setting model; "achievable" is sometimes "acceptable," "reviewed" is sometimes "recorded," and "exciting" is sometimes "ethical." Based on the earlier SMART model, the SMARTER goal-setting model seems to originate in British sports psychology writing around the mid-1990s. For early examples, see P. Butler, *Performance Profiling* (Leeds, UK: The National Coaching Foundation, 1996), 36; R. C. Thelwell and I. A. Greenlees, "The Effects of a Mental Skills Training Program Package on Gymnasium Triathlon Performance," *The Sports Psychologist* 15, no. 2 (2001): 127–41.

61. The value and limitations of measurement are discussed in J. M. Henshaw, *Does Measurement Measure Up? How Numbers Reveal and Conceal the Truth* (Baltimore, MD: Johns Hopkins Press, 2006).

62. A. C. Crossley, C. Cooper, and T. Wernsing, "Making Things Happen through Challenging Goals: Leader Proactivity, Trust, and Business-Unit Performance," *Journal of Applied Psychology* 98, no. 3 (2013): 540–49; A. Kruglanski et al., "The Rocky Road from Attitudes to Behaviors: Charting the Goal Systemic Course of Actions," *Psychological Review* 122, no. 4 (2015): 598–620.

63. Z. Zhang and M. Jia, "How Can Companies Decrease the Disruptive Effects of Stretch Goals? The Moderating Role of Interpersonal—and Informational—Justice Climates," *Human Relations* 66, no. 7 (2013): 993–1020; L. D. Ordóñez and D. T. Welsh, "Immoral Goals: How Goal Setting May Lead to Unethical Behavior," *Current Opinion in Psychology* 6 (2015): 93–96.

64. E. A. Locke and G. P. Latham, *A Theory of Goal Setting and Task Performance* (Englewood Cliffs, NJ: Prentice Hall, 1990), chaps. 6 and 7; H. Klein, J. T. Cooper, and C. A. Monahan, "Goal Commitment," in *New Developments in Goal Setting and Task Performance*, ed. E. A. Locke and G. P. Latham (London: Taylor and Francis, 2012), 65–89.

65. M. London, E. M. Mone, and J. C. Scott, "Performance Management and Assessment: Methods for Improved Rater Accuracy and Employee Goal Setting," *Human Resource Management* 43, no. 4 (2004): 319–36; G. P. Latham and C. C. Pinder, "Work Motivation Theory and Research at the Dawn of the Twenty-First Century," *Annual Review of Psychology* 56 (2005): 485–516.

66. G. P. Latham, *Work Motivation: History, Theory, Research, and Practice* (Thousand Oaks, CA: Sage, 2007), 198–203; A. Baker et al., "Feedback and Organizations: Feedback Is Good, Feedback-Friendly Culture Is Better," *Canadian Psychology* 54, no. 4 (2013): 260–68.

67. Adobe Systems, *Adobe Check-In: Career Grows When Feedback Flows* (San Jose, CA: Adobe Systems, 2014), YouTube video; A. Fisher, "How Adobe Keeps Key Employees from Quitting," *Fortune*, June 16, 2015; P. Cappelli and A. Tavis, "The Performance Management Revolution," *Harvard Business Review* 94 (2016): 58–67; D. Morris, "2017: The Year Performance Reviews Get the Axe," *Conversations*, Adobe Systems, January 11, 2017, https://blogs.adobe.com/conversations; D. Morris, "Yes, You Can Reward Employees without Ratings and Rankings," *Conversations*, Adobe Systems, February 16, 2017, https://blogs.adobe.com/conversations.

68. P. Drucker, *The Effective Executive* (Oxford, UK: Butterworth-Heinemann, 2007), 22. Drucker's emphasis on strengths also was noted in D. K. Whitney and A. Trosten-Bloom, *The Power of Appreciative Inquiry: A Practical Guide to Positive Change*, 2nd ed. (San Francisco: Berrett-Koehler, 2010), xii.

69. M. Buckingham, *Go Put Your Strengths to Work* (New York: Free Press, 2007); A. L. Clancy and J. Binkert, "Appreciative Coaching: Pathway to Flourishing," in *Excellence in Coaching: The Industry Guide*, ed. J. Passmore (London: Kogan Page, 2010), 147–56; H. Aguinis, R. K. Gottfredson, and H. Joo, "Delivering Effective Performance Feedback: The Strengths-Based Approach," *Business Horizons* 55, no. 2 (2012): 105–11.

70. A. N. Kluger and D. Nir, "The Feedforward Interview," *Human Resource Management Review* 20, no. 3 (2010): 235–46; H. Aguinis, R. K. Gottfredson, and H. Joo, "Delivering Effective Performance Feedback: The Strengths-Based Approach," *Business Horizons* 55, no. 2 (2012): 105–11.

71. A. Terracciano, P. T. Costa, and R. R. McCrae, "Personality Plasticity after Age 30," *Personality and Social Psychology Bulletin* 32, no. 8 (2006): 999–1009; M. R. Leary, "Motivational and Emotional Aspects of the Self," *Annual Review of Psychology* 58, no. 1 (2007): 317–44.

72. Cited in H. Aguinis, R. K. Gottfredson, and H. Joo, "Delivering Effective Performance Feedback: The Strengths-Based Approach," *Business Horizons* 55, no. 2 (2012): 105–11.

73. J. W. Smither, M. London, and R. R. Reilly, "Does Performance Improve Following Multisource Feedback? A Theoretical Model, Meta-Analysis, and Review of Empirical Findings," *Personnel Psychology* 58, no. 1 (2005): 33–66; L. E. Atwater, J. F. Brett, and A. C. Charles, "Multisource Feedback: Lessons Learned and Implications for Practice," *Human Resource Management* 46, no. 2 (2007): 285–307; M. C. Campion, E. D. Campion, and M. A. Campion, "Improvements in Performance Management through the Use of 360 Feedback," *Industrial and Organizational Psychology* 8, no. 1 (2015): 85–93.

74. S. J. Ashford and G. B. Northcraft, "Conveying More (or Less) Than We Realize: The Role of Impression Management in Feedback Seeking," *Organizational Behavior and Human Decision Processes* 53 (1992): 310–34; J. R. Williams et al., "Increasing Feedback Seeking in Public Contexts: It Takes Two (or More) to Tango," *Journal of Applied Psychology* 84 (1999): 969–76.

75. J. B. Miner, "The Rated Importance, Scientific Validity, and Practical Usefulness of Organizational Behavior Theories: A Quantitative Review," *Academy of Management Learning and Education* 2, no. 3 (2003): 250–68. Also see C. C. Pinder, *Work Motivation in Organizational Behavior* (Upper Saddle River, NJ: Prentice Hall, 1998), 384.

76. P. M. Wright, "Goal Setting and Monetary Incentives: Motivational Tools That Can Work Too Well," *Compensation and Benefits Review* 26 (1994): 41–49; S. Kerr and D. LePelley, "Stretch Goals: Risks, Possibilities, and Best Practices," in *New Developments in Goal Setting and Task Performance*, ed. E. A. Locke and G. P. Latham (London: Taylor and Francis, 2012), 21–32; L. D. Ordóñez and D. T. Welsh, "Immoral Goals: How Goal Setting May Lead to Unethical Behavior," *Current Opinion in Psychology* 6 (2015): 93–96.

77. G. P. Latham, *Work Motivation: History, Theory, Research, and Practice* (Thousand Oaks, CA: Sage, 2007), 188.

78. J. A. Colquitt et al., "Justice at the Millennium, a Decade Later: A Meta-Analytic Test of Social Exchange and Affect-Based Perspectives," *Journal of Applied Psychology* 98, no. 2 (2013): 199–236; J. Brockner et al., "Riding the Fifth Wave: Organizational Justice as Dependent Variable," *Research in Organizational Behavior* 35 (2015): 103–21. The literature identifies up to six types of justice. However, we focus on the two main types and subsume interpersonal justice within procedural justice based on the idea that interpersonal justice is a procedural characteristic.

79. M. Deutsch, "Equity, Equality, and Need: What Determines Which Value Will Be Used as the Basis of Distributive Justice?," *Journal of Social Issues* 31, no. 3 (1975): 137–49; D.A. Morand and K.K. Merriman, "Equality Theory" as a Counterbalance to Equity Theory in Human Resource Management," *Journal of Business Ethics* 111, no. 1 (2012): 133–44; T. Reeskens and W. van Oorschot, "Equity, Equality, or Need? A Study of Popular Preferences for Welfare Redistribution Principles across 24 European Countries," *Journal of European Public Policy* 20, no. 8 (2013): 1174–95.

80. "B&T Salary Survey," *B&T Magazine* 64, no. 2812 (2015): 56–63; G. Plimmer and C. Cantal, *Workplace Dynamics in New Zealand Public Services*, Centre for Labour, Employment and Work (Wellington, NZ: Victoria University of Wellington, November 2016); Willis Towers Watson, "Only Half of U.S. Employees Think They Are Paid Fairly Compared to Counterparts," news release (Arlington, VA: Willis Towers Watson, November 10, 2016); *Comp Is Culture: 2017 Compensation Best Practices Report* (Seattle: PayScale, February 14, 2017).

81. J. S. Adams, "Toward an Understanding of Inequity," *Journal of Abnormal and Social Psychology* 67 (1963): 422–36; P. H. Siegel, M. Schraeder, and R. Morrison, "A Taxonomy of Equity Factors," *Journal of Applied Social Psychology* 38, no. 1 (2008): 61–75; R. Cropanzana, D. E. Bowen, and S. W. Gilliland, "The Management of Organizational Justice," *Academy of Management Perspectives* 21, no. 4 (2007): 34–48.

82. C. T. Kulik and M. L. Ambrose, "Personal and Situational Determinants of Referent Choice," *Academy of Management Review* 17 (1992): 212–37; J. Shin and Y. W. Sohn, "Effects of Employees' Social Comparison Behaviors on Distributive Justice Perception and Job Satisfaction," *Social Behavior and Personality* 43, no. 7 (2015): 1071–83; C. M. Sterling and G. Labianca, "Costly Comparisons: Managing Envy in the Workplace," *Organizational Dynamics* 44, no. 4 (2015): 296–305.

83. T. P. Summers and A. S. DeNisi, "In Search of Adams' Other: Reexamination of Referents Used in the Evaluation of Pay," *Human Relations* 43 (1990): 497–511.

84. The emotive dynamics of feelings of inequity are studied in A. W. Cappelen et al., "Equity Theory and Fair Inequality: A Neuroeconomic Study," *Proceedings of the National Academy of Sciences* 111, no. 43 (2014): 15368–72.

85. Y. Cohen-Charash and P. E. Spector, "The Role of Justice in Organizations: A Meta-Analysis," *Organizational Behavior and Human Decision Processes* 86 (2001): 278–321; B. Walker and R. T. Hamilton, "Employee–Employer Grievances: A Review," *International Journal of Management Reviews* 13, no. 1 (2011): 40–58; R. Cropanzana and C. Moliner, "Hazards of Justice: Egocentric Bias, Moral Judgments, and Revenge-Seeking," in *Deviant and Criminal Behavior in the Workplace*, ed. S. M. Elias (New York: New York University Press, 2013), 155–77; B. C. Holtz and C. M. Harold, "Interpersonal Justice and Deviance: The Moderating Effects of Interpersonal Justice Values and Justice Orientation," *Journal of Management* 39, no. 2 (2013): 339–65; C. L. Wilkin and C. E. Connelly, "Green with Envy and Nerves of Steel: Moderated Mediation between Distributive Justice and Theft," *Personality and Individual Differences* 72 (2015): 160–64.

86. Canadian Press, "Pierre Berton, Canadian Cultural Icon, Enjoyed Long and Colourful Career," *Times Colonist* (Victoria, BC), November 30, 2004.

87. J. Fizel, A. C. Krautman, and L. Hadley, "Equity and Arbitration in Major League Baseball," *Managerial and Decision Economics* 23, no. 7 (2002): 427–35; M. Ezzamel and R. Watson, "Pay Comparability across and within UK Boards: An Empirical Analysis of the Cash Pay Awards to CEOs and Other Board Members," *Journal of Management Studies* 39, no. 2 (2002): 207–32.

88. D. R. Bobocel and L. Gosse, "Procedural Justice: A Historical Review and Critical Analysis," in *Oxford Handbook of Justice in the Workplace*, ed. R. S. Cropanzano and M. L. Ambrose (New York: Oxford University Press, 2015), 51–88.

89. J. Greenberg and E. A. Lind, "The Pursuit of Organizational Justice: From Conceptualization to Implication to Application," in *Industrial and Organizational Psychology: Linking Theory with Practice*, ed. C. L. Cooper and E. A. Locke (London: Blackwell, 2000), 72–108 ; C. B. Goldberg, M. A. Clark, and A. B. Henley, "Speaking Up: A Conceptual Model of Voice Responses Following the Unfair Treatment of Others in Non-Union Settings," *Human Resource Management* 50, no. 1 (2011): 75–94; M. R. Bashshur, "When Voice Matters: A Multilevel Review of the Impact of Voice in Organizations," *Journal of Management* 41, no. 5 (2015): 1530–54.

How should people make decisions in organizations? Most business leaders would likely answer this question by saying that effective decision making involves identifying, selecting, and applying the best possible alternative. In other words, the best decisions use pure logic and all available information to choose the alternative with the highest value—such as highest expected profitability, customer satisfaction, employee well-being, or some combination of these outcomes. These decisions sometimes involve complex calculations of data to produce a formula that points to the best choice.

In its extreme form, rational choice decision making has dominated in Western societies for most of written history.[4] It was established 2,500 years ago when Plato and his contemporaries in ancient Greece raised logical debate and reasoning to a fine art. About 400 years ago, Descartes and other European philosophers emphasized that the ability to make logical decisions is one of the most important accomplishments of human beings. In the 1700s, Scottish philosophers refined the notion that the best choice is the one that offers the greatest satisfaction.

Rational choice decision making selects the best alternative by calculating the probability that various outcomes will occur from the choices and the expected satisfaction from each of those outcomes.[5] We have already seen how similar calculations of probability and valences are used in two earlier organizational behavior theories, namely the attitude model in Chapter 4 and expectancy theory of motivation in Chapter 5.

To understand the rational choice calculation, consider the example in Exhibit 6.1.[6] Your company wants to choose a new supplier of a particular raw material, and the preferred supplier should be the best based on three outcomes (called selection criteria): Does the supplier provide a high-quality product (+9) with low prices (+6) and on-time delivery (+4)?[7] The numbers, which are on a plus or minus 10-point scale, indicate each outcome's importance or expected satisfaction (valence). You discover that supplier A has excellent on-time delivery (about 90 percent probability of exceeding the company's expectations) whereas it has a 70 percent probability of reliably providing a product with exceptional quality. Supplier B has a 90 percent chance of providing very high product quality but a lower likelihood (40 percent) of offering the best prices.

Which of these two suppliers should be selected? A rational choice decision maker would choose Supplier A because that company offers the greatest satisfaction (expected positive emotions). This satisfaction is calculated by multiplying the

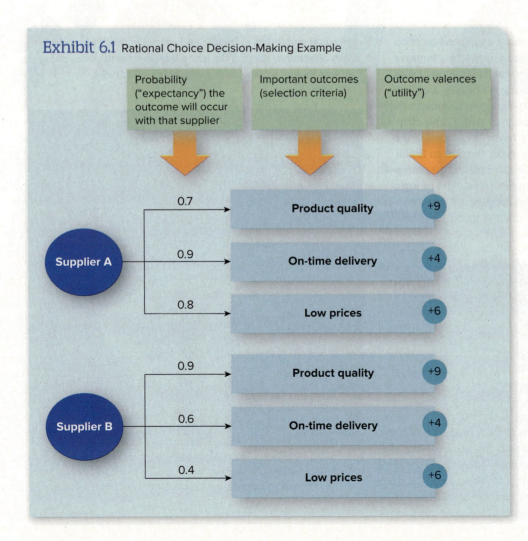

Exhibit 6.1 Rational Choice Decision-Making Example

valence of each outcome with the probability of that outcome occurring, then adding those results across all three outcomes. The supplier with the higher score is the better choice, given available information. The key point from this example is that all rational decisions rely primarily on two pieces of information: (a) the probability that each outcome will occur and (b) the valence or expected satisfaction of each outcome.

Rational Choice Decision-Making Process

Calculating the best alternative is at the heart of rational choice decision making, but it goes hand-in-hand with the systematic decision process illustrated in Exhibit 6.2.[8] The first step is to identify the problem or recognize an opportunity. A *problem* is a deviation between the current and the desired situation—the gap between "what is" and "what ought to be." This deviation is a symptom of more fundamental causes that need to be corrected.[9] The "ought to be" refers to goals, and these goals later help evaluate the selected choice. For instance, if a customer contact center's goal is to answer incoming client calls within 30 seconds, the problem is the gap between that goal and the actual time the contact center takes to answer most client calls. An *opportunity* is a deviation between current expectations and a potentially better situation that was not previously expected. In other words, an opportunity exists when decision makers discover that some choices may produce better results than current goals or expectations.

The second step involves choosing the best decision process. This step is really a meta-decision—deciding how to decide— because it refers to choosing among the different approaches and processes to make the decision.[10] One meta-decision is whether to solve the problem alone or involve others in the process.

Later in this chapter, we'll examine the contingencies of employee involvement in decision making. Another meta-decision is whether to assume the decision is programmed or nonprogrammed. *Programmed decisions* follow standard operating procedures; they have been resolved in the past, so the optimal solution has already been identified and documented. In contrast, *nonprogrammed decisions* require all steps in the decision model because the problems are new, complex, or ill-defined.

The third step in the rational choice decision process is to identify and/or develop a list of possible choices. This usually begins by searching for ready-made solutions, such as practices that have worked well on similar problems. If an acceptable solution cannot be found, then decision makers need to design a custom-made solution or modify an existing one. The fourth step is to select the best choice by applying the rational choice calculation we described in Exhibit 6.1. Choosing the alternative that offers the greatest satisfaction or value requires the decision maker to have information about all possible alternatives and their outcomes. That condition is usually impossible, but the rational choice view of decision making assumes this can be accomplished with ease.

The fifth step is to implement the selected alternative. Rational choice decision making assumes that implementation occurs without any problems. The final step is to evaluate whether the gap has narrowed between "what is" and "what ought to be." Ideally, this information should come from systematic benchmarks so that relevant feedback is objective and easily observed.

Problems with Rational Choice Decision Making

The rational choice view of decision making seems so logical, yet there are several reasons why it is impossible to apply in reality.[11] Therefore, we need to understand why people have imperfect rationality. Over the next several pages we reexamine each step in the rational choice decision-making process, but with more detail about what really happens through the lens of "imperfect rationality."

> **LO6-2** Explain why people differ from rational choice decision making when identifying problems/opportunities, evaluating/choosing alternatives, and evaluating decision outcomes.

IDENTIFYING PROBLEMS AND OPPORTUNITIES

When Albert Einstein was asked how he would save the world in one hour, he replied that the first 55 minutes should be spent defining the problem and the last 5 minutes solving it.[12] Einstein's point is that problem identification is not just the first step in decision making; it is arguably the most important step. But problems and opportunities are not clearly labeled objects

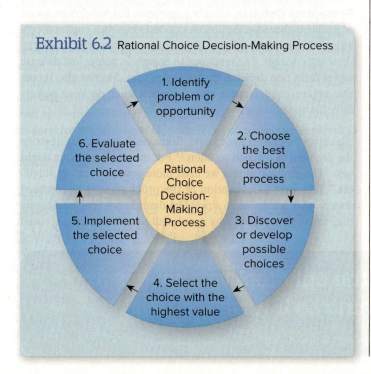

Exhibit 6.2 Rational Choice Decision-Making Process

1. Identify problem or opportunity
2. Choose the best decision process
3. Discover or develop possible choices
4. Select the choice with the highest value
5. Implement the selected choice
6. Evaluate the selected choice

Rational Choice Decision-Making Process

candidates have found other jobs. Consequently, decision makers rely on sequential evaluation of new alternatives against an implicit favorite. This necessarily calls for a satisficing decision rule—choose the first alternative that is "good enough."

Maximization—or at least human attempts to choose the best alternative—can result in better decisions when some alternatives are clearly better than others. But maximizing decision makers run into trouble where there are many alternatives, those alternatives have many features, and the quality of those features for each alternative is ambiguous. For example, it is difficult to choose the best possible car because of the large number of choices, the many features to consider for each choice, and the unclear qualities of some of those features. Under those conditions, maximization leads to a spiral of endless trade-offs among features across the various choices, which can actually result in worse decisions and less satisfied decision makers.[36]

When presented with a large number of choices, people often choose a decision strategy that is even less cognitively challenging than satisficing; they don't make any decision at all! In one study, grocery store customers saw one of two jam-tasting booths. Thirty percent of consumers who visited the booth displaying 6 types of jam purchased one of those products. In contrast, only 3 percent of customers who saw the booth displaying 24 types of jam made a purchase. The larger number of choices discouraged them from making any decision. Other studies revealed similar results in decisions about chocolates, term essays, and pension plan investment options.[37]

Selecting Opportunities

Opportunities are just as important as problems, but what happens when an opportunity is "discovered" and selected is quite different from the process of problem solving. Decision makers seldom choose from among several opportunities; after all, the opportunity *is* the solution, so why look for others! An opportunity is usually experienced as an exciting and rare revelation, so decision makers tend to have an emotional attachment to the opportunity. Unfortunately, this emotional preference motivates decision makers to implement the opportunity and short-circuit any detailed assessment of it.[38]

LO6-3 Discuss the roles of emotions and intuition in decision making.

Emotions and Making Choices

Over the previous pages, we described the findings by Herbert Simon and other experts about how people are far from perfect at rational decision making. However, these scholars neglected

Moods and specific emotions influence the process of evaluating alternatives.
©Ned Frisk/Blend Images LLC

to mention another problem: The rational choice view completely ignores the effect of emotions in human decision making. Just as both the rational and emotional brain centers alert us to problems, they also influence our choice of alternatives.[39] Emotions affect the evaluation of alternatives in three ways.

Emotions Form Early Preferences The emotional marker process described in previous chapters (Chapters 3, 4, and 5) shapes our preference for each alternative before we consciously evaluate those alternatives. Our brain very quickly attaches specific emotions to information about each alternative, and our preferred alternative is strongly influenced by those initial emotional markers.[40] Of course, logical analysis also influences which alternative we choose, but it requires strong logical evidence to change our initial preferences (initial emotional markers). Yet even logical analysis depends on emotions to sway our decision. Specifically, neuroscientific evidence says that information produced from logical analysis is tagged with emotional markers that then motivate us to choose or avoid a particular alternative. Ultimately, emotions, not rational logic, energize us to make the preferred choice. In fact, people with damaged emotional brain centers have difficulty making choices.

Emotions Change the Decision Evaluation Process Moods and specific emotions influence the *process* of evaluating alternatives.[41] For instance, we pay more attention to details when in a negative mood, possibly because a negative mood signals that there is something wrong that requires attention. When in a positive mood, on the other hand, we pay less attention to details and rely on a more programmed decision routine. This phenomenon explains why executive teams in successful companies are often less vigilant about competitors and other environmental threats.[42] Research also suggests that decision makers rely on stereotypes and other shortcuts to speed up the choice process when they experience anger. Anger also makes them more optimistic about the success of risky alternatives, whereas the emotion of fear tends to make them less optimistic. Overall, emotions shape *how* we evaluate information, not just which choice we select.

Emotions Serve as Information When We Evaluate Alternatives The third way that emotions influence the evaluation of alternatives is through a process called "emotions as information." Marketing experts have found that we listen in on our emotions to gain guidance when making choices.[43] This intuition the ability to know when a problem or opportunity exists and to select the best course of action without conscious reasoning

process is similar to having a temporary improvement in emotional intelligence. Most emotional experiences remain below the level of conscious awareness, but people actively try to be more sensitive to these subtle emotions when making a decision.

When buying a new car, for example, you not only logically evaluate each vehicle's features; you also try to gauge your emotions when visualizing what it would be like to own each of the cars on your list of choices. Even if you have solid information about the quality of each vehicle on key features (purchase price, fuel efficiency, maintenance costs, resale value, etc.), you are swayed by your emotional reaction and actively try to sense that emotional response when thinking about it. Everyone consciously pays attention to his or her emotions to some degree when choosing alternatives. This phenomenon ties directly into our next topic, intuition.

Intuition and Making Choices

Do you rely on your "gut instinct" to help make decisions? These emotional experiences potentially (but not necessarily) indicate your **intuition**—the ability to know when a problem or opportunity exists and to select the best course of action without conscious reasoning.[44] Some people rely more on intuition, whereas others rely more on logical analysis when making decisions (see Chapter 2 on the MBTI thinking versus feeling orientation). However, emotions are always present in human decision making, so intuition and logical analysis are not opposites and never completely replace each other.[45] Some people pay more attention to emotional signals, whereas others pay more attention to logic, but emotions are always involved.

Intuition is both an emotional experience and a rapid non-conscious analytic process. The gut feelings we experience are emotional signals that have enough intensity to make us consciously aware of them. These signals warn us of impending danger or motivate us to take advantage of an opportunity. Some intuition also directs us to preferred choices relative to other alternatives in the situation.

All gut feelings are emotional signals, but not all emotional signals are intuition. The main distinction is that intuition involves rapidly comparing our observations with deeply held patterns learned through experience.[46] These "templates of the mind" represent tacit knowledge that has been implicitly acquired over time. They are mental models that help us understand whether the current situation is good or bad, depending on how well that situation fits our mental model. When a template fits or doesn't fit the current situation, emotions are produced that motivate us to act. Studies have found that when chess masters quickly scan a chessboard, they experience emotional signals that the chess configuration poses an opportunity or threat. These emotional signals motivate closer observation to logically confirm the situation and to act on it. Thus, intuition signals that a problem or opportunity exists long before conscious rational analysis has occurred.

A key message here is that some emotional signals are not intuition, so gut feelings shouldn't always guide our decisions. The problem is that emotional responses are not always based on well-grounded mental models. Instead, we sometimes compare the current situation to more remote templates, which may or may not be relevant. A new employee might feel confident about relations with a supplier, whereas an experienced employee senses potential problems. The difference is that the new employee relies on templates from other experiences or industries that might not work well in this situation. Thus, the extent to which our gut feelings in a situation represent intuition depends on our level of experience in that situation.

So far, we have described intuition as an emotional experience (gut feeling) and a process in which we compare the current situation with well-established templates of the mind. Intuition also relies on *action scripts*—programmed decision routines that speed up our response to pattern matches or mismatches.[47] Action scripts effectively shorten the decision-making process by jumping from problem identification to selection of a solution. In other words, action scripting is a form of programmed decision making. Action scripts are generic, so we need to consciously adapt them to the specific situation.

> The extent to which our gut feelings in a situation represent intuition depends on our level of experience in that situation.

Making Choices More Effectively

It is very difficult to get around the human limitations of making choices, but a few strategies help minimize these concerns. One important discovery is that decisions tend to have a higher failure rate when leaders are decisive rather than contemplative about the available options. Of course, decisions also can be ineffective when leaders take too long to make a choice, but research indicates that a lack of logical evaluation of alternatives is a greater concern. By systematically assessing alternatives against relevant factors, decision makers minimize the implicit favorite and satisficing problems that occur when they rely on general subjective judgments. This recommendation does not suggest that we ignore intuition; rather, it suggests that we use it in combination with careful analysis of relevant information.[48]

A second piece of advice is to remember that decisions are influenced by both rational and emotional processes. Therefore, some decision makers deliberately revisit important issues later when their initial emotions have subsided and they can look at the information in a different mood. For example, if you sense that your team is feeling somewhat too self-confident when making an important competitive decision, you might decide to have the team members revisit the decision a few days later when they are thinking more critically.

Another strategy is **scenario planning**, which is a disciplined method for imagining possible futures.[50] It typically involves thinking about what would happen if a significant environmental condition changed and what the organization should do to anticipate and react to such an outcome. Scenario planning is a useful vehicle for choosing the best solutions under possible scenarios long before they occur because alternative courses of action are evaluated without the pressure and emotions that occur during real emergencies.

IMPLEMENTING DECISIONS

Implementing decisions is often skipped over in most writing about decision making. Yet leading business writers emphasize that execution—translating decisions into action—is one of the most important and challenging tasks in the decision-making process.[51] Implementing decisions is mainly about organizational change, which we discuss in Chapter 14, but also relates to leadership (Chapter 11) and several other topics throughout this book.

Intuition versus Data Analysis: Crunch Your Hunch[49]

84% of 300 UK recruitment professionals surveyed identify intuition as the most cost-efficient recruitment tool (but only the third most effective tool).

61% of 2,037 professionals surveyed globally somewhat or strongly agree that there is pressure from senior management for the organization to become more data driven and analytical.

68% of 600 American and UK executives surveyed say senior management in their organization is highly or totally committed to analytics and fact-based decision making.

70% of 1,018 Australian small to medium enterprise owners surveyed say they trusted their gut instinct over any professional advice.

©Jonathan Evans/Photographer's Choice RF/Getty Images

EVALUATING DECISIONS

Contrary to the rational choice view, decision makers aren't completely honest with themselves when evaluating the effectiveness of their decisions. Earlier in this chapter, we explained that decision makers engage in confirmation bias to support their implicit favorite during the decision-making process. This bias continues long after the decision has been made (which is why it is also called *postdecisional justification*). Decision makers ignore or underemphasize negative outcomes of the choice they made and overemphasize new information about its positive features. Confirmation bias gives people an excessively optimistic evaluation of their decisions, but only until they receive very clear and undeniable information to the contrary.

Escalation of Commitment

Another reason why decision makers don't evaluate their decisions very well is due to **escalation of commitment**—the tendency to repeat an apparently bad decision or allocate more resources to a failing course of action.[52] Why are decision makers led deeper and deeper into failing projects? Several explanations have been identified and discussed over the years, but the four main influences are self-justification effect, self-enhancement effect, prospect theory effect, and sunk costs effect.

Self-Justification Effect People try to convey a positive public image of themselves. In decision making, this self-justification typically involves appearing to be rational and competent. Decision makers are therefore motivated to demonstrate that their choices will be successful, which includes continuing to support a decision even when it is not having the desired outcomes. In contrast, pulling the plug symbolizes the project's failure and the decision maker's incompetence. This self-justification effect is particularly evident when decision makers are personally identified with the project, have staked their reputations to some extent on the project's success, and have low self-esteem.[53]

Self-Enhancement Effect People have a natural tendency to feel good about themselves—to feel luckier, more competent, and more successful than average—regarding things that are important to them (see Chapter 3).[54] This **self-enhancement** supports a positive self-concept, but it also increases the risk of escalation of commitment. When presented with evidence that a project is in trouble, the self-enhancement process biases our interpretation of the information as a temporary aberration from an otherwise positive

trend line. And when we eventually realize that the project isn't going as well as planned, we continue to invest in the project because our probability of rescuing the project is above average.

Self-justification and self-enhancement often occur together, but they are different mechanisms. Self-justification is a deliberate attempt to maintain a favorable public image, whereas self-enhancement operates mostly nonconsciously, distorting information so we do not recognize the problem sooner and biasing our probabilities of success so we continue to invest in the losing project.[55]

Prospect Theory Effect **Prospect theory effect** is the tendency to experience stronger negative emotions when losing something of value than the positive emotions when gaining something of equal value. This prospect theory effect motivates us to avoid losses, which typically occurs by taking the risk of investing more in that losing project. Stopping a project is a certain loss, which evokes more negative emotions to most people than the uncertainty of success associated with continuing to fund the project. Given the choice, decision makers choose escalation of commitment, which is the less painful option at the time.[56]

Sunk Costs Effect Another disincentive to axing a failing project is sunk costs—the value of resources already invested in the decision.[57] The rational choice view states that investing resources should be determined by expected future gains and risk, not the size of earlier resources invested in the project. Yet people inherently feel motivated to invest more resources in projects that have high sunk costs. A variation of sunk costs is time investment. Time is a resource, so the more time decision makers have devoted to a project, the more motivated they are to continue investing in that project. Finally, sunk costs can take the form of closing costs, that is, the financial or nonfinancial penalties associated with shutting down a project. As with other forms of sunk costs, the higher the closing costs, the more motivated decision makers are to engage in escalation of commitment.

Escalation of commitment occurs partly because people are motivated to invest resources in projects with high sunk costs (large amounts already spent), whereas they should consider only the expected future gains.
©pogonici/Shutterstock

creativity the development of original ideas that make a socially recognized contribution

divergent thinking reframing a problem in a unique way and generating different approaches to the issue

Escalation of commitment is usually framed as poor decision making, but persistence may be the better choice under some circumstances.[58] Indeed, many breakthroughs have occurred because of the decision makers' persistence and optimism. Continuing with a losing project may be prudent when the cost overruns are small relative to the project cost, the benefits of success are high, and the rewards of a successful project are received quickly. Some experts also suggest that throwing more money into a failing project is sometimes a logical attempt to further understand an ambiguous situation. By adding more resources, the decision maker gains new information about the project's development, which provides more feedback about the project's future success. This strategy is particularly common where the project has high closing costs.

Evaluating Decision Outcomes More Effectively

One of the most effective ways to minimize escalation of commitment and confirmation bias is to ensure that the people who made the original decision are not the same people who later evaluate that decision. Target Corporation was able to withdraw early from the ill-fated Canadian expansion probably because Target's CEO did not make the original decision. This separation of roles minimizes the self-justification effect. A second strategy is to publicly establish a preset level at which the decision is abandoned or reevaluated. This is similar to a stop-loss order in the stock market, whereby the stock is sold if it falls below a certain price. The problem with this solution is that conditions are often so complex that it is difficult to identify an appropriate point to abandon a project.[59]

A third strategy is to find a source of systematic and clear feedback.[60] At some point, even the strongest escalation and confirmation bias effects deflate when the evidence highlights the project's failings. A fourth strategy to improve the decision evaluation process is to involve several people in the evaluation. Coworkers continuously monitor each other and might notice problems sooner than someone working alone on the project.

OB THEORY TO PRACTICE

Evaluating Decision Outcomes More Effectively

▶ Decision reviewers (evaluating the decision's success) should be different from those who made the decision.

▶ Publicly establish a preset level at which the decision is abandoned or reevaluated.

▶ Seek out sources of systematic and clear feedback for the decision's outcomes.

▶ Involve several people in the decision evaluation process.

LO6-4 Describe employee characteristics, workplace conditions, and specific activities that support creativity.

CREATIVITY

The entire decision-making process described over the preceding pages depends on **creativity** —the development of original ideas that make a socially recognized contribution.[61] Creativity operates when imagining opportunities such as how Infosys's expertise can improve value for its clients. It is also applied when developing and selecting alternatives because we need to visualize the future in different ways and to figure out how each choice might be useful or a liability in those scenarios.

The Creative Process

How does creativity occur? That question has puzzled experts for hundreds of years and has been the fascination of many scientists who saw how creative thinking led to their own important discoveries. The four-stage model shown in Exhibit 6.4 was introduced nearly a century ago, yet is still considered the most elegant representation of the creative process.[62]

The first stage, *preparation,* involves developing a clear understanding of what you are trying to achieve through a novel solution and then actively studying information seemingly related to the topic. The second stage, called *incubation*, is the period of reflective thought. We put the problem aside, but our mind is still working on it in the background.[63] The important condition here is to maintain a low-level awareness by frequently revisiting the problem. Incubation does not mean that you forget about the problem or issue.

Incubation assists **divergent thinking**—reframing the problem

Exhibit 6.4 The Creative Process Model

Preparation	Incubation	Illumination	Verification
• Understand the problem or opportunity • Investigate information that seems relevant to the issue	• Period of reflective thought • Nonconscious or low-level awareness, not direct attention to the issue • Active divergent thinking process	• Sudden awareness of a novel, although vague and incomplete, idea entering one's consciousness • May include an initial period of "fringe" awareness	• Detailed logical and experimental evaluation of the illuminated idea • Further creative thinking

Source: Based on G. Wallas, *The Art of Thought* (London: Jonathan Cape, 1926), chap. 4.

in a unique way and generating different approaches to the issue. This contrasts with *convergent thinking*—calculating the conventionally accepted "right answer" to a logical problem. Divergent thinking breaks us away from existing mental models so that we can apply concepts or processes from completely different areas of life.

The third stage of creativity, called *illumination* (or *insight*), refers to the experience of suddenly becoming aware of a unique idea.[64] Illumination is often visually depicted as a lightbulb, but a better image would be a flash of light or perhaps a briefly flickering candle because this stage begins with a "fringe" awareness before the idea fully enters our consciousness. These bits of inspiration are fleeting and can be quickly lost if not documented. For this reason, many creative people keep a journal or notebook nearby so they can jot down their ideas before they disappear. Also, flickering ideas don't keep a particular schedule; they might come to you at any time of day or night.

Illumination presents ideas that are usually vague, roughly drawn, and untested. *Verification* therefore provides the essential final stage of creativity, whereby we flesh out the illuminated ideas and subject them to detailed logical evaluation and experimentation. This stage often calls for further creativity as the ideas evolve into finished products or services. Thus, although verification is labeled the final stage of creativity, it is really the beginning of a long process of creative decision making toward development of an innovative product or service.

Characteristics of Creative People

Everyone is creative, but some people have a higher potential for creativity. Four of the main characteristics that give individuals more creative potential are intelligence, persistence, knowledge and experience, and a cluster of personality traits and values representing independent imagination (see Exhibit 6.5).

- *Cognitive and practical intelligence.* Creative people have above-average intelligence to synthesize information, analyze ideas, and apply

The Creativity Advantage[65]

85% of 1,068 hiring managers believe that creativity is valuable to society.

80% of 2,606 U.S. workers polled believe there is increasing pressure to be productive rather than creative at work.

27% of 2,606 U.S. workers polled say their organization does nothing to encourage employee creativity (support employee curiosity).

73% of 175 public sector creative professionals polled in the U.S. and Canada believe that creativity is undervalued in government.

28% of 7,800 Millennials surveyed across 26 countries say their organization does NOT (not at all or not very much) reward its people for innovative ideas.

51% of 1,068 hiring managers believe businesses grasp the importance of creativity.

©ansonsaw/Getty Images

Exhibit 6.5 Characteristics of Creative People

Characteristics of Creative People

Independent Imagination
- High openness to experience
- Moderately low need for affiliation
- Strong self-direction value
- Strong stimulation value

Cognitive and Practical Intelligence
- Ability to synthesize, analyze, and apply ideas
- Ability to evaluate potential usefulness of ideas

Knowledge and Experience
- Prerequisite knowledge and experience
- Not locked into a fixed knowledge mindset

Persistence
- High need for achievement
- Strong task motivation
- Moderately high self-esteem and optimism

> **People have a general tendency to dismiss or criticize creative ideas, so creative people need persistence to withstand these negative social forces.**

their ideas.[66] They recognize the significance of small bits of information and are able to connect them in ways that few others can imagine. They also have *practical intelligence*—the capacity to evaluate the potential usefulness of their ideas.

- *Persistence*. Creative people have persistence, which is based on a higher need for achievement, a strong motivation from the task itself, and a moderate or high degree of self-esteem. Persistence is vital because people need this motivation to continue working on and investing in a project in spite of failures and advice from others to quit. In fact, people have a general tendency to dismiss or criticize creative ideas, so creative people need persistence to withstand these negative social forces.[67]

- *Knowledge and experience*. Creative people require a foundation of knowledge and experience to discover or acquire new knowledge.[68] However, this expertise is a double-edged sword. As people acquire knowledge and experience about a specific topic, their mental models tend to become more rigid. They are less adaptable to new information or rules about that knowledge domain. Some writers suggest that expertise also increases "mindless behavior" because expertise reduces the tendency to question why things happen.[69] To overcome the limitations of expertise, some corporate leaders like to hire people from other industries and areas of expertise.

- *Independent imagination*. Creative people possess a cluster of personality traits and values that support an independent imagination: high openness to experience, moderately low need for affiliation, and strong values around self-direction and stimulation.[70] Openness to experience is a Big Five personality dimension representing the extent to which a person is imaginative, curious, sensitive, open-minded, and original (see Chapter 2). Creative people have a moderately low need for affiliation so they are less embarrassed when making mistakes. Self-direction includes the values of creativity and independent thought; stimulation includes the values of excitement and challenge. Together, these values form openness to change—representing the motivation to pursue innovative ways (see Chapter 2).

Organizational Conditions Supporting Creativity

Intelligence, persistence, expertise, and independent imagination represent a person's creative potential, but the extent to which these characteristics produce more creative output depends on how well the work environment supports the creative process.[71] Several job and workplace characteristics have been identified in the literature, and different combinations of situations can equally support creativity; there isn't one best work environment.[73]

One of the most important conditions for creativity is a **learning orientation**. The workplace supports a learning orientation when reasonable mistakes are tolerated and expected as part of the discovery process. A second condition for creativity is motivation from the job itself.[74] Employees tend to be more creative when they believe their work benefits the organization and/or larger society (i.e., task significance) and when they have the freedom to pursue novel ideas without bureaucratic delays (i.e., autonomy). Creativity is about changing things, and change is possible only when employees have the authority to experiment. More generally, jobs encourage creativity when they are challenging and aligned with the employee's knowledge and skills.

Along with a learning orientation and intrinsically motivating jobs, creativity blossoms through open communication and sufficient resources. Creative organizations also provide a comfortable degree of job security, which explains why creativity suffers during times of downsizing and corporate restructuring.[75] Some companies also support creativity by designing nontraditional workspaces, such as unique building design or unconventional office areas.[76] Google is one example. The Internet innovator has funky offices in several countries that include hammocks, gondola- and hive-shaped privacy spaces, slides, and brightly painted walls.

To some degree, creativity also improves with support from leaders and coworkers. One study reported that effective product champions provide enthusiastic support for new ideas. Other studies suggest that coworker support can improve creativity in some situations whereas competition among coworkers improves creativity in other situations.[77] Similarly, it isn't clear how much pressure should be exerted on employees to produce creative ideas. Extreme time pressures are well-known creativity inhibitors, but lack of pressure doesn't seem to produce the highest creativity either.

Activities That Encourage Creativity

We have described two cornerstones of creativity in organizations: hiring people with strong creative potential and providing a work environment that supports creativity. The third cornerstone is activities that help employees think more creatively. Four types of creativity-building activities are redefining the problem, associative play, cross-pollination, and design thinking.

- *Redefining the problem*. Revisit projects that have been set aside. After a period of neglect, these projects might be seen in new ways.[78] You also can see the problem from different perspectives by asking coworkers

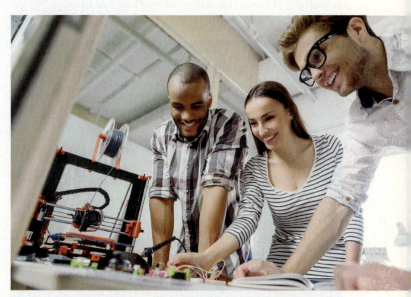

Along with hiring people with strong creative potential and providing a work environment that supports creativity, companies rely on activities that stimulate creative thinking.
©Olena Yakobchuk/Shutterstock

35. S. Botti and S. S. Iyengar, "The Dark Side of Choice: When Choice Impairs Social Welfare," *Journal of Public Policy and Marketing* 25, no. 1 (2006): 24–38; K. D. Vohs et al., "Making Choices Impairs Subsequent Self-Control: A Limited-Resource Account of Decision Making, Self-Regulation, and Active Initiative," *Journal of Personality and Social Psychology* 94, no. 5 (2008): 883–98.

36. K. Jain, J. N. Bearden, and A. Filipowicz, "Do Maximizers Predict Better Than Satisficers?," *Journal of Behavioral Decision Making* 26, no. 1 (2013): 41–50; W. Mao, "When One Desires Too Much of a Good Thing: The Compromise Effect under Maximizing Tendencies," *Journal of Consumer Psychology* 26, no. 1 (2016): 66–80.

37. S. Botti and S. S. Iyengar, "The Dark Side of Choice: When Choice Impairs Social Welfare," *Journal of Public Policy & Marketing* 25, no. 1 (2006): 24–38; S. Iyengar, *The Art of Choosing* (New York: Hachette, 2010), 177–95.

38. P. C. Nutt, "Search during Decision Making," *European Journal of Operational Research* 160 (2005): 851–76.

39. P. Winkielman et al., "Affective Influence on Judgments and Decisions: Moving towards Core Mechanisms," *Review of General Psychology* 11, no. 2 (2007): 179–92.

40. P. Winkielman and K. C. Berridge, "Unconscious Emotion," *Current Directions in Psychological Science* 13, no. 3 (2004): 120–23; A. Bechara and A. R. Damasio, "The Somatic Marker Hypothesis: A Neural Theory of Economic Decision," *Games and Economic Behavior* 52, no. 2 (2005): 336–72; T. S. Saunders and M. J. Buehner, "The Gut Chooses Faster Than the Mind: A Latency Advantage of Affective over Cognitive Decisions," *Quarterly Journal of Experimental Psychology* 66, no. 2 (2013): 381–88; A. Moors, "Automaticity: Componential, Causal, and Mechanistic Explanations," *Annual Review of Psychology* 67, no. 1 (2016): 263–87.

41. J. P. Forgas and J. M. George, "Affective Influences on Judgments and Behavior in Organizations: An Information Processing Perspective," *Organizational Behavior and Human Decision Processes* 86 (2001): 3–34; G. Loewenstein and J. S. Lerner, "The Role of Affect in Decision Making," in *Handbook of Affective Sciences*, ed. R. J. Davidson, K. R. Scherer, and H. H. Goldsmith (New York: Oxford University Press, 2003), 619–42; M. T. Pham, "Emotion and Rationality: A Critical Review and Interpretation of Empirical Evidence," *Review of General Psychology* 11, no. 2 (2007): 155–78; J. P. Forgas and A. S. Koch, "Mood Effects on Cognition," in *Handbook of Cognition and Emotion*, ed. M. D. Robinson, E. R. Watkins, and E. Harmon-Jones (New York: Guilford, 2013), 231–51.

42. D. Miller, *The Icarus Paradox* (New York: HarperBusiness, 1990); D. Miller, "What Happens after Success: The Perils of Excellence," *Journal of Management Studies* 31, no. 3 (1994): 325–68; A. C. Amason and A. C. Mooney, "The Icarus Paradox Revisited: How Strong Performance Sows the Seeds of Dysfunction in Future Strategic Decision-Making," *Strategic Organization* 6, no. 4 (2008): 407–34.

43. M. T. Pham, "The Logic of Feeling," *Journal of Consumer Psychology* 14 (2004): 360–69; N. Schwarz, "Feelings-as-Information Theory," in *Handbook of Theories of Social Psychology*, ed. P. Van Lange, A. Kruglanski, and E. T. Higgins (London: Sage, 2012), 289–308.

44. O. Behling and N. L. Eckel, "Making Sense out of Intuition," *Academy of Management Executive* 5 (1991): 46–54; R. M. Hogarth, "Intuition: A Challenge for Psychological Research on Decision Making," *Psychological Inquiry* 21, no. 4 (2010): 338–53; S. Epstein, "Demystifying Intuition: What It Is, What It Does, and How It Does It," *Psychological Inquiry* 21, no. 4 (2010): 295–312.

45. Y. Wang et al., "Meta-Analytic Investigations of the Relation between Intuition and Analysis," *Journal of Behavioral Decision Making* 30, no. 1 (2017): 15–25; K. Hamilton, S.-I. Shih, and S. Mohammed, "The Development and Validation of the Rational and Intuitive Decision Styles Scale," *Journal of Personality Assessment* (2016): 1–13.

46. W. G. Chase and H. A. Simon, "Perception in Chess," *Cognitive Psychology* 4, no. 1 (1973): 55–81; G. Klein, *Intuition at Work* (New York: Currency/Doubleday, 2003); E. Dane, K. W. Rockmann, and M. G. Pratt, "When Should I Trust My Gut? Linking Domain Expertise to Intuitive Decision-Making Effectiveness," *Organizational Behavior and Human Decision Processes* 119, no. 2 (2012): 187–94; A. Linhares and D. M. Chada, "What Is the Nature of the Mind's Pattern-Recognition Process?," *New Ideas in Psychology* 31, no. 2 (2013): 108–21.

47. G. Klein, *Intuition at Work* (New York: Currency/Doubleday, 2003), 12–13, 16–17.

48. Y. Ganzach, A. H. Kluger, and N. Klayman, "Making Decisions from an Interview: Expert Measurement and Mechanical Combination," *Personnel Psychology* 53 (2000): 1–20; A. M. Hayashi, "When to Trust Your Gut," *Harvard Business Review* 79 (2001): 59–65. Evidence of high failure rates from quick decisions is reported in P. C. Nutt, *Why Decisions Fail* (San Francisco, CA: Berrett-Koehler, 2002); P. C. Nutt, "Search during Decision Making," *European Journal of Operational Research* 160 (2005): 851–76; P. C. Nutt, "Investigating the Success of Decision Making Processes," *Journal of Management Studies* 45, no. 2 (2008): 425–55.

49. Accenture, "Organizations Make Strides in Adoption of Analytics, but Struggle to Capitalize on Investments, Accenture Research Finds," news release (New York: Accenture, March 5, 2013); Wolters Kluwer, "Survey Finds Most SMEs Shun Professional Advice, Possibly at Their Peril," news release (Sydney: Wolters Kluwer, April 11, 2013); *The Recruitment Reality Check* (London: Monster UK and University College London, March 17, 2014); D. Kiron, K. Prentice, and R. B. Ferguson, *The Analytics Mandate* (Cambridge, MA: MIT Sloan Management Review and SAS Institute, May 12, 2014).

50. R. Bradfield et al., "The Origins and Evolution of Scenario Techniques in Long Range Business Planning," *Futures* 37, no. 8 (2005): 795–812; G. Wright, G. Cairns, and P. Goodwin, "Teaching Scenario Planning: Lessons from Practice in Academe and Business," *European Journal of Operational Research* 194, no. 1 (2009): 323–35; T. J. Chermack, *Scenario Planning in Organizations* (San Francisco: Berrett-Koehler, 2011).

51. J. Pfeffer and R. I. Sutton, "Knowing 'What' to Do Is Not Enough: Turning Knowledge into Action," *California Management Review* 42, no. 1 (1999): 83–108; R. Charan, C. Burke, and L. Bossidy, *Execution: The Discipline of Getting Things Done* (New York: Crown Business, 2002).

52. B. M. Staw and J. Ross, "Behavior in Escalation Situations: Antecedents, Prototypes, and Solutions," in *Research in Organizational Behavior*, ed. L. L. Cummings and B. M. Staw (Greenwich, CT: JAI, 1987), 39–78; J. Brockner, "The Escalation of Commitment to a Failing Course of Action: Toward Theoretical Progress," *Academy of Management Review* 17, no. 1 (1992): 39–61; D. J. Sleesman et al., "Cleaning up the Big Muddy: A Meta-Analytic Review of the Determinants of Escalation of Commitment," *Academy of Management Journal* 55, no. 3 (2012): 541–62.

53. F. D. Schoorman and P. J. Holahan, "Psychological Antecedents of Escalation Behavior: Effects of Choice, Responsibility, and Decision Consequences," *Journal of Applied Psychology* 81 (1996): 786–93; D. Steinkühler, M. D. Mahlendorf, and M. Brettel, "How Self-Justification Indirectly Drives Escalation of Commitment– A Motivational Perspective," *Schmalenbach Business Review: ZFBF* 66, no. 2 (2014): 191–222.

54. C. L. Guenther and M. D. Alicke, "Deconstructing the Better-Than-Average Effect," *Journal of Personality and Social Psychology* 99, no. 5 (2010): 755–70; S. Loughnan et al., "Universal Biases in Self-Perception: Better and More Human Than Average," *British Journal of Social Psychology* 49 (2010): 627–36.

55. M. Keil, G. Depledge, and A. Rai, "Escalation: The Role of Problem Recognition and Cognitive Bias," *Decision Sciences* 38, no. 3 (2007): 391–421.

56. G. Whyte, "Escalating Commitment in Individual and Group Decision Making: A Prospect Theory Approach," *Organizational Behavior and Human Decision Processes* 54 (1993): 430–55; D. Kahneman and J. Renshon, "Hawkish Biases," in *American Foreign Policy and the Politics of Fear: Threat Inflation Since 9/11*, ed. T. Thrall and J. Cramer (New York: Routledge, 2009), 79–96.

57. D. J. Sleesman et al., "Cleaning up the Big Muddy: A Meta-Analytic Review of the Determinants of Escalation of Commitment," *Academy of Management Journal* 55, no. 3 (2012): 541–62.

58. J. D. Bragger et al., "When Success Breeds Failure: History, Hysteresis, and Delayed Exit Decisions," *Journal of Applied Psychology* 88, no. 1 (2003): 6–14; H. Drummond, "Escalation of Commitment: When to Stay the Course?," *The Academy of Management Perspectives* 28, no. 4 (2014): 430–46.

59. I. Simonson and B. M. Staw, "De-Escalation Strategies: A Comparison of Techniques for Reducing Commitment to Losing Courses of Action," *Journal of Applied Psychology* 77 (1992): 419–26; W. Boulding, R. Morgan, and R. Staelin, "Pulling the Plug to Stop the New Product Drain," *Journal of Marketing Research*, no. 34 (1997): 164–76; B. M. Staw, K. W. Koput, and S. G. Barsade, "Escalation at the Credit Window: A Longitudinal Study of Bank Executives' Recognition and Write-Off of Problem Loans," *Journal of Applied Psychology* 82, no. 1 (1997): 130–42; M. Keil and D. Robey, "Turning around Troubled Software Projects: An Exploratory Study of the Deescalation of Commitment to Failing Courses of Action," *Journal of Management Information Systems* 15 (1999): 63–87; B. C. Gunia, N. Sivanathan, and A. D. Galinsky, "Vicarious Entrapment: Your Sunk Costs, My Escalation of Commitment," *Journal of Experimental Social Psychology* 45, no. 6 (2009): 1238–44.

60. D. Ghosh, "De-Escalation Strategies: Some Experimental Evidence," *Behavioral Research in Accounting* 9 (1997): 88–112.

61. M. I. Stein, "Creativity and Culture," *Journal of Psychology* 36 (1953): 311–22; M. A. Runco and G. J. Jaeger, "The Standard Definition of Creativity," *Creativity Research Journal* 24, no. 1 (2012): 92–96.

62. G. Wallas, *The Art of Thought* (London: Jonathan Cape, 1926). For recent applications of Wallas's classic model, see T. Kristensen, "The Physical Context of Creativity," *Creativity and Innovation Management* 13, no. 2 (2004): 89–96; U. E. Haner, "Spaces for Creativity and Innovation in Two Established Organizations," *Creativity and Innovation Management* 14, no. 3 (2005): 288–98.

63. R. S. Nickerson, "Enhancing Creativity," in *Handbook of Creativity,* ed. R. J. Sternberg (New York: Cambridge University Press, 1999), 392–430.

64. For a thorough discussion of illumination or insight, see R. J. Sternberg and J. E. Davidson, *The Nature of Insight* (Cambridge, MA: MIT Press, 1995).

65. *Big Demands and High Expectations*, The Deloitte Millennial Survey (New York: Deloitte Touche Tohmatsu, January 2014); *Seeking Creative Candidates: Hiring for the Future* (San Jose, CA: Adobe, September 2014); Adobe, "New Adobe Study Uncovers Creativity Gap in Government," news release (San Jose, CA: Adobe, March 30, 2016); M. Hvisdos, "How to Foster Curiosity and Creativity in the Workplace," *Training*, June 8, 2016.

66. R. J. Sternberg and L. A. O'Hara, "Creativity and Intelligence," in *Handbook of Creativity*, ed. R. J. Sternberg (New York: Cambridge University Press, 1999), 251–72; S. Taggar, "Individual Creativity and Group Ability to Utilize Individual Creative Resources: A Multilevel Model," *Academy of Management Journal* 45 (2002): 315–30.

67. G. J. Feist, "The Influence of Personality on Artistic and Scientific Creativity," in *Handbook of Creativity*, ed. R. J. Sternberg (New York: Cambridge University Press, 1999), 273–96; T. Åsterbro, S. A. Jeffrey, and G. K. Adomdza, "Inventor Perseverance after Being Told to Quit: The Role of Cognitive Biases," *Journal of Behavioral Decision Making* 20 (2007): 253–72; J. S. Mueller, S. Melwani, and J. A. Goncalo, "The Bias against Creativity: Why People Desire but Reject Creative Ideas," *Psychological Science* 23, no. 1 (2012): 13–17.

68. R. W. Weisberg, "Creativity and Knowledge: A Challenge to Theories," in *Handbook of Creativity*, ed. R. J. Sternberg (New York: Cambridge University Press, 1999), 226–50.

69. E. Dane, "Reconsidering the Trade-Off between Expertise and Flexibility: A Cognitive Entrenchment Perspective," *Academy of Management Review* 35, no. 4 (2010): 579–603; R. I. Sutton, *Weird Ideas That Work* (New York: Free Press, 2002), 53–54, 121.

70. G. J. Feist, "The Influence of Personality on Artistic and Scientific Creativity," in *Handbook of Creativity*, ed. R. J. Sternberg (New York: Cambridge University Press, 1999), 273–96; C. E. Shalley, J. Zhou, and G. R. Oldham, "The Effects of Personal and Contextual Characteristics on Creativity: Where Should We Go from Here?," *Journal of Management* 30, no. 6 (2004): 933–58; S. J. Dollinger, K. K. Urban, and T. A. James, "Creativity and Openness to Experience: Validation of Two Creative Product Measures," *Creativity Research Journal* 16, no. 1 (2004): 35–47; T. S. Schweizer, "The Psychology of Novelty-Seeking, Creativity and Innovation: Neurocognitive Aspects within a Work-Psychological Perspective," *Creativity and Innovation Management* 15, no. 2 (2006): 164–72; S. Acar and M. A. Runco, "Creative Abilities: Divergent Thinking," in *Handbook of Organizational Creativity*, ed. M. Mumford (Waltham, MA: Academic Press, 2012), 115–39.

71. C. E. Shalley, J. Zhou, and G. R. Oldham, "The Effects of Personal and Contextual Characteristics on Creativity: Where Should We Go from Here?," *Journal of Management* 30, no. 6 (2004): 933–58; S. J. Dollinger, K. K. Urban, and T. A. James, "Creativity and Openness to Experience: Validation of Two Creative Product Measures," *Creativity Research Journal* 16, no. 1 (2004): 35–47; T. M. Amabile et al., "Leader Behaviors and the Work Environment for Creativity: Perceived Leader Support," *The Leadership Quarterly* 15, no. 1 (2004): 5–32; S. T. Hunter, K. E. Bedell, and M. D. Mumford, "Climate for Creativity: A Quantitative Review," *Creativity Research Journal* 19, no. 1 (2007): 69–90; T. C. DiLiello and J. D. Houghton, "Creative Potential and Practised Creativity: Identifying Untapped Creativity in Organizations," *Creativity and Innovation Management* 17, no. 1 (2008): 37–46.

72. "BNY Mellon Looks to Tap in to UK Startup Culture with New EMEA Innovation Centre," *Finextra*, November 11, 2015; S. Kumar, "Relaunching Innovation: Lessons from Silicon Valley," *Banking Perspective*, March 2016, 18–23; BNY Mellon, "Rewarding 'Intrapreneurship,'" BNY Mellon, 2016, http://www.bnymellon.com/us/en/who-we-are/people-report/lead/rewarding-intrapreneurship.jsp (accessed April 26, 2016).

73. R. Westwood and D.R. Low, "The Multicultural Muse: Culture, Creativity and Innovation," *International Journal of Cross Cultural Management* 3, no. 2 (2003): 235–59.

74. T. M. Amabile, "Motivating Creativity in Organizations: On Doing What You Love and Loving What You Do," *California Management Review* 40 (1997): 39–58; A. Cummings and G. R. Oldham, "Enhancing Creativity: Managing Work Contexts for the High Potential Employee," *California Management Review*, no. 40 (1997): 22–38; F. Coelho and M. Augusto, "Job Characteristics and the Creativity of Frontline Service Employees," *Journal of Service Research* 13, no. 4 (2010): 426–38.

75. T. M. Amabile, "Changes in the Work Environment for Creativity during Downsizing," *Academy of Management Journal* 42 (1999): 630–40.

76. J. Moultrie et al., "Innovation Spaces: Towards a Framework for Understanding the Role of the Physical Environment in Innovation," *Creativity & Innovation Management* 16, no. 1 (2007): 53–65.

77. J. M. Howell and K. Boies, "Champions of Technological Innovation: The Influence of Contextual Knowledge, Role Orientation, Idea Generation, and Idea Promotion on Champion Emergence," *The Leadership Quarterly* 15, no. 1 (2004): 123–43; C. E. Shalley, J. Zhou, and G. R. Oldham, "The Effects of Personal and Contextual Characteristics on Creativity: Where Should We Go from Here?," *Journal of Management* 30, no. 6 (2004): 933–58; S. J. Dollinger, K. K. Urban, and T. A. James, "Creativity and Openness to Experience: Validation of Two Creative Product Measures," *Creativity Research Journal* 16, no. 1 (2004): 35–47; S. Powell, "The Management and Consumption of Organisational Creativity," *Journal of Consumer Marketing* 25, no. 3 (2008): 158–66.

78. A. Hiam, "Obstacles to Creativity—and How You Can Remove Them," *Futurist* 32 (1998): 30–34.

79. M. A. West, *Developing Creativity in Organizations* (Leicester, UK: BPS Books, 1997), 33–35.

80. For discussion of how play affects creativity, see S. Brown, *Play: How It Shapes the Brain, Opens the Imagination, and Invigorates the Soul* (New York: Avery, 2009); C. Mainemelis and D. D. Dionysiou, "Play, Flow, and Timelessness," in *The Oxford Handbook of Creativity, Innovation, and Entrepreneurship*, ed. C. Shalley, M. Hitt, and J. Zhou (New York: Oxford University Press, 2015), 121–40.

81. T. Ritchey, *Wicked Problems—Social Messes: Decision Support Modelling with Morphological Analysis*, Risk, Governance and Society (Berlin: Springer-Verlag, 2011); S. Seidenstricker and C. Linder, "A Morphological Analysis-Based Creativity Approach to Identify and Develop Ideas for BMI: A Case Study of a High-Tech Manufacturing Company," *International Journal of Entrepreneurship and Innovation Management* 18, no. 5–6 (2014): 409–24.

82. A. Hargadon and R. I. Sutton, "Building an Innovation Factory," *Harvard Business Review* 78 (2000): 157–66; T. Kelley, *The Art of Innovation* (New York: Currency Doubleday, 2001), 158–62; P. F. Skilton and K. J. Dooley, "The Effects of Repeat Collaboration on Creative Abrasion," *Academy of Management Review* 35, no. 1 (2010): 118–34.

83. C. Meinel and L. Leifer, "Introduction—Design Thinking Is Mainly about Building Innovators," in *Design Thinking Research: Building Innovators*, ed. H. Plattner, C. Meinel, and L. Leifer (Cham, Switzerland: Springer International, 2015), 1–11.

84. E. Köppen and C. Meinel, "Empathy Via Design Thinking: Creation of Sense and Knowledge," in *Design Thinking Research: Building Innovators*, ed. H. Plattner, C. Meinel, and L. Leifer (Cham, Switzerland: Springer International, 2015), 15–28.

85. J. Kolko, "Design Thinking Comes of Age," *Harvard Business Review* 93, no. 9 (2015): 66–71; C. Vetterli et al., "How Deutsche Bank's IT Division Used Design Thinking to Achieve Customer Proximity," *MIS Quarterly Executive* 15, no. 1 (2016): 37–53.

86. M. Fenton-O'Creevy, "Employee Involvement and the Middle Manager: Saboteur or Scapegoat?," *Human Resource Management Journal*, no. 11 (2001): 24–40. Also see V. H. Vroom and A. G. Jago, *The New Leadership: Managing Participation in Organizations* (Englewood Cliffs, NJ: Prentice Hall, 1988).

87. V. H. Vroom and A. G. Jago, *The New Leadership: Managing Participation in Organizations* (Englewood Cliffs, NJ: Prentice Hall, 1988).

88. Some of the early OB writing on employee involvement includes C. Argyris, *Personality and Organization* (New York: Harper & Row, 1957); D. McGregor, *The Human Side of Enterprise* (New York: McGraw-Hill, 1960); R. Likert, *New Patterns of Management* (New York: McGraw-Hill, 1961).

89. A. G. Robinson and D. M. Schroeder, *Ideas Are Free* (San Francisco: Berrett-Koehler, 2004).

90. R. J. Ely and D. A. Thomas, "Cultural Diversity at Work: The Effects of Diversity Perspectives on Work Group Processes and Outcomes," *Administrative Science Quarterly* 46 (2001): 229–73; E. Mannix and M. A. Neale, "What Differences Make a Difference?: The Promise and Reality of Diverse Teams in Organizations," *Psychological Science in the Public Interest* 6, no. 2 (2005): 31–55.

91. D. Berend and J. Paroush, "When Is Condorcet's Jury Theorem Valid?," *Social Choice and Welfare* 15, no. 4 (1998): 481–88.

92. This quotation has a long and convoluted history. It has been attributed (incorrectly) to Benjamin Franklin and to Native Americans. The quotation stated here was popular in education during the 1960s and is cited in the 1975 source below. However, this quotation is almost certainly an adaptation of writing by Chinese Confucian philosopher Xun Kuang (circa 250 BC). A simplified version of his original statement is: "I hear and I forget; I see and I remember; I do and I understand." R. E. Keeton, "Tell Me, Show Me, Involve Me," *Learning and the Law* 2 (1975): 16–21, 64–65.

93. K. T. Dirks, L. L. Cummings, and J. L. Pierce, "Psychological Ownership in Organizations: Conditions under Which Individuals Promote and Resist Change," *Research in Organizational Change and Development*, no. 9 (1996): 1–23; J. P. Walsh and S. F. Tseng, "The Effects of Job Characteristics on Active Effort at Work," *Work & Occupations* 25, no. 1 (1998): 74–96; B. Scott-Ladd and V. Marshall, "Participation in Decision Making: A Matter of Context?," *Leadership & Organization Development Journal* 25, no. 8 (2004): 646–62.

94. V. H. Vroom and A. G. Jago, *The New Leadership: Managing Participation in Organizations* (Englewood Cliffs, NJ: Prentice Hall, 1988).

PART 3

7 | Team Dynamics

©Moopixel/Shutterstock

Learning Objectives

After you read this chapter, you should be able to:

LO7-1 Explain why employees join informal groups, and discuss the benefits and limitations of teams.

LO7-2 Outline the team effectiveness model and discuss how task characteristics, team size, and team composition influence team effectiveness.

LO7-3 Discuss how the four team processes—team development, norms, cohesion, and trust—influence team effectiveness.

LO7-4 Discuss the characteristics and factors required for the success of self-directed teams and virtual (remote) teams.

LO7-5 Identify four constraints on team decision making and discuss the advantages and disadvantages of four structures aimed at improving team decision making.

Buurtzorg Nederland employs approximately 8,000 professionals (mostly registered nurses) in more than 700 self-directed teams across the Netherlands. "There are no managers to call for help or to take responsibility; teams resolve issues for themselves," observes a British nurse who recently studied the nonprofit community health care organization's team structure. In fact, the company's motto is (translated): "How do you manage professionals? You don't!" The head office has only 45 people in administration and another 15 coaches to help teams improve their work relationships.

Each team consists of up to 12 nurses responsible for between 50 and 60 home care patients, most of whom are elderly, disabled, or terminally ill. Patients are usually served by a subteam of employees rather than by one team member alone. Team members have considerable autonomy to care for patients. Issues are discussed and creatively resolved by team members at weekly meetings.

Team members also use the company's secure social network system to share information and solutions with other Buurtzorg teams.

Buurtzorg measures performance at the team level, including patient satisfaction, work efficiency, and cost savings. Every employee can view a dashboard that provides feedback on the team's performance compared with other teams across the organization. Independent studies have reported that the company's self-directed teams are significantly more cost-efficient than traditional (mostly nonteam) services, even though Buurtzorg employees have higher education and more training. Buurtzorg's employees also enjoy the team structure. The company has been the top employer in the Netherlands for several consecutive years.[1]

Teamwork is woven into the organizational structure at Buurtzorg Nederland. Why are teams so important at this company and many others, and how can organizations strengthen their potential for organizational effectiveness? We find the answers to these and other questions in this chapter on team dynamics. This chapter begins by defining *teams,* examining the reasons why organizations rely on teams, and explaining why people join informal groups in organizational settings. A large segment of this chapter examines a model of team effectiveness, which includes team and organizational environment; team design; and the team processes of development, norms, cohesion, and trust. We then turn our attention to two specific types of teams: self-directed teams and virtual (also called remote) teams. The final section of this chapter looks at the challenges and strategies for making better decisions in teams.

LO7-1 Explain why employees join informal groups, and discuss the benefits and limitations of teams.

TEAMS AND INFORMAL GROUPS

Teams are groups of two or more people who interact with and influence each other, are mutually accountable for achieving common goals associated with organizational objectives, and perceive themselves as a social entity within an organization.[2]

This definition has a few important components worth repeating. First, all teams exist to fulfill some purpose, such as creating an industrial mold, assembling a product, designing a new social welfare program, or making an important decision. Second, team members are held together by their interdependence and need for collaboration to achieve common goals. All teams require some form of communication so that members can coordinate and share common objectives. Third, team members influence each other, although some members may be more influential than others regarding the team's goals and activities. Finally, a team exists when its members perceive themselves to be a team. They feel connected to each other through a common interest or purpose.

There are many types of teams in organizations, and each type can be distinguished by three characteristics: team permanence, skill diversity, and authority dispersion (see Exhibit 7.1).[3] Team permanence refers to how long that type of team usually exists. Accounting, marketing, and other departments are usually long-lasting structures, so these teams have high permanence. In contrast, task forces usually have low permanence because most are formed temporarily to solve a problem, realize an opportunity, or design a product or service. An emerging trend is the formation of teams that exist even more briefly, sometimes only for one eight-hour shift.[4]

A second distinguishing characteristic is the team's skill diversity. A team has high skill diversity when its members possess different skills and knowledge, whereas low diversity exists when team members have similar abilities and, therefore, are interchangeable. Most functional departments have low skill diversity because they organize employees around their common

Exhibit 7.1 Team Permanence, Skill Diversity, and Authority Dispersion for Selected Team Types

Team Type	Description	Typical Characteristics
Departmental teams	Teams that consist of employees who have similar or complementary skills and are located in the same unit of a functional structure; usually minimal task interdependence because each person works with clients or with employees in other departments.	*Team permanence:* High—departments continue indefinitely. *Skill diversity:* Low to medium—departments are often organized around common skills (e.g., accounting staff located in the accounting department). *Authority dispersion:* Low—departmental power is usually concentrated in the departmental manager.
Self-directed teams	Teams whose members are organized around work processes that complete an entire piece of work requiring several interdependent tasks and have substantial autonomy over the execution of those tasks (i.e., they usually control inputs, flow, and outputs with little or no supervision).	*Team permanence:* High—teams are usually assigned indefinitely to a specific cluster of production or service activities. *Skill diversity:* Medium to high—members typically perform different tasks requiring diverse skill sets, but cross-training can somewhat reduce skill diversity. *Authority dispersion:* High—team members share power, usually with limited hierarchical authority.
Task force (project) teams	Cross-functional teams whose members are usually drawn from several disciplines to solve a specific problem, realize an opportunity, or design a product or service.	*Team permanence:* Low—teams typically disband on completion of a specific project. *Skill diversity:* Medium to high—members are typically drawn from several functional specializations associated with the complexity of the problem or opportunity. *Authority dispersion:* Medium—teams often have someone with formal authority (project leader), but members also have moderate power due to their expertise and functional representation.

skill sets (e.g., people with accounting expertise are located in the accounting department). In contrast, self-directed teams, which we discuss later in this chapter, are responsible for producing an entire product or service, which usually requires members with dissimilar skills and knowledge to perform the diverse tasks in that work. Cross-training increases interchangeability of team members to some extent, but moderately high skill diversity is still likely where the team's work is complex.

Authority dispersion, the third distinguishing characteristic of teams, refers to the degree to which decision-making responsibility is distributed throughout the team (high dispersion) or is vested in one or a few members of the team (low dispersion). Departmental teams tend to have low authority dispersion because power is somewhat concentrated in a formal manager. Self-directed teams usually have high authority dispersion because the entire team makes key decisions and hierarchical authority is limited.

Informal Groups

This chapter mainly focuses on formal teams, but employees also belong to informal groups. All teams are groups; however, many groups do not satisfy our definition of teams. Groups include people assembled together, whether or not they have any interdependence or organizationally focused objective. The friends you meet for lunch are an *informal group*, but they wouldn't be called a team because they have little or no interdependence (each

person could just as easily eat lunch alone) and no organizationally mandated purpose. Instead, they exist primarily for the benefit of their members.

Why do informal groups exist? One reason is that human beings are social animals. Our drive to bond is hardwired through

Informal groups exist in organizations because people have a drive to bond, define themselves partly by their social identity, need others to help accomplish nontask goals, and rely on social interaction to minimize stress.
©Jetta Productions/Blend Images/Getty Images

evolutionary development, creating a need to belong to informal groups.[5] This is evident by the fact that people invest considerable time and effort forming and maintaining social relationships without any special circumstances or ulterior motives. A second reason why people join informal groups is provided by social identity theory, which states that individuals define themselves by their group affiliations (see Chapter 3). Thus, we join groups—particularly those that are viewed favorably by others and that have values similar to our own—because they shape and reinforce our self-concept.[6]

A third reason why informal groups exist is that they accomplish personal objectives that cannot be achieved by individuals working alone. For example, employees will sometimes congregate to oppose organizational changes because this collective effort has more power than individuals who try to bring about change alone. These informal groups, called *coalitions*, are discussed in Chapter 9. A fourth explanation for informal groups is that we are comforted by the mere presence of other people and are therefore motivated to be near them in stressful situations. When in danger, people congregate near each other even though doing so serves no protective purpose. Similarly, employees tend to mingle more often after hearing rumors that the company

ADVANTAGES AND DISADVANTAGES OF TEAMS

Why are teams becoming so important in so many other companies around the world? The answer to this question has a long history.[9] Early research on British coal mining in the 1940s, the Japanese economic miracle of the 1970s, and a huge number of investigations since then have revealed that *under the right conditions*, teams make better decisions, develop better products and services, and create a more engaged workforce than do employees working alone.[10] Similarly, team members can quickly share information and coordinate tasks, whereas these processes are slower and prone to more errors in traditional departments led by supervisors. Teams typically provide superior customer service because they offer clients more knowledge and expertise than individuals working alone can offer.

Research on the changing nature of scientific research provides further evidence that teams outperform individuals, at least in complex work. A study of almost 20 million research

> ## Talent wins games, but teamwork and intelligence win championships.[11]
>
> —Michael Jordan, professional basketball player and sports executive

might be acquired by a competitor. As Chapter 4 explained, this social support minimizes stress by providing emotional and/or informational resources to buffer the stress experience.[7]

Informal Groups and Organizational Outcomes Informal groups are not created to serve corporate objectives, yet they have a profound influence on the organization and its employees. Informal groups potentially minimize employee stress because, as mentioned, group members provide emotional and informational social support. This stress-reducing capability of informal groups improves employee well-being, which potentially increases organizational effectiveness. Informal groups are also the backbone of *social networks*, which are important sources of trust building, information sharing, power, influence, and employee well-being in the workplace.[8] Chapter 8 describes the increasing popularity of enterprise social networking sites similar to Facebook and LinkedIn that encourage employees to form informal groups. Chapter 9 explains how social networks are a source of influence in organizational settings. Employees with strong informal networks tend to have more power and influence because they receive better information and preferential treatment from others and their talent is more visible to key decision makers.

publications reported that the percentage of journal articles written by teams rather than individuals has increased substantially over the past five decades. Team-based articles also had a much higher number of subsequent citations, suggesting that journal articles written by teams are superior to articles written by individuals.[12]

Teams are potentially more productive because, in many situations, their members are more motivated than when working alone.[13] There are three motivating forces at work. First, employees have a drive to bond and are motivated to fulfill the goals of groups to which they belong. This felt obligation is particularly strong when the employee's social identity is connected to the team. Second, members have high accountability to fellow team members, who monitor performance more closely than a traditional supervisor. This accountability is particularly strong when the team's performance depends on the worst performer, such as on an assembly line. Third, each team member creates a moving performance standard for the others. When a few employees complete tasks faster, other team members recognize that they could work faster. This benchmark effect also motivates because employees are often apprehensive that their performance will be compared to others' performance.

> ## Insanity in individuals is something rare—but in groups, parties, nations, and epochs, it is the rule.[96]
>
> —Friedrich Nietzsche

LO7-5 Identify four constraints on team decision making and discuss the advantages and disadvantages of four structures aimed at improving team decision making.

TEAM DECISION MAKING

Self-directed teams, virtual/remote teams, and practically all other groups are expected to make decisions. Teams are potentially more effective than individuals at identifying problems, choosing alternatives, and evaluating their decisions. To leverage these benefits, however, we first need to understand the constraints on effective team decision making. Then, we look at specific team structures that try to overcome these constraints.

Constraints on Team Decision Making

Anyone who has spent enough time in the workplace can recite several ways in which teams stumble in decision making. The four most common problems are time constraints, evaluation apprehension, pressure to conform, and overconfidence.

Time Constraints There's a saying that committees keep minutes and waste hours. This reflects the fact that teams take longer than individuals to make decisions.[93] Teams consume time organizing, coordinating, and maintaining relationships (i.e., process losses). Team members require time to build rapport, agree on rules and norms of behavior in the decision process, and understand each other's ideas.

Another time-related constraint in most team structures is that only one person can speak at a time.[94] This problem, known as **production blocking**, undermines idea generation in a few ways. First, team members need to listen in on the conversation to find an opportune time to speak up, but this monitoring makes it difficult for them to concentrate on their own ideas. Second, ideas are fleeting, so the longer they wait to speak up, the more likely their flickering ideas will die out. Third, team members might remember their fleeting thoughts by concentrating on them, but this causes them to pay less attention to the conversation. By ignoring what others are saying, team members miss other potentially good ideas.

Evaluation Apprehension Team members are often reluctant to mention ideas that seem silly because they believe (often correctly) that other team members are silently evaluating them.[95] This **evaluation apprehension** is based on the individual's desire to create a favorable self-presentation and need to protect self-esteem. It is most common when meetings are attended by people with different levels of status or expertise or when members formally evaluate each other's performance throughout the year (as in 360-degree feedback). Creative ideas often sound bizarre or illogical when first presented, so evaluation apprehension tends to discourage employees from mentioning them in front of coworkers.

Pressure to Conform Team cohesion leads employees to conform to the team's norms. This control keeps the group organized around common goals, but it also may cause team members to suppress their dissenting opinions, particularly when a strong team norm is related to the issue. When someone does state a point of view that violates the majority opinion, other members might punish the violator or try to persuade him or her that the opinion is incorrect. Conformity also can be subtle. To some extent, we depend on the opinions that others hold to validate our own views. If coworkers don't agree with us, we begin to question our own opinions even without overt peer pressure.

Overconfidence (Inflated Team Efficacy) Teams are more successful when their members have collective confidence in how well they work together and the likely success of their team effort.[97] This **team efficacy** is similar to the power of individual self-efficacy, which we discussed in Chapter 3. High-efficacy teams set more challenging goals and are more motivated to achieve them, both of which increase team performance. Unfortunately, teams make worse decisions when they become overconfident and develop a false sense of invulnerability.[98] In other words, the team's efficacy far exceeds reality regarding its abilities and the favorableness of the situation. Overconfident teams are less vigilant when making decisions, partly because they have more positive than negative emotions and moods during these events. They also engage in less-constructive debate and are less likely to seek out or accept information located outside the team, both of which undermine the quality of team decisions.

Why do teams become overconfident? The main reason is a team-level variation of self-enhancement (see Chapter 3), whereby team members have a natural motivation to believe the team's capabilities and situation are above average. Overconfidence is more common in highly cohesive teams

> Creative ideas often sound bizarre or illogical when first presented, so evaluation apprehension tends to discourage employees from mentioning them in front of coworkers.

because people engage in self-enhancement for things that are important to them (such as a cohesive team). It is also stronger when the team has external threats or competition because these adversaries generate "us–them" differentiation. Team efficacy is further inflated by the mutually reinforcing beliefs among team members. We develop a clearer and higher opinion of the team when others echo that opinion.

Improving Creative Decision Making in Teams

Team decision making is fraught with problems, but several solutions also emerge from these bad-news studies. Team members need to be confident in their decision making but not so confident that they collectively feel invulnerable. This calls for team norms that encourage critical thinking as well as team membership with sufficient diversity. Checks and balances need to be in place to prevent the leader or other individuals from dominating the discussion. The team also should be large enough to possess the collective knowledge to resolve the problem yet small enough that the team doesn't consume too much time or restrict individual input.

Along with these general recommendations, OB studies have identified four team structures that encourage creativity in a team setting: brainstorming, brainwriting, electronic brainstorming, and nominal group technique:

- *Brainstorming*. **Brainstorming** is a team event in which participants try to think up as many ideas as possible.[99] The process consists of four rules to maximize the number and quality of ideas presented: (1) Speak freely—describe even the craziest ideas; (2) don't criticize others or their ideas; (3) provide as many ideas as possible—the quality of ideas increases with the quantity of ideas; and (4) build on the ideas that others have presented. Brainstorming rules potentially increase divergent thinking and minimize evaluation apprehension, but field research indicates that these benefits require an experienced facilitator and participants who work together in a supportive culture.[100]

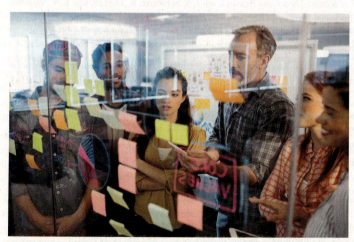

Brainstorming rules potentially increase divergent thinking and minimize evaluation apprehension, but field research indicates that these benefits require an experienced facilitator and participants who work together in a supportive culture.
©wavebreakmedia/Shutterstock

- *Brainwriting*. **Brainwriting** is a variation of brainstorming that minimizes the problem of production blocking by removing conversation during idea generation.[101] There are many forms of brainwriting, but they all have the common feature that individuals write down their ideas rather than verbally describe them. In one version, participants write their ideas on cards and place them in the center of the table. At any time, participants can pick up one or more cards in the center to spark their thinking or further build (piggyback) on those ideas. The limited research on brainwriting suggests that it produces more and better-quality ideas than brainstorming due to the lack of production blocking.

- *Electronic Brainstorming*. **Electronic brainstorming** is similar to brainwriting but uses computer technology rather than handwritten cards to document and share ideas. After receiving the question or issue, participants enter their ideas using special computer software. The ideas are distributed anonymously to other participants, who are encouraged to piggyback on those ideas. Team members eventually vote electronically on the ideas presented. Face-to-face discussion usually follows. Electronic brainstorming tends to minimize production blocking, evaluation apprehension, and conformity problems because participants' ideas are anonymous.[102] However, many executives consider electronic brainstorming too structured and technology-bound.

- *Nominal Group Technique*. Another variation of brainwriting, **nominal group technique**, adds a verbal element to the process.[103] The problem is described, team members silently and independently write down as many solutions as they can, then they describe their solutions to the other team members, usually in a round-robin format. As with brainstorming, there is no criticism or debate, just clarification. Finally, participants silently and independently rank-order or vote on each proposed solution. Nominal group technique has been used in real-world decisions and tends to improve the quality of ideas generated. However, production blocking and evaluation apprehension still occur to some extent. Training improves this structured approach to team decision making.[104]

production blocking a time constraint in team decision making due to the procedural requirement that only one person may speak at a time

evaluation apprehension a decision-making problem that occurs when individuals are reluctant to mention ideas that seem silly because they believe (often correctly) that other team members are silently evaluating them

team efficacy the collective belief among team members in the team's capability to successfully complete a task

brainstorming a freewheeling, face-to-face meeting where team members aren't allowed to criticize but are encouraged to speak freely, generate as many ideas as possible, and build on the ideas of others

brainwriting a variation of brainstorming whereby participants write (rather than speak about) and share their ideas

electronic brainstorming a form of brainstorming that relies on networked computers for submitting and sharing creative ideas

nominal group technique a variation of brainwriting consisting of three stages in which participants (1) silently and independently document their ideas, (2) collectively describe these ideas to the other team members without critique, and then (3) silently and independently evaluate the ideas presented the United States and similar cultures avoid silence and interpret those incidents as a sign of disagreement. Conversational overlaps are considered rude in Japan, but people in Brazil, France, and a few other countries tend to view them favorably as an indication of the other person's interest and involvement in the conversation. Meetings in countries that expect overlapping conversations can seem like a chaotic cacophony to those from other cultures.

Nonverbal Differences across Cultures

Nonverbal communication represents another potential area for misunderstanding across cultures. Many nonconscious or involuntary nonverbal cues (such as smiling) have the same meaning around the world, but deliberate gestures often have different interpretations. For example, most of us shake our head from side to side to say, "No," but a variation of head shaking means "I understand" to many people in India. Filipinos raise their eyebrows to give an affirmative answer, yet Arabs interpret this expression (along with clicking one's tongue) as a negative response. Most Americans are taught to maintain eye contact with the speaker to show interest and respect, whereas some North American native groups learn at an early age to show respect by looking down when an older or more senior person is talking to them.[66]

Gender Differences in Communication

Men and women have similar communication practices, but there are subtle distinctions that can occasionally lead to misunderstanding and conflict (see Exhibit 8.5).[67] One distinction is that men are more likely than women to view conversations as negotiations of relative status and power. They assert their power by directly giving advice to others (e.g., "You should do the following") and using combative language. There is also evidence that men dominate the talk time in conversations with women, as well as interrupt more and adjust their speaking style less than do women.

Men engage in more "report talk," in which the primary function of the conversation is impersonal and efficient information exchange. Women also do report talk, particularly when conversing with men, but conversations among women have a higher incidence of relationship building through "rapport talk."[68] Women use more tentative speech patterns, including modifiers ("It might be a good idea . . ."), disclaimers ("I'm not certain, but . . ."), and tag questions ("This works, doesn't it?"). They also make more use of indirect requests ("Do you think you should . . . ?"), apologize more often, and seek advice from others more quickly than do men. These gender differences are modest, however, mainly because men also use these speech patterns to some extent. Research does clearly indicate that women are more sensitive than men to nonverbal cues in face-to-face meetings. Together, these conditions can create communication conflicts. Women who describe problems get frustrated that men offer advice rather than rapport, whereas men become frustrated because they can't understand why women don't appreciate their advice.

LO8-5 Explain how to get your message across more effectively, and summarize the elements of active listening.

IMPROVING INTERPERSONAL COMMUNICATION

Effective interpersonal communication depends on the sender's ability to get the message across and the receiver's performance as an active listener. In this section, we outline these two essential features of effective interpersonal communication.

Exhibit 8.5 Gender Differences in Communication

When Men Communicate	When Women Communicate
• Report talk—give advice, assert power	• Rapport talk—relationship building
• Give advice directly	• Give advice indirectly
• Dominant conversation style	• Flexible conversation style
• Apologize less often	• Apologize more often
• Less sensitive to nonverbal cues	• More sensitive to nonverbal cues

Photos: ©McGraw-Hill Education

Getting Your Message Across

This chapter began with the statement that effective communication occurs when the other person receives and understands the message. This is more difficult to accomplish than most people believe. To get your message across to the other person, you first need to empathize with the receiver, such as being sensitive to words that may be ambiguous or trigger the wrong emotional response. Second, be sure that you repeat the message, such as by rephrasing the key points a couple of times. Third, your message competes with other messages and noise, so find a time when the receiver is less likely to be distracted by these other matters. Finally, if you are communicating bad news or criticism, focus on the problem, not the person.

Exhibit 8.6 Active Listening Process and Strategies

Sensing
• Postpone evaluation
• Avoid interruptions
• Maintain interest

Active Listening

Responding
• Show interest
• Clarify the message

Evaluating
• Empathize
• Organize information

> ❝Nature gave us one tongue, but two ears, so we may listen twice as much as we speak.❞[69]
>
> —Epictetus, Greek philosopher

Active Listening

Active listening is a process of mindfully sensing the sender's signals, evaluating them accurately, and responding appropriately. These three components of listening—sensing, evaluating, and responding—reflect the listener's side of the communication model described at the beginning of this chapter. Listeners receive the sender's signals, decode them as intended, and provide appropriate and timely feedback to the sender (see Exhibit 8.6). Active listeners constantly cycle through sensing, evaluating, and responding during the conversation and engage in various activities to improve these processes.[70]

• *Sensing.* Sensing is the process of receiving signals from the sender and paying attention to them. Active listeners improve sensing in three ways. First, they postpone evaluation by not forming an opinion until the speaker has finished. Second, they avoid interrupting the speaker's conversation. Third, they remain motivated to listen to the speaker.

• *Evaluating.* This component of listening includes understanding the message meaning, evaluating the message, and remembering the message. To improve their evaluation of the conversation, active listeners empathize with the speaker—they try to understand and be sensitive to the speaker's feelings, thoughts, and situation. Evaluation also improves by organizing the speaker's ideas during the communication episode.

• *Responding.* This third component of listening involves providing feedback to the sender, which motivates and directs the speaker's communication. Active listeners accomplish this by maintaining sufficient eye contact and sending back channel signals (e.g., "I see"), both of which show interest. They also respond by clarifying the message—rephrasing the speaker's ideas at appropriate breaks ("So you're saying that . . . ?").

IMPROVING COMMUNICATION THROUGHOUT THE HIERARCHY

So far, we have looked at micro-level issues in the communication process, namely, sending and receiving information between two employees or the informal exchanges of information across several people. But in this era where knowledge is competitive advantage, corporate leaders also need to maintain an open flow of communication up, down, and across the entire organization. In this section, we discuss three organizationwide communication strategies: workspace design, Internet-based communication, and direct communication with top management.

Workspace Design

To improve information sharing and create a more sociable work environment, many organizations have torn down the cubicle walls. In addition, they have incorporated informal spaces for small teams and happenstance gatherings.[71] The location and design of hallways, offices, cubicles, and communal areas (cafeterias, elevators) all shape to whom we speak as well as the frequency of that communication. Although these open-space arrangements increase the amount of face-to-face communication,

Communicating Up and Down the Hierarchy[75]

52% of 451 internal communications **professionals** surveyed across several countries say their biggest barrier to successful internal communication is the lack of line manager communication skills.

50% of 1,900 managers surveyed in Singapore, Hong Kong, and China say that lack of communication from their senior management is a key barrier to successful organizational change.

33% of more than 423,000 UK National Health System employees surveyed report good communication between senior managers and staff.

47% of 182,165 Canadian federal government employees surveyed say that essential information flows effectively from senior management to staff in their department.

60% of 407,789 U.S. federal government employees surveyed agree that their managers communicate the goals and priorities of their organization.

©Robert Churchill/Getty Images

they also potentially produce more noise, distractions, and loss of privacy.[72] Open workspaces can potentially have minimal noise problems because employees tend to speak more softly and white noise technology blocks out most voices. Still, the challenge is to increase social interaction without raising noise and distraction levels.

Another workspace strategy is to cloister employees into team spaces, but also encourage sufficient interaction with people from other teams. Pixar Animation Studios constructed its campus in Emeryville, California, with these principles in mind. The building encourages communication among team members. At the same time, the campus encourages happenstance interactions with people on other teams. Pixar executives call this the "bathroom effect" because team members must leave their isolated pods to fetch their mail, have lunch, or visit the restroom.[73]

Internet-Based Organizational Communication

For decades, employees received official company news through hard-copy newsletters and magazines. Some firms still use these communication devices, but most have supplemented or replaced them completely with web-based sources of information. The traditional company magazine is now typically published on web pages or distributed in PDF format. The advantage of these *e-zines* is that company news can be prepared and distributed quickly.

Employees are increasingly skeptical of information that has been screened and packaged by management, so a few companies such as IBM are encouraging employees to post their own news on internal blogs and wikis. Wikis are collaborative web spaces in which anyone in a group can write, edit, or remove material from the website. *Wikipedia*, the popular online encyclopedia, is a massive public example of a wiki. The accuracy of wikis depends on the quality of participants, but IBM experts say that errors are quickly identified by IBM's online community. Another concern is that wikis have failed to gain employee support, likely because wiki involvement takes time and the company does not reward or recognize those who provide this time to wiki development.[74]

management by walking around (MBWA)
a communication practice in which executives get out of their offices and learn from others in the organization through face-to-face dialogue

Direct Communication with Top Management

According to various surveys, effective organizational communication includes regular interaction directly between senior executives and employees further down the hierarchy. One form of direct communication is through town hall meetings, where executives brief a large gathering of staff on the company's current strategy and results. Although the communication is mostly from executives to employees, town hall meetings are more personal and credible than video or written channels. Also, these events usually provide some opportunity for employees to ask questions. Another strategy is for senior executives to hold roundtable forums with a small representation of employees, mainly to hear their opinions on various issues.

A less formal approach to direct communication is management by walking around (MBWA). Coined by people at Hewlett-Packard four decades ago, this is essentially the practice in which senior executives get out of their offices and casually chat with employees on a daily or regular basis.[76] Some executives, such as Jet.com cofounder and CEO Marc Lore, don't even have an office or a desk; they move around to different workspaces, which makes MBWA a natural part of their daily activity. These direct communication strategies

OB THEORY TO PRACTICE

Google Keeps Employees Informed through Weekly All-Hands TGIF Meetings

Google has becomes one of the world's largest technology companies, yet its cofounders still hold town hall sessions every Friday (called TGIF all-hands meetings). Thousands of employees attend in person or by video link; many others watch the recorded broadcast later. Google executives update employees on strategic and operational developments. They also devote half an hour to answering questions that employees submit through an online system. There are more questions than time allows, but Google has a transparent way to choose the best questions. Before each session, Google employees vote on which submitted questions are most important. The executives answer the questions that receive the most votes.[77]

©Tzido/iStock/Getty Images Plus

grapevine an unstructured and informal communication network founded on social relationships rather than organizational charts or job descriptions

potentially minimize filtering because executives listen directly to employees. They also help executives acquire a deeper meaning and quicker understanding of internal organizational problems. A third benefit of direct communication is that employees might have more empathy for decisions made further up the corporate hierarchy.

COMMUNICATING THROUGH THE GRAPEVINE

Organizational leaders may try their best to quickly communicate breaking news to employees through emails, Twitter tweets, and other direct formal channels, but employees still rely to some extent on the corporate **grapevine**. The grapevine is an unstructured and informal network founded on social relationships rather than organizational charts or job descriptions. What do employees think about the grapevine? Surveys have found that almost all employees use the grapevine, but very few of them prefer this source of information. In one survey, only one-third of employees believe grapevine information is credible. In other words, employees turn to the grapevine when they have few other options.[78]

Grapevine Characteristics

Research conducted several decades ago reported that the grapevine transmits information very rapidly in all directions throughout the organization. The typical pattern is a cluster chain, whereby a few people actively transmit information to many others. The grapevine works through informal social networks, so it is more active where employees have similar backgrounds and are able to communicate easily. Many rumors seem to have at least a kernel of truth, possibly because they are transmitted through media-rich communication channels (e.g., face-to-face) and employees are motivated to communicate effectively. Nevertheless, the grapevine distorts information by deleting fine details and exaggerating key points of the story.[79]

Some of these characteristics might still be true, but the grapevine almost certainly has changed as email, social networking sites, and Twitter tweets have replaced the traditional water cooler as sources of gossip. For example, several Facebook sites are unofficially themed around specific companies, allowing employees and customers to vent their complaints about the organization. Along with altering the speed and network of corporate grapevines, the Internet has expanded these networks around the globe, not just around the next cubicle.

Grapevine Benefits and Limitations

Should the grapevine be encouraged, tolerated, or quashed? The difficulty in answering this question is that the grapevine has both benefits and limitations.[80] One benefit, as was mentioned earlier, is that employees rely on the grapevine when information is not available through formal channels. It is also the main conduit through which organizational stories and other symbols of the organization's culture are communicated. A third benefit of the grapevine is that this social interaction relieves anxiety. This explains why rumor mills are most active during times of uncertainty.[81] Finally, the grapevine is associated with the drive to bond. Being a recipient of gossip is a sign of inclusion, according to evolutionary psychologists. Trying to quash the grapevine is, in some respects, an attempt to undermine the natural human drive for social interaction.[82]

While the grapevine offers these benefits, it is not a preferred communication medium. Grapevine information is sometimes so distorted that it escalates rather than reduces employee anxiety. Furthermore, employees develop more negative attitudes toward the organization when management is slower than the grapevine in communicating information. What should corporate leaders do with the grapevine? The best advice seems to be to listen to the grapevine as a signal of employee anxiety, then correct the cause of this anxiety. Some companies also listen to the grapevine and step in to correct blatant errors and fabrications. Most important, corporate leaders need to view the grapevine as a competitor and meet this challenge by directly informing employees of news before it spreads throughout the grapevine.

> The grapevine works through informal social networks, so it is more active where employees have similar backgrounds and are able to communicate easily.

Study Checklist

Connect® Management is available for *M Organizational Behavior.* Additional resources include:

✓ Interactive Applications:

- **Case Analysis:** Apply concepts within the context of a real-world situation.
- **Drag and Drop:** Work through an interactive example to test your knowledge of the concepts.
- **Video Case:** See management in action through interactive videos.

✓ **SmartBook™**—SmartBook is the first and only adaptive reading experience available today. Distinguishing what you know from what you don't, and honing in on concepts you are most likely to forget, SmartBook personalizes content for you in a continuously adapting reading experience. Reading is no longer a passive and linear experience, but an engaging and dynamic one where you are more likely to master and retain important concepts and go to class better prepared.

©Natthawat Jamnapa/123RF

Notes

1. A. H. Van de Ven, A. L. Delbecq, and R. Koenig Jr., "Determinants of Coordination Modes within Organizations," *American Sociological Review* 41, no. 2 (1976): 322–38; J. H. Gittell, R. Seidner, and J. Wimbush, "A Relational Model of How High-Performance Work Systems Work," *Organization Science* 21, no. 2 (2010): 490–506; R. Foy et al., "Meta-Analysis: Effect of Interactive Communication between Collaborating Primary Care Physicians and Specialists," *Annals of Internal Medicine* 152, no. 4 (2010): 247–58.

2. C. Barnard, *The Functions of the Executive* (Cambridge, MA: Harvard University Press, 1938), 82. Barnard's entire statement also refers to the other features of organizations that we describe in Chapter 1, namely that (a) people are willing to contribute their effort to the organization and (b) they have a common purpose.

3. M. T. Hansen, M. L. Mors, and B. Løvås, "Knowledge Sharing in Organizations: Multiple Networks, Multiple Phases," *Academy of Management Journal* 48, no. 5 (2005): 776–93; S. R. Murray and J. Peyrefitte, "Knowledge Type and Communication Media Choice in the Knowledge Transfer Process," *Journal of Managerial Issues* 19, no. 1 (2007): 111–33; S. L. Hoe and S. L. McShane, "Structural and Informal Knowledge Acquisition and Dissemination in Organizational Learning: An Exploratory Analysis," *Learning Organization* 17, no. 4 (2010): 364–86.

4. J. O'Toole and W. Bennis, "What's Needed Next: A Culture of Candor," *Harvard Business Review* 87, no. 6 (2009): 54–61.

5. W. J. L. Elving, "The Role of Communication in Organisational Change," *Corporate Communications* 10, no. 2 (2005): 129–38; P. M. Leonardi, T. B. Neeley, and E. M. Gerber, "How Managers Use Multiple Media: Discrepant Events, Power, and Timing in Redundant Communication," *Organization Science* 23, no. 1 (2012): 98–117; D. A. Tucker, P. Yeow, and G. T. Viki, "Communicating during Organizational Change Using Social Accounts: The Importance of Ideological Accounts," *Management Communication Quarterly* 27, no. 2 (2013): 184–209.

6. N. Ellemers, R. Spears, and B. Doosje, "Self and Social Identity," *Annual Review of Psychology* 53 (2002): 161–86; S. A. Haslam and S. Reicher, "Stressing the Group: Social Identity and the Unfolding Dynamics of Responses to Stress," *Journal of Applied Psychology* 91, no. 5 (2006): 1037–52; M. T. Gailliot and R. F. Baumeister, "Self-Esteem, Belongingness, and Worldview Validation: Does Belongingness Exert a Unique Influence Upon Self-Esteem?," *Journal of Research in Personality* 41, no. 2 (2007): 327–45.

7. A. M. Saks, K. L. Uggerslev, and N. E. Fassina, "Socialization Tactics and Newcomer Adjustment: A Meta-Analytic Review and Test of a Model," *Journal of Vocational Behavior* 70, no. 3 (2007): 413–46.

8. S. Cohen, "The Pittsburgh Common Cold Studies: Psychosocial Predictors of Susceptibility to Respiratory Infectious Illness," *International Journal of Behavioral Medicine* 12, no. 3 (2005): 123–31; B. N. Uchino, "Social Support and Health: A Review of Physiological Processes Potentially Underlying Links to Disease Outcomes," *Journal of Behavioral Medicine* 29, no. 4 (2006): 377–87.

9. C. E. Shannon and W. Weaver, *The Mathematical Theory of Communication* (Urbana: University of Illinois Press, 1949); R. M. Krauss and S. R. Fussell, "Social Psychological Models of Interpersonal Communication," in *Social Psychology: Handbook of Basic Principles,* ed. E. T. Higgins and A. Kruglanski (New York: Guilford Press, 1996), 655–701.

10. R. Cross and R. J. Thomas, *Driving Results through Social Networks: How Top Organizations Leverage Networks for Performance and Growth* (San Francisco: Jossey-Bass, 2009); R. McDermott and D. Archibald, "Harnessing Your Staff's Informal Networks," *Harvard Business Review* 88, no. 3 (2010): 82–89; J. Nieves and J. Osorio, "The Role of Social Networks in Knowledge Creation," *Knowledge Management Research & Practice* 11, no. 1 (2013): 62–77.

11. P. Shachaf and N. Hara, "Behavioral Complexity Theory of Media Selection: A Proposed Theory for Global Virtual Teams," *Journal of Information Science* 33 (2007): 63–75.

12. One study found that email was the first or second choice for almost every situation (urgency, confidentiality, accountability, integrity, and social interaction). See P. Palvia et al., "Contextual Constraints in Media Choice: Beyond Information Richness," *Decision Support Systems* 51, no. 3 (2011): 657–70.

13. N. B. Ducheneaut and L. A. Watts, "In Search of Coherence: A Review of E-Mail Research," *Human-Computer Interaction* 20, no. 1–2 (2005): 11–48; R. S. Mano and G. S. Mesch, "E-Mail Characteristics, Work Performance and Distress," *Computers in Human Behavior* 26, no. 1 (2010): 61–69.

14. W. Lucas, "Effects of E-mail on the Organization," *European Management Journal* 16, no. 1 (1998): 18–30; G. de La Rupelle, C. Guthrie, and M. Kalika, "La relation entre l'intensité perçue d'utilisation de la messagerie électronique et la qualité de la relation hiérarchique," *Relations Industrielles* 70, no. 1 (2015): 157–85; C. M. Brotheridge, D. J. Neufeld, and B. Dyck, "Communicating Virtually in a Global Organization," *Journal of Managerial Psychology* 30, no. 8 (2015): 909–24.

15. N. Panteli, "Richness, Power Cues and Email Text," *Information & Management* 40, no. 2 (2002): 75–86; C. T. Carr and C. Stefaniak, "Sent from My iPhone: The Medium and Message as Cues of Sender Professionalism in Mobile Telephony," *Journal of Applied Communication Research* 40, no. 4 (2012): 403–24; D. C. DeAndrea, "Advancing Warranting Theory," *Communication Theory* 24, no. 2 (2014): 186–204; C. M. Brotheridge, D. J. Neufeld, and B. Dyck, "Communicating Virtually in a Global Organization," *Journal of Managerial Psychology* 30, no. 8 (2015): 909–24.

16. J. B. Walther et al., "Computer-Mediated Communication and the Reduction of Prejudice: A Controlled Longitudinal Field Experiment among Jews and Arabs in Israel," *Computers in Human Behavior* 52 (2015): 550–58.

17. J. Kruger et al., "Egocentrism over E-Mail: Can We Communicate as Well as We Think?," *Journal of Personality and Social Psychology* 89, no. 6 (2005): 925–36.

18. J. B. Walther, "Language and Communication Technology: Introduction to the Special Issue," *Journal of Language and Social Psychology* 23, no. 4 (2004): 384–96; J. B. Walther, T. Loh, and L. Granka, "Let Me Count the Ways: The Interchange of Verbal and Nonverbal Cues in Computer-Mediated and Face-to-Face Affinity," *Journal of Language and Social Psychology* 24, no. 1 (2005): 36–65; K. Byron, "Carrying Too Heavy a Load? The Communication and Miscommunication of Emotion by Email," *Academy of Management Review* 33, no. 2 (2008): 309–27; J. M. Whalen, P. M. Pexman, and A. J. Gill, "'Should Be Fun—Not!': Incidence and Marking of Nonliteral Language in E-Mail," *Journal of Language and Social Psychology* 28, no. 3 (2009): 263–80.

19. K. Byron, "Carrying Too Heavy a Load? The Communication and Miscommunication of Emotion by Email," *Academy of Management Review* 33, no. 2 (2008): 309–27.

20. G. Hertel, S. Geister, and U. Konradt, "Managing Virtual Teams: A Review of Current Empirical Research," *Human Resource Management Review* 15 (2005): 69–95; H. Lee, "Behavioral Strategies for Dealing with Flaming in an Online Forum," *The Sociological Quarterly* 46, no. 2 (2005): 385–403.

21. S. R. Barley, D. E. Meyerson, and S. Grodal, "E-Mail as a Source and Symbol of Stress," *Organization Science* 22, no. 4 (2011): 887–906; N. Sobotta and M. Hummel, "A Capacity Perspective on E-Mail Overload: How E-Mail Use Contributes to Information Overload" (paper presented at the 2015 48th Hawaii International Conference on System Sciences, January 5–8, 2015), 692–701.

22. The Radicati Group, *Email Statistics Report, 2014–2018* (Palo Alto, CA: April 2014); Symantec, *Symantec Intelligence Report* (Mountain View, CA: January 2014).

23. R. D. Waters et al., "Engaging Stakeholders through Social Networking: How Nonprofit Organizations Are Using Facebook," *Public Relations Review* 35, no. 2 (2009): 102–106; J. Cunningham, "New Workers, New Workplace? Getting the Balance Right," *Strategic Direction* 26, no. 1 (2010): 5; A. M. Kaplan and M. Haenlein, "Users of the World, Unite! The Challenges and Opportunities of Social Media," *Business Horizons* 53, no. 1 (2010): 59–68.

24. J. H. Kietzmann et al., "Social Media? Get Serious! Understanding the Functional Building Blocks of Social Media," *Business Horizons* 54, no. 3 (2011): 241–51; J. W. Treem and P. M. Leonardi, "Social Media Use in Organizations: Exploring the Affordances of Visibility, Editability, Persistence, and Association," *Communication Yearbook* 36 (2012): 143–89.

25. "The Coworker Network," *Kellogg Insight,* June 3, 2013; W. van Zoonen, T. G. L. A. van der Meer, and J. W. M. Verhoeven, "Employees Work-Related Social-Media Use: His Master's Voice," *Public Relations Review* 40, no. 5 (2014): 850–52; G. Martin, E. Parry, and P. Flowers, "Do Social Media Enhance Constructive Employee Voice All of the Time or Just Some of the Time?," *Human Resource Management Journal* 25, no. 4 (2015): 541–62; W. van Zoonen, J. W. M. Verhoeven, and R. Vliegenthart, "How Employees Use Twitter to Talk about Work: A Typology of Work-Related Tweets," *Computers in Human Behavior* 55, pt. A (2016): 329–39.

26. P. W. Cardon and B. Marshall, "The Hype and Reality of Social Media Use for Work Collaboration and Team Communication," *International Journal of Business Communication* 52, no. 3 (2015): 273–93; C. Li, "Why No One Uses the Corporate Social Network," *Harvard Business Review Online,* April 7, 2015, https://hbr.org/2015/04/why-no-one-uses-the-corporate-socialnetwork.

27. M. Göhring and K. Perschke, "Internal Community Management @ Bosch," in *KnowTech 2014* (Hanau, Germany: BitKom KnowTech, 2014); R. Roewekamp, "Bosch Bricht Ins Vernetzte Arbeiten Auf (Bosch Launches into Connected Work)," *CIO* (German edition), November 19, 2015; Robert Bosch GmbH, "Boosting Agility on the Job: Bosch Invests in the Workplace of the Future," news release (Stuttgart, Germany: ENP Newswire, June 15, 2015); J. Heinz and A. Kumar, "Enterprise Social Networks—The Nerve-Center of Future Organizations," in *Connect2016* (Orlando, FL: IBM, 2016).

28. D. G. Leathers and M. H. Eaves, *Successful Nonverbal Communication: Principles and Applications,* 4th ed. (New York: Routledge, 2015).

29. L. Z. Tiedens and A. R. Fragale, "Power Moves: Complementarity in Dominant and Submissive Nonverbal Behavior," *Journal of Personality and Social Psychology* 84, no. 3 (2003): 558–68.

30. CareerBuilder, "Careerbuilder Releases Annual List of Strangest Interview and Body Language Mistakes," news release (Chicago: CareerBuilder, January 12, 2017).

31. P. Ekman and E. Rosenberg, *What the Face Reveals: Basic and Applied Studies of Spontaneous Expression Using the Facial Action Coding System* (Oxford, UK: Oxford University Press, 1997); P. Winkielman and K. C. Berridge, "Unconscious Emotion," *Current Directions in Psychological Science* 13, no. 3 (2004): 120–23.

32. J. Champy, *What I Learned from Peter Drucker* (Boston: New Word City, 2010), chap. 4.

33. W. J. Becker and R. Cropanzano, "Organizational Neuroscience: The Promise and Prospects of an Emerging Discipline," *Journal of Organizational Behavior* 31, no. 7 (2010): 1055–59.

34. M. Sonnby-Borgstrom, P. Jonsson, and O. Svensson, "Emotional Empathy as Related to Mimicry Reactions at Different Levels of Information Processing," *Journal of Nonverbal Behavior* 27 (2003): 3–23; S. K. Johnson, "I Second That Emotion: Effects of Emotional Contagion and Affect at Work on Leader and Follower

Outcomes," *Leadership Quarterly* 19, no. 1 (2008): 1–19; V. Vijayalakshmi and S. Bhattacharyya, "Emotional Contagion and Its Relevance to Individual Behavior and Organizational Processes: A Position Paper," *Journal of Business and Psychology* 27, no. 3 (2012): 363–74.

35. J. R. Kelly and S. G. Barsade, "Mood and Emotions in Small Groups and Work Teams," *Organizational Behavior and Human Decision Processes* 86 (2001): 99–130; T. L. Chartrand and J. L. Lakin, "The Antecedents and Consequences of Human Behavioral Mimicry," *Annual Review of Psychology* 64, no. 1 (2013): 285–308.

36. A. R. Dennis, R. M. Fuller, and J. S. Valacich, "Media, Tasks, and Communication Processes: A Theory of Media Synchronicity," *MIS Quarterly* 32, no. 3 (2008): 575–600; S. Taipale, "Synchronicity Matters: Defining the Characteristics of Digital Generations," *Information, Communication & Society* 19, no. 1 (2016): 80–94.

37. R. E. Rice, "Media Appropriateness: Using Social Presence Theory to Compare Traditional and New Organizational Media," *Human Communication Research* 19, no. 4 (1993): 451–84; D. Gooch and L. Watts, "The Impact of Social Presence on Feelings of Closeness in Personal Relationships," *Interacting with Computers* 27, no. 6 (2015): 661–74.

38. J. Fulk, "Social Construction of Communication Technology," *Academy of Management Journal* 36, no. 5 (1993): 921–50; L. K. Treviño, J. Webster, and E. W. Stein, "Making Connections: Complementary Influences on Communication Media Choices, Attitudes, and Use," *Organization Science* 11, no. 2 (2000): 163–82; B. van den Hooff, J. Groot, and S. de Jonge, "Situational Influences on the Use of Communication Technologies," *Journal of Business Communication* 42, no. 1 (2005): 4–27; J. W. Turner et al., "Exploring the Dominant Media: How Does Media Use Reflect Organizational Norms and Affect Performance?," *Journal of Business Communication* 43, no. 3 (2006): 220–50; M. B. Watson-Manheim and F. Bélanger, "Communication Media Repertoires: Dealing with the Multiplicity of Media Choices," *MIS Quarterly* 31, no. 2 (2007): 267–93.

39. Z. Lee and Y. Lee, "Emailing the Boss: Cultural Implications of Media Choice," *IEEE Transactions on Professional Communication* 52, no. 1 (2009): 61–74; D. Holtbrügge, A. Weldon, and H. Rogers, "Cultural Determinants of Email Communication Styles," *International Journal of Cross Cultural Management* 13, no. 1 (2013): 89–110.

40. R. C. King, "Media Appropriateness: Effects of Experience on Communication Media Choice," *Decision Sciences* 28, no. 4 (1997): 877–910.

41. A. K. C. Au and D. K. S. Chan, "Organizational Media Choice in Performance Feedback: A Multifaceted Approach," *Journal of Applied Social Psychology* 43, no. 2 (2013): 397–407; K. K. Stephens, A. K. Barrett, and M. J. Mahometa, "Organizational Communication in Emergencies: Using Multiple Channels and Sources to Combat Noise and Capture Attention," *Human Communication Research* 39, no. 2 (2013): 230–51.

42. K. Griffiths, "KPMG Sacks 670 Employees by E-Mail," *The Independent* (London), November 5, 2002, 19; "Shop Worker Sacked by Text Message," *The Post* (Claremont/Nedlands, Western Australia), July 28, 2007, 1, 78.

43. R. L. Daft and R. H. Lengel, "Information Richness: A New Approach to Managerial Behavior and Organization Design," *Research in Organizational Behavior* 6 (1984): 191–233; R. H. Lengel and R. L. Daft, "The Selection of Communication Media as an Executive Skill," *Academy of Management Executive* 2 (1988): 225–32.

44. H. Rodriguez et al., "Huddle Up!: The Adoption and Use of Structured Team Communication for VA Medical Home Implementation," *Health Care Management Review* 40, no. 4 (2015): 286–99; R. W. Quinn and J. S. Bunderson, "Could We Huddle on This Project? Participant Learning in Newsroom Conversations," *Journal of Management* 42, no. 2 (2016): 386–418.

45. R. E. Rice, "Task Analyzability, Use of New Media, and Effectiveness: A Multi-Site Exploration of Media Richness," *Organization Science* 3 (1992): 475–500.

46. V. W. Kupritz and E. Cowell, "Productive Management Communication: Online and Face-to-Face," *Journal of Business Communication* 48, no. 1 (2011): 54–82.

47. R. F. Otondo et al., "The Complexity of Richness: Media, Message, and Communication Outcomes," *Information & Management* 45, no. 1 (2008): 21–30.

48. N. L. Reinsch Jr., J. W. Turner, and C. H. Tinsley, "Multicommunicating: A Practice Whose Time Has Come?," *Academy of Management Review* 33, no. 2 (2008): 391–403; A. F. Cameron and J. Webster, "Multicommunicating: Juggling Multiple Conversations in the Workplace," *Information Systems Research* 24, no. 2 (2013): 352–71.

49. S. Xu, Z. Wang, and P. David, "Media Multitasking and Well-Being of University Students," *Computers in Human Behavior* 55, pt. A (2016): 242–50.

50. J. R. Carlson and R. W. Zmud, "Channel Expansion Theory and the Experiential Nature of Media Richness Perceptions," *Academy of Management Journal* 42 (1999): 153–70; N. Kock, "Media Richness or Media Naturalness? The Evolution of Our Biological Communication Apparatus and Its Influence on Our Behavior toward E-Communication Tools," *IEEE Transactions on Professional Communication* 48, no. 2 (2005): 117–30.

51. V. W. Kupritz and E. Cowell, "Productive Management Communication: Online and Face-to-Face," *Journal of Business Communication* 48, no. 1 (2011): 54–82.

52. D. Muller, T. Atzeni, and F. Butera, "Coaction and Upward Social Comparison Reduce the Illusory Conjunction Effect: Support for Distraction–Conflict Theory," *Journal of Experimental Social Psychology* 40, no. 5 (2004): 659–65; L. P. Robert and A. R. Dennis, "Paradox of Richness: A Cognitive Model of Media Choice," *IEEE Transactions on Professional Communication* 48, no. 1 (2005): 10–21.

53. E. V. Wilson, "Perceived Effectiveness of Interpersonal Persuasion Strategies in Computer-Mediated Communication," *Computers in Human Behavior* 19, no. 5 (2003): 537–52; K. Sassenberg, M. Boos, and S. Rabung, "Attitude Change in Face-to-Face and Computer-Mediated Communication: Private Self-Awareness as Mediator and Moderator," *European Journal of Social Psychology* 35 (2005): 361–74; P. Di Blasio and L. Milani, "Computer-Mediated Communication and Persuasion: Peripheral vs. Central Route to Opinion Shift," *Computers in Human Behavior* 24, no. 3 (2008): 798–815.

54. J. Kruger et al., "Egocentrism over E-Mail: Can We Communicate as Well as We Think?," *Journal of Personality and Social Psychology* 89, no. 6 (2005): 925–36.

55. Most sources incorrectly attribute this famous quotation (usually with "accomplished" rather than "achieved") to the Irish playwright and social critic George Bernard Shaw. To the best of our knowledge, it was first uttered in the late 1950s by Joe Coffman, president of Tecnifax Corporation (which made visual education technology). Coffman held patents for specialized slide transparencies and related apparatus on overhead projectors. Given the company's products,

Coffman was also an enthusiast of visual and interpersonal communication. Twice each year at its head office in Holyoke, Massachusetts, Tecnifax held international seminars on communication practices. This quotation was originally published in a 1960 article summarizing a public health conference, during which one of the speakers credited Coffman as the originator of this quotation. There is one more twist to the origins of this quotation. Coffman may have adapted it from the following passage in William H. Whyte's 1950 *Fortune* magazine article on communication, which became one of *Fortune*'s most-read articles: "The great enemy of communication, we find, is the illusion of it." See W. H. Whyte, "Is Anybody Listening," *Fortune*, September 1950, 77-83, 167-78; "Web of Mutual Anticipations: Conference Report," *Public Health Reports* 75, no. 10 (1960): 927-32; D. M. Davis, *A Biased Biography: Mine* (Lincoln, NE: iUniverse, 2004); "The Biggest Problem in Communication Is the Illusion That It Has Taken Place," *Quote Investigator,* August 31, 2014, http://quoteinvestigator.com/2014/08/31/illusion/.

56. R. M. Krauss, "The Psychology of Verbal Communication," in *International Encyclopedia of the Social and Behavioral Sciences,* ed. N. Smelser and P. Baltes (London: Elsevier, 2002), 16161-65.

57. A. M. Carton, C. Murphy, and J. R. Clark, "A (Blurry) Vision of the Future: How Leader Rhetoric about Ultimate Goals Influences Performance," *Academy of Management Journal* 57, no. 6 (2014): 1544-70; P. D. Joshi et al., "Communicating with Distant Others: The Functional Use of Abstraction," *Social Psychological and Personality Science* 7, no. 1 (2016): 37-44.

58. D. Goleman, R. Boyatzis, and A. McKee, *Primal Leaders* (Boston: Harvard Business School Press, 2002), 92-95.

59. J. O'Toole and W. Bennis, "What's Needed Next: A Culture of Candor," *Harvard Business Review* 87, no. 6 (2009): 54-61.

60. T. W. Jackson and P. Farzaneh, "Theory-Based Model of Factors Affecting Information Overload," *International Journal of Information Management* 32, no. 6 (2012): 523-32.

61. A. G. Schick, L. A. Gordon, and S. Haka, "Information Overload: A Temporal Approach," *Accounting, Organizations & Society* 15 (1990): 199-220; A. Edmunds and A. Morris, "The Problem of Information Overload in Business Organisations: A Review of the Literature," *International Journal of Information Management* 20 (2000): 17-28; R. Pennington, "The Effects of Information Overload on Software Project Risk Assessment," *Decision Sciences* 38, no. 3 (2007): 489-526.

62. D. C. Thomas and K. Inkson, *Cultural Intelligence: People Skills for Global Business* (San Francisco: Berrett-Koehler, 2004), chap. 6; D. Welch, L. Welch, and R. Piekkari, "Speaking in Tongues," *International Studies of Management & Organization* 35, no. 1 (2005): 10-27.

63. T. Craig, "Different Strokes," *Personnel Today,* November 25, 2008, 190.

64. D. C. Barnlund, *Communication Styles of Japanese and Americans: Images and Realities* (Belmont, CA: Wadsworth, 1988); H. Yamada, *American and Japanese Business Discourse: A Comparison of Interaction Styles* (Norwood, NJ: Ablex, 1992), chap. 2; T. Hasegawa and W. B. Gudykunst, "Silence in Japan and the United States," *Journal of Cross-Cultural Psychology* 29, no. 5 (1998): 668-84; M. Fujio, "Silence during Intercultural Communication: A Case Study," *Corporate Communications* 9, no. 4 (2004): 331-39.

65. Adapted from M. Nakamoto, "Cross-Cultural Conversations," *Financial Times* (London), January 12, 2012, 16.

66. P. Harris and R. Moran, *Managing Cultural Differences* (Houston, TX: Gulf, 1987); H. Blagg, "A Just Measure of Shame?," *British Journal of Criminology* 37 (1997): 481-501; R. E. Axtell, *Gestures: The Do's and Taboos of Body Language around the World,* rev. ed. (New York: Wiley, 1998).

67. D. Tannen, *You Just Don't Understand: Men and Women in Conversation* (New York: Ballantine Books, 1990); J. L. Locke, *Duels and Duets: Why Men and Women Talk So Differently* (Cambridge, UK: Cambridge University Press, 2011); M. R. Atai and F. Chahkandi, "Democracy in Computer-Mediated Communication: Gender, Communicative Style, and Amount of Participation in Professional Listservs," *Computers in Human Behavior* 28, no. 3 (2012): 881-88; A. B. Hancock and B. A. Rubin, "Influence of Communication Partner's Gender on Language," *Journal of Language and Social Psychology* 34, no. 1 (2015): 46-64.

68. A. Mulac et al., "'Uh-Huh. What's That All About?' Differing Interpretations of Conversational Backchannels and Questions as Sources of Miscommunication across Gender Boundaries," *Communication Research* 25 (1998): 641-68; N. M. Sussman and D. H. Tyson, "Sex and Power: Gender Differences in Computer-Mediated Interactions," *Computers in Human Behavior* 16 (2000): 381-94; C. Leaper and R. D. Robnett, "Women Are More Likely Than Men to Use Tentative Language, Aren't They? A Meta-Analysis Testing for Gender Differences and Moderators," *Psychology of Women Quarterly* 35, no. 1 (2011): 129-42.

69. This quotation is varied slightly from the original translations by E. Carter, *All the Works of Epictetus, Which Are Now Extant,* 3rd ed., vol. 2 (London: J. and F. Rivington, 1768), 333; T. W. Higginson, *The Works of Epictetus* (Boston: Little, Brown, and Company, 1866), 428.

70. L. B. Comer and T. Drollinger, "Active Empathetic Listening and Selling Success: A Conceptual Framework," *Journal of Personal Selling & Sales Management* 19 (1999): 15-29; T. Drollinger, L. B. Comer, and P. T. Warrington, "Development and Validation of the Active Empathetic Listening Scale," *Psychology and Marketing* 23, no. 2 (2006): 161-80; P. JungKun et al., "The Role of Listening in E-Contact Center Customer Relationship Management," *Journal of Services Marketing* 29, no. 1 (2015): 49-58.

71. T. J. Allen, "Architecture and Communication among Product Development Engineers," *California Management Review* 49, no. 2 (2007): 23-41; M. C. Davis, D. J. Leach, and C. W. Clegg, "The Physical Environment of the Office: Contemporary and Emerging Issues," in *International Review of Industrial and Organizational Psychology 2011* (Wiley, 2011), 193-237; J. Kim and R. de Dear, "Workspace Satisfaction: The Privacy-Communication Trade-Off in Open-Plan Offices," *Journal of Environmental Psychology* 36 (2013): 18-26.

72. G. Evans and D. Johnson, "Stress and Open-Office Noise," *Journal of Applied Psychology* 85 (2000): 779-83; A. Seddigh et al., "The Association between Office Design and Performance on Demanding Cognitive Tasks," *Journal of Environmental Psychology* 42 (2015): 172-81; M. Pierrette et al., "Noise Effect on Comfort in Open-Space Offices: Development of an Assessment Questionnaire," *Ergonomics* 58, no. 1 (2015): 96-106.

73. S. P. Means, "Playing at Pixar," *Salt Lake Tribune* (Utah), May 30, 2003, D1; G. Whipp, "Swimming against the Tide," *Los Angeles Daily News,* May 30, 2003, U6.

74. C. Wagner and A. Majchrzak, "Enabling Customer-Centricity Using Wikis and the Wiki Way," *Journal of Management Information Systems* 23, no. 3 (2006): 17-43; C. Karena, "Working the Wiki Way," *Sydney Morning Herald,* March 6, 2007; R. B. Ferguson, "Build a Web 2.0 Platform and Employees Will Use It," *eWeek,* June 20, 2007.

75. Treasury Board of Canada Secretariat, "2014 Public Service Employee Survey: Summary Report," *Public Service Employee Surveys* (Ottawa: Government of Canada, March 5, 2015) (accessed June 30, 2017); U.S. Office of Personnel Management, *Federal Employee Viewpoint Survey* (Washington, DC: Office of Personnel Management, September 2016); S. Gopal and D. Lucy, Profile Search and Selection and Roffey Park, *Working in Asia: Key HR and Leadership Priorities for 2016,* (Horsham, UK: Roffey Park Institute, May 2016); National Health Service, "Staff Survey 2016 Detailed Spreadsheets" (London: National Health Service, 2016); *State of the Sector 2017* (London: Gatehouse, February 2017).

76. The original term is "management by *wandering* around," but this has been replaced with "walking around" over the years. See W. Ouchi, *Theory Z* (New York: Avon Books, 1981), 176–77; T. Peters and R. Waterman, *In Search of Excellence* (New York: Harper and Row, 1982), 122.

77. L. Bock, *Work Rules! Insights from Google That Will Transform How You Live and Lead* (New York: Hachette, 2015), 42.

78. R. Rousos, "Trust in Leaders Lacking at Utility," *The Ledger* (Lakeland, FL), July 29, 2003, B1; B. Whitworth and B. Riccomini, "Management Communication: Unlocking Higher Employee Performance," *Communication World,* March/April 2005, 18–21.

79. K. Davis, "Management Communication and the Grapevine," *Harvard Business Review* 31 (1953): 43–49; W. L. Davis and J. R. O'Connor, "Serial Transmission of Information: A Study of the Grapevine," *Journal of Applied Communication Research* 5 (1977): 61–72.

80. S. R. Clegg and A. van Iterson, "Dishing the Dirt: Gossiping in Organizations," *Culture and Organization* 15, no. 3/4 (2009): 275–89; C. Mills, "Experiencing Gossip: The Foundations for a Theory of Embedded Organizational Gossip," *Group & Organization Management* 35, no. 2 (2010): 213–40.

81. R. L. Rosnow, "Inside Rumor: A Personal Journey," *American Psychologist* 46 (1991): 484–96; C. J. Walker and C. A. Beckerle, "The Effect of State Anxiety on Rumor Transmission," *Journal of Social Behavior & Personality* 2 (1987): 353–60; M. Noon and R. Delbridge, "News from Behind My Hand: Gossip in Organizations," *Organization Studies* 14 (1993): 23–36.

82. N. Nicholson, "Evolutionary Psychology: Toward a New View of Human Nature and Organizational Society," *Human Relations* 50 (1997): 1053–78; E. K. Foster, "Research on Gossip: Taxonomy, Methods, and Future Directions," *Review of General Psychology* 8, no. 2 (2004): 78–99; B. Beersma and G. A. Van Kleef, "Why People Gossip: An Empirical Analysis of Social Motives, Antecedents, and Consequences," *Journal of Applied Social Psychology* 42, no. 11 (2012): 2640–70.

9 | Power and Influence in the Workplace

©Hero Images/Getty Images

Learning Objectives

After you read this chapter, you should be able to:

LO9-1 Describe the dependence model of power and the five sources of power in organizations.

LO9-2 Discuss the four contingencies of power.

LO9-3 Explain how people and work units gain power through social networks.

LO9-4 Describe eight types of influence tactics, three consequences of influencing others, and three contingencies to consider when choosing an influence tactic.

LO9-5 Identify the organizational conditions and personal characteristics associated with organizational politics, as well as ways to minimize organizational politics.

One of the most popular topics in organizational behavior classes is about managing your boss. The theme may sound manipulative, but managing your boss is actually a valuable process of gaining power and using influence for the benefit of the organization. Most executives say it is a key factor in everyone's career success.

"Managing up is about setting boundaries and rules on how you and your manager work together," explains Tomas Kucera, vice president of business operations at SolarWinds, the Austin, Texas, firm that develops enterprise information technology infrastructure management software. "It is about understanding the needs of the other person and helping them to achieve their goals."

There are many ways to manage your boss—or anyone else in and around organizations—such as aligning communication and work styles, becoming a valuable resource, being solution-oriented rather than problem-oriented, and supporting your manager's career success by performing your own job well. These and other practices develop power bases and apply influence tactics that ultimately change (or stabilize) the behavior of others. These activities are not unusual. On the contrary, OB experts point out that power and influence are inherent in all organizations. They exist in every business and in every decision and action.[1]

This chapter unfolds as follows: First, we define power and present a basic model depicting the dynamics of power in organizational settings. The chapter then discusses the five bases of power. Next, we look at the contingencies necessary to translate those sources into meaningful power. Our attention then turns to social networks and how they provide power to members through social capital. The latter part of this chapter examines the various types of influence in organizational settings as well as the contingencies of effective influence strategies. The final section of this chapter looks at situations in which influence becomes organizational politics, as well as ways of minimizing political behavior.

LO9-1 Describe the dependence model of power and the five sources of power in organizations.

THE MEANING OF POWER

Power is the capacity of a person, team, or organization to influence others.[2] There are a few important features of this definition. First, power is not the act of changing someone's attitudes or behavior; it is only the *potential* to do so. People frequently have power they do not use; they might not even know they have power. Second, power is based on the target's *perception* that the power holder controls (i.e., possesses, has access to, or regulates) a valuable resource that can help the target achieve his or her goals.[3] People might generate power by convincing others that they control something of value, whether or not they actually control that resource. This perception also is formed from the power holder's behavior, such as someone who is not swayed by authority or norms. For instance, people are perceived as more powerful just by engaging in behavior that deviates from norms, such as putting their feet on a table.[4] However, power is not your own perception or feeling of power; it exists only when others believe you have power.

Third, power involves asymmetric (unequal) *dependence* of one party on another party.[5] This dependent relationship is illustrated in Exhibit 9.1. The line from Person B to the goal shows that he or she believes Person A controls a resource that can help or hinder Person B in achieving that goal. Person A—the power holder in this illustration—might have power over Person B by controlling a desired job assignment, useful information, rewards, or even the privilege of being associated with Person A! For example, if you believe a coworker

Exhibit 9.1 Dependence Model of Power

Person A (power holder)

Countervailing power

Power

Person B

Person A is perceived as controlling resources that help or hinder Person B's goal achievement.

Person B's goal

has expertise (the resource) that would substantially help you write a better report (your goal), then that coworker has some power over you because you value that expertise to achieve your goal. Whatever the resource is, Person B is *dependent* on Person A (the power holder) to provide the resource so Person B can reach his or her goal.

Although dependence is a key element of power relationships, we use the phrase *asymmetric dependence* because the less powerful party still has some degree of power—called **countervailing power**—over the stronger power holder. In Exhibit 9.1, Person A dominates the power relationship, but Person B has enough countervailing power to keep Person A in the exchange relationship and ensure that person uses his or

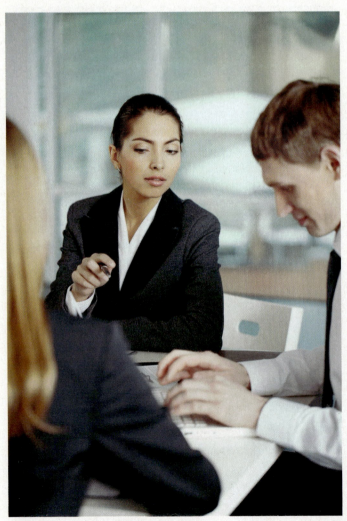

Power involves asymmetric dependence of one party on another party because the less powerful party has countervailing power over the stronger power holder.
©Image Source/Getty Images

her dominant power judiciously. For example, although managers have power over subordinates in many ways (e.g., control of job security and preferred work assignments), employees have countervailing power by possessing skills and knowledge to keep production humming and customers happy, something that management can't accomplish alone.

One other key feature is that all power relationships depend on some minimum level of trust. Trust indicates a level of expectation that the more powerful party will deliver the resource. For example, you trust your employer to give you a paycheck at the end of each pay period. Even those in extremely dependent situations will usually walk away from the relationship if they lack a minimum level of trust in the more powerful party.

Let's look at this power dependence model in the employee–manager relationship. You depend on your boss to support your continued employment, satisfactory work arrangements, and other valued resources. At the same time, the manager depends on you to complete required tasks and to work effectively with others in the completion of their work. Managers (and the companies they represent) typically have more power, whereas employees have weaker countervailing power. But sometimes employees do have more power than their bosses in the employment relationship. Notice that the strength of your power in the employee–manager relationship doesn't depend on your actual control over valued resources; it depends on the perceptions that your boss and others have about your control of these resources. Finally, trust is an essential ingredient in this relationship. Even with strong power, the employee–manager relationship comes apart when one party no longer sufficiently trusts the other.

The dependence model reveals only the core features of power dynamics between people and work units in organizations. We also need to learn about the specific sources of power and contingencies that effectively convert power into influence. As Exhibit 9.2 illustrates, power is derived from five sources: legitimate, reward, coercive, expert, and referent. The model also identifies four contingencies of power: the employee's or department's substitutability, centrality, visibility, and discretion. Over the next few pages, we will discuss each of these sources and contingencies of power in the context of organizations.

SOURCES OF POWER IN ORGANIZATIONS

There are five main sources of power in human interactions.[6] Three of these—legitimate, reward, and coercive—originate mostly (but not completely) from the power holder's formal position or informal role. In other words, the person is granted these sources of power formally by the organization or informally by coworkers. Two other sources of power—expert and referent—originate mainly from the power holder's own characteristics; in other words, people carry these power bases around with them. However, even personal sources of power are not

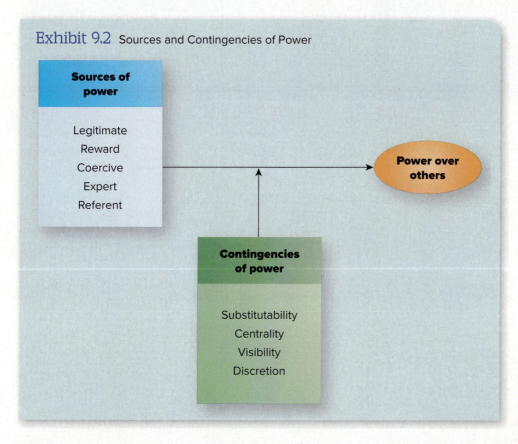

Exhibit 9.2 Sources and Contingencies of Power

Sources of power

Legitimate
Reward
Coercive
Expert
Referent

Power over others

Contingencies of power

Substitutability
Centrality
Visibility
Discretion

usually the most important source of power in organizational settings, particularly between employees and managers.[7] For example, managers have a legitimate right to tell employees what tasks to perform, whom to work with, what company resources they can use, and so forth. Employees follow the boss's requests because they have agreed to follow a range of requests from people in positions of higher authority. Employee motivation to comply with these requests occurs separately from the manager's ability to reward or punish employees.

Notice that legitimate power has restrictions; it gives the power holder only the right to ask others to perform a limited domain of behaviors. This domain—known as the "zone of indifference"—is the set of behaviors that individuals are willing to engage in at the other person's request.[8] Although most employees accept the boss's right to deny them access to Facebook during company time, some might draw the line when the boss asks them to work several hours beyond the regular workday. They either overtly refuse to follow orders or engage in delaying and other evasive tactics.

The size of the zone of indifference (and, consequently, the magnitude of legitimate power) increases with the level of trust in the power holder. Some values and personality traits also make people more obedient to authority. Those who value conformity and tradition as well as have high power

completely within the person because they depend on how others perceive them.

Legitimate Power

Legitimate power is an agreement among organizational members that people in certain roles can request a set of behaviors from others. This perceived right or obligation originates from formal job descriptions as well as informal rules of conduct. It is

---

OB THEORY TO PRACTICE

Deference to Authority Leads People to the Extreme

A French television program revealed how far people are willing to follow orders. As a variation of the 1960s experiments conducted by Stanley Milgram, 80 contestants administered electric shocks whenever a volunteer (an actor who didn't receive the shocks at all) answered a question incorrectly. Shocks increased in 20-volt increments, from 20 volts for the first mistake through to 460 volts. Contestants often hesitated after hearing the volunteer screaming for them to stop, yet continued the shocks after the television host reminded them that their job was to apply punishment for wrong answers. Only 16 of the 80 contestants refused to administer the strongest shocks.[10]

©Yami 2

distance (i.e., they accept an unequal distribution of power) tend to have higher deference to authority. The organization's culture represents another influence on the willingness of employees to follow orders. A 3M scientist might continue to work on a project after being told by superiors to stop working on it because the 3M culture supports an entrepreneurial spirit, which includes ignoring your boss's authority from time to time.[9]

Managers are not the only people with legitimate power in organizations. Employees also have legitimate power over their bosses and coworkers through legal and administrative rights as well as informal norms.[11] For example, an organization might give employees the right to request information that is required for their job. Laws give employees the right to refuse to work in unsafe conditions. Subtler forms of legitimate power also exist.[12] Human beings have a **norm of reciprocity**—a feeling of obligation to help someone who has helped you. If a coworker previously helped you handle a difficult client, that coworker has power because you feel an obligation to help the coworker on something of similar value in the future. The norm of reciprocity is a form of legitimate power because it is an informal rule of conduct that we are expected to follow.

Legitimate Power through Information Control A particularly potent form of legitimate power occurs when people have the right to control information that others receive.[14] These information gatekeepers have power in two ways. First, information is a resource, so those who need information are dependent on the gatekeeper to provide that resource. For example, the map department of a mining company has considerable power when other departments are dependent on the map department to deliver maps required for exploration projects.

Second, information gatekeepers gain power by selectively distributing information in a way that affects how those receiving the information perceive the situation compared to their perception if they received all of the information.[15] As we learned in the previous chapter on communication, information is often filtered as it flows up the hierarchy, which enables those transmitting the information to frame the situation in a more positive light. This framing allows the information gatekeeper to steer the executive team toward one decision rather than another.

Reward Power

Reward power is derived from the person's ability to control the allocation of rewards valued by others and to remove negative sanctions (i.e., negative reinforcement). Managers have formal authority that gives them power over the distribution of organizational rewards such as pay, promotions, time off, vacation schedules, and work assignments. Employees also have reward power over their bosses through their feedback and ratings in 360-degree feedback systems. These ratings affect supervisors' promotions and other rewards, so supervisors tend to pay more attention to employee needs after 360-degree feedback is introduced.

Coercive Power

Coercive power is the ability to apply punishment. This occurs when managers warn employees about the consequences of poor performance, yet employees also have coercive power. For example, employees might criticize coworkers when they disregard team norms.[16] Some firms rely on this coercive power from other team members to control coworker behavior in team settings.

Expert Power

Legitimate, reward, and coercive power originate mostly from the position.[17] Expert power, on the other hand, originates from within the power holder. It is an individual's or work unit's capacity to influence others by possessing knowledge or skills valued by others. An important form of expert power is the perceived ability to manage uncertainties in the business environment. Organizations are more effective when they operate in predictable environments, so they value people who can cope with turbulence in consumer trends, societal changes, unstable supply lines, and so forth. Expertise can help companies cope with uncertainty in three ways. These coping strategies are

An important form of expert power is the perceived ability to manage uncertainties in the business environment.
©Darren Greenwood/DesignPics

arranged in a hierarchy of importance, with prevention being the most powerful:[18]

- *Prevention*—The most effective strategy is to prevent environmental changes from occurring. For example, financial experts acquire power by preventing the organization from experiencing a cash shortage or breaching debt covenants.

- *Forecasting*—The next best strategy is to predict environmental changes or variations. In this respect, trendspotters and other marketing specialists gain power by predicting changes in consumer preferences.

- *Absorption*—People and work units also gain power by absorbing or neutralizing the impact of environmental shifts as they occur. An example is the ability of maintenance crews to come to the rescue when machines break down.

Many people respond to expertise just as they respond to authority—they mindlessly follow the guidance of these experts.[19] In one classic study, for example, a researcher posing as a hospital physician telephoned on-duty nurses to prescribe a specific dosage of medicine to a hospitalized patient. None of the nurses knew the person calling, and hospital policy forbade them from accepting treatment by telephone (i.e., the caller lacked legitimate power). Furthermore, the medication was unauthorized and the prescription was twice the maximum daily dose. Yet, almost all 22 nurses who received the telephone call followed the "doctor's" orders until stopped by researchers.[20]

This doctor–nurse study is a few decades old, but the power of expertise remains just as strong today, sometimes with tragic consequences. Not long ago, the Canadian justice system discovered that one of its "star" expert witnesses—the head of pediatric forensic pathology at a children's hospital in Toronto—had provided inaccurate cause of death evaluations in at least 20 cases, a dozen of which resulted in wrongful or highly questionable criminal convictions. The pathologist's reputation as a renowned authority was the main reason why his often-weak evidence was accepted without question. "Experts in a courtroom—we give great deference to experts," admits a Canadian defense lawyer familiar with this situation.[21]

Referent Power

People have **referent power** when others identify with them, like them, or otherwise respect them. As with expert power, referent power originates within the power holder. It is largely a function of the person's interpersonal skills. Referent power is also associated with **charisma**. Experts have difficulty agreeing on the meaning of charisma, but it is most often described as a form of

interpersonal attraction whereby followers ascribe almost magical powers to the charismatic individual.[22] Some writers describe charisma as a special "gift" or trait within the charismatic person, while others say it is mainly in the eyes of the beholder. However, all agree that charisma produces a high degree of trust, respect, and devotion toward the charismatic individual.

LO9-2 Discuss the four contingencies of power.

CONTINGENCIES OF POWER

Let's say that you have expert power because of your ability to forecast and possibly even prevent dramatic changes in the organization's environment. Does this expertise mean that you are influential? Not necessarily. As was illustrated earlier in Exhibit 9.2, sources of power generate power only under certain conditions. Four important contingencies of power are substitutability, centrality, visibility, and discretion.[23]

Substitutability

Power is strongest when the individual or work unit has a monopoly over a valued resource. In other words, they are nonsubstitutable. Conversely, power decreases as the number of alternative sources of the critical resource increases. If you—and no one else—have expertise across the organization on an important issue, you would be more powerful than if several people in your company possess this valued knowledge. Substitutability refers not only to other sources that offer the resource, but also to substitutions of the resource itself. For instance, the power of a labor union weakens when the company introduces technologies that replace the need for the union's members. Technology is a substitute for employees and, consequently, reduces union power.

Controlling access to the resource increases nonsubstitutability. Professions and labor unions gain power by controlling knowledge,

> **Many people respond to expertise just as they respond to authority—they mindlessly follow the guidance of these experts.**

more distant roles that managers and employees expect in high power distance cultures.

LO9-5 Identify the organizational conditions and personal characteristics associated with organizational politics, as well as ways to minimize organizational politics.

ORGANIZATIONAL POLITICS

You might have noticed that organizational politics has not been mentioned yet, even though some of the practices or examples described over the past few pages are usually considered political tactics. The phrase was carefully avoided because, for the most part, organizational politics is in the eye of the beholder. You might perceive a coworker's attempt to influence the boss as acceptable behavior for the good of the organization, whereas someone else might perceive the coworker's tactic as brazen organizational politics.

This perceptual issue explains why OB experts increasingly discuss influence tactics as behaviors and organizational politics as perceptions.[72] The influence tactics described earlier are perceived as **organizational politics** when they seem to be self-serving behaviors at the expense of others and possibly contrary to the interests of the entire organization. Of course, some tactics are so blatantly selfish and counterproductive that almost everyone correctly sees them as organizational politics. In other situations, however, a person's behavior might be viewed as political or in the organization's best interest, depending on the observer's point of view.

Employees who experience organizational politics from others have lower job satisfaction, organizational commitment, organizational citizenship, and task performance, as well as higher levels of work-related stress and motivation to leave the organization. "A politically charged work environment can hinder productivity, erode trust, and lead to morale and retention issues," says Renan Silva, a corporate project management office specialist at Serasa Experian, a credit bureau in São Paulo, Brazil.[74] And because political tactics serve individuals rather than organizations, they potentially divert resources away from the organization's effective functioning and may threaten its survival.

OB THEORY TO PRACTICE

Playing Politics with the Vacation Schedule

The vacation roster is a scarce resource, and resource scarcity brings out the worst office politics. One recent poll reported that 13 percent of British employees refused to reveal when they would take their vacations so coworkers wouldn't book the same dates. Another 7 percent said they protected their vacation plans by lying to coworkers about those plans. Five percent were even more Machiavellian; they strategically booked vacation dates that scuttled the plans of a disliked coworker. "I know this is true," says an employee from Newport, Wales, who was not part of the survey. "I had a colleague who knew my holiday habits and would go in on January the 2nd and book every week that he knew I habitually had for holidays because he knew my wife's holidays were fixed and could not be changed. He didn't really need those days; he did it out of spite."[75]

©Ferran Traite Soler/E+/Getty Images

Minimizing Organizational Politics

Researchers have identified several conditions that encourage organizational politics, so we can identify corresponding strategies to keep political activities to a minimum.[76] First, organizational politics are triggered by scarce resources in the workplace. When budgets are slashed, people rely on political tactics to safeguard their resources and maintain the status quo. Although it is not easy to maintain or add resources, sometimes this action is less costly than the consequences of organizational politics.

> **Keep your friends close and your enemies closer.**[73]
>
> —Attributed to Sun-Tzu, Chinese general, circa 500 B.C.

SELF-ASSESSMENT 9.3: How Politically Charged is Your School?

Every organization has some degree of organizational politics. Depending on behavioral norms and organizational culture, employees in some companies actively use influence tactics to get their own way for personal gain. In other workplaces, employees who engage in organizational politics are quickly reminded to avoid these tactics, or are eventually asked to work somewhere else. Students can usually sense the level of organizational politics at the college where they are taking courses. You can discover the degree to which you believe the school where you attend classes has a politicized culture by locating this self-assessment in Connect if it is assigned by your instructor.

SELF-ASSESSMENT 9.4: How Machiavellian Are You?

One of the best-known individual differences in organizational politics is Machiavellianism, named after the 16th-century Italian philosopher who wrote a famous treatise about political behavior (*The Prince*). Machiavellian employees take a perspective of situations and other people that motivates them to apply influence tactics more for personal gain. Although few people want to be viewed as Machiavellian, measures suggest that most of us apply these practices to some extent. You can discover your level of Machiavellianism by locating this self-assessment in Connect if it is assigned by your instructor.

Second, political tactics are fueled by ambiguous or complex rules, or the absence of formal rules, because those tactics help people get what they want when decisions lack structural guidelines. Consequently, organizational politics are suppressed when resource allocation decisions are clear and simplified. Third, organizational change tends to bring out more organizational politics, mainly because change creates ambiguity and threatens the employee's power and other valued resources.[77] Consequently, leaders need to apply the organizational change strategies that we describe in Chapter 14, particularly through communication, learning, and involvement. Research has found that employees who are kept informed of what is going on in the organization and who are involved in organizational decisions are less likely to engage in organizational politics.

Fourth, political behavior is more common in work units and organizations where it is tolerated and reinforced. Some companies seem to nurture self-serving behavior through reward systems and the role modeling of organizational leaders. To minimize political norms, the organization needs to diagnose and alter systems and role modeling that support self-serving behavior. They should support organizational values that oppose political tactics, such as altruism and focusing on the customer. One of the most important strategies is for leaders to become role models of organizational citizenship rather than symbols of successful organizational politicians.

Personal Characteristics

Several personal characteristics affect an individual's motivation to engage in self-serving behavior.[79] This includes a strong need for personal as opposed to socialized power. Those with a need for personal power seek power for its own sake and try to acquire more power. Some individuals have strong **Machiavellian values**. Machiavellianism is named after Niccolò Machiavelli, the 16th-century Italian philosopher who wrote *The Prince*, a famous treatise about political behavior.

Office Politics By the Numbers[78]

68% of 1,125 Taiwanese office workers polled say they have experienced workplace politics.

54% of 1,100 16–25 year olds polled in the UK say they are not prepared or informed about office politics.

46% of more than 1,000 American office workers polled say that gossiping or spreading rumors is the most common form of office politics where they work.

©SchulteProductions/Getty Images

33% of 1,102 employed Americans polled who don't normally work at a desk say that an important advantage of a non-desk job is not having to deal with office politics.

28% of 2,200 chief financial officers polled say that gossiping or engaging in office politics is the most annoying behavior by coworkers (second highest, following sloppy work).

19% of 7,000 American employees polled believe that office politics are more vicious than national (elected government) politics.

People with high Machiavellian values are comfortable with getting more than they deserve, and they believe that deceit is a natural and acceptable way to achieve this goal. They seldom trust coworkers and tend to use cruder influence tactics to get their own way, such as bypassing their boss or being assertive.[80]

Study Checklist

Connect® Management is available for *M Organizational Behavior.* Additional resources include:

✓ Interactive Applications:
- **Case Analysis:** Apply concepts within the context of a real-world situation.
- **Drag and Drop:** Work through an interactive example to test your knowledge of the concepts.
- **Video Case:** See management in action through interactive videos.

✓ **SmartBook™**—SmartBook is the first and only adaptive reading experience available today. Distinguishing what you know from what you don't, and honing in on concepts you are most likely to forget, SmartBook personalizes content for you in a continuously adapting reading experience. Reading is no longer a passive and linear experience, but an engaging and dynamic one where you are more likely to master and retain important concepts and go to class better prepared.

©Natthawat Jamnapa/123RF

Notes

1. J. J. Gabarro and J. P. Kotter, "Managing Your Boss," *Harvard Business Review* 58, no. 1 (1980): 92–100; B. Tulgan, *It's Okay to Manage Your Boss* (San Francisco: Jossey-Bass, 2010); T. Kucera, "How to Manage Your Manager," *LinkedIn Pulse*, March 5, 2017.

2. J. R. French and B. Raven, "The Bases of Social Power," in *Studies in Social Power*, ed. D. Cartwright (Ann Arbor: University of Michigan Press, 1959), 150–67; A. D. Galinsky et al., "Power and Perspectives Not Taken," *Psychological Science* 17, no. 12 (2006): 1068–74. Also see H. Mintzberg, *Power in and around Organizations* (Englewood Cliffs, NJ: Prentice Hall, 1983), chap. 1; J. Pfeffer, *Managing with Power: Politics and Influence in Organizations* (Boston: Harvard Business School Press, 1992), 17, 30; A. Guinote and T. K. Vescio, "Introduction: Power in Social Psychology," in *The Social Psychology of Power*, ed. A. Guinote and T. K. Vescio (New York: Guilford Press, 2010), 1–18.

3. R. A. Dahl, "The Concept of Power," *Behavioral Science* 2 (1957): 201–18; R. M. Emerson, "Power-Dependence Relations," *American Sociological Review* 27 (1962): 31–41; A. M. Pettigrew, *The Politics of Organizational Decision-Making* (London: Tavistock, 1973).

4. G. A. van Kleef et al., "The Social Dynamics of Breaking the Rules: Antecedents and Consequences of Norm-Violating Behavior," *Current Opinion in Psychology* 6 (2015): 25–31.

5. J. Pfeffer and G. R. Salancik, *The External Control of Organizations* (New York: Harper & Row, 1978), 52–54; K. Cowan, A. K. Paswan, and E. Van Steenburg, "When Inter-Firm Relationship Benefits Mitigate Power Asymmetry," *Industrial Marketing Management* 48 (2015): 140–48.

6. J. R. French and B. Raven, "The Bases of Social Power," in *Studies in Social Power*, ed. D. Cartwright (Ann Arbor: University of Michigan Press, 1959), 150–67; P. M. Podsakoff and C. Schreisheim, "Field Studies of French and Raven's Bases of Power: Critique, Analysis, and Suggestions for Future Research," *Psychological Bulletin* 97 (1985): 387–411; P. P. Carson and K. D. Carson, "Social Power Bases: A Meta-Analytic Examination of Interrelationships and Outcomes," *Journal of Applied Social Psychology* 23 (1993): 1150–69. Most alternative models of power bases parallel French and Raven's list. See P. Heinemann, *Power Bases and Informational Influence Strategies: A Behavioral Study on the Use of Management Accounting Information* (Wiesbaden, Germany: Deutscher Universitäts-Verlag, 2008). Raven subsequently proposed information power as a sixth source of power. We present information power as forms of legitimate and expert power rather than as a distinct sixth power base.

7. Legitimate power and expert power are also consistently the strongest sources of power that coaches have over players in sports. See P. Rylander, "Coaches' Bases of Power: Developing Some Initial Knowledge of Athletes' Compliance with Coaches in Team Sports," *Journal of Applied Sport Psychology* 27, no. 1 (2015): 110–21.

8. C. Barnard, *The Function of the Executive* (Cambridge, MA: Harvard University Press, 1938), 167–70; B. J. Tepper, "What Do Managers Do When Subordinates Just Say, 'No'?: An Analysis of Incidents Involving Refusal to Perform Downward Requests," in *Power and Influence in Organizations*, ed. L. L. Neider and C. A. Schreisheim (Charlotte, NC: IAP/Information Age Publishing, 2006), 1–20.

9. A. I. Shahin and P. L. Wright, "Leadership in the Context of Culture: An Egyptian Perspective," *Leadership & Organization Development Journal* 25, no. 5/6 (2004): 499–511; Y. J. Huo et al., "Leadership and the Management of Conflicts in Diverse Groups: Why Acknowledging versus Neglecting Subgroup Identity Matters," *European Journal of Social Psychology* 35, no. 2 (2005): 237–54.

10. B. Crumley, "Game of Death: France's Shocking TV Experiment," *Time*, March 17, 2010; M. Portillo, "Would You Torture This Man?," *Sunday Telegraph* (London), March 21, 2010, 22. A recent variation of deference to authority occurred on British television. Four strangers were individually encouraged to assist the head of a (fictitious) charity by impersonating a wealthy would-be donor who died before making the donation, then kicking the supposedly dead body, and later throwing the body off a roof. See H. Mount, "Could You Be Talked into Murder?," *Daily Mail* (London), January 14, 2016, 16.

11. B. H. Raven, "Kurt Lewin Address: Influence, Power, Religion, and the Mechanisms of Social Control," *Journal of Social Issues* 55 (1999): 161–86.

12. A. W. Gouldner, "The Norm of Reciprocity: A Preliminary Statement," *American Sociological Review* 25 (1960): 161–78; M. Koslowsky and J. Schwarzwald, "Power Tactics Preference in Organizations: Individual and Situational Factors," in *Power and Interdependence in Organizations*, ed. D. Tjosvold and B. Wisse (New York: Cambridge University Press, 2009), 244–61.

13. A. Einstein, *The Ultimate Quotable Einstein*, ed. A. Calaprice (Princeton, NJ: Princeton University Press, 2011), 161. Originally in a letter to Swiss teacher Jost Winteler on July 8, 1901.

14. G. Yukl and C. M. Falbe, "Importance of Different Power Sources in Downward and Lateral Relations," *Journal of Applied Psychology* 76 (1991): 416–23; B. H. Raven, "Kurt Lewin Address: Influence, Power, Religion, and the Mechanisms of Social Control," *Journal of Social Issues* 55 (1999): 161–86.

15. A. M. Pettigrew, "Information Control as a Power Resource," *Sociology* 6, no. 2 (1972): 187–204; P. L. Dawes, D. Y. Lee, and G. R. Dowling, "Information Control and Influence in Emergent Buying Centers," *Journal of Marketing* 62, no. 3 (1998): 55–68; J. Webster et al., "Beyond Knowledge Sharing: Withholding Knowledge at Work," *Research in Personnel and Human Resources Management* 27 (2008): 1–37; C. E. Connelly et al., "Knowledge Hiding in Organizations," *Journal of Organizational Behavior* 33, no. 1 (2012): 64–88.

16. S. L. Robinson, J. O'Reilly, and W. Wang, "Invisible at Work: An Integrated Model of Workplace Ostracism," *Journal of Management* 39, no. 1 (2013): 203–31.

17. J. M. Peiro and J. L. Melia, "Formal and Informal Interpersonal Power in Organisations: Testing a Bifactorial Model of Power in Role-Sets," *Applied Psychology* 52, no. 1 (2003): 14–35.

18. C. R. Hinings et al., "Structural Conditions of Intraorganizational Power," *Administrative Science Quarterly* 19 (1974): 22–44. Also see C. S. Saunders, "The Strategic Contingency Theory of Power: Multiple Perspectives," *Journal of Management Studies* 27 (1990): 1–21.

19. R. B. Cialdini and N. J. Goldstein, "Social Influence: Compliance and Conformity," *Annual Review of Psychology* 55 (2004): 591–621.

20. C. K. Hofling et al., "An Experimental Study in Nurse-Physician Relationships," *Journal of Nervous and Mental Disease* 143, no. 2 (1966): 171–77.

21. C. Perkel, "It's Not CSI," *Canadian Press*, November 10, 2007; "Dr. Charles Smith: The Man behind the Public Inquiry," *CBC News* (Toronto), August 10, 2010; J. Chipman, *Death in the Family* (Toronto: Doubleday Canada, 2017).

22. K. Miyahara, "Charisma: From Weber to Contemporary Sociology," *Sociological Inquiry* 53, no. 4 (1983): 368–88; J. D. Kudisch and M. L. Poteet, "Expert Power, Referent Power, and Charisma: Toward the Resolution of a Theoretical Debate," *Journal of Business & Psychology* 10 (1995): 177–95; D. Ladkin, "The Enchantment of the Charismatic Leader: Charisma Reconsidered as Aesthetic Encounter," *Leadership* 2, no. 2 (2006): 165–79.

23. D. J. Hickson et al., "A Strategic Contingencies' Theory of Intraorganizational Power," *Administrative Science Quarterly* 16 (1971): 216–27; C. R. Hinings et al., "Structural Conditions of Intraorganizational Power," *Administrative Science Quarterly* 19 (1974): 22–44; R. M. Kanter, "Power Failure in Management Circuits," *Harvard Business Review* (1979): 65–75.

24. A. Bryant, "The Right Job? It's Much Like the Right Spouse," *The New York Times*, May 22, 2011, 2.

25. D. J. Hickson et al., "A Strategic Contingencies' Theory of Intraorganizational Power," *Administrative Science Quarterly* 16 (1971): 219–21; J. D. Hackman, "Power and Centrality in the Allocation of Resources in Colleges and Universities," *Administrative Science Quarterly* 30 (1985): 61–77; D. J. Brass and M. E. Burkhardt, "Potential Power and Power Use: An Investigation of Structure and Behavior," *Academy of Management Journal* 36 (1993): 441–70.

26. A. Caza, "Typology of the Eight Domains of Discretion in Organizations," *Journal of Management Studies* 49, no. 1 (2012): 144–77.

27. B. E. Ashforth, "The Experience of Powerlessness in Organizations," *Organizational Behavior and Human Decision Processes* 43 (1989): 207–42; D. B. Wangrow, D. J. Schepker, and V. L. Barker, "Managerial Discretion: An Empirical Review and Focus on Future Research Directions," *Journal of Management* 41, no. 1 (2015): 99–135.

28. S. Wasserman and K. Faust, *Social Network Analysis: Methods and Applications*, Structural Analysis in the Social Sciences (Cambridge, UK: Cambridge University Press, 1994), chap. 1; D. J. Brass et al., "Taking Stock of Networks and Organizations: A Multilevel Perspective," *Academy of Management Journal* 47, no. 6 (2004): 795–817.

29. M. Grossetti, "Where Do Social Relations Come From?: A Study of Personal Networks in the Toulouse Area of France," *Social Networks* 27, no. 4 (2005): 289–300.

30. R. J. Taormina and J. H. Gao, "A Research Model for Guanxi Behavior: Antecedents, Measures, and Outcomes of Chinese Social Networking," *Social Science Research* 39, no. 6 (2010): 1195–212; J. Barbalet, "Guanxi, Tie Strength, and Network Attributes," *American Behavioral Scientist* 59, no. 8 (2015): 1038–50; X.-A. Zhang, N. Li, and T. B. Harris, "Putting Non-Work Ties to Work: The Case of Guanxi in Supervisor–Subordinate Relationships," *Leadership Quarterly* 26, no. 1 (2015): 37–54. For problems with guanxi, see W. R. Vanhonacker, "When Good Guanxi Turns Bad," *Harvard Business Review* 82, no. 4 (2004): 18–19; F. Yang, "Guanxi Human Resource Management Practices as a Double-Edged Sword: The Moderating Role of Political Skill," *Asia Pacific Journal of Human Resources* 52, no. 4 (2014): 496–510.

31. A. Portes, "Social Capital: Its Origins and Applications in Modern Society," *Annual Review of Sociology* 24 (1998): 1–24; P. S. Adler and S. W. Kwon, "Social Capital: Prospects for a New Concept," *Academy of Management Review* 27, no. 1 (2002): 17–40; R. Lee, "Social Capital and Business and Management: Setting a Research Agenda," *International Journal of Management Reviews* 11, no. 3 (2009): 247–73.

32. R. F. Chisholm, *Developing Network Organizations: Learning from Practice and Theory* (Reading, MA: Addison-Wesley Longman, 1998); W. S. Chow and L. S. Chan, "Social Network, Social Trust and Shared Goals in Organizational Knowledge Sharing," *Information & Management* 45, no. 7 (2008): 458–65.

33. R. S. Burt, *Structural Holes: The Social Structure of Competition* (Cambridge, MA: Harvard University Press, 1992).

34. M. T. Rivera, S. B. Soderstrom, and B. Uzzi, "Dynamics of Dyads in Social Networks: Assortative, Relational, and Proximity Mechanisms," *Annual Review of Sociology* 36 (2010): 91–115.

35. R. Cross and R. J. Thomas, *Driving Results through Social Networks: How Top Organizations Leverage Networks for Performance and Growth* (San Francisco: Jossey-Bass, 2009); R. McDermott and D. Archibald, "Harnessing Your Staff's Informal Networks," *Harvard Business Review* 88, no. 3 (2010): 82–89.

36. M. Kilduff and D. Krackhardt, *Interpersonal Networks in Organizations: Cognition, Personality, Dynamics, and Culture* (New York: Cambridge University Press, 2008).

37. T. Gibbs, S. Heywood, and L. Weiss, "Organizing for an Emerging World," *McKinsey Quarterly* (2012): 1–11.

38. N. B. Ellison, C. Steinfield, and C. Lampe, "The Benefits of Facebook 'Friends': Social Capital and College Students' Use of Online Social Network Sites," *Journal of Computer-Mediated Communication* 12, no. 4 (2007): 1143–68.

39. D. J. Brass et al., "Taking Stock of Networks and Organizations: A Multilevel Perspective," *Academy of Management Journal* 47, no. 6 (2004): 795-817; D. Melamed and B. Simpson, "Strong Ties Promote the Evolution of Cooperation in Dynamic Networks," *Social Networks* 45 (2016): 32-44.

40. M. S. Granovetter, "The Strength of Weak Ties," *American Journal of Sociology* 78 (1973): 1360-80; B. Erickson, "Social Networks," in *The Blackwell Companion to Sociology*, ed. J. R. Blau (Malden, MA: Blackwell, 2004), 314-26.

41. B. Uzzi and S. Dunlap, "How to Build Your Network," *Harvard Business Review* 83, no. 12 (2005): 53-60.

42. S. C. de Janasz and M. L. Forret, "Learning the Art of Networking: A Critical Skill for Enhancing Social Capital and Career Success," *Journal of Management Education* 32, no. 5 (2008): 629-50; Y. Zenou, "A Dynamic Model of Weak and Strong Ties in the Labor Market," *Journal of Labor Economics* 33, no. 4 (2015): 891-932.

43. C. Phelps, R. Heidl, and A. Wadhwa, "Knowledge, Networks, and Knowledge Networks: A Review and Research Agenda," *Journal of Management* 38, no. 4 (2012): 1115-66.

44. R. S. Burt, *Structural Holes: The Social Structure of Competition* (Cambridge, MA: Harvard University Press, 1992); D. J. Brass and D. M. Krackhardt, "Power, Politics, and Social Networks in Organizations," in *Politics in Organizations: Theory and Research Considerations*, ed. G. R. Ferris and D. C. Treadway (New York: Routledge, 2012), 355-75.

45. B. R. Ragins and E. Sundstrom, "Gender and Power in Organizations: A Longitudinal Perspective," *Psychological Bulletin* 105 (1989): 51-88; S. McDonald et al., "Frontiers of Sociological Research on Networks, Work, and Inequality," in *Networks, Work and Inequality*, ed. S. McDonald, Research in the Sociology of Work (Bingley, UK: Emerald Group Publishing Limited, 2013), 1-41.

46. S. Ritchey, "The Biggest Mistake Women Make When Networking," *Fortune*, February 1, 2016.

47. D. M. McCracken, "Winning the Talent War for Women: Sometimes It Takes a Revolution," *Harvard Business Review* (2000): 159-67.

48. Y. Amichai-Hamburger, G. Wainapel, and S. Fox, "'On the Internet No One Knows I'm an Introvert': Extroversion, Neuroticism, and Internet Interaction," *Cyber-Psychology & Behavior* 5, no. 2 (2002): 125-28; K. Brooks, "Networking 101 for Introverts," *Psychology Today* (2010); D. Zack, *Networking for People Who Hate Networking* (San Francisco: Berret-Koehler, 2010).

49. J. Lammers, J. I. Stoker, and D. A. Stapel, "Differentiating Social and Personal Power: Opposite Effects on Stereotyping, but Parallel Effects on Behavioral Approach Tendencies," *Psychological Science* 20, no. 12 (2009): 1543-49.

50. J. Lammers et al., "Power and Morality," *Current Opinion in Psychology* 6 (2015): 15-19.

51. A. D. Galinsky et al., "Acceleration with Steering: The Synergistic Benefits of Combining Power and Perspective-Taking," *Social Psychological and Personality Science* 5, no. 6 (2014): 627-35.

52. K. Atuahene-Gima and H. Li, "Marketing's Influence Tactics in New Product Development: A Study of High Technology Firms in China," *Journal of Product Innovation Management* 17 (2000): 451-70; A. Somech and A. Drach-Zahavy, "Relative Power and Influence Strategy: The Effects of Agent/Target Organizational Power on Superiors' Choices of Influence Strategies," *Journal of Organizational Behavior* 23 (2002): 167-79.

53. D. Kipnis, S. M. Schmidt, and I. Wilkinson, "Intraorganizational Influence Tactics: Explorations in Getting One's Way," *Journal of Applied Psychology* 65 (1980): 440-52; G. Yukl, "Power and the Interpersonal Influence of Leaders," in *Power and Interdependence in Organizations*, ed. D. Tjosvold and B. Wisse (New York: Cambridge University Press, 2009), 207-23.

54. R. B. Cialdini and N. J. Goldstein, "Social Influence: Compliance and Conformity," *Annual Review of Psychology* 55 (2004): 591-621.

55. A. Rao and K. Hashimoto, "Universal and Culturally Specific Aspects of Managerial Influence: A Study of Japanese Managers," *Leadership Quarterly* 8 (1997): 295-312. Silent authority as an influence tactic in non-Western cultures also is discussed in S. F. Pasa, "Leadership Influence in a High Power Distance and Collectivist Culture," *Leadership & Organization Development Journal* 21 (2000): 414-26.

56. C. de Gaulle, *The Edge of the Sword (Le fil de l'epée)*, trans. G. Hopkins (London: Faber, 1960), 59.

57. CareerBuilder, "Office Bullying Plagues Workers across Races, Job Levels and Educational Attainment, According to Careerbuilder's New Study," news release (Chicago: CareerBuilder, September 18, 2014); Trades Union Congress, "Nearly a Third of People Are Bullied at Work, Says TUC," news release (London: Trades Union Congress, November 12, 2015); Family Lives, "Family Lives Extended News Release: Bullying in the Workplace," news release (Hatfield, UK: Family Lives, January 12, 2015); Australian Public Service Commission, *State of the Service Report* (Canberra: Commonwealth of Australia, December 2016); "Workplace Bullying Widespread at Fire Departments, Survey Shows," *Japan Times*, March 29, 2017.

58. S. Maitlis, "Taking It from the Top: How CEOs Influence (and Fail to Influence) Their Boards," *Organization Studies* 25, no. 8 (2004): 1275-311. This type of influence is a form of manipulation. See P. Fleming and A. Spicer, "Power in Management and Organization Science," *The Academy of Management Annals* 8, no. 1 (2014): 237-98.

59. A. T. Cobb, "Toward the Study of Organizational Coalitions: Participant Concerns and Activities in a Simulated Organizational Setting," *Human Relations* 44 (1991): 1057-79; E. A. Mannix, "Organizations as Resource Dilemmas: The Effects of Power Balance on Coalition Formation in Small Groups," *Organizational Behavior and Human Decision Processes* 55 (1993): 1-22; D. J. Terry, M. A. Hogg, and K. M. White, "The Theory of Planned Behavior: Self-Identity, Social Identity and Group Norms," *British Journal of Social Psychology* 38 (1999): 225-44.

60. A. P. Brief, *Attitudes in and around Organizations* (Thousand Oaks, CA: Sage, 1998), 69-84; D. J. O'Keefe, *Persuasion: Theory and Research* (Thousand Oaks, CA: Sage, 2002); R. H. Gass and J. S. Seiter, *Persuasion: Social Influence and Compliance Gaining*, 5th ed. (New York: Routledge, 2014).

61. These and other features of message content in persuasion are detailed in R. Petty and J. Cacioppo, *Attitudes and Persuasion: Classic and Contemporary Approaches* (Dubuque, IA: W. C. Brown, 1981); M. Pfau, E. A. Szabo, and J. Anderson, "The Role and Impact of Affect in the Process of Resistance to Persuasion," *Human Communication Research* 27 (2001): 216-52; D. J. O'Keefe, *Persuasion: Theory and Research* (Thousand Oaks, CA: Sage, 2002), chap. 9; R. Buck et al., "Emotion and Reason in Persuasion: Applying the ARI Model and the CASC Scale," *Journal of Business Research* 57, no. 6 (2004): 647-56; W. D. Crano and R. Prislin, "Attitudes and Persuasion," *Annual Review of Psychology* 57 (2006): 345-74.

62. N. Rhodes and W. Wood, "Self-Esteem and Intelligence Affect Influenceability: The Mediating Role of Message Reception," *Psychological Bulletin* 111, no. 1 (1992): 156-71.

63. M. Bolino, D. Long, and W. Turnley, "Impression Management in Organizations: Critical Questions, Answers, and Areas for Future Research," *Annual Review of Organizational Psychology and Organizational Behavior* 3, no. 1 (2016): 377–406.

64. T. Peters, "The Brand Called You," *Fast Company*, August 1997; J. Sills, "Becoming Your Own Brand," *Psychology Today* 41, no. 1 (2008): 62–63.

65. D. Strutton and L. E. Pelton, "Effects of Ingratiation on Lateral Relationship Quality within Sales Team Settings," *Journal of Business Research* 43 (1998): 1–12; R. Vonk, "Self-Serving Interpretations of Flattery: Why Ingratiation Works," *Journal of Personality and Social Psychology* 82 (2002): 515–26.

66. C. A. Higgins, T. A. Judge, and G. R. Ferris, "Influence Tactics and Work Outcomes: A Meta-Analysis," *Journal of Organizational Behavior* 24 (2003): 90–106.

67. D. Strutton, L. E. Pelton, and J. F. Tanner, "Shall We Gather in the Garden: The Effect of Ingratiatory Behaviors on Buyer Trust in Salespeople," *Industrial Marketing Management* 25 (1996): 151–62; J. O'Neil, "An Investigation of the Sources of Influence of Corporate Public Relations Practitioners," *Public Relations Review* 29 (2003): 159–69.

68. J. Foster, "Here Are Best Answers to Job Interview Questions," *The Herald (Rock Hill, S.C.)*, April 4, 2010; "Common Interview Questions and How to Answer Them," *Advice & Tips* (Sydney: Seek, September 19, 2013), https://www.seek.com.au/career-advice/common-interview-questions-and-how-to-answer-them (accessed July 3, 2017); J. Haden, "27 Most Common Job Interview Questions and Answers," *Inc.*, June 20, 2016; "Ten Tough Interview Questions and Ten Great Answers," *Job Search Advice* (Seattle: CollegeGrad, 2017), https://collegegrad.com/jobsearch/mastering-the-interview/ten-tough-interview-questions-and-ten-great-answers (accessed July 3, 2017); M. Cheary, "Common Interview Questions and Answers," *Interview Techniques* (London: Reed, 2017) (accessed July 3, 2017).

69. C. M. Falbe and G. Yukl, "Consequences for Managers of Using Single Influence Tactics and Combinations of Tactics," *Academy of Management Journal* 35 (1992): 638–52.

70. G. Yukl and J. Tracey, "Consequences of Influence Tactics Used with Subordinates, Peers, and the Boss," *Journal of Applied Psychology* 77, no. 4 (1992): 525–35; B. Oc and M. R. Bashshur, "Followership, Leadership and Social Influence," *Leadership Quarterly* 24, no. 6 (2013): 919–34; M. B. Wadsworth and A. L. Blanchard, "Influence Tactics in Virtual Teams," *Computers in Human Behavior* 44 (2015): 386–93.

71. P. P. Fu et al., "The Impact of Societal Cultural Values and Individual Social Beliefs on the Perceived Effectiveness of Managerial Influence Strategies: A Meso Approach," *Journal of International Business Studies* 35, no. 4 (2004): 284–305; A. N. Smith et al., "Gendered Influence: A Gender Role Perspective on the Use and Effectiveness of Influence Tactics," *Journal of Management* 39, no. 5 (2013): 1156–83; C. C. Lewis and J. Ryan, "Age and Influence Tactics: A Life-Stage Development Theory Perspective," *The International Journal of Human Resource Management* 25, no. 15 (2014): 2146–58.

72. Organizational politics is a badly convoluted construct. Early literature defined it as influence tactics outside the formal role that could be either selfish or altruistic. Unfortunately, that definition fails to recognize the highly subjective nature of the definition and doesn't distinguish political behavior from other influence behavior. See J. Pfeffer, *Power in Organizations* (Boston: Pitman, 1981); H. Mintzberg, *Power in and around Organizations* (Englewood Cliffs, NJ: Prentice Hall, 1983). More recent scholars recognized that behavior is political or not depending on whether it is perceived by others as self-serving. From this definition, organizational politics benefit the politician, not the organization or coworkers. Yet, some scholars are returning to the view that organizational politics can be good or bad, suggesting that political tactics are just influence tactics with a different name. See G. R. Ferris and D. C. Treadway, "Politics in Organizations: History, Construct Specification, and Research Directions," in *Politics in Organizations: Theory and Research Considerations*, ed. G. R. Ferris and D. C. Treadway (New York: Routledge, 2012), 3–26; D. A. Lepisto and M. G. Pratt, "Politics in Perspective: On the Theoretical Challenges and Opportunities in Studying Organizational Politics," in *Politics in Organizations: Theory and Research Considerations*, ed. G. R. Ferris and D. C. Treadway (New York: Routledge, 2012), 67–98.

73. This famous quotation is attributed to both Nicolo Machiavelli and Sun-tzu. None of Machiavelli's five main books (translated) has any statement close to this quotation. Sun-tzu's book *Art of War* (translated) does not have this quotation either, but he makes a similar statement about spies: "Hence it is that with none in the whole army are more intimate relations to be maintained than with spies." See Sun-tzu, *The Art of War*, trans. L. Giles (Mineola, NY: Dover, 2002), 98.

74. K. M. Kacmar and R. A. Baron, "Organizational Politics: The State of the Field, Links to Related Processes, and an Agenda for Future Research," in *Research in Personnel and Human Resources Management*, ed. G. R. Ferris (Greenwich, CT: JAI Press, 1999), 1–39; E. Vigoda, "Stress-Related Aftermaths to Workplace Politics," *Journal of Organizational Behavior* 23, no. 5 (August 2002): 571–91. C. H. Chang, C. C. Rosen, and P. E. Levy, "The Relationship between Perceptions of Organizational Politics and Employee Attitudes, Strain, and Behavior: A Meta-Analytic Examination," *Academy of Management Journal* 52, no. 4 (2009): 779–801. The quotation is from M. Landry, "Navigating the Political Minefield," *PM Network*, March 2013, 38–43.

75. L. Hull, "Covert War in the Workplace . . . over the Holiday Rota," *Mail Online*, August 7, 2013; "Office Wars: Tis the Season to Be Spiteful," *Officebroker Blog*, 2013, www.officebroker.com/blog/.

76. C. Hardy, *Strategies for Retrenchment and Turnaround: The Politics of Survival* (Berlin: Walter de Gruyter, 1990), chap. 14; G. R. Ferris et al., "Perceptions of Organizational Politics: Prediction, Stress-Related Implications, and Outcomes," *Human Relations* 49 (1996): 233–63; M. C. Andrews and K. M. Kacmar, "Discriminating among Organizational Politics, Justice, and Support," *Journal of Organizational Behavior* 22 (2001): 347–66.

77. S. Blazejewski and W. Dorow, "Managing Organizational Politics for Radical Change: The Case of Beiersdorf-Lechia S.A., Poznan," *Journal of World Business* 38 (2003): 204–23.

78. Robert Walters Australia, *Robert Walters Employee Insights Newsletter* (Sydney: Robert Walters, August 2012); CareerBuilder, "More Than One-Third of Workers Discuss Politics at Work," news release (Chicago: CareerBuilder, March 1, 2012); "Wasting Time at Work 2012," salary.com, 2012, www.salary.com/wasting-time-at-work-2012/slide/11/ (accessed May 28, 2014); "Nearly 70% Experience 'Workplace Politics': Poll" (Taiwan: Focus Taiwan News Channel, September 30, 2013), http://focustaiwan.tw/news/asoc/201309300033.aspx (accessed May 28, 2014); CareerBuilder, "New CareerBuilder Study Explores the Perks and Pitfalls of Working in a Desk Job vs. a Non-Desk Job," news release (Chicago: CareerBuilder, May 22, 2014).

79. L. W. Porter, R. W. Allen, and H. L. Angle, "The Politics of Upward Influence in Organizations," *Research in Organizational Behavior* 3 (1981): 120–22; R. J. House, "Power and Personality in Complex Organizations," *Research in Organizational Behavior* 10 (1988): 305–57.

80. R. Christie and F. Geis, *Studies in Machiavellianism* (New York: Academic Press, 1970); S. R. Kessler et al., "Re-Examining Machiavelli: A Three-Dimensional Model of Machiavellianism in the Workplace," *Journal of Applied Social Psychology* 40, no. 8 (2010): 1868–96; E. O'Boyle et al., "A Meta-Analysis of the Dark Triad and Work Behavior: A Social Exchange Perspective," *Journal of Applied Psychology* 97, no. 3 (2012): 557–79.

from productive activities. Disagreement with one's supervisor, for example, wastes productive time, violates the hierarchy of command, and questions the efficient assignment of authority (where managers make the decisions and employees follow them).

Although the "conflict-is-bad" perspective is now considered too simplistic, conflict can indeed have negative consequences under some circumstances (see Exhibit 10.1).[5] Conflict has been criticized for reducing employee performance by consuming otherwise productive time. It is often stressful, which consumes personal energy and distracts employees from their work. It also increases job dissatisfaction, resulting in higher turnover and lower customer service.[6]

People who experience conflict also tend to reduce their information sharing and other forms of coordination with each other. Ironically, with less communication, the feuding parties are more likely to escalate their disagreement because each side relies increasingly on distorted perceptions and stereotypes of the other party. Conflict fuels organizational politics, such as motivating employees to find ways to undermine the credibility of their opponents. Finally, conflict among team members may undermine team cohesion and performance.

Benefits of Conflict In the 1920s, when most organizational scholars viewed conflict as inherently dysfunctional, a few experts argued that conflict can have positive outcomes.[7] But it wasn't until the 1970s that conflict management experts began to embrace the notion that some level of conflict can be beneficial.[8] They formed an "optimal conflict" perspective, which states that organizations are most effective when employees experience some level of conflict, but become less effective with high levels of conflict.[9]

What are the benefits of conflict? Conflict energizes people to debate issues and evaluate alternatives more thoroughly. They probe and test each other's way of thinking to better understand the underlying issues that need to be addressed. This discussion and debate tests the logic of arguments and encourages participants to reexamine their basic assumptions about the problem and its possible solution. It prevents individuals and teams from making inferior decisions and potentially helps them develop sounder and more creative solutions.[11]

A second potential benefit is that moderate levels of conflict prevent organizations from becoming nonresponsive to their external environment. Differences of opinion encourage employees to engage in active thinking, and this often involves ongoing questioning and vigilance about how the organization can be more closely aligned with its customers, suppliers, and other stakeholders.[12] A third benefit of conflict occurs when team members have a dispute or competition with external sources. This form of conflict represents an external challenge that potentially increases cohesion within the team (see Chapter 7). People are more motivated to work together when faced with an external threat, such as conflict with people outside the team.

> Conflict is the gadfly of thought. It stirs us to observation and memory. It instigates to invention. It shocks us out of sheeplike passivity, and sets us at noting and contriving.[10]
>
> —John Dewey, educational philosopher/psychologist

Exhibit 10.1 Consequences of Workplace Conflict

Negative Consequences	Positive Consequences
• Lower performance	• Better decision making
• Higher stress, dissatisfaction, and turnover	—Tests logic of arguments
• Less information sharing and coordination	—Questions assumptions
• Increased organizational politics	• More responsive to changing environment
• Wasted resources	• Stronger team cohesion (conflict between the team and outside opponents)
• Weakened team cohesion (conflict among team members)	

THE EMERGING VIEW: TASK AND RELATIONSHIP CONFLICT

The "optimal conflict" perspective remains popular and may be true in some respects; too much of any conflict is probably dysfunctional. However, the emerging school of thought is that there are various types of conflict with different consequences. The two dominant types are task conflict and relationship conflict.[13]

Task Conflict

Task conflict (also called *constructive conflict*) occurs when people focus their discussion around the issue (i.e., the "task") while showing respect for people with other points of view. We view task conflict as an umbrella term for disagreements about the task or decision, including what task should be performed, how should it be done, and who should perform the various task roles.[14] This type of conflict debates the various alternatives and questioning the competence of the people who introduce or support that idea. It also occurs when someone uses status to defend a position ("My suggestion is better because I have the most experience!") because status-based arguments inherently undermine the worth of others in the debate. Relationship conflict even occurs when someone is abrasive or assertive to the extent that the behavior demeans others in the conversation. For example, relationship conflict can occur when a manager bangs his or her fist on the desk while making a logical argument; the physical action implies that the speaker has more power and the followers need harsh signals to get their attention.

Relationship conflict is dysfunctional because it threatens self-esteem, self-enhancement, and self-verification processes (see Chapter 3). It usually triggers defense mechanisms and a competitive orientation between the parties. Relationship conflict also reduces mutual trust because it emphasizes interpersonal differences that weaken any bond that exists between the parties.[17] Relationship conflict escalates more easily than task conflict because the adversaries become less motivated to communicate and share information, making it more difficult for them to discover common

> ## Task conflict keeps the debate focused on the issue and avoids any attention to the competence or power of the participants.

arguments so they can be clarified, redesigned, and tested for logical soundness. The focus is on the assumptions and logical foundation of the ideas presented, not on the characteristics of the people who presented them. In other words, task conflict keeps the debate focused on the issue and avoids any attention to the competence or power of the participants.

Research indicates that task conflict tends to produce the beneficial outcomes described earlier, particularly better decision making.[15] However, there is increasing evidence of an upper limit to the beneficial intensity of any disagreement, above which it would be difficult to remain constructive. In other words, there is likely an optimal level of task conflict.[16]

Relationship Conflict

Whereas task conflict focuses on the issues, **relationship conflict** focuses on characteristics of the people in the dispute. This type of conflict occurs when someone tries to dismiss an idea by

ground and ultimately resolve the conflict. Instead, they rely increasingly on distorted perceptions and stereotypes, which tend to reinforce their perceptions of threat.

Separating Task from Relationship Conflict

From our discussion so far, the logical recommendation is for organizations to encourage task conflict and minimize relationship conflict. This idea sounds good in theory, but separating these two types of conflict isn't easy in practice. Research indicates that we experience some degree of relationship conflict whenever we are engaged in constructive debate.[18] No matter how diplomatically someone questions our ideas and actions, he or she potentially threatens our self-esteem and our public image, which usually triggers our drive to defend. The stronger the level of debate and the more the issue is tied to our self-view, the

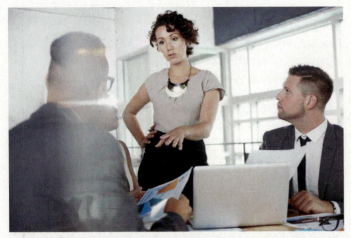

People experience some degree of relationship conflict whenever they engage in constructive debate, but relationship conflict can be minimized through team-level emotional intelligence, cohesion, and supportive norms.
©ESB Basic/Shutterstock

more likely that task conflict will evolve into (or mix with) relationship conflict. Fortunately, three conditions potentially minimize the level of relationship conflict during task conflict episodes.[19]

- *Emotional intelligence and emotional stability.* Relationship conflict is less likely to occur, or is less likely to escalate, when team members have high levels of emotional intelligence and its associated personality characteristic: emotional stability.[20] Employees with higher emotional intelligence and stability are better able to regulate their emotions during debate, which reduces the risk of escalating perceptions of interpersonal hostility. They are also more likely to view a coworker's emotional reaction as valuable information about that person's needs and expectations, rather than as a personal attack.

- *Cohesive team.* Relationship conflict is suppressed when the conflict occurs within a highly cohesive team. The longer people work together, get to know each other, and develop mutual trust, the more latitude they give to each other to show emotions without being personally offended. This might explain why task conflict is more effective in top management teams than in teams of more junior staff.[21] Strong cohesion also allows each person to know about and anticipate the behaviors and emotions of his or her teammates. Another benefit is that cohesion produces a stronger social identity with the group, so team members are motivated to avoid escalating relationship conflict during otherwise emotionally turbulent discussions.

- *Supportive team norms.* Various team norms can hold relationship conflict at bay during task-focused debate. When team norms encourage openness, for instance, team members learn to appreciate honest dialogue without personally reacting to any emotional display during the disagreements.[22] Other norms might discourage team members from displaying negative emotions toward coworkers. Team norms also encourage tactics that diffuse relationship conflict when it first appears. For instance, research has found that teams with low relationship conflict use humor to maintain positive group emotions, which offsets negative feelings team members might develop toward some coworkers during debate.

LO10-3 Diagram the conflict process model and describe six structural sources of conflict in organizations.

CONFLICT PROCESS MODEL

Now that we have outlined the history and current perspectives of conflict and its outcomes, let's look at the model of the conflict process, shown in Exhibit 10.2.[23] This model begins with the sources of conflict, which we will describe in the next section. At some point, the sources of conflict lead one or both

Exhibit 10.2 Model of the Conflict Process

parties to perceive that conflict exists. They become aware that one party's statements and actions are incompatible with their own goals or beliefs. These perceptions usually interact with emotions experienced about the conflict.[24]

Conflict perceptions and emotions produce manifest conflict—the decisions and behaviors of one party toward the other. These *conflict episodes* may range from subtle nonverbal behaviors to warlike aggression. Particularly when people experience high levels of conflict-generated emotions, they have difficulty finding the words and expressions that communicate effectively without further irritating the relationship.[25] Conflict is also behaviorally revealed by the style each side uses to resolve the conflict. Some people tend to avoid the conflict whereas others try to defeat those with opposing views. We discuss different conflict handling styles later in this chapter.

Exhibit 10.2 shows arrows looping back from manifest conflict to conflict perceptions and emotions. These arrows illustrate that the conflict process is really a series of episodes that potentially cycle into conflict escalation.[26] It doesn't take much to start this conflict cycle—just an inappropriate comment, a misunderstanding, or an action that lacks diplomacy.

People experience conflict because their different training, values, beliefs, and experiences (differentiation) produce divergent beliefs about the best way to achieve their common goals.
©Barbara Penoyar/Getty Images

These behaviors cause the other party to perceive that conflict exists. Even if the first party did not intend to demonstrate conflict, the second party's response may create that perception.

STRUCTURAL SOURCES OF CONFLICT IN ORGANIZATIONS

The conflict model starts with the sources of conflict, so we need to understand these sources to effectively diagnose conflict episodes and subsequently resolve the conflict or occasionally to generate conflict where it is lacking. The six main conditions that cause conflict in organizational settings are incompatible goals, differentiation, interdependence, scarce resources, ambiguous rules, and communication problems.

Incompatible Goals

Goal incompatibility occurs when the goals of one person or department seem to interfere with another person's or department's goals.[27] For example, the production department strives for cost-efficiency by scheduling long production runs whereas the sales team emphasizes customer service by delivering the client's product as quickly as possible. If the company runs out of a particular product, the production team would prefer to have clients wait until the next production run. This infuriates sales representatives, who would rather change production quickly to satisfy consumer demand.

Differentiation

Another source of conflict is differentiation—differences among people and work units regarding their training, values, beliefs, and experiences. Differentiation can be distinguished from goal incompatibility; two people or departments may agree on a common goal (serving customers better) but have different beliefs about how to achieve that goal (e.g., standardize employee behavior versus give employees autonomy in customer interactions). Differentiation produces the classic tension between employees from two companies brought together through a merger.[28] Even when people from both companies want the integrated organization to succeed, they fight over the "right way" to do things because of their unique experiences in the separate companies.

Differentiation is also usually a factor in intergenerational conflict. Younger and older employees have different needs, different expectations, and different workplace practices, which sometimes produce conflicting preferences and actions. Studies suggest that these intergenerational differences occur because people develop social identities around technological

> **Every generation needs a new revolution.**[30]
>
> —Attributed to Thomas Jefferson, American Founding Father and third president

developments and other pivotal social events that are unique to their era.[29]

Interdependence

All conflict is caused to some extent by interdependence because conflict exists only when one party perceives that its interests are being opposed or negatively affected by another party. Task interdependence refers to the extent to which employees must share materials, information, or expertise to perform their jobs (see Chapter 7). Conflict is inherently about relationships because people and work units are affected by others only when they have some level of interdependence.

The risk of conflict increases with the level of interdependence.[31] Employees usually have the lowest risk of conflict when working with others in a pooled interdependence relationship. Pooled interdependence occurs where individuals operate independently except for reliance on a common resource or authority. The potential for conflict is higher in sequential interdependence work relationships, such as an assembly line. The highest risk of conflict tends to occur in reciprocal interdependence situations. With reciprocal interdependence, employees have high mutual dependence on each other as well as higher centrality. Consequently, relationships with reciprocal interdependence have the strongest and most immediate risk of interfering with each other's objectives.

Scarce Resources

Resource scarcity generates conflict because each person or unit requiring the same resource necessarily undermines others who also need that resource to fulfill their goals. Most labor strikes, for instance, occur because there aren't enough financial and other resources for employees and company owners to each receive the outcomes they seek, such as higher pay (employees) and higher investment returns (stockholders). Budget deliberations within organizations also produce conflict because there aren't enough funds to satisfy the goals of each work unit. The more resources one group receives, the fewer resources other groups will receive. Fortunately, these interests aren't perfectly opposing in complex negotiations, but limited resources are typically a major source of friction.

Ambiguous Rules

Ambiguous rules—or the complete lack of rules—breed conflict. This occurs because uncertainty increases the risk that one party intends to interfere with the other party's goals. Ambiguity also encourages political tactics and, in some cases, employees enter a free-for-all battle to win decisions in their favor. This explains why conflict is more common during mergers and acquisitions. Employees from both companies have conflicting practices and values, and few rules have developed to minimize the maneuvering for power and resources.[32] When clear rules exist, on the other hand, employees know what to expect from each other and have agreed to abide by those rules.

Ambiguous rules or the complete lack of rules breeds conflict because uncertainty increases the risk that one party intends to interfere with the other party's goals.
©T.Dallas/Shutterstock

Communication Problems

Conflict often occurs due to the lack of opportunity, ability, or motivation to communicate effectively. Let's look at each of these causes. First, when two parties lack the opportunity to communicate, they tend to rely more on stereotypes to understand the other party in the conflict. Unfortunately, stereotypes are sufficiently subjective that emotions can negatively distort the meaning of an opponent's actions, thereby escalating perceptions of conflict. Second, some people lack the necessary skills to communicate in a diplomatic, nonconfrontational manner. When one party communicates its disagreement arrogantly, opponents are more likely to heighten their perception of the conflict. This may lead opponents to reciprocate with a similar response, which further escalates the conflict.[33]

A third problem is that relationship conflict is uncomfortable, so people are less motivated to communicate with others in a disagreement. Unfortunately, less communication can further escalate the conflict because each side has less accurate information about the other side's intentions. To fill in the missing pieces, they rely on distorted images and stereotypes of the other party. Perceptions are further distorted because people in conflict situations tend to engage in more differentiation with those who are unlike themselves (see Chapter 3). This differentiation creates a more positive self-concept and a more negative image of the opponent. We begin to see competitors less favorably so our self-concept remains positive during these conflict episodes.[34]

Flashpoints of Conflict in the Workplace[35]

33% of 617 American and 1,007 UK office employees surveyed say that miscommunication and lack of communication are the most common sources of conflict with other departments (less than 1% difference between results in these two countries).

48% of 1,000 Australian and New Zealand professionals surveyed say they have experienced conflict caused by intergenerational differences (most often due to differing expectations about the company's values and culture).

44% of 2,195 UK employees say the most serious recent conflict incident focused on differences in personality or styles of working.

56% of 427 working Americans surveyed identify personality clashes as a major source of conflict (highest source).

23% of 617 American and 1,007 UK office employees surveyed say that conflicting priorities are the most common sources of conflict with other departments (same percent within each country).

10% of 617 American office employees say they don't experience conflict with any department, group, or team in their organization (12% of 1,007 UK employees say the same).

©donskarpo/Shutterstock

LO10-4 Outline the five conflict-handling styles and discuss the circumstances in which each would be most appropriate.

INTERPERSONAL CONFLICT-HANDLING STYLES

The six sources of conflict lead to conflict perceptions and emotions that, in turn, motivate people to respond in some way to the conflict. More than 70 years ago, organizational behavior pioneer Mary Parker Follett observed that people

respond to perceived and felt conflict through various conflict-handling strategies. Follett's original list was expanded and refined over the years into the five-category model shown in Exhibit 10.3. This model recognizes that how people respond behaviorally to a conflict situation depends on the relative importance they place on maximizing outcomes for themselves and for the other party.[36]

- *Problem solving.* Problem solving tries to find a solution that is beneficial for both parties. This is known as the **win–win orientation** because people using this style believe the resources at stake are expandable rather than fixed if the parties work together to find a creative solution. Information sharing is an important feature of this style because both parties collaborate to identify common ground and potential solutions that satisfy everyone involved.

- *Forcing.* Forcing tries to win the conflict at the other's expense. People who use this style typically have a **win–lose orientation**—they believe the parties are drawing from a fixed pie, so the more one party receives, the less the other party will receive. Consequently, this style relies on assertiveness and other hard influence tactics (see Chapter 9) to get one's own way.

- *Avoiding.* Avoiding tries to smooth over or evade conflict situations altogether. A common avoidance strategy is to steer clear of the coworkers associated with the conflict. A second avoidance strategy is to minimize discussion of the sensitive topic when interacting with the other person in the conflict. Notice from these examples that avoidance does not necessarily mean that we have a low concern for both one's own and the other party's interests. We might be very concerned about the issue but conclude that avoidance is the best solution, at least in the short term.[37]

> **People who use the forcing style typically have a win-lose orientation—they believe the parties are drawing from a fixed pie, so the more one party receives, the less the other party will receive.**

Exhibit 10.3 Interpersonal Conflict-Handling Styles

High

Forcing　　　　　　　　　　　**Problem solving**

Assertiveness
(motivation to
satisfy one's
own interests)

Compromising

Avoiding　　　　　　　　　　　**Yielding**

Low

Low　　　　　　　　　　　　　　　High

Cooperativeness
(motivation to satisfy
other party's interests)

Source: C. K. W. de Dreu, A. Evers, B. Beersma, E. S. Kluwer and A. Nauta, "A Theory-Based Measure of Conflict Management Strategies in the Workplace," *Journal of Organizational Behavior* 22 (2001): 645–68. Reprinted with permission of John Wiley & Sons, Inc.

- *Yielding.* Yielding involves giving in completely to the other side's wishes, or at least cooperating with little or no attention to your own interests. This style involves making unilateral concessions and unconditional promises, as well as offering help with no expectation of reciprocal help.

- *Compromising.* Compromising involves looking for a position in which your losses are offset by equally valued gains. It involves actively searching for a middle ground between the interests of the two parties. Compromising also is associated with matching the other party's concessions and making conditional offers ("If you do X, I'll do Y.").

Choosing the Best Conflict-Handling Style

Chances are that you prefer one or two conflict-handling styles more than the others. You might typically engage in avoiding or yielding because disagreement makes you feel uncomfortable and is contrary to your self-view as someone who likes to get along with everyone. Or perhaps you prefer the compromising and forcing strategies because they reflect your strong need for achievement and to control your environment. People usually gravitate toward one or two conflict-handling styles that match their personality, personal and cultural values, and past experience.[38] However, the best style depends on the situation, so we need to understand and develop the capacity to use any of the five styles for the appropriate occasions.[39] The contingencies, as well as problems with using each conflict-handling style, are outlined in Exhibit 10.4.

Exhibit 10.4 Conflict-Handling Style Contingencies and Problems

Conflict-Handling Style	Preferred Style When . . .	Problems with this Style
Problem solving	• Interests are not perfectly opposing (i.e., not pure win–lose) • Parties have trust, openness, and time to share information • Issues are complex	• Sharing information that the other party might use to his or her advantage
Forcing	• You have a deep conviction about your position (e.g., believe other person's behavior is unethical) • Dispute requires a quick solution • Other party would take advantage of more cooperative strategies	• Highest risk of relationship conflict • May damage long-term relations, reducing future problem solving
Avoiding	• Conflict has become too emotionally charged • Cost of trying to resolve the conflict outweighs the benefits	• Doesn't usually resolve the conflict • May increase other party's frustration
Yielding	• Other party has substantially more power • Issue is much less important to you than to the other party • The value and logic of your position aren't as clear	• Increases other party's expectations in future conflict episodes
Compromising	• Parties have equal power • Time pressure to resolve the conflict • Parties lack trust/openness for problem solving	• Suboptimal solution where mutual gains are possible

Problem solving is widely recognized as the preferred conflict-handling style, whenever possible, because it is the best strategy to guide the parties toward a win–win solution. In addition, the problem-solving style tends to improve long-term relationships, reduce stress, and minimize emotional defensiveness and other indications of relationship conflict.[40] This style works best when there are opportunities for mutual gains, such as when the conflict is complex with multiple elements.

The problem-solving style is not optimal in all situations, however. If the conflict is simple and perfectly opposing (each party wants more of a single fixed pie), then the problem-solving style will waste time and increase frustration. It also takes more time and requires a fairly high degree of trust because there is a risk that the other party will take advantage of the information you have openly shared. The problem-solving style can be stressful and

The problem-solving style of conflict handling is less effective when the conflict is simple and perfectly opposing (each party wants more of a single fixed pie).
©Pandora Studio/Shutterstock

difficult when people experience strong feelings of conflict, likely because these negative emotions undermine trust in the other party.[41]

The conflict-avoidance style is often ineffective because it doesn't resolve the conflict and may increase the other party's frustration. However, avoiding may be the best strategy where conflict has become emotionally charged or where conflict resolution would cost more than its benefits.[42] The forcing style is usually inappropriate because it frequently generates relationship conflict more quickly or intensely than other conflict-handling styles. However, forcing may be necessary when you know you are correct (e.g., the other party's position is unethical or based on obviously flawed logic), the dispute requires a quick solution, or the other party would take advantage of a more cooperative conflict-handling style.

The yielding style may be appropriate when the other party has substantially more power, the issue is not as important to

The more arguments you win, the fewer friends you will have.[43]
—Unknown source, popular adage since late 1800s

you as to the other party, and you aren't confident that your position has superior logical or ethical justification.[44] On the other hand, yielding behaviors may give the other side unrealistically high expectations, thereby motivating them to seek more from you in the future. In the long run, yielding may produce more conflict, rather than resolve it. "Raised voices, red faces, and table thumping is a far less dysfunctional way of challenging each other than withdrawal, passivity and sullen acceptance," explains one conflict management consultant. "It doesn't mean that people agree with you: they just take their misgivings underground and spread them throughout the organization, which has a corrosive effect."[45]

The compromising style may be best when the problem-solving approach offers little hope for mutual gain, both parties have equal power, and both are under time pressure to settle their differences. However, we rarely know whether the parties have perfectly opposing interests, yet the compromise approach assumes this win–lose orientation. Therefore, entering a conflict with the compromising style may cause the parties to overlook better solutions because they have not attempted to share enough information and creatively look for win–win alternatives.

Cultural and Gender Differences in Conflict-Handling Styles

Cultural values and norms influence the conflict-handling style used most often in a society, so they also represent an important contingency when choosing the preferred conflict-handling approach in that culture. For example, people who frequently use the conflict avoidance style might have more problems in cultures where the forcing style is common.[47]

Men and women also rely on different conflict-handling styles to some degree.[48] The clearest difference is that men are more likely than women to use the forcing style, whether as managers or nonmanagement employees. Female managers are more likely than male managers to use the avoiding style, whereas this difference is less pronounced between female and male nonmanagement employees. The male preference for forcing has a logical foundation. Compared to men, women pay more attention to the relationship between the parties, so their preferred style tries to protect the relationship. This is apparent in less use of the forcing and more use of the avoiding styles of conflict handling. Women are also slightly more likely than men to use the compromising and yielding styles.

LO10-5 Apply the six structural approaches to conflict management and describe the three types of third-party dispute resolution.

STRUCTURAL APPROACHES TO CONFLICT MANAGEMENT

Conflict-handling styles describe how we approach the other party in a conflict situation. But conflict management also involves altering the underlying structural causes of potential conflict. The main structural approaches parallel the sources of conflict discussed earlier. These structural approaches include emphasizing superordinate goals, reducing differentiation, improving communication and understanding, reducing task interdependence, increasing resources, and clarifying rules and procedures.

Emphasizing Superordinate Goals

One of the oldest recommendations for resolving conflict is to refocus the parties' attention around superordinate goals and away from the conflicting subordinate goals.[49] **Superordinate goals** are goals that the conflicting employees or departments value and whose attainment requires the joint resources and effort of those parties.[50] These goals are called superordinate because they are higher-order aspirations such as the organization's strategic objectives rather than objectives specific to the individual or work unit. Research indicates that the most effective executive teams frame their

Steering Clear of Workplace Conflict[46]

37% of 616 American managers surveyed say they are uncomfortable giving direct performance feedback/criticism to their employees that they might respond badly to.

46% of 1,554 Australian employees polled say they would rather seek a new job than deal with a workplace conflict.

25% of 2,195 UK employees say the most common negative behavior resulting from recent conflict episodes was the refusal to work together or cooperate with each other.

20% of 926 American employees surveyed say they avoid some coworkers because of their political views (54% of employees say they avoid talking about politics at all with colleagues).

©Alhovik/Shutterstock

Reducing Differentiation

Differentiation—differences regarding training, values, beliefs, and experiences—was identified earlier as one of the main sources of workplace conflict. Therefore, reducing differentiation is a logical approach to reducing dysfunctional conflict. As people develop common experiences and beliefs, they become more motivated to coordinate activities and resolve their disputes through constructive discussion.[53] One way to reduce differentiation is to rotate key staff to different departments or regions throughout their career. This career development process develops common experiences around the entire company rather than within different areas. Another way to reduce differentiation is to have employees from different parts of the organization work together on important (and hopefully successful) projects. These projects become a common ground for otherwise diverse employee groups. A third strategy is to build and maintain a strong organizational culture. Employees have shared values and assumptions in a company with a strong culture, and Chapter 13 describes specific activities to support a strong culture.

Improving Communication and Mutual Understanding

A third way to resolve dysfunctional conflict is to give the conflicting parties more opportunities to communicate and understand each other. This recommendation applies two principles and practices introduced in Chapter 3: the Johari Window model and meaningful interaction. Although both were previously described as ways to improve self-awareness, they are equally valuable to improve other-awareness.

In the Johari Window process, individuals disclose more about themselves so others have a better understanding of the underlying causes of their behavior. A variation of Johari Window occurs in "lunch and learn" sessions, where employees in one functional area describe work and its challenges to co-workers in other areas. Meaningful interaction potentially improves mutual understanding through the contact hypothesis, which says that we develop a more person-specific and accurate understanding of others by working closely with them.[54]

Although communication and mutual understanding can work well, there are two important warnings. First, these interventions should be applied only where differentiation is sufficiently low or *after* differentiation has been reduced. If perceived differentiation remains high, attempts to manage conflict through dialogue might escalate rather than reduce relationship conflict. The reason is that when forced to interact with people who we believe are quite different and in conflict with us, we tend to select information that reinforces that view.[55]

The second warning is that people in collectivist and high power distance cultures are less comfortable with the practice of resolving differences through direct and open communication.[56] Recall that people in collectivist cultures prefer an avoidance conflict-handling style because it is the most consistent with harmony and face saving. Direct communication is a high-risk

One of the oldest recommendations for resolving conflict is to refocus the parties' attention around superordinate goals and away from the conflicting subordinate goals.
©Pixtal/age fotostock

decisions as superordinate goals that rise above each executive's departmental or divisional goals. Similarly, effective leaders reduce conflict through an inspirational vision that unifies employees and makes them less preoccupied with their subordinate goal differences.[51]

Suppose that marketing staff members want a new product released quickly, whereas engineers want more time to test and add new features. Leaders can potentially reduce this interdepartmental conflict by reminding both groups of the company's mission to serve customers, or by pointing out that competitors currently threaten the company's leadership in the industry. By increasing commitment to companywide goals (customer focus, competitiveness), engineering and marketing employees pay less attention to their competing departmental-level goals, which reduces their perceived conflict with each other. Superordinate goals also potentially reduce the problem of differentiation because they establish feelings of a shared social identity (work for the same company).[52]

shared leadership the view that leadership is a role, not a position assigned to one person; consequently, people within the team and organization lead each other

transformational leadership a leadership perspective that explains how leaders change teams or organizations by creating, communicating, and modeling a vision for the organization or work unit and inspiring employees to strive for that vision

hierarchy. Formal leaders are responsible for "leading" others, but companies are far more effective when everyone assumes leadership responsibilities in various ways and at various times. This emerging view, called **shared leadership**, is based on the idea that leadership is a role, not a position.[6] It doesn't belong to just one individual in the work unit. Instead, when Gore employees are asked, "Are you a leader?" in annual surveys, more than 50 percent of them answer yes.[8]

Shared leadership flourishes in organizations where the formal leaders are willing to delegate power and encourage employees to take initiative and risks without fear of failure (i.e., a learning orientation culture). Shared leadership also calls for a collaborative rather than internally competitive culture because employees succeed in shared leadership roles only when their coworkers support them in these roles. Furthermore, shared leadership lacks formal authority, so it operates best when employees learn to influence others through their enthusiasm, logical analysis, and involvement of coworkers in their idea or vision.

> " We've abandoned the Great Man model of leadership that long characterized Fiat and have created a culture where everyone is expected to lead.[9] "
>
> —Sergio Marchionne, CEO of Fiat Chrysler Automobiles and Ferrari

employees lead each other as the occasion arises. Shared leadership exists when employees champion the introduction of new technologies and products.[7] It also exists when employees engage in organizational citizenship behaviors to assist the performance and well-being of coworkers and the overall team.

Shared leadership typically supplements formal leadership; that is, employees lead along with the formal manager, rather than as a replacement for that manager. However, W. L. Gore & Associates, Semco SA, Valve Corporation, and a few other unique companies rely almost completely on shared leadership because they don't have any formal managers on the organizational chart. In fact,

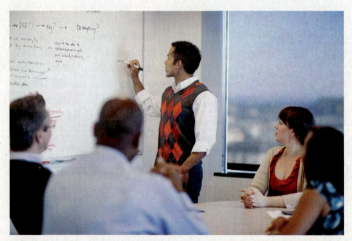

Shared leadership is based on the idea that leadership is a role, not a position; everyone assumes leadership responsibilities in various ways and at various times.
©Inti St Clair/Blend Images

LO11-2 Describe the four elements of transformational leadership and explain why they are important for organizational change.

TRANSFORMATIONAL LEADERSHIP PERSPECTIVE

Most leadership concepts and practices can be organized into four perspectives: transformational, managerial, implicit, and personal attributes. By far the most popular of these perspectives today—and arguably the most important in the domain of leadership—is transformational leadership. **Transformational leadership** views leaders as change agents. They move the organization or work unit in a new direction that will provide better opportunities and alignment with the external environment.

The four elements of transformational leadership models most frequently identified in the literature are develop and communicate a strategic vision, model the vision, encourage experimentation, and build commitment to the vision (see Exhibit 11.1).[10] Transformational leaders create, communicate, and model a shared vision for the team or organization. They encourage experimentation so employees find a better path to the future. Through these and other activities, transformational leaders also build commitment in followers to strive for that vision.

Exhibit 11.1 Elements of Transformational Leadership

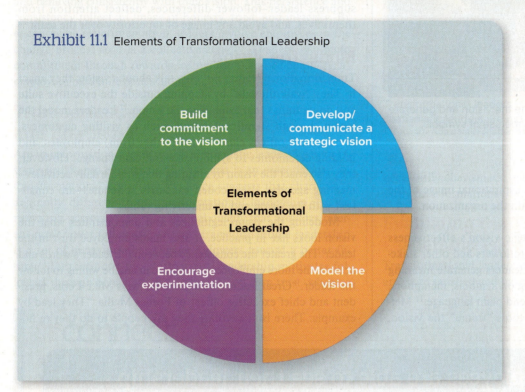

Build commitment to the vision

Develop/communicate a strategic vision

Elements of Transformational Leadership

Encourage experimentation

Model the vision

vision is particularly meaningful and appealing to employees, which energizes them to strive for that ideal. Another reason why a strategic vision motivates employees is because it is a distant goal that is both challenging and abstract. A vision is challenging because it requires substantial transformation, such as new work practices and belief systems.

A strategic vision is necessarily abstract for two reasons. One reason is that the vision hasn't yet been experienced (at least, not in this company or industry), so it isn't possible to detail exactly what the vision looks like. The other reason is that an abstract description enables the vision to remain stable over time, yet is sufficiently flexible to accommodate operational adjustments in a shifting external environment.

Another feature of an effective vision is that it is unifying. It is a superordinate objective that bonds employees together and aligns their personal values with the organization's values. In fact, a successful vision is really a shared vision because employees

Develop and Communicate a Strategic Vision

The heart of transformational leadership is a strategic *vision*.[11] A vision is a positive image or model of the future that energizes and unifies employees.[12] Sometimes this vision is created by the leader; at other times, it is formed by employees or other stakeholders and then adopted and championed by the formal leader. William Rogers, CEO of British radio station group UKRD, emphasizes that one of the key features of successful leaders is their "clarity of vision, so people can say: 'I know where we're going, what this journey is about, what our noble cause is.' For us, it's not just running a radio group and commercial success—it's about changing people's lives, impacting on communities."[13]

An effective strategic vision has several identifiable features.[15] It refers to an idealized future with a higher purpose. This purpose is associated with personal values that directly or indirectly fulfill the needs of multiple stakeholders. A values-based

Not Quite Leading with Vision[16]

47% of 1,200 Canadian employees surveyed strongly or somewhat agree that senior management in their organization communicates a clear vision.

42% of more than 40,000 employees surveyed in 300 global companies say they know their organization's vision, mission, and values.

©Barbara Penoyar/Stockbyte/Getty Images

61% of 32,000 employees surveyed globally say their company's leaders communicate a clear and compelling vision of the future.

40% of 1,061 American employees surveyed say they don't get (understand) the company's vision or have never seen it.

38% of 168,000 employees surveyed across 30 countries say they either do not believe in their employer's mission/purpose (vision) or don't understand it.

managerial leadership a leadership perspective stating that effective leaders help employees improve their performance and well-being toward current objectives and practices

concept; the theory implies that it should be applied in all situations. Only a few studies have investigated whether this transformational leadership is more valuable in some situations than others.[36] Preliminary evidence suggests that the transformational leadership perspective is relevant across cultures. However, there may be specific elements of transformational leadership, such as the way visions are communicated and modeled, that are more appropriate in North America than in other cultures.

LO11-3 Compare managerial leadership with transformational leadership, and describe the features of task-oriented, people-oriented, and servant leadership.

MANAGERIAL LEADERSHIP PERSPECTIVE

Leaders don't spend all (or even most) of their time transforming the organization or work unit. They also engage in **managerial leadership**—daily activities that support and guide the performance and well-being of individual employees and the work unit toward current objectives and practices. Leadership experts recognize that leading (transformational leadership) differs from managing (managerial leadership).[37] Although the distinction between these two perspectives remains somewhat fuzzy, each cluster has a reasonably clear set of activities and strong research foundation.

contrast, leaders "do the right thing," which means that transformational leadership behaviors change the organization or work unit so its objectives are aligned more closely with the external environment.

A second distinction is that managerial leadership is more micro-focused and concrete because it relates to the specific performance and well-being objectives of individual employees and the immediate work unit. Transformational leadership is more macro-focused and abstract. It is directed toward an imprecise strategic vision for an entire organization, department, or team.

Interdependence of Managerial and Transformational Leadership

Although transformational and managerial leadership are discussed as two leadership perspectives, they are more appropriately viewed as *interdependent* perspectives.[40] In other words, transformational leadership and managerial leadership depend on each other. Transformational leadership identifies, communicates, and builds commitment to a better future for the organization or work unit. But these transformational leadership behaviors are not enough for organizational success. That success also requires managerial leadership to translate the abstract vision into more specific operational behaviors and practices, and to continuously improve employee performance and well-being in the pursuit of that future ideal. Managerial leadership also depends on transformational leadership to set the right direction. Otherwise, managers might produce operational excellence toward goals that are misaligned with the organization's long-term survival.

Senior executive positions call for more transformational leadership behavior than do managerial positions further down the hierarchy, likely because transformational leadership requires

---

> ## Managers are people who do things right and leaders are people who do the right thing.[38]
>
> —Warren Bennis, leadership scholar (based on earlier writing by Peter Drucker)

One distinction between these two perspectives is that managerial leadership assumes the organization's (or department's) objectives are stable and aligned with the external environment, whereas transformational leadership assumes the organization (or department) is misaligned with its environment and therefore needs to change its direction.[39] An often-cited saying is that managers "do things right," which means that managerial leadership behaviors focus on making employees and work units more effective at established objectives and practices. In

more discretion to enable macro-level change. However, managerial and transformational leadership are not embodied in different people or positions in the organization. Every manager needs to apply both transformational and managerial leadership behaviors to varying degrees. Indeed, even frontline nonmanagement employees who engage in shared leadership may be managerial (helping coworkers through a difficult project) or transformational (championing more customer-friendly norms in the work unit).

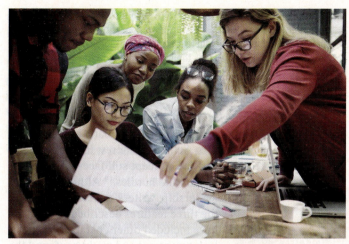

Transformational leadership requires managerial leadership to translate the abstract vision into more specific operational behaviors and practices; managerial leadership requires transformational leadership to set the right direction.
©Rawpixel.com/Shutterstock

Task-Oriented and People-Oriented Leadership

Managerial leadership research began in the 1940s when several universities launched intensive investigations to answer the question "What behaviors make leaders effective?" They studied first-line supervisors by asking subordinates to rate their bosses

on many behaviors. These independent research teams essentially identified the same two clusters of leadership behavior from literally thousands of items (Exhibit 11.2).[41]

One cluster, called *task-oriented leadership*, includes behaviors that define and structure work roles. Task-oriented leaders assign employees to specific tasks, set goals and deadlines, clarify work duties and procedures, define work procedures, and plan work activities. The other cluster represents *people-oriented leadership*. This cluster includes behaviors such as listening to employees' ideas, creating a pleasant physical work environment, showing interest in staff, appreciating employees for their contributions, and showing consideration of employee needs.

These early managerial leadership studies tried to find out whether effective managers are more task-oriented or more people-oriented. This proved to be a difficult question to answer because each style has its advantages and disadvantages. In fact, recent evidence suggests that effective leaders rely on both styles, but in different circumstances.[42] When leaders apply high levels of people-oriented leadership behavior, their employees tend to have more positive attitudes as well as lower absenteeism, grievances, stress, and turnover. When leaders apply task-oriented leadership behaviors, their employees tend to have higher job performance. Not surprisingly, employees generally prefer people-oriented bosses and they form negative attitudes toward bosses who are mostly task-oriented. However, task-oriented leadership also is appreciated to some degree. For example, college students value task-oriented instructors because those instructors provide clear expectations and well-prepared lectures that abide by the course objectives.[43]

Servant Leadership

Servant leadership is an extension or variation of people-oriented leadership because it defines leadership as serving others. In particular, servant leaders assist others in their need fulfillment, personal development, and growth.[44] Servant leaders ask, "How can I help you?" rather than expecting employees to serve them. Servant leaders have been described as selfless, egalitarian, humble, nurturing, empathetic, and ethical coaches. The main objective of servant leadership is to help followers and other

servant leadership the view that leaders serve followers, rather than vice versa; leaders help employees fulfill their needs and are coaches, stewards, and facilitators of employee development

Exhibit 11.2 Task- and People-Oriented Leadership Styles

Leaders are task-oriented when they . . .	Leaders are people-oriented when they . . .
• Assign work and clarify responsibilities. • Set goals and deadlines. • Evaluate and provide feedback on work quality. • Establish well-defined best work procedures. • Plan future work activities.	• Show interest in others as people. • Listen to employees. • Make the workplace more pleasant. • Show appreciation to employees for their performance contribution. • Are considerate of employee needs.

Knowledge of the Business

Effective leaders possess tacit and explicit knowledge of the business environment in which they operate, including subtle indications of emerging trends. Knowledge of the business also includes a good understanding of how their organization works effectively.

Cognitive and Practical Intelligence

Leaders have above-average cognitive ability to process enormous amounts of information. Leaders aren't necessarily geniuses; rather, they have a superior ability to analyze a variety of complex alternatives and opportunities. Furthermore, leaders have practical intelligence. This means that they can think through the relevance and application of ideas in real-world settings. Practical intelligence is particularly evident where problems are poorly defined, information is missing, and more than one solution may be plausible.[84]

Emotional Intelligence

Effective leaders have a high level of emotional intelligence. They are able to recognize and regulate emotions in themselves and in other people (see Chapter 4).[85] For example, effective leaders can tell when their conversations are having the intended emotional effect on employees. They also are able to recognize and change their own emotional state to suit the situation, such as feeling optimistic and determined in spite of recent business setbacks.

Authentic Leadership

A few paragraphs ago, we said that successful leaders have a complex, internally consistent, and clear self-concept as a leader, and that they have a strong positive self-evaluation. These characteristics lay the foundation for **authentic leadership**, which refers to how well leaders are aware of, feel comfortable with, and act consistently with their values, personality, and self-concept.[86] Authenticity is mainly about knowing yourself and being yourself (see Exhibit 11.5). Leaders learn more about their personality, values, thoughts, and habits by reflecting on various situations and personal experiences. They also improve this self-awareness by receiving feedback from trusted

Authentic leadership begins by knowing yourself better through self-reflection and receptivity to feedback from trusted sources.
©michaeljung/Shutterstock

people inside and outside the organization. Both self-reflection and receptivity to feedback require high levels of emotional intelligence.

As people learn more about themselves, they gain a greater understanding of their inner purpose, which, in turn, generates a long-term passion for achieving something worthwhile for the organization or society. Some leadership experts suggest that this inner purpose emerges from a life story, typically initiated by a transformative event or experience earlier in life.[87]

Authentic leadership is more than self-awareness; it also involves behaving in ways that are consistent with that self-concept rather than pretending to be someone else. It is difficult enough to lead others as your natural self; to lead others while pretending to be someone else is nearly impossible. To be themselves, great leaders regulate their decisions and behavior in several ways. First, they develop their own style and, where appropriate, move into positions where that style is most effective. Although effective leaders adapt their behavior to the situation to some extent, they invariably understand and rely on decision methods and interpersonal styles that feel most comfortable to them.

Second, effective leaders continually think about and consistently apply their stable hierarchy of personal values to those decisions and behaviors. Leaders face many pressures and temptations, such as achieving short-term stock price targets at the cost of long-term profitability. Experts note that authentic leaders demonstrate self-discipline by remaining anchored to their values. Third, leaders maintain consistency around their self-concept by having a strong, positive core self-evaluation. They have high self-esteem and self-efficacy as well as an internal locus of control (Chapter 3).

Exhibit 11.5 Authentic Leadership

Know yourself:	Be yourself:
• Engage in self-reflection. • Receive feedback from trusted sources. • Understand your life story.	• Develop your own style. • Apply your values. • Maintain a positive core self-evaluation.

Personal Attributes Perspective Limitations and Practical Implications

Personality, experience, self-concept, and other personal characteristics potentially contribute to a leader's effectiveness. Still, the leadership attributes perspective has a few limitations.[88] First, it assumes that all effective leaders have the same personal characteristics that are equally important in all situations. This is probably a false assumption; leadership is far too complex to have a universal list of traits that apply to every condition. Some attributes might not be important all the time. Second, alternative combinations of attributes may be equally successful; two people with different sets of personal characteristics might be equally good leaders. Third, the personal attributes perspective views leadership as something within a person, yet experts emphasize that leadership is relational. People are effective leaders because of their favorable relationships with followers, not just because they possess specific personal characteristics.[89]

Also remember from our discussion earlier in this chapter that, in the short term, followers tend to define others as effective or ineffective leaders based on their personal characteristics rather than whether the leader actually makes a difference to the organization's success. People who exhibit self-confidence, extraversion, and other traits are called leaders because they fit the widely held prototype of an effective leader. Alternatively, if someone is successful, observers might assign several nonobservable personal characteristics to him or her, such as intelligence, confidence, and drive. In short, the link between personal characteristics and effective leadership is muddied by several perceptual distortions.

One important final point: The personal attributes perspective of leadership does not necessarily imply that leadership is a talent acquired at birth. On the contrary, attributes indicate only leadership *potential*, not leadership performance. People with these characteristics become effective leaders only after they have developed and mastered the necessary leadership behaviors. However, even those with fewer leadership attributes may become very effective leaders by more fully developing their potential.

LO11-7 Discuss cultural and gender similarities and differences in leadership.

CROSS-CULTURAL AND GENDER ISSUES IN LEADERSHIP

Along with the four perspectives of leadership presented throughout this chapter, cultural values and practices affect what leaders do. Culture shapes the leader's values and norms, which influence his or her decisions and actions. Cultural values

Cultural values influence the leader's decisions and actions; they also shape the expectations that followers have of their leaders.
©Rawpixel.com/Shutterstock

also shape the expectations that followers have of their leaders. An executive who acts inconsistently with cultural expectations is more likely to be perceived as an ineffective leader. Furthermore, leaders who deviate from those values may experience various forms of influence to get them to conform to the leadership norms and expectations of the society. Thus, differences in leadership practices across cultures are partly explained by implicit leadership theory, which was described earlier in this chapter.

A major global research project over the past two decades has found that some features of leadership are universal and some differ across cultures.[90] One leadership category, called "charismatic visionary," is a universally recognized concept and middle managers around the world believe it is characteristic of effective leaders. Charismatic visionary represents a cluster of concepts including visionary, inspirational, performance orientation, integrity, and decisiveness.[91] In contrast, participative leadership is perceived as characteristic of effective leadership in low power distance cultures but less so in high power distance cultures. In summary, some features of leadership are universal and some differ across cultures.

Gender and Leadership

Studies in work settings have generally found that male and female leaders do not differ in their levels of task-oriented or people-oriented leadership. The main explanation is that real-world jobs require similar behavior from male and female job incumbents.[92] However, women do adopt a participative leadership style more readily than their male counterparts. One possible reason is that, compared to boys, girls are often raised to be more egalitarian and less status-oriented, which is consistent with being participative. There is also some evidence that, compared to men, women have somewhat better interpersonal skills, and this translates into their relatively greater use of the participative leadership style. A third explanation is that employees, on the basis of their own gender stereotypes, expect female leaders to be more participative, so female leaders comply with follower expectations to some extent.

Surveys report that women are rated higher than men on the emerging leadership qualities of coaching, teamwork, and empowering employees.[93] Yet research also suggests that women are evaluated negatively when they try to apply the full range of leadership styles, particularly more directive and autocratic approaches. Thus, ironically, women may be well suited to contemporary leadership roles, yet they often continue to face limitations of leadership due to followers' gender stereotypes and prototypes of leaders.[94] Overall, both male and female leaders must be sensitive to the fact that followers have expectations about how leaders should act. Leaders who deviate from those expectations may discover that followers evaluate them more harshly.

Study Checklist

Connect® Management is available for *M Organizational Behavior*. Additional resources include:

✓ Interactive Applications:
- **Decision Generator**
- **Drag and Drop:** Work through an interactive example to test your knowledge of the concepts.
- **Video Case:** See management in action through interactive videos

✓ **SmartBook™**—SmartBook is the first and only adaptive reading experience available today. Distinguishing what you know from what you don't, and honing in on concepts you are most likely to forget, SmartBook personalizes content for you in a continuously adapting reading experience. Reading is no longer a passive and linear experience, but an engaging and dynamic one where you are more likely to master and retain important concepts and go to class better prepared.

©Natthawat Jamnapa/123RF

Notes

1. C. McMorrow, *Entrepreneurs Turn Us On: 20 Years of Recognizing Bright Ideas,* EY Entrepreneur of the year—Ontario 2013, Ernst & Young (October 2013); D. Ovsey, "'Get out of the Way,'" *National Post,* February 18, 2014.

2. Most of these statistics were collected in March 2017. Library of Congress data were collected in 2010.

3. Many of these perspectives are summarized in R. N. Kanungo, "Leadership in Organizations: Looking Ahead to the 21st Century," *Canadian Psychology* 39 (1998): 71–82; G. A. Yukl, *Leadership in Organizations,* 8th ed. (Upper Saddle River, NJ: Pearson Education, 2013).

4. *State of the American Manager: Analytics and Advice for Leaders* (Washington, DC: Gallup, March 2015); CareerBuilder, "4 in 10 Indian Employees Believe Their Boss Has Room for Improvement," news release (Noida, India: CareerMuse, August 6, 2015); *Connecting the Dots between Retention and Employee Development,* Saba Global Workforce Survey (Redwood Shores, CA: Saba, November 2015); CareerBuilder, "Bosses in the Western U.S. Receive Higher Praise from Their Employees," news release (Chicago: PR Newswire, May 25, 2016); *Rewriting the Rules for the Digital Age,* 2017 Deloitte Global Human Capital Trends, Deloitte (New York: Deloitte University Press, February 2017).

5. R. House, M. Javidan, and P. Dorfman, "Project GLOBE: An Introduction," *Applied Psychology: An International Review* 50 (2001): 489–505; R. House et al., "Understanding Cultures and Implicit Leadership Theories across the Globe: An Introduction to Project GLOBE," *Journal of World Business* 37 (2002): 3–10.

6. J. A. Raelin, "We the Leaders: In Order to Form a Leaderful Organization," *Journal of Leadership & Organizational Studies* 12, no. 2 (2005): 18–30; C. L. Pearce, J. A. Conger, and E. A. Locke, "Shared Leadership Theory," *Leadership Quarterly* 19, no. 5 (2008): 622–28; E. Engel Small and J. R. Rentsch, "Shared Leadership in Teams: A Matter of Distribution," *Journal of Personnel Psychology* 9, no. 4 (2010): 203–11.

7. C. A. Beatty, "Implementing Advanced Manufacturing Technologies: Rules of the Road," *Sloan Management Review* (1992): 49–60; J. M. Howell, "The Right Stuff: Identifying and Developing Effective Champions of Innovation," *Academy of Management Executive* 19, no. 2 (2005): 108–19; J. M. Howell and C. M. Shea, "Effects of Champion Behavior, Team Potency, and External Communication Activities on Predicting Team Performance," *Group & Organization Management* 31, no. 2 (2006): 180–211.

8. D. Anfuso, "Core Values Shape W. L. Gore's Innovative Culture," *Workforce* 78, no. 3 (1999): 48–53.

9. S. Marchionne, "Fiat's Extreme Makeover," *Harvard Business Review* (2008): 45–48.

10. Most or all of these elements are included in W. Bennis and B. Nanus, *Leaders: The Strategies for Taking Charge* (New York: Harper & Row, 1985); N. M. Tichy and M. A. Devanna, *The Transformational Leader* (New York: Wiley, 1986); B. M. Bass and R. E. Riggio, *Transformational Leadership,* 2nd ed. (Mahwah, NJ: Erlbaum, 2006); J. M. Kouzes and B. Z. Posner, *The Leadership Challenge,* 5th ed. (San Francisco: Jossey-Bass, 2012).

11. Strategic collective vision has been identified as a key factor in leadership since Chester Barnard's seminal book in organizational behavior. See C. Barnard, *The Functions of the Executive* (Cambridge, MA: Harvard University Press, 1938), 86–89.

12. W. Bennis and B. Nanus, *Leaders: The Strategies for Taking Charge* (New York: Harper & Row, 1985), 27-33, 89; R. E. Quinn, *Building the Bridge as You Walk on It: A Guide for Leading Change* (San Francisco: Jossey-Bass, 2004), chap. 11; R. Gill, *Theory and Practice of Leadership* (London: Sage, 2011), chap. 4; D. O'Connell, K. Hickerson, and A. Pillutla, "Organizational Visioning: An Integrative Review," *Group & Organization Management* 36, no. 1 (2011): 103-25.

13. J. Faragher, "Employee Engagement: The Secret of UKRD's Success," *Personnel Today*, May 3, 2013; S. Waite, "Warm Hearts Bring Cheer and Rewards," *Sunday Times* (London), March 3, 2013.

14. N. Augustine, *Augustine's Laws,* 3rd ed. (New York: Viking, 1986), 32.

15. J. M. Strange and M. D. Mumford, "The Origins of Vision: Effects of Reflection, Models, and Analysis," *Leadership Quarterly* 16, no. 1 (2005): 121-48; S. Kantabutra, "Toward a Behavioral Theory of Vision in Organizational Settings," *Leadership & Organization Development Journal* 30, no. 4 (2009): 319-37; S. A. Kirkpatrick, "Lead through Vision and Values," in *Handbook of Principles of Organizational Behavior*, ed. E. A. Locke (Chichester, UK: Wiley, 2010), 367-87; R. Gill, *Theory and Practice of Leadership* (London: Sage, 2011), chap. 4.

16. Canadian Management Centre, *Build a Better Workplace: Employee Engagement Edition* (Toronto: Canadian Management Centre, August 23, 2012); Kelly Services, *The Leadership Disconnect* (Troy, MI: Kelly Services, August 2012); TINYpulse, *7 Vital Trends Disrupting Today's Workplace*, 2013 TINYpulse Employment Engagement Survey (Seattle: TINYpulse, December 2013); Root, "New Study Reveals What U.S. Employees Think about Today's Workplace," news release (Sylvania, OH: Root, March 26, 2013); Towers Watson, *Global Workforce Study: At a Glance*, (London: Towers Watson, August 2014).

17. J. A. Conger and R. N. Kanungo, *Charismatic Leadership in Organizations* (Thousand Oaks, CA: Sage, 1998), 173-83; M. Venus, D. Stam, and D. van Knippenberg, "Leader Emotion as a Catalyst of Effective Leader Communication of Visions, Value-Laden Messages, and Goals," *Organizational Behavior and Human Decision Processes* 122, no. 1 (2013): 53-68; J. Mayfield, M. Mayfield, and W. C. Sharbrough, "Strategic Vision and Values in Top Leaders' Communications: Motivating Language at a Higher Level," *International Journal of Business Communication* 52, no. 1 (2015): 97-121.

18. D. A. Waldman, P. A. Balthazard, and S. J. Peterson, "Leadership and Neuroscience: Can We Revolutionize the Way That Inspirational Leaders Are Identified and Developed?," *Academy of Management Perspectives* 25, no. 1 (2011): 60-74; S. Denning, *The Leader's Guide to Storytelling: Mastering the Art and Discipline of Business Narrative*, rev. ed. (San Francisco: Jossey-Bass, 2011); J. C. Sarros et al., "Leaders and Their Use of Motivating Language," *Leadership & Organization Development Journal* 35, no. 3 (2014): 226-40; A. M. Carton, C. Murphy, and J. R. Clark, "A (Blurry) Vision of the Future: How Leader Rhetoric About Ultimate Goals Influences Performance," *Academy of Management Journal* 57, no. 6 (2014): 1544-70.

19. R. Shook, *Heart & Soul: Five American Companies That Are Making the World a Better Place* (Dallas: BenBella Books, 2010), 155-222.

20. L. Black, "Hamburger Diplomacy," *Report on Business Magazine*, August 1988, 30-36.

21. J. E. Baur et al., "More Than One Way to Articulate a Vision: A Configurations Approach to Leader Charismatic Rhetoric and Influence," *Leadership Quarterly* 27, no. 1 (2016): 156-71.

22. D. E. Berlew, "Leadership and Organizational Excitement," *California Management Review* 17, no. 2 (1974): 21-30; W. Bennis and B. Nanus, *Leaders: The Strategies for Taking Charge* (New York: Harper & Row, 1985), 43-55; T. Simons, "Behavioral Integrity: The Perceived Alignment between Managers' Words and Deeds as a Research Focus," *Organization Science* 13, no. 1 (2002): 18-35.

23. S. Kolesnikov-Jessop, "You're the Conductor: Listen to the Music You Can Create with the Group," *The New York Times*, April 11, 2016.

24. For a discussion of trust in leadership, see C. S. Burke et al., "Trust in Leadership: A Multi-Level Review and Integration," *Leadership Quarterly* 18, no. 6 (2007): 606-32. The surveys on leading by example are reported in J. C. Maxwell, "People Do What People See," *BusinessWeek*, November 19, 2007, 32; Kronos, "Who's the Boss of Workplace Culture?," news release (Chelmsford, MA: Kronos, March 9, 2016). In the earlier survey, "leading by example" was the most important attribute of effective leaders. In the recent survey, HR professionals and managers rated "leading by example" as the top attribute of a company's culture, whereas employees ranked it below pay, coworker respect, and work-life balance.

25. D. Ossip, "Create a Culture of Engagement for Successful Customer Outcomes," *The CEO Forum* 2015, 30-31.

26. B. M. Bass and R. E. Riggio, *Transformational Leadership*, 2nd ed. (Mahwah, NJ: Erlbaum, 2006), 7; J. M. Kouzes and B. Z. Posner, *The Leadership Challenge*, 5th ed. (San Francisco: Jossey-Bass, 2012), chaps. 6 and 7.

27. W. E. Baker and J. M. Sinkula, "The Synergistic Effect of Market Orientation and Learning Orientation on Organizational Performance," *Academy of Marketing Science Journal* 27, no. 4 (1999): 411-27; Z. Emden, A. Yaprak, and S. T. Cavusgil, "Learning from Experience in International Alliances: Antecedents and Firm Performance Implications," *Journal of Business Research* 58, no. 7 (2005): 883-92.

28. J. M. Kouzes and B. Z. Posner, *The Leadership Challenge*, 5th ed. (San Francisco: Jossey-Bass, 2012).

29. R. J. House, "A 1976 Theory of Charismatic Leadership," in *Leadership: The Cutting Edge*, ed. J. G. Hunt and L. L. Larson (Carbondale: Southern Illinois University Press, 1977), 189-207; J. A. Conger, "Charismatic Leadership," in *The Sage Handbook of Leadership*, ed. A. Bryman et al. (London: Sage, 2011), 86-102.

30. J. E. Barbuto Jr., "Taking the Charisma out of Transformational Leadership," *Journal of Social Behavior & Personality* 12 (1997): 689-97; Y. A. Nur, "Charisma and Managerial Leadership: The Gift That Never Was," *Business Horizons* 41 (1998): 19-26; M. D. Mumford and J. R. Van Doorn, "The Leadership of Pragmatism: Reconsidering Franklin in the Age of Charisma," *Leadership Quarterly* 12, no. 3 (2001): 279-309; A. Fanelli, "Bringing Out Charisma: CEO Charisma and External Stakeholders," *Academy of Management Review* 31, no. 4 (2006): 1049-61; M. J. Platow et al., "A Special Gift We Bestow on You for Being Representative of Us: Considering Leader Charisma from a Self-Categorization Perspective," *British Journal of Social Psychology* 45, no. 2 (2006): 303-20.

31. B. Shamir et al., "Correlates of Charismatic Leader Behavior in Military Units: Subordinates' Attitudes, Unit Characteristics, and Superiors' Appraisals of Leader Performance," *Academy of Management Journal* 41, no. 4 (1998): 387-409; R. E. de Vries, R. A. Roe, and T. C. B. Taillieu, "On Charisma and Need for Leadership," *European Journal of Work and Organizational Psychology* 8 (1999): 109-33; R. Khurana, *Searching for a Corporate Savior: The Irrational Quest for Charismatic CEOs* (Princeton, NJ: Princeton University Press, 2002); R. E. de Vries, R. D. Pathak, and A. R. Paquin, "The Paradox of Power Sharing: Participative Charismatic Leaders Have Subordinates with More Instead of Less Need for Leadership," *European Journal of Work and Organizational Psychology* 20, no. 6

(2010): 779-804. The effect of charismatic leadership on follower dependence also was noted earlier by U.S. government leader John Gardner. See J. W. Gardner, *On Leadership* (New York: Free Press, 1990), 34-36.

32. J. Lipman-Blumen, "A Pox on Charisma: Why Connective Leadership and Character Count," in *The Drucker Difference: What the World's Greatest Management Thinker Means to Today's Business Leaders*, ed. C. L. Pearce, J. A. Maciariello, and H. Yamawaki (New York: McGraw-Hill, 2010), 149-74.

33. A. Mackey, "The Effect of CEOs on Firm Performance," *Strategic Management Journal* 29, no. 12 (2008): 1357-67; J. Barling, T. Weber, and E. K. Kelloway, "Effects of Transformational Leadership Training on Attitudinal and Financial Outcomes: A Field Experiment," *Journal of Applied Psychology* 81 (1996): 827-32. However, one study reported that transformational leadership is less effective than authoritarian (command-control with punishment) leadership in resource scarcity environments. See X. Huang et al., "When Authoritarian Leaders Outperform Transformational Leaders: Firm Performance in a Harsh Economic Environment," *Academy of Management Discoveries* 1, no. 2 (2015): 180-200.

34. A. Bryman, "Leadership in Organizations," in *Handbook of Organization Studies*, ed. S. R. Clegg, C. Hardy, and W. R. Nord (Thousand Oaks, CA: Sage, 1996), 276-92; D. van Knippenberg and S. B. Sitkin, "A Critical Assessment of Charismatic–Transformational Leadership Research: Back to the Drawing Board?," *Academy of Management Annals* 7, no. 1 (2013): 1-60.

35. G. Yukl and J. W. Michel, "A Critical Assessment of Research on Effective Leadership Behavior," in *Advances in Authentic and Ethical Leadership*, ed. L. L. Neider and C. A. Schriesheim (Charlotte, NC: Information Age, 2014), 209-30.

36. B. S. Pawar and K. K. Eastman, "The Nature and Implications of Contextual Influences on Transformational Leadership: A Conceptual Examination," *Academy of Management Review* 22 (1997): 80-109; C. P. Egri and S. Herman, "Leadership in the North American Environmental Sector: Values, Leadership Styles, and Contexts of Environmental Leaders and Their Organizations," *Academy of Management Journal* 43, no. 4 (2000): 571-604.

37. A. Zaleznik, "Managers and Leaders: Are They Different?," *Harvard Business Review* 55, no. 3 (1977): 67-78; J. P. Kotter, *A Force for Change: How Leadership Differs from Management* (New York: Free Press, 1990); E. A. Locke, *The Essence of Leadership* (New York: Lexington Books, 1991); G. Yukl and R. Lepsinger, "Why Integrating the Leading and Managing Roles Is Essential for Organizational Effectiveness," *Organizational Dynamics* 34, no. 4 (2005): 361-75; D. V. Simonet and R. P. Tett, "Five Perspectives on the Leadership–Management Relationship: A Competency-Based Evaluation and Integration," *Journal of Leadership & Organizational Studies* 20, no. 2 (2013): 199-213.

38. W. Bennis and B. Nanus, *Leaders: The Strategies for Taking Charge* (New York: Harper & Row, 1985), 20. Peter Drucker also is widely cited as the source of this quotation. The closest passage we could find, however, is in the first two pages of *The Effective Executive* (1966) where Drucker states that effective executives "get the right things done." On the next page, he states that manual workers only need efficiency, "that is, the ability to do things right rather than the ability to get the right things done." See P. F. Drucker, *The Effective Executive* (New York: Harper Business, 1966), 1-2.

39. R. J. House and R. N. Aditya, "The Social Scientific Study of Leadership: Quo Vadis?," *Journal of Management* 23, no. 3 (1997): 409-73.

40. G. Yukl and R. Lepsinger, "Why Integrating the Leading and Managing Roles Is Essential for Organizational Effectiveness," *Organizational Dynamics* 34, no. 4 (2005): 361-75. One recent critique of leadership theories suggests that scholars need to further clarify the distinction, if any exists, between leading and managing. See S. T. Hannah et al., "Debunking the False Dichotomy of Leadership Idealism and Pragmatism: Critical Evaluation and Support of Newer Genre Leadership Theories," *Journal of Organizational Behavior* 35, no. 5 (2014): 598-621.

41. E. A. Fleishman, "The Description of Supervisory Behavior," *Journal of Applied Psychology* 37, no. 1 (1953): 1-6. For discussion on methodological problems with the development of these people-versus-task-oriented leadership constructs, see C. A. Schriesheim, R. J. House, and S. Kerr, "Leader Initiating Structure: A Reconciliation of Discrepant Research Results and Some Empirical Tests," *Organizational Behavior and Human Performance* 15, no. 2 (1976): 297-321; L. Tracy, "Consideration and Initiating Structure: Are They Basic Dimensions of Leader Behavior?," *Social Behavior and Personality* 15, no. 1 (1987): 21-33.

42. A. K. Korman, "Consideration, Initiating Structure, and Organizational Criteria—a Review," *Personnel Psychology* 19 (1966): 349-62; E. A. Fleishman, "Twenty Years of Consideration and Structure," in *Current Developments in the Study of Leadership*, ed. E. A. Fleishman and J. C. Hunt (Carbondale: Southern Illinois University Press, 1973), 1-40; T. A. Judge, R. F. Piccolo, and R. Ilies, "The Forgotten Ones?: The Validity of Consideration and Initiating Structure in Leadership Research," *Journal of Applied Psychology* 89, no. 1 (2004): 36-51; D. S. DeRue et al., "Trait and Behavioral Theories of Leadership: An Integration and Meta-Analytic Test of Their Relative Validity," *Personnel Psychology* 64, no. 1 (2011): 7-52; G. A. Yukl, *Leadership in Organizations*, 8th ed. (Upper Saddle River, NJ: Pearson Education, 2013), 62-75.

43. V. V. Baba, "Serendipity in Leadership: Initiating Structure and Consideration in the Classroom," *Human Relations* 42 (1989): 509-25.

44. S. J. Peterson, B. M. Galvin, and D. Lange, "CEO Servant Leadership: Exploring Executive Characteristics and Firm Performance," *Personnel Psychology* 65, no. 3 (2012): 565-96.

45. R. K. Greenleaf, *Servant Leadership: A Journey into the Nature of Legitimate Power & Greatness* (Mahwah, NJ: Paulist Press, 1977; repr., 2002), 27.

46. S. Sendjaya, J. C. Sarros, and J. C. Santora, "Defining and Measuring Servant Leadership Behaviour in Organizations," *Journal of Management Studies* 45, no. 2 (2008): 402-24; R. C. Liden et al., "Servant Leadership: Development of a Multidimensional Measure and Multi-Level Assessment," *Leadership Quarterly* 19, no. 2 (2008): 161-77; D. van Dierendonck, "Servant Leadership: A Review and Synthesis," *Journal of Management* 37, no. 4 (2011): 1228-61; R. VanMeter et al., "In Search of Clarity on Servant Leadership: Domain Specification and Reconceptualization," *AMS Review* 6, no. 1 (March 29, 2016): 59-78.

47. J. Mattson, "'Sergeant' Means 'Servant': How NCOs Typify the Servant Leader," *NCO Journal*, May 14, 2013. For a more detailed discussion of servant leadership in the military, see D. Campbell, *The Leader's Code: Mission, Character, Service, and Getting the Job Done* (New York: Random House, 2013).

48. R. VanMeter et al., "In Search of Clarity on Servant Leadership: Domain Specification and Reconceptualization," *AMS Review* 6, no. 1 (March 29, 2016): 59-78.

49. S. J. Peterson, B. M. Galvin, and D. Lange, "CEO Servant Leadership: Exploring Executive Characteristics and Firm Performance," *Personnel Psychology* 65, no. 3 (2012): 565-96.

50. S. Kerr et al., "Towards a Contingency Theory of Leadership Based Upon the Consideration and Initiating Structure Literature," *Organizational Behavior and Human Performance* 12 (1974): 62–82; L. L. Larson, J. G. Hunt, and R. N. Osborn, "The Great Hi-Hi Leader Behavior Myth: A Lesson from Occam's Razor," *Academy of Management Journal* 19 (1976): 628–41.

51. R. J. House, "A Path Goal Theory of Leader Effectiveness," *Administrative Science Quarterly* 16, no. 3 (1971): 321–39; M. G. Evans, "Extensions of a Path–Goal Theory of Motivation," *Journal of Applied Psychology* 59 (1974): 172–78; R. J. House and T. R. Mitchell, "Path–Goal Theory of Leadership," *Journal of Contemporary Business* (1974): 81–97; M. G. Evans, "Path Goal Theory of Leadership," in *Leadership*, ed. L. L. Neider and C. A. Schriesheim (Greenwich, CT: Information Age, 2002), 115–38.

52. For a thorough study of how expectancy theory of motivation relates to leadership, see R. G. Isaac, W. J. Zerbe, and D. C. Pitt, "Leadership and Motivation: The Effective Application of Expectancy Theory," *Journal of Managerial Issues* 13 (2001): 212–26.

53. R. J. House, "Path–Goal Theory of Leadership: Lessons, Legacy, and a Reformulated Theory," *The Leadership Quarterly* 7, no. 3 (1996): 323–52.

54. J. Indvik, "Path-Goal Theory of Leadership: A Meta-Analysis," *Academy of Management Proceedings* (1986): 189–92; J. C. Wofford and L. Z. Liska, "Path-Goal Theories of Leadership: A Meta-Analysis," *Journal of Management* 19 (1993): 857–76.

55. J. D. Houghton and S. K. Yoho, "Toward a Contingency Model of Leadership and Psychological Empowerment: When Should Self-Leadership Be Encouraged?," *Journal of Leadership & Organizational Studies* 11, no. 4 (2005): 65–83.

56. R. T. Keller, "A Test of the Path–Goal Theory of Leadership with Need for Clarity as a Moderator in Research and Development Organizations," *Journal of Applied Psychology* 74 (1989): 208–12.

57. R. P. Vecchio, J. E. Justin, and C. L. Pearce, "The Utility of Transactional and Transformational Leadership for Predicting Performance and Satisfaction within a Path–Goal Theory Framework," *Journal of Occupational and Organizational Psychology* 81 (2008): 71–82.

58. B. Carroll and L. Levy, "Defaulting to Management: Leadership Defined by What It Is Not," *Organization* 15, no. 1 (2008): 75–96; I. Holmberg and M. Tyrstrup, "Well Then—What Now? An Everyday Approach to Managerial Leadership," *Leadership* 6, no. 4 (2010): 353–72.

59. C. A. Schriesheim and L. L. Neider, "Path–Goal Leadership Theory: The Long and Winding Road," *Leadership Quarterly* 7 (1996): 317–21.

60. The earliest contingency theory of leadership in the 1960s introduced the notion that managers have preferred styles and limited flexibility to use other styles. That theory had various flaws (so is not described here) but deserves recognition for proposing that it is better to move managers to situations that fit their leadership style than to expect managers to fluidly change style with the situation. See F. E. Fiedler, "Engineer the Job to Fit the Manager," *Harvard Business Review* 43, no. 5 (1965): 115–22; F. E. Fiedler, *A Theory of Leadership Effectiveness* (New York: McGraw-Hill, 1967); F. E. Fiedler and M. M. Chemers, *Leadership and Effective Management* (Glenview, IL: Scott, Foresman, 1974).

61. N. Nicholson, *Executive Instinct* (New York: Crown, 2000).

62. T. A. Judge, R. F. Piccolo, and R. Ilies, "The Forgotten Ones?: The Validity of Consideration and Initiating Structure in Leadership Research," *Journal of Applied Psychology* 89, no. 1 (2004): 36–51; T. A. Judge, R. F. Piccolo, and T. Kosalka, "The Bright and Dark Sides of Leader Traits: A Review and Theoretical Extension of the Leader Trait Paradigm," *Leadership Quarterly* 20 (2009): 855–75.

63. S. Kerr and J. M. Jermier, "Substitutes for Leadership: Their Meaning and Measurement," *Organizational Behavior and Human Performance* 22 (December 1978): 375–403.

64. This observation also has been made by C. A. Schriesheim, "Substitutes-for-Leadership Theory: Development and Basic Concepts," *Leadership Quarterly* 8 (1997): 103–08.

65. D. F. Elloy and A. Randolph, "The Effect of Superleader Behavior on Autonomous Work Groups in a Government Operated Railway Service," *Public Personnel Management* 26 (1997): 257–72; C. C. Manz and H. Sims Jr., *The New SuperLeadership: Leading Others to Lead Themselves* (San Francisco: Berrett-Koehler, 2001).

66. M. L. Loughry, "Coworkers Are Watching: Performance Implications of Peer Monitoring," *Academy of Management Proceedings* (2002): O1–O6.

67. P. M. Podsakoff and S. B. MacKenzie, "Kerr and Jermier's Substitutes for Leadership Model: Background, Empirical Assessment, and Suggestions for Future Research," *Leadership Quarterly* 8 (1997): 117–32; S. D. Dionne et al., "Neutralizing Substitutes for Leadership Theory: Leadership Effects and Common-Source Bias," *Journal of Applied Psychology* 87, no. 3 (2002): 454–64; J. R. Villa et al., "Problems with Detecting Moderators in Leadership Research Using Moderated Multiple Regression," *Leadership Quarterly* 14, no. 1 (2003): 3–23; S. D. Dionne et al., "Substitutes for Leadership, or Not," *Leadership Quarterly* 16, no. 1 (2005): 169–93.

68. J. R. Meindl, "On Leadership: An Alternative to the Conventional Wisdom," *Research in Organizational Behavior* 12 (1990): 159–203; L. R. Offermann, J. K. Kennedy, and P. W. Wirtz, "Implicit Leadership Theories: Content, Structure, and Generalizability," *Leadership Quarterly* 5, no. 1 (1994): 43–58; R. J. Hall and R. G. Lord, "Multi-Level Information Processing Explanations of Followers' Leadership Perceptions," *Leadership Quarterly* 6 (1995): 265–87; O. Epitropaki and R. Martin, "Implicit Leadership Theories in Applied Settings: Factor Structure, Generalizability, and Stability over Time," *Journal of Applied Psychology* 89, no. 2 (2004): 293–310. For a broader discussion of the social construction of leadership, see G. T. Fairhurst and D. Grant, "The Social Construction of Leadership: A Sailing Guide," *Management Communication Quarterly* 24, no. 2 (2010): 171–210.

69. R. G. Lord et al., "Contextual Constraints on Prototype Generation and Their Multilevel Consequences for Leadership Perceptions," *Leadership Quarterly* 12, no. 3 (2001): 311–38; K. A. Scott and D. J. Brown, "Female First, Leader Second? Gender Bias in the Encoding of Leadership Behavior," *Organizational Behavior and Human Decision Processes* 101 (2006): 230–42; S. J. Shondrick, J. E. Dinh, and R. G. Lord, "Developments in Implicit Leadership Theory and Cognitive Science: Applications to Improving Measurement and Understanding Alternatives to Hierarchical Leadership," *Leadership Quarterly* 21, no. 6 (2010): 959–78.

70. S. F. Cronshaw and R. G. Lord, "Effects of Categorization, Attribution, and Encoding Processes on Leadership Perceptions," *Journal of Applied Psychology* 72 (1987): 97–106; J. L. Nye and D. R. Forsyth, "The Effects of Prototype-Based Biases on Leadership Appraisals: A Test of Leadership Categorization Theory," *Small Group Research* 22 (1991): 360–79.

71. R. Meindl, "On Leadership: An Alternative to the Conventional Wisdom," *Research in Organizational Behavior* 12 (1990): 163; B. Schyns, J. R. Meindl, and M. A. Croon, "The Romance of Leadership Scale: Cross-Cultural Testing and Refinement," *Leadership* 3, no. 1 (2007): 29–46; J. Felfe and L. E. Petersen, "Romance of Leadership and Management Decision Making," *European Journal of Work and Organizational Psychology* 16, no. 1 (2007): 1–24.

72. J. Pfeffer, "The Ambiguity of Leadership," *Academy of Management Review* 2 (1977): 102–12.

73. R. Weber et al., "The Illusion of Leadership: Misattribution of Cause in Coordination Games," *Organization Science* 12, no. 5 (2001): 582–98; N. Ensari and S. E. Murphy, "Cross-Cultural Variations in Leadership Perceptions and Attribution of Charisma to the Leader," *Organizational Behavior and Human Decision Processes* 92 (2003): 52–66; M. L. A. Hayward, V. P. Rindova, and T. G. Pollock, "Believing One's Own Press: The Causes and Consequences of CEO Celebrity," *Strategic Management Journal* 25, no. 7 (2004): 637–53.

74. The history of the trait perspective of leadership, as well as current research on this topic, is nicely summarized in S. J. Zaccaro, C. Kemp, and P. Bader, "Leader Traits and Attributes," in *The Nature of Leadership*, ed. J. Antonakis, A. T. Cianciolo, and R. J. Sternberg (Thousand Oaks, CA: Sage, 2004), 101–24.

75. R. M. Stogdill, *Handbook of Leadership* (New York: Free Press, 1974), chap. 5.

76. This list is based on S. A. Kirkpatrick and E. A. Locke, "Leadership: Do Traits Matter?," *Academy of Management Executive* 5 (1991): 48–60; S. J. Zaccaro, C. Kemp, and P. Bader, "Leader Traits and Attributes," in *The Nature of Leadership*, ed. J. Antonakis, A. T. Cianciolo, and R. J. Sternberg (Thousand Oaks, CA: Sage, 2004), 101–24; G. A. Yukl, *Leadership in Organizations*, 8th ed. (Upper Saddle River, NJ: Pearson Education, 2013), chap. 6.

77. T. A. Judge et al., "Personality and Leadership: A Qualitative and Quantitative Review," *Journal of Applied Psychology* 87, no. 4 (2002): 765–80; D. S. Derue et al., "Trait and Behavioral Theories of Leadership: An Integration and Meta-Analytic Test of Their Relative Validity," *Personnel Psychology* 64, no. 1 (2011): 7–52; A. Deinert et al., "Transformational Leadership Sub-Dimensions and Their Link to Leaders' Personality and Performance," *Leadership Quarterly* 26, no. 6 (2015): 1095–120; A. D. Parr, S. T. Lanza, and P. Bernthal, "Personality Profiles of Effective Leadership Performance in Assessment Centers," *Human Performance* 29, no. 2 (2016): 143–57.

78. D. V. Day, M. M. Harrison, and S. M. Halpin, *An Integrative Approach to Leader Development: Connecting Adult Development, Identity, and Expertise* (New York: Routledge, 2009); D. S. DeRue and S. J. Ashford, "Who Will Lead and Who Will Follow? A Social Process of Leadership Identity Construction in Organizations," *Academy of Management Review* 35, no. 4 (2010): 627–47; H. Ibarra et al., "Leadership and Identity: An Examination of Three Theories and New Research Directions," in *The Oxford Handbook of Leadership and Organizations*, ed. D. V. Day (New York: Oxford University Press, 2014), 285–301; L. Guillén, M. Mayo, and K. Korotov, "Is Leadership a Part of Me? A Leader Identity Approach to Understanding the Motivation to Lead," *Leadership Quarterly* 26, no. 5 (2015): 802–20.

79. B. Carroll and L. Levy, "Defaulting to Management: Leadership Defined by What It Is Not," *Organization* 15, no. 1 (2008): 75–96.

80. One recent study suggests that leaders retain their power by undermining followers' power. See C. Case and J. Maner, "Divide and Conquer: When and Why Leaders Undermine the Cohesive Fabric of Their Group," *Journal of Personality and Social Psychology* 107, no. 6 (2014): 1033–50.

81. J. B. Miner, "Twenty Years of Research on Role Motivation Theory of Managerial Effectiveness," *Personnel Psychology* 31 (1978): 739–60; C. J. Vinkenburg et al., "Arena: A Critical Conceptual Framework of Top Management Selection," *Group & Organization Management* 39, no. 1 (2014): 33–68; B. L. Connelly et al., "Tournament Theory: Thirty Years of Contests and Competitions," *Journal of Management* 40, no. 1 (2014): 16–47; Y. Baruch and Y. Vardi, "A Fresh Look at the Dark Side of Contemporary Careers: Toward a Realistic Discourse," *British Journal of Management* 27, no. 2 (2016): 355–72.

82. For surveys on the importance of leader integrity, see J. M. Kouzes and B. Z. Posner, *The Leadership Challenge*, 5th ed. (San Francisco: Jossey-Bass, 2012), chap. 2; Robert Half, "What Is the Most Important Leadership Attribute?," news release (Menlo Park, CA: PR Newswire, September 22, 2016); S. Giles, "The Most Important Leadership Competencies, According to Leaders around the World," *Harvard Business Review Digital Articles*, March 2016, 2–6.

83. Treasury Board of Canada, *2014 Public Service Employee Survey: Summary Report* (Ottawa: Treasury Board of Canada, February 2015); "New Globoforce Survey Shows Recognition Creates More Human-Focused Workplaces," news release (Southborough, MA and Dublin, Ireland: Business Wire, March 24, 2016); U.S. Office of Personnel Management, *Federal Employee Viewpoint Survey* (Washington, DC: Office of Personnel Management, September 2016); Robert Half, "What Is the Most Important Leadership Attribute?," news release (Menlo Park, CA: PR Newswire, September 22, 2016); *Work and Well-Being Survey*, Center for Organizational Excellence (Washington, DC: American Psychological Association, May 30, 2017).

84. J. Hedlund et al., "Identifying and Assessing Tacit Knowledge: Understanding the Practical Intelligence of Military Leaders," *Leadership Quarterly* 14, no. 2 (2003): 117–40; R. J. Sternberg, "A Systems Model of Leadership: WICS," *American Psychologist* 62, no. 1 (2007): 34–42.

85. J. M. George, "Emotions and Leadership: The Role of Emotional Intelligence," *Human Relations* 53 (2000): 1027–55; D. Goleman, R. Boyatzis, and A. McKee, *Primal Leaders* (Boston: Harvard Business School Press, 2002); R. G. Lord and R. J. Hall, "Identity, Deep Structure and the Development of Leadership Skill," *Leadership Quarterly* 16, no. 4 (2005): 591–615; C. Skinner and P. Spurgeon, "Valuing Empathy and Emotional Intelligence in Health Leadership: A Study of Empathy, Leadership Behaviour and Outcome Effectiveness," *Health Services Management Research* 18, no. 1 (2005): 1–12.

86. B. George, *Authentic Leadership* (San Francisco: Jossey-Bass, 2004); W. L. Gardner et al., "'Can You See the Real Me?' A Self-Based Model of Authentic Leader and Follower Development," *Leadership Quarterly* 16 (2005): 343–72; B. George, *True North* (San Francisco: Jossey-Bass, 2007), chap. 4; M. E. Palanski and F. J. Yammarino, "Integrity and Leadership: Clearing the Conceptual Confusion," *European Management Journal* 25, no. 3 (2007): 171–84; F. O. Walumbwa et al., "Authentic Leadership: Development and Validation of a Theory-Based Measure," *Journal of Management* 34, no. 1 (2008): 89–126.

87. W. G. Bennis and R. J. Thomas, "Crucibles of Leadership," *Harvard Business Review* 80, no. 9 (2002): 39–45; R. J. Thomas, *Crucibles of Leadership: How to Learn from Experience to Become a Great Leader* (Boston: Harvard Business Press, 2008).

88. R. Jacobs, "Using Human Resource Functions to Enhance Emotional Intelligence," in *The Emotionally Intelligent Workplace*, ed. C. Cherniss and D. Goleman (San Francisco: Jossey-Bass, 2001), 161–63; J. A. Conger and D. A. Ready, "Rethinking Leadership Competencies," *Leader to Leader* (2004): 41–47.

89. R. G. Lord and D. J. Brown, *Leadership Processes and Self-Identity: A Follower-Centered Approach to Leadership* (Mahwah, NJ: Erlbaum, 2004); R. Bolden and J. Gosling, "Leadership Competencies: Time to Change the Tune?," *Leadership* 2, no. 2 (2006): 147–63.

90. Six of the Project GLOBE clusters are described in a special issue of the *Journal of World Business* 37 (2000). For an overview of Project GLOBE, see R. House, M. Javidan, and P. Dorfman, "Project GLOBE: An Introduction," *Applied Psychology: An International Review* 50 (2001): 489–505; R. House et al., "Understanding Cultures and Implicit Leadership Theories across the Globe: An Introduction to Project GLOBE," *Journal of World Business* 37 (2002): 3–10.

91. J. C. Jesuino, "Latin Europe Cluster: From South to North," *Journal of World Business* 37 (2002): 88. Another GLOBE study, of Iranian managers, also reported that "charismatic visionary" stands out as a primary leadership dimension. See A. Dastmalchian, M. Javidan, and K. Alam, "Effective Leadership and Culture in Iran: An Empirical Study," *Applied Psychology: An International Review* 50 (2001): 532–58.

92. G. N. Powell, "One More Time: Do Female and Male Managers Differ?," *Academy of Management Executive* 4 (1990): 68–75; M. L. van Engen and T. M. Willemsen, "Sex and Leadership Styles: A Meta-Analysis of Research Published in the 1990s," *Psychological Reports* 94, no. 1 (2004): 3–18.

93. A. H. Eagly, M. C. Johannesen-Schmidt, and M. L. van Engen, "Transformational, Transactional, and Laissez-Faire Leadership Styles: A Meta-Analysis Comparing Women and Men," *Psychological Bulletin* 129 (2003): 569–91; S. Paustian-Underdahl, L. Walker, and D. Woehr, "Gender and Perceptions of Leadership Effectiveness: A Meta-Analysis of Contextual Moderators," *Journal of Applied Psychology* 99, no. 6 (2014): 1129–45.

94. A. H. Eagly, S. J. Karau, and M. G. Makhijani, "Gender and the Effectiveness of Leaders: A Meta-Analysis," *Psychological Bulletin* 117 (1995): 125–45; M. E. Heilman et al., "Penalties for Success: Reactions to Women Who Succeed at Male Gender-Typed Tasks," *Journal of Applied Psychology* 89, no. 3 (2004): 416–27; A. H. Eagly, "Achieving Relational Authenticity in Leadership: Does Gender Matter?," *Leadership Quarterly* 16, no. 3 (2005): 459–74; A. J. Anderson et al., "The Effectiveness of Three Strategies to Reduce the Influence of Bias in Evaluations of Female Leaders," *Journal of Applied Social Psychology* 45, no. 9 (2015): 522–39.

PART 4

12 | Designing Organizational Structures

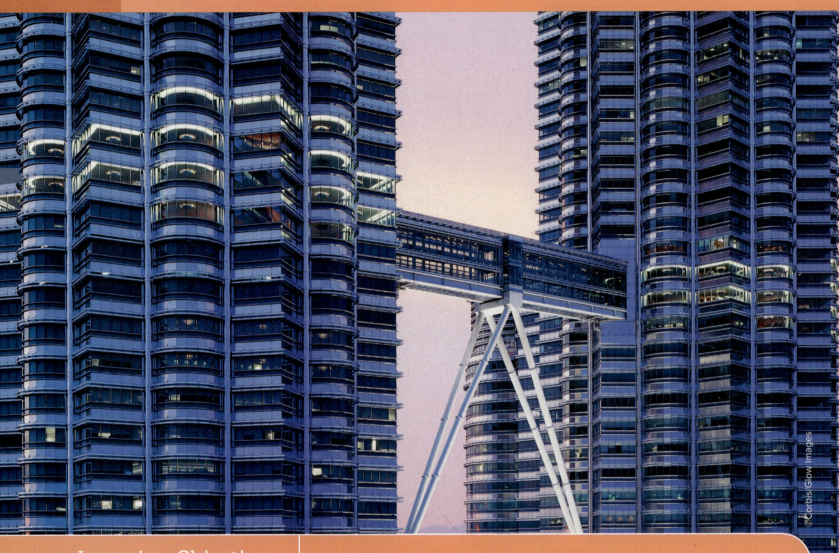

©Corbis/Glow Images

Learning Objectives

After you read this chapter, you should be able to:

LO12-1   Describe three types of coordination in organizational structures.

LO12-2   Discuss the role and effects of span of control, centralization, and formalization, and relate these elements to organic and mechanistic organizational structures.

LO12-3   Identify and evaluate five types of departmentalization.

LO12-4   Explain how the external environment, organizational size, technology, and strategy are relevant when designing an organizational structure.

Samsung Electronics is one of the world's largest technology companies, yet the South Korean maker of smartphones, tablets, televisions, and home appliances wants to be as nimble as a high-tech startup. The magic ingredient for this transformation is a new organizational structure. "Samsung will stay away from top-down structures and build bottom-up structures, while the company will put more focus on improving efficiency by introducing programs to self-motivate employees," the company explains.

This transformation, called "Start-up Samsung," will be challenging because the conglomerate's existing organizational structure is almost the opposite of what most startups look like. As with most large Korean firms, Samsung has had a tall, rigid hierarchy with power centralized at the top of the organization and seven well-defined status titles below the executive level. Samsung employees tended to follow orders without question, communicated with other departments mainly through their manager, routinely wrote detailed reports to management, and attended endless meetings.

Samsung's new organizational structure has a flatter hierarchy with only four career levels. Employees are expected to speak up about new ideas and to use the company's internal communications portal to coordinate informally and spontaneously with co-workers elsewhere in the company. Formal reports and meetings with management are now discouraged. "Samsung's top management plans to kill unnecessary internal meetings and require executives to end the rigidity of internal reporting systems," says Samsung's statement about the changes.[1]

Samsung Electronics is relying on its new organizational structure to keep the South Korean technology giant nimble and competitive. **Organizational structure** refers to the division of labor as well as the patterns of coordination, communication, workflow, and formal power that direct organizational activities. It formally dictates what activities receive the most attention as well as financial, power, and information resources. At Samsung, for example, power and resources previously concentrated around the top of the hierarchy, whereas the company now wants to delegate some of that authority and accountability to frontline employees and lower levels of management.

The topic of organizational structure typically conjures up images of an organizational chart. Organizational structure includes these reporting relationships, but it also includes other features that relate to work standards and rules, team dynamics, power relationships, information flow, and job design. The organization's structure is an important instrument in an executive's toolkit for organizational change because it establishes new communication patterns and aligns employee behavior with the corporate vision.

Indeed, one recent global survey of 7,000 business and human resources leaders in 130 countries reported that organizational design was their firm's most important trend or priority to improve human capital (leadership and corporate culture were second and third most important, respectively).[2]

This chapter begins by introducing the two fundamental processes in organizational structure: division of labor and coordination. This is followed by a detailed investigation of the four main elements of organizational structure: span of control, centralization, formalization, and departmentalization. The latter part of this chapter examines the contingencies of organizational design, including external environment, organizational size, technology, and strategy.

LO12-1 Describe three types of coordination in organizational structures.

DIVISION OF LABOR AND COORDINATION

All organizational structures include two fundamental requirements: the division of labor into distinct tasks and the coordination of that labor so employees are able to accomplish common goals.[3] Organizations are groups of people who work interdependently toward some purpose. To effectively accomplish this common purpose, most work is divided into manageable chunks, particularly when there are many different tasks required to complete the work. Organizations also introduce various coordinating mechanisms to ensure that everyone is working effectively toward the same objectives.

Division of Labor

Division of labor refers to the subdivision of work into separate jobs assigned to different people. Subdivided work leads to job

All organizational structures include two fundamental requirements: the division of labor into distinct tasks and the coordination of that labor.
©Vetta/Getty Images

specialization because each job now includes a narrow subset of the tasks necessary to complete the product or service. Samsung divides its employees into thousands of specific jobs to more effectively design, manufacture, and market new products. As companies get larger, this horizontal division of labor is usually accompanied by vertical division of labor. Some people are assigned the task of supervising employees, others are responsible for managing those supervisors, and so on.

Why do companies divide the work into several jobs? As we described in Chapter 5, job specialization increases work efficiency.[4] Job incumbents can master their tasks more quickly when work cycles are shorter. Less time is wasted changing from one task to another. Training costs are lower because employees require fewer physical and mental skills to accomplish the assigned work. Finally, job specialization makes it easier to match people with specific aptitudes or skills to the jobs for which they are best suited. It is almost impossible for one person working alone to design, manufacture, and sell a new smartphone; instead, this enterprise requires hundreds of people with diverse knowledge and skills.

Coordination of Work Activities

When people divide work among themselves, they require coordinating mechanisms to ensure that everyone works in concert. In fact, the extent to which work can be effectively divided among several people and work units depends on how well the divided work can be coordinated. When an organization divides work beyond its capacity to coordinate that work, individual effort is wasted due to misalignment, duplication, and mistiming of tasks. Coordination also tends to become more expensive and difficult as the division of labor increases. Therefore, companies specialize jobs only to the point where it isn't too costly or challenging to coordinate the people in those jobs.[5]

Every organization—from the two-person corner convenience store to the largest corporate entity—uses one or more of the following coordinating mechanisms:[6] informal communication, formal hierarchy, and standardization (see Exhibit 12.1). These forms of coordination align the work of staff within the same department as well as across work units. The coordinating mechanisms are also critical when several organizations work together, such as in joint ventures and humanitarian aid programs.[7]

Coordination through Informal Communication All organizations rely on informal communication as a coordinating mechanism. This process includes sharing information on mutual tasks as well as forming common mental models so that employees synchronize work activities using the same mental road map.[8] Informal communication is vital in nonroutine and ambiguous situations because employees need to exchange a large volume of information through face-to-face communication and other media-rich channels. Samsung's new structure encourages more informal communication because much of the work among engineers relates to novel ideas, which are nonroutine and ambiguous.

Although coordination through informal communication is easiest in small firms, information technologies have further enabled this coordinating mechanism at Samsung and in other large organizations.[9] Companies employing thousands of people also support informal communication by keeping each production site small. Magna International follows this principle by keeping most of its plants to no more than 200 employees. The global auto-parts manufacturer has found that employees have difficulty remembering each other's names in plants that are any larger, a situation that makes informal communication more difficult as a coordinating mechanism.[10]

Larger organizations also encourage coordination through informal communication by assigning *liaison roles* to employees,

---

Exhibit 12.1 Coordinating Mechanisms in Organizations

Form of Coordination	Description	Subtypes/Strategies
Informal communication	Sharing information on mutual tasks; forming common mental models to synchronize work activities	Direct communication Liaison roles Integrator roles Temporary teams
Formal hierarchy	Assigning legitimate power to individuals, who then use this power to direct work processes and allocate resources	Direct supervision Formal communication channels
Standardization	Creating routine patterns of behavior or output	Standardized skills Standardized processes Standardized output

Sources: Based on information in J. Galbraith, *Designing Complex Organizations* (Reading, MA: Addison-Wesley, 1973), 8–19; H. Mintzberg, *The Structuring of Organizations* (Englewood Cliffs, NJ: Prentice Hall, 1979), chap. 1; D. A. Nadler and M. L. Tushman, *Competing by Design: The Power of Organizational Architecture* (New York: Oxford University Press, 1997), chap. 6.

Organizations encourage coordination through informal communication by forming temporary cross-functional teams in which employees are given considerable authority and autonomy.
©Pressmaster/Shutterstock

who are expected to communicate and share information with coworkers in other work units. Where coordination is required among several work units, companies create *integrator roles*. These people are responsible for coordinating a work process by encouraging employees in each work unit to share information and informally coordinate work activities. Integrators do not have authority over the people involved in that process, so they must rely on persuasion and commitment. Brand managers for luxury perfumes have integrator roles because they ensure that the work of fragrance developers, bottle designers, advertising creatives, production, and other groups are aligned with the brand's image and meaning.[11]

Another way that organizations—particularly large businesses—encourage coordination through informal communication is by forming temporary cross-functional teams in which employees are given considerable authority and autonomy. This process is now common in vehicle design, which Toyota pioneered more than three decades ago. As design engineers work on product specifications, team members from production engineering, manufacturing, marketing, purchasing, and other departments provide immediate feedback as well as begin their contribution to the process. Without the informal coordination available through teams, the preliminary car design would pass from one department to the next—a much slower process.[12]

Coordination through Formal Hierarchy
Informal communication is the most flexible form of coordination, but it can become chaotic as the number of employees increases.

Consequently, as organizations grow, they rely increasingly on a second coordinating mechanism: formal hierarchy.[13] Hierarchy assigns legitimate power to individuals, who then use this power to direct work processes and allocate resources. In other words, work is coordinated through direct supervision—the chain of command. For instance, Walmart stores have managers and assistant managers who are responsible for ensuring that employees are properly trained, perform their respective tasks, and coordinate effectively with other staff.

A century ago, management scholars applauded the formal hierarchy as the best coordinating mechanism for large organizations. They argued that organizations are most effective when managers exercise their authority and employees receive orders from only one supervisor. The chain of command—in which information flows across work units only through supervisors and managers—was viewed as the backbone of organizational strength.

Although still important, formal hierarchy is much less popular today. One problem, which Samsung is trying to minimize with its new structure, is that hierarchical organizations are not as agile for coordination in complex and novel situations. Formal communication through the chain of command is rarely as fast or accurate as informal direct communication among employees. Another concern with formal hierarchy is that managers are able to closely supervise only a limited number of employees. As the business grows, the number of supervisors and layers of management must increase, resulting in a costly bureaucracy. A third problem is that today's workforce demands more autonomy over work and more involvement in company decisions. Coordination through formal hierarchy tends to limit employee autonomy and involvement, which increases employee complaints of being "micromanaged."

Coordination through Micromanagement[14]

44% of 434 American human resource professionals polled identify micromanaging as a major complaint or concern that younger employees have about older managers.

59% of 450 American employees surveyed say they have worked for a micromanager.

31% of 97,000 employees surveyed in 30 countries describe their company's leadership as oppressive or authoritative.
©Steve Hamblin/Corbis

18% of 300 American human resource managers say that micromanaging employees has the most negative effect on employee morale (second only to lack of open, honest communication).

25% of 500 American employees surveyed say they currently work for a "micromanager."

Coordination through Standardization Standardization, the third means of coordination, involves creating routine patterns of behavior or output. This coordinating mechanism takes three distinct forms:

- *Standardized processes.* Quality and consistency of a product or service often can be improved by standardizing work activities through job descriptions and procedures.[15] For example, flowcharts represent coordination through standardized processes. This coordinating mechanism works best when the task is routine (such as mass production) or simple (such as stocking shelves), but it is less effective in nonroutine and complex work such as product design (which occurs among employees at Samsung's creativity center).

- *Standardized outputs.* This form of standardization involves ensuring that individuals and work units have clearly defined goals and output measures (e.g., customer satisfaction, production efficiency). For instance, to coordinate the work of salespeople, companies assign sales targets rather than specific behaviors.

- *Standardized skills.* When work activities are too complex to standardize through processes or goals, companies often coordinate work effort by extensively training employees or hiring people who have learned precise role behaviors from educational programs. Samsung and other technology companies rely on coordination through standardized skills. They carefully hire people for their skills in software engineering and other disciplines so they can perform tasks without continuous supervision, precise job descriptions, or exacting work process guidelines. Training is also a form of standardization through skills. Many companies have in-house training programs where employees learn how to perform tasks consistent with company expectations.

Division of labor and coordination of work represent the two fundamental ingredients of all organizations. But how work is divided, which coordinating mechanisms are emphasized, who makes decisions, and other issues are related to the four elements of organizational structure that we discuss over the next two sections of this chapter.

LO12-2 Discuss the role and effects of span of control, centralization, and formalization, and relate these elements to organic and mechanistic organizational structures.

ELEMENTS OF ORGANIZATIONAL STRUCTURE

Organizational structure has four elements that apply to every organization. This section introduces three of them: span of control, centralization, and formalization. The fourth element—departmentalization—is presented in the next section.

Span of Control

Span of control (also called *span of management*) refers to the number of people directly reporting to the next level above in the hierarchy. A narrow span of control exists when very few people report directly to a manager, whereas a wide span exists when a manager has many direct reports.[16] A century ago, French engineer and management scholar Henri Fayol strongly recommended a relatively narrow span of control, typically no more than 20 employees per supervisor and 6 supervisors per manager. Fayol championed formal hierarchy as the primary coordinating mechanism, so he believed that supervisors should closely monitor and coach employees. His views were similar to those of Napoleon, who declared that senior military leaders should have no more than five officers directly reporting to them. These prescriptions were based on the belief that managers simply could not monitor and control any more subordinates closely enough.[17]

Today, we know better. The best-performing manufacturing plants currently have an average of 38 production employees per supervisor (see Exhibit 12.2).[18] What's the secret here? Did Fayol, Napoleon, and others miscalculate the optimal span of control? The answer is that those sympathetic to hierarchical control believed that employees should perform the physical tasks, whereas supervisors and other management personnel should make the decisions and monitor employees to make sure they performed their tasks. In contrast, the best-performing manufacturing operations today rely on self-directed teams, so direct supervision (formal hierarchy) is supplemented with other coordinating mechanisms. Self-directed teams coordinate mainly through informal communication and various forms of standardization (i.e., training and processes), so formal hierarchy plays more of a supporting role.

Managers often can accommodate a wider span of control because staff members are self-managing and coordinate mainly through standardized skills. For example, more than two dozen employees, ranging from project specialists to sales support staff, report directly to Amy Geiger, director of sales operations at Sunrise Identity. "Amy is a big proponent of letting her employees be self-led," says one of Geiger's direct reports at the Bellevue, Washington, marketing and merchandising agency. "She is against micromanaging and wants her employees to grow from their own learned experiences."[20]

A second factor influencing the best span of control is whether employees perform routine tasks. A wider span of control is possible when employees perform routine jobs because they require less direction or advice from supervisors. A narrow span of control is necessary when employees perform novel or complex tasks because these employees tend to require more supervisory decisions and coaching. This principle is illustrated in a survey of property and casualty insurers. The average span of control in commercial-policy processing departments is around 15 employees per supervisor, whereas the span of control is 6.1 in claims service and 5.5 in commercial underwriting. Staff members in the latter two departments perform more

Exhibit 12.2 Recommended, Actual, Estimated, and Enforced Spans of Control[19]

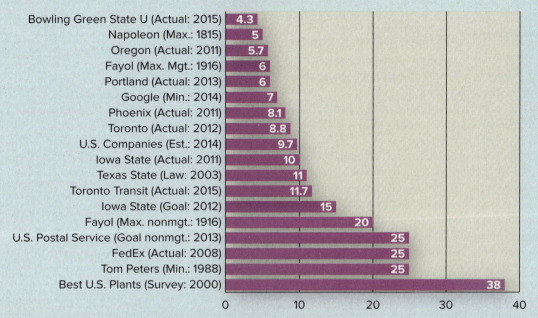

	Span of control
Bowling Green State U (Actual: 2015)	4.3
Napoleon (Max.: 1815)	5
Oregon (Actual: 2011)	5.7
Fayol (Max. Mgt.: 1916)	6
Portland (Actual: 2013)	6
Google (Min.: 2014)	7
Phoenix (Actual: 2011)	8.1
Toronto (Actual: 2012)	8.8
U.S. Companies (Est.: 2014)	9.7
Iowa State (Actual: 2011)	10
Texas State (Law: 2003)	11
Toronto Transit (Actual: 2015)	11.7
Iowa State (Goal: 2012)	15
Fayol (Max. nonmgt.: 1916)	20
U.S. Postal Service (Goal nonmgt.: 2013)	25
FedEx (Actual: 2008)	25
Tom Peters (Min.: 1988)	25
Best U.S. Plants (Survey: 2000)	38

(Axis: 0, 10, 20, 30, 40)

Note: Data represent the average number of direct reports per manager. "Max." is the maximum spans of control recommended by Napoleon Bonaparte and Henri Fayol. "Min." is the minimum span of control applied to teams by Google and recommended by Tom Peters. "Est." is the estimated average span of control across all major U.S. companies, according to consulting firm Deloitte. "Goal" refers to the span of control targets that the U.S. Postal Service and State of Iowa are trying to achieve. (USPS currently exceeds its goal.) The State of Texas number is the span of control mandated by law. The Best U.S. Plants number is the average span of control in American manufacturing facilities identified by *Industry Week* magazine as the most effective. "Actual" refers to the spans of control reported in the cities of Phoenix, Portland, and Toronto; the public service of the U.S. states of Oregon and Iowa; Bowling Green State University; the Toronto Transit Commission; and FedEx Corporation in the years indicated. The City of Toronto number excludes firefighters and parks, which have unusually high spans of control. When these units are included, Toronto's span of control is 16.29.

technical work, so they have more novel and complex tasks, which requires more active supervision. Commercial-policy processing, on the other hand, is like production work. Tasks are routine and have few exceptions, so managers have less coordinating to do with each employee.[21]

A third influence on span of control is the degree of interdependence among employees within the department or team.[22] Generally, a narrow span of control is necessary for highly interdependent jobs because employees tend to experience more conflict with each other, which requires more of a manager's time to resolve. Also, employees are less clear on their personal work performance in highly interdependent tasks, so supervisors spend more time providing coaching and feedback.

Tall versus Flat Structures Span of control is interconnected with organizational size (number of employees) and the number of layers in the organizational hierarchy. Consider two companies with the same number of employees. If Company A

As companies grow, they usually build taller structures to enable some degree of direct supervision as a coordinating mechanism.
©Ilya Terentyev/Getty Images

has a wider span of control (more direct reports per manager) than Company B, then Company A necessarily has fewer layers of management (i.e., a flatter structure). The reason for this relationship is that a company with a wider span of control has more employees per supervisor, more supervisors for each middle manager, and so on. This larger number of direct reports, compared to a company with a narrower span of control, is possible only by removing layers of management.

The interconnection of span of control, organizational size (number of employees), and number of management layers has important implications for companies. As organizations grow, they typically employ more people, which means they must widen the span of control, build a taller hierarchy, or both. Most companies end up building taller structures because they rely on direct supervision to some extent as a coordinating mechanism and there are limits to how many people each manager can coordinate.

Unfortunately, building a taller hierarchy (more layers of management) creates problems. One concern is that executives in tall structures tend to receive lower-quality and less timely information. People tend to filter, distort, and simplify information before it is passed to higher levels in the hierarchy because they are motivated to frame the information in a positive light or to summarize it more efficiently. In contrast, in flat hierarchies, information is manipulated less and is usually transmitted much more quickly than in tall hierarchies.

A second problem is that taller structures have higher overhead costs. With more managers per employee, tall hierarchies necessarily have more people administering the company, thereby reducing the percentage of staff who are actually making the product or providing the service. A third issue with tall hierarchies is that employees usually feel less empowered and engaged in their work. Hierarchies are power structures, so more levels of hierarchy tend to draw power away from people at the bottom of that hierarchy. Indeed, the size of the hierarchy itself tends to focus power around managers rather than employees.[23]

These problems with tall hierarchies have prompted companies to reduce management layers. For example, McDonald's Corp. and BCE (Canada's largest telecommunications company) recently sliced out three layers of management. McDonald's CEO Steve Easterbrook says that the delayering "has meant the visibility and the flow of ideas and the transparency was just much, much quicker for all of us as we're making our business decisions." Conagra Foods also recently restructured into a flatter organization. CEO Sean Connolly says the packaged food company now has "fewer layers, broader spans of control and the workforce, we believe, is right-sized for speed, empowerment, agility, all the things we need to do."[25]

There are potential negative consequences of flattening the hierarchy, however.[26] Critics warn that all companies need managers to translate corporate strategy into coherent daily operations. Delayering widens the span of control, leaving managers with less time to effectively coach employees, resolve conflicts, and make operational decisions within the work unit. Fewer layers also reduce the company's ability to develop managerial skills because there are fewer positions and steps to develop management talent. Promotions are also riskier because they involve a larger jump in responsibility in flatter, compared to taller, hierarchies.

OB THEORY TO PRACTICE

BBC Further Flattens the Hierarchy

The British Broadcasting Corporation (BBC) has one of the lowest overhead costs among public-sector and regulated companies in the United Kingdom. Overhead (management and administration) represents less than 8 percent of total costs. Yet, with declining television license fee income, the BBC is further reducing management numbers and flattening the corporate hierarchy. "In some places there are currently 10 layers of people and management and this will be cut to a maximum of seven in the future," advises BBC Director-General Tony Hall.

Lord Hall warns that, in addition to being a source of overhead costs, hierarchy "slows down decision making." He suggests that reducing management layers will improve the BBC because the organization excels with "as few barriers as possible to creativity, allowing people, teams and ideas to come together to do their best work. It is not one which allows bureaucracy, layers, and box-ticking to get in the way."[27]

©David Pearson/Alamy Stock Photo

Centralization and Decentralization

Centralization means that formal decision-making authority is held by a small group of people, typically those at the top of the organizational hierarchy. Most organizations begin with centralized structures because the founder makes most of the decisions and tries to direct the business toward his or her vision. As organizations grow, however, they diversify and their environments

> Any new idea condemned to struggle upward through multiple levels of rigidly hierarchical, risk-averse management is an idea that won't see daylight . . . until it's too late.[24]
>
> —Sergio Marchionne, CEO of Fiat Chrysler Automobiles and Ferrari

become more complex. Senior executives aren't able to process all the decisions that significantly influence the business. Consequently, larger organizations typically *decentralize*; that is, they disperse decision authority and power throughout the organization.

The optimal level of centralization or decentralization depends on several contingencies that we will examine later in this chapter. However, different degrees of decentralization can occur simultaneously in different parts of an organization. For instance, 7-Eleven centralizes decisions about information technology and supplier purchasing to improve buying power, increase cost-efficiencies, and minimize complexity across the organization. Yet it decentralizes local inventory decisions to store managers because they have the best information about their customers and can respond quickly to local market needs. "We could never predict a busload of football players on a Friday night, but the store manager can," explains a 7-Eleven executive.[28]

Formalization

Formalization is the degree to which organizations standardize behavior through rules, procedures, formal training, and related mechanisms.[29] In other words, companies become more formalized as they increasingly rely on various forms of standardization to coordinate work. McDonald's restaurants and most other efficient fast-food chains typically have a high degree of formalization because they rely on standardization of work processes as a coordinating mechanism. Employees have precisely defined roles, right down to how much mustard should be dispensed, how many pickles should be applied, and how long each hamburger should be cooked.

Older companies tend to become more formalized because work activities become routinized, making them easier to document into standardized practices. Larger companies also tend to have more formalization because direct supervision and informal communication among employees do not operate as easily when large numbers of people are involved. External influences, such as government safety legislation and strict accounting rules, also encourage formalization.

Formalization may increase efficiency and compliance, but it also can create problems.[30] Rules and procedures reduce organizational flexibility, so employees follow prescribed behaviors even when the situation clearly calls for a customized response. High levels of formalization tend to undermine organizational

> **Companies become more formalized as they increasingly rely on various forms of standardization to coordinate work.**

learning and creativity. Some work rules become so convoluted that organizational efficiency would decline if they were actually followed as prescribed. Formalization is also a source of job dissatisfaction and work stress. Finally, rules and procedures have been known to take on a life of their own in some organizations. They become the focus of attention rather than the organization's ultimate objectives of producing a product or service and serving its dominant stakeholders.

Mechanistic versus Organic Structures

We discussed span of control, centralization, and formalization together because they cluster around two broader organizational forms: mechanistic and organic structures (see Exhibit 12.3).[31] A **mechanistic structure** is characterized by a narrow span of control and a high degree of formalization and centralization. Mechanistic structures have many rules and procedures, limited decision making at lower levels, tall hierarchies of people in specialized roles, and vertical rather than horizontal communication flows. Tasks are rigidly defined and are altered only when sanctioned by higher authorities. Although now changing its structure, Samsung has traditionally had a mechanistic structure, which is apparent by the Korean firm's centralized decision making, clearly defined job descriptions, and work activities heavily guided by established rules and procedures.

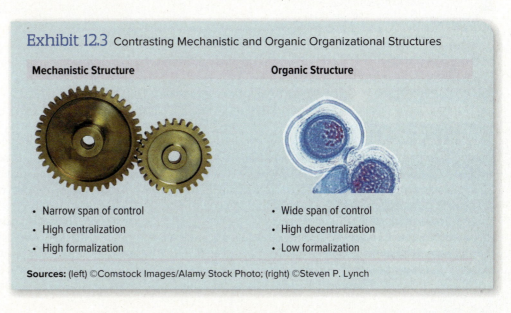

Exhibit 12.3 Contrasting Mechanistic and Organic Organizational Structures

Mechanistic Structure
- Narrow span of control
- High centralization
- High formalization

Organic Structure
- Wide span of control
- High decentralization
- Low formalization

Sources: (left) ©Comstock Images/Alamy Stock Photo; (right) ©Steven P. Lynch

organic structure an organizational structure with a wide span of control, little formalization, and decentralized decision making

functional structure an organizational structure in which employees are organized around specific knowledge or other resources

Companies with an **organic structure** have the opposite characteristics. They operate with a wide span of control, decentralized decision making, and little formalization. Tasks are fluid, adjusting to new situations and organizational needs. In extremely organic organizations, decision making is decentralized down to teams and individuals, and employees have enough autonomy to adapt their job duties to fit the situation.

As a general rule, mechanistic structures operate better in stable environments because they rely on efficiency and routine behaviors. Organic structures work better in rapidly changing (i.e., dynamic) environments because they are more flexible and responsive to the changes. Organic structures are also more compatible with organizational learning and high-performance workplaces because they emphasize information sharing and an empowered workforce rather than hierarchy and status.[32] However, the effectiveness of organic structures depends on how well employees have developed their roles and expertise.[33] Without these conditions, employees are unable to coordinate effectively with each other, resulting in errors and gross inefficiencies.

strategy for coordinating organizational activities because it influences organizational behavior in the following ways:[34]

- Departmentalization establishes the chain of command—the system of common supervision among positions and units within the organization. It frames the membership of formal work teams and typically determines which positions and units must share resources. Thus, departmentalization establishes interdependencies among employees and subunits.

- Departmentalization focuses people around common mental models or ways of thinking, such as serving clients, developing products, or supporting a particular skill set. This focus is typically anchored around the common budgets and measures of performance assigned to employees within each departmental unit.

- Departmentalization encourages specific people and work units to coordinate through informal communication. With common supervision and resources, members within each configuration typically work near each other, so they can use frequent and informal interaction to get the work done.

There are almost as many organizational charts as there are businesses, but the five most common pure types of departmentalization are simple, functional, divisional, team-based, and matrix.

Simple Structure

Most companies begin with a *simple structure*.[35] They employ only a few people and typically offer only one distinct product or service. There is minimal hierarchy—usually just employees reporting to the owners. Employees perform broadly defined roles because there are insufficient economies of scale to assign them to specialized jobs. The simple structure is highly flexible and minimizes the walls that form between employees in other structures. However, the simple structure usually depends on the owner's direct supervision to coordinate work activities, so it is very difficult to operate as the company grows and becomes more complex.

LO12-3 Identify and evaluate five types of departmentalization.

FORMS OF DEPARTMENTALIZATION

Span of control, centralization, and formalization are important elements of organizational structure, but most people think about organizational charts when the discussion of organizational structure arises. The organizational chart represents the fourth element in the structuring of organizations, called *departmentalization*. Departmentalization specifies how employees and their activities are grouped together. It is a fundamental

Functional Structure

As organizations grow, they typically shift from a simple structure to a functional structure. Even after they adopt more complex organizational structures that we discuss later, they will have a functional structure at some level of the hierarchy. A **functional structure** organizes employees around specific knowledge or other resources (see Exhibit 12.4). Employees with marketing expertise are grouped into a marketing unit, those with production skills are located in manufacturing, engineers are found in product development, and so on. Organizations with functional structures are typically centralized to coordinate their activities effectively.

Exhibit 12.4 A Functional Organizational Structure

formal controls and coordination when people are organized around functions.

Divisional Structure

The **divisional structure** (sometimes called the *multidivisional* or *M-form* structure) groups employees around geographic areas, outputs (products or services), or clients. Exhibit 12.5 illustrates these three variations of divisional structure.[38] The *geographic divisional structure* organizes employees around distinct regions of the country or world. Exhibit 12.5(a) illustrates a simplified version of the geographic divisional structure adopted by Kone, the Finland-based global elevator and escalator company. The *product/service divisional structure* organizes employees around distinct outputs. Exhibit 12.5(b) illustrates the four product divisions at Danone, the France-based global food company. The *client divisional structure* organizes employees around specific customer groups. Exhibit 12.5(c) illustrates a customer-focused divisional structure adopted by the U.S. Internal Revenue Service.[39]

Which form of divisional structure should large organizations adopt? The answer depends mainly on the primary source of environmental diversity or uncertainty.[40] Suppose an organization has one type of product sold to people across the country. If customers have different needs across regions, or if state governments impose different regulations on the product, then a geographic structure would be best so the company can be more vigilant about this diversity. On the other hand, if the company sells several types of products across the country and customer preferences and government regulations are similar everywhere, then a product structure would likely work best.

Kone, the global elevator and escalator company, is organized mainly around geographic regions, likely because regulations and sales channels vary much more by region than by product. McDonald's is organized into four geographic divisions (high growth, established, franchised) and is further organized by specific countries or zones within each of these divisions. This geographic organization makes sense because even though it makes the same Big Mac throughout the world, McDonald's has more fish products in Hong Kong and more vegetarian products in India, in line with traditional diets in those countries. Danone has dozens of country managers to anticipate and respond to cultural differences. However, the French dairy products maker places product groups (waters, dairy, medical, early life) at the top of its organizational structure, possibly because marketing and manufacturing activities vary much more across product divisions than across regions.

Evaluating the Functional Structure The functional structure creates specialized pools of talent that typically serve everyone in the organization. Pooling talent into one group improves economies of scale compared to dispersing functional specialists over different parts of the organization. The functional structure also increases employee identity with the specialization or profession. Direct supervision is easier in a functional structure because managers oversee people with common issues and expertise.[36]

The functional structure also has limitations.[37] Grouping employees around their skills tends to focus attention on those skills and related professional needs rather than on the company's products, services, or client needs. Unless people are transferred from one function to the next, they might not develop a broader understanding of the business. Compared with other structures, the functional structure usually produces more dysfunctional conflict and poorer coordination in serving clients or developing products. These problems occur because employees need to work with coworkers in other departments to complete organizational tasks, yet they have different subgoals and mental models about how to perform the work effectively. Together, these problems require substantial

By grouping employees around their skills, the functional structure focuses attention on those skills rather than on the company's products, services, or client needs.
©tkemot/Shutterstock

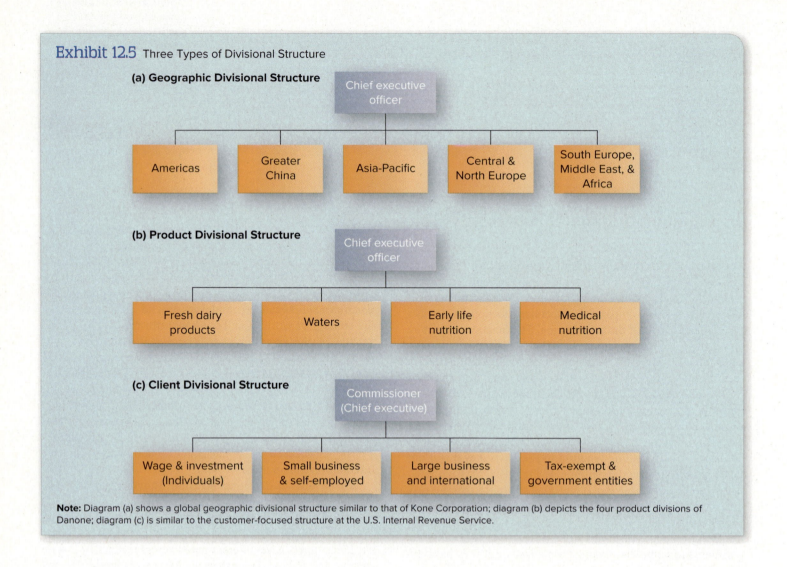

Exhibit 12.5 Three Types of Divisional Structure

(a) Geographic Divisional Structure

Chief executive officer

- Americas
- Greater China
- Asia-Pacific
- Central & North Europe
- South Europe, Middle East, & Africa

(b) Product Divisional Structure

Chief executive officer

- Fresh dairy products
- Waters
- Early life nutrition
- Medical nutrition

(c) Client Divisional Structure

Commissioner (Chief executive)

- Wage & investment (Individuals)
- Small business & self-employed
- Large business and international
- Tax-exempt & government entities

Note: Diagram (a) shows a global geographic divisional structure similar to that of Kone Corporation; diagram (b) depicts the four product divisions of Danone; diagram (c) is similar to the customer-focused structure at the U.S. Internal Revenue Service.

Many companies are moving away from structures that organize people around geographic clusters.[41] One reason is that clients can purchase products online and communicate with businesses from almost anywhere in the world, so local representation is becoming less important. Reduced geographic variation is another reason for the shift away from geographic structures; freer trade has reduced government intervention, and consumer preferences for many products and services are becoming more similar (converging) around the world. The third reason is that large companies increasingly have global business customers who demand one global point of purchase, not one in every country or region.

Evaluating the Divisional Structure The divisional organizational structure is a building-block structure; it accommodates growth relatively easily. As the company develops new products, services, or clients, it can sprout new divisions. The divisional structure is also outcome-focused. It directs employee attention to customers and products, rather than to their own specialized knowledge.[42]

Whether an organization should adopt a geographic, product, or client-focused structure depends mainly on the primary source of environmental diversity or uncertainty.
©David Pearson/REX/Shutterstock

team-based organizational structure an organizational structure built around self-directed teams that complete an entire piece of work

These advantages are offset by a number of limitations. First, the divisional structure tends to duplicate resources, such as production equipment and engineering or information technology expertise. Also, unless the division is quite large, resources are not used as efficiently as they are in functional structures where resources are pooled across the entire organization. The divisional structure also creates silos of knowledge. Expertise is spread across several autonomous business units, and this reduces the ability and perhaps motivation of the people in one division to share their knowledge with counterparts in other divisions. In contrast, a functional structure organizes experts together, thereby supporting knowledge sharing.

Finally, the preferred divisional structure depends on the company's primary source of environmental diversity or uncertainty. This principle seems to be applied easily enough at McDonald's and the U.S. Internal Revenue Service, but many global organizations experience diversity and uncertainty in terms of geography, product, *and* clients. Consequently, some organizations revise their structures back and forth or create complex structures that attempt to give all three dimensions equal status. This waffling generates further complications because organizational structure decisions shift power and status among executives. If the company switches from a geographic to a product structure, people who lead the geographic fiefdoms suddenly get demoted under the product chiefs. In short, leaders of global organizations struggle to find the best divisional structure, often resulting in the departure of some executives and frustration among those who remain.

Team-Based Structure

A **team-based organizational structure** is built around self-directed teams that complete an entire piece of work, such as manufacturing a product or developing an electronic game. This type of structure is usually organic. There is a wide span of control because teams operate with minimal supervision. There is no formal leader in its most extreme variation, just someone selected by other team members to help coordinate the work and liaise with top management.

Team structures are highly decentralized because almost all day-to-day decisions are made by team members rather than someone further up the organizational hierarchy. Many team-based structures also have low formalization because teams are given relatively few rules about how to organize their work. Instead, executives assign quality and quantity output targets, and often productivity improvement goals, to each team. Teams are then encouraged to use available resources and their own initiative to achieve those objectives.

Team-based structures are usually found within the manufacturing or service operations of larger divisional structures. Several GE Aircraft Engines plants are organized as team-based structures, but these plants operate within GE's larger divisional structure. However, a small number of firms apply the team-based structure from top to bottom, including W. L. Gore & Associates, Semco SA, Morning Star Company, and Valve Corporation, where almost all employees work in teams.

Evaluating the Team-Based Structure

The team-based structure has gained popularity because it is more flexible and responsive in turbulent environments.[43] It tends to reduce costs because teams have less reliance on formal hierarchy (direct supervision). A cross-functional team structure improves communication and cooperation across traditional boundaries. With greater autonomy, this structure also allows quicker and more informed decision making.[44] For this reason, some hospitals have shifted from functional departments to cross-functional teams. Teams composed of nurses, radiologists, anesthetists, a pharmacology representative, possibly social workers, a rehabilitation therapist, and other specialists communicate and coordinate more efficiently, thereby reducing delays and errors.[45]

Some hospitals have shifted from functional departments to cross-functional teams to improve communication and cooperation across traditional specialist boundaries.
©Fuse/Getty Images

> One limitation of the divisional structure is that, unless the division is quite large, resources are not used as efficiently as they are in functional structures where resources are pooled across the entire organization.

The team-based structure also has several limitations. It can be costly to maintain due to the need for ongoing interpersonal skills training. Teamwork potentially takes more time to coordinate than formal hierarchy during the early stages of team development. Employees may experience more stress due to increased ambiguity in their roles. Team leaders also experience more stress due to increased conflict, loss of functional power, and unclear career progression ladders. In addition, team structures suffer from duplication of resources and potential competition (and lack of resource sharing) across teams.[46]

Matrix Structure

ABB Group, one of the world's largest power and automation technology engineering firms, has four product divisions, such as power grids and process automation. It employs more than 140,000 people across 100 countries, so the global giant also has several regional groups (Americas, AMEA, and Europe). What organizational structure would work best for ABB? For example, should the head of power grids in North America report to the worldwide head of power products in Zurich, Switzerland, or to the head of the Americas operations?

For ABB, the answer is to have a **matrix structure**, which overlays two structures (in this case, a product divisional and geographic divisional structure) to leverage the benefits of both.[47] Exhibit 12.6 shows a product–geographic matrix structure, which is a simplified version of ABB's structure. The dots represent the individuals who have two bosses. For example, the head of power grids in Europe reports to ABB's worldwide president of power grids as well as to ABB's president of European regional operations.

A common mistake is to assume that everyone in this type of matrix organizational structure reports to two bosses. In reality, only managers at one level in the organization (typically country-specific product managers) have two bosses. For example, as mentioned, ABB's executive responsible for power grids in Europe reports to both the product and regional leaders. However, employees below that country product leader report to only one manager in the European operations.

The product–geographic matrix structure is the most common matrix design among global companies. For instance, Shiseido, Procter & Gamble, and Shell have variations of this matrix structure because these firms recognize that regional groups and product/services groups are equally important. Other variations of matrix structures also exist in global businesses. H&M, the Swedish fast-fashion retail group, has a matrix organizational structure that intersects its brands-based divisions (H&M, H&M Home, Cheap Monday, Monki, Cos, etc.) with almost a dozen functional groups (logistics, production, accounting, human resources, etc).[48]

Exhibit 12.6 Matrix Organizational Structure at ABB Group

Regional Groups

Product Groups

	Americas	Asia, Middle East, Africa (AMEA)	Europe
Power Grids	●	●	●
Electrification Products	●	●	●
Discrete Automation and Motion	●	●	●
Process Automation	●	●	●

● Product leader in that region

Note: This diagram is for illustrative purposes only. It represents a simplified version of ABB's most recent structure. The complete top-level structure also has three nonmatrixed functional groups (finance, legal, HR) reporting to the CEO. In addition, this diagram assumes ABB has a pure matrix structure, in which both product and regional chiefs have equal power. ABB says it continues to have a matrix structure, but its recent reorganization seems to give more direct line authority to product groups rather than regional groups.

Global organizations tend to have complex designs that combine different types of structures, so a "pure" matrix design is relatively uncommon. A pure matrix gives equal power to leaders of both groups (products and regions, for example), whereas in reality companies often give more power to one set of groups while the other set of groups has mostly "dotted line" or advisory authority. So, although ABB's head of power grids has two bosses, the global president of power grids might have more final say or line authority than the regional leader on most issues.

Some companies also deviate from the pure matrix structure by applying it only to some regions. One such example is Cummins Inc., which is mainly organized around product divisions but has a matrix structure in China, India, and Russia. These markets are large, have high potential, and tend to be less visible to headquarters, so the country leaders are given as much authority as the product leaders within those regions. "I think in China there's still enough lack of transparency, there's still enough uniqueness to the market that having some kind of coordination across business units gets the greatest synergies," explains Michael Barbalas, a board member of the American Chamber of Commerce in China.[49]

A second type of matrix structure, which can be applied to small or large companies, overlays a functional structure with a project structure.[50] BioWare adopted this project–functional matrix structure soon after the electronic games company was born two decades ago. Most BioWare employees have two managers. One manager leads the specific project to which employees are assigned, such as *Star Wars*, *Mass Effect*, and *Dragon Age*; the other manager is head of the employee's functional specialization, such as art, programming, audio, quality assurance, and design.[51] Employees are assigned permanently to their functional unit but physically work with the temporary project team. When the project nears completion, the functional boss reassigns employees in his or her functional specialization to another project.

Evaluating the Matrix Structure The project–functional matrix structure usually makes very good use of resources and expertise, making it ideal for project-based organizations with fluctuating workloads. When properly managed, it improves communication efficiency, project flexibility, and innovation, compared to purely functional or divisional designs. It focuses employees on serving clients or creating products, yet keeps people organized around their specialization. The result is that knowledge sharing improves and human resources are used more efficiently.

Matrix structures for global organizations are also a logical choice when, as in the case of ABB Group, two different dimensions (regions and products) are equally important. Structures determine executive power and what should receive priority; the matrix structure works best when the business environment is complex and two different dimensions deserve equal attention and integration. Executives who have worked in a global matrix also say they have more freedom, likely because their two bosses are more advisory and less oriented toward command-and-control leadership.[52]

The many advantages of the matrix structure are offset by well-known problems.[54] One concern is that it increases conflict among managers who equally share power. Employees working at the matrix level have two bosses and, consequently, two sets of priorities that aren't always aligned with each other. Project leaders might squabble with functional leaders regarding the assignment of specific employees to projects as well as regarding the employee's technical competence. However, successful companies manage this conflict by developing and promoting leaders who can work effectively in matrix structures. "Of course there's potential for friction," says an executive at IBM India. "In fact, one of the prerequisites to attaining a leadership position at IBM is the ability to function in a matrix structure."[55]

Ambiguous accountability is another challenge with matrix structures. In a functional or divisional structure, one manager is responsible for everything, even the most unexpected issues. But in a matrix structure, the unusual problems don't get resolved because neither manager takes ownership of them.[56] Due to this ambiguous accountability, matrix structures have been blamed for corporate ethical misconduct, such as embezzlement at Hana Financial Group in Korea and massive bribery at Siemens AG in Germany. The combination of dysfunctional conflict and ambiguous accountability in matrix structures also explains why some employees experience more stress and why some managers are less satisfied with their work arrangements.

CONTINGENCIES OF ORGANIZATIONAL DESIGN

Most organizational behavior theories and concepts have contingencies: Ideas that work well in one situation might not work as well in another situation. This contingency approach is certainly relevant when choosing the most appropriate organizational structure.[57] In this section, we introduce four contingencies of organizational design: external environment, size, technology, and strategy.

External Environment

The best structure for an organization depends on its external environment. The external environment includes anything outside the organization, including most stakeholders (e.g., clients, suppliers, government), resources (e.g., raw materials, human resources, information, finances), and competitors. Four characteristics of external environments influence the type of organizational structure best suited to a particular situation: dynamism, complexity, diversity, and hostility.[58]

Dynamic versus Stable Environments Dynamic environments have a high rate of change, leading to novel situations and a lack of identifiable patterns. Organic structures, particularly those in which employees are experienced and coordinate well in teams, are better suited to dynamic environments, so the organization can adapt more quickly to changes.[59] In contrast, stable environments are characterized by regular cycles of activity and steady changes in supply and demand for inputs and outputs. Events are more predictable, enabling the firm to apply rules and procedures. Mechanistic structures are more efficient when the environment is predictable, so they tend to be more profitable than organic structures under these conditions.

Complex versus Simple Environments Complex environments have many elements, whereas simple environments have few things to monitor. As an example, a major university library operates in a more complex environment than a small-town public library. The university library's clients require several types of services—book borrowing, online full-text databases, research centers, course reserve collections, and so on. A small-town public library has fewer of these demands placed on it. The more complex the environment, the more decentralized the

Mechanistic structures are better suited to stable environments, which have regular cycles of activity and predictable changes in supply and demand for inputs and outputs.
©Monty Rakusen/Cultura/Getty Images

organization should become. Decentralization is a logical choice for complex environments because decisions are pushed down to people and subunits who possess the information needed to make informed choices.

Diverse versus Integrated Environments Organizations located in diverse environments have a greater variety of products or services, clients, and regions. In contrast, an integrated environment has only one client, product, and geographic area. The more diversified the environment, the more the firm needs to use a divisional structure aligned with that diversity. If it sells a single product around the world, a geographic divisional structure would align best with the firm's geographic diversity, for example. Diverse environments also call for decentralization. By pushing decision making further down the hierarchy, the company can adapt better and more quickly to diverse clients, government requirements, and other circumstances related to that diversity.

Hostile versus Munificent Environments Firms located in hostile environments face resource scarcity and more competition in the marketplace. These conditions are typically dynamic

organizational strategy
the way the organization positions itself in its environment in relation to its stakeholders, given the organization's resources, capabilities, and mission

as well because they reduce the predictability of access to resources and demand for outputs. Organic structures tend to be best in hostile environments. However, when the environment is extremely unfavorable—such as a severe shortage of supplies or tumbling market share—organizations tend to temporarily centralize so that decisions can be made more quickly and executives feel more comfortable being in control.[60] Ironically, centralization may result in lower-quality decisions during organizational crises because top management has less information, particularly when the environment is complex.

Organizational Size

Larger organizations have different structures than do smaller organizations, for good reason.[61] As the number of employees increases, job specialization increases due to a greater division of labor. The greater division of labor requires more elaborate coordinating mechanisms. Thus, larger firms make greater use of standardization (particularly work processes and outcomes) to coordinate work activities. These coordinating mechanisms create an administrative hierarchy and greater formalization. Historically, larger organizations make less use of informal communication as a coordinating mechanism. However, emerging information technologies and increased emphasis on empowerment have caused informal communication to regain its importance in large firms.[62]

Larger organizations also tend to be more decentralized than are smaller organizations. Executives have neither sufficient time nor expertise to process all the decisions that significantly influence the business as it grows. Therefore, decision-making authority is pushed down to lower levels, where employees are able to make decisions on issues within their narrower range of responsibility.

Technology

Technology is another factor to consider when designing the best organizational structure for the situation.[63] *Technology* refers to the mechanisms or processes an organization relies on to make its products or services. In other words, technology isn't just the equipment used to make something; it also includes how the production process is physically arranged and how the production work is divided among employees.

The two main technological contingencies are task variability and task analyzability, both of which we described as job characteristics in Chapter 5. *Task variability* refers to how predictable the job duties are from one day to the next. In jobs with high variability, employees perform several types of tasks, but they don't know which of those tasks are required from one day to the next. Low variability occurs when the work is highly routine and predictable. *Task analyzability* refers to how much the job can be performed using known procedures and rules. In jobs with high task analyzability, employees have well-defined guidelines to direct them through the work process. In jobs with low task analyzability, employees tackle unique situations with few (if any) guidelines to help them determine the best course of action.

An organic, rather than a mechanistic, structure should be introduced where employees perform tasks with high variability and low analyzability, such as in a research setting. The reason is that employees face unique situations with little opportunity for repetition. In contrast, a mechanistic structure is preferred where the technology has low variability and high analyzability, such as an assembly line. Assembly work is routine, is highly predictable, and has well-established procedures—an ideal situation for a mechanistic structure to operate efficiently.

Organizational Strategy

Organizational strategy refers to the way the organization positions itself in its environment in relation to its stakeholders,

Organizations tend to be more decentralized as they grow because executives have neither sufficient time nor expertise to process all the decisions that significantly influence a large business.
©Matej Kastelic/Shutterstock

given the organization's resources, capabilities, and mission.[64] In other words, strategy represents the decisions and actions applied to achieve the organization's goals. Although size, technology, and environment influence the optimal organizational structure, these contingencies do not necessarily determine structure. Instead, corporate leaders formulate and implement strategies that shape both the characteristics of these contingencies as well as the organization's resulting structure.

This concept is summed up with the simple phrase "structure follows strategy."[65] Organizational leaders decide how large to grow and which technologies to use. They take steps to define and manipulate their environments, rather than let the organization's fate be entirely determined by external influences (see the open systems perspective in Chapter 1). Furthermore, organizational structures don't evolve as a natural response to environmental conditions; they result from conscious human decisions. Thus, organizational strategy influences both the contingencies of structure and the structure itself.

If a company's strategy is to compete through innovation, a more organic structure would be preferred because it is easier for employees to share knowledge and be creative. If a company chooses a low-cost strategy, a mechanistic structure is preferred because it maximizes production and service efficiency.[66] Overall, it is now apparent that organizational structure is influenced by size, technology, and environment, but the organization's strategy may reshape these elements and loosen their connection to organizational structure.

Study Checklist

Connect® Management is available for *M Organizational Behavior.* Additional resources include:

✓ Interactive Applications:
- **Decision Generator**
- **Drag and Drop:** Work through an interactive example to test your knowledge of the concepts.
- **Video Case:** See management in action through interactive videos.

✓ **SmartBook™**—SmartBook is the first and only adaptive reading experience available today. Distinguishing what you know from what you don't, and honing in on concepts you are most likely to forget, SmartBook personalizes content for you in a continuously adapting reading experience. Reading is no longer a passive and linear experience, but an engaging and dynamic one where you are more likely to master and retain important concepts and go to class better prepared.

©Natthawat Jamnapa/123RF

Notes

1. "Samsung Emulates Silicon Valley by Letting Staff Take on Pet Projects," *Today* (Singapore), November 20, 2015, 55; Y.-C. Kim, "Samsung to Overhaul Rigid Business Structure," *Korea Times*, March 24, 2016; "Korean Companies Seek to Drop Job Titles," *Korea Herald*, April 6, 2016; "Samsung to Streamline Job Titles," *The Nation* (Bangkok), February 11, 2017; "Samsung to Demolish Rigid, Top-Down Corporate Culture," *Korea Times*, February 11, 2017.

2. S. Ranson, R. Hinings, and R. Greenwood, "The Structuring of Organizational Structure," *Administrative Science Quarterly* 25 (1980): 1–14; J. E. Johanson, "Intraorganizational Influence," *Management Communication Quarterly* 13 (2000): 393–435; K. Walsh, "Interpreting the Impact of Culture on Structure," *Journal of Applied Behavioral Science* 40, no. 3 (2004): 302–22. The recent survey is reported in J. Bersin et al., "The New Organization: Different by Design," in *Global Human Capital Trends 2016* (Westlake, TX: Deloitte University Press, 2016), 1–14.

3. H. Mintzberg, *The Structuring of Organizations* (Englewood Cliffs, NJ: Prentice Hall, 1979), 2–3.

4. E. E. Lawler III, *Motivation in Work Organizations* (Monterey, CA: Brooks/Cole, 1973); M. A. Campion, "Ability Requirement Implications of Job Design: An Interdisciplinary Perspective," *Personnel Psychology* 42 (1989): 1–24.

5. G. S. Becker and K. M. Murphy, "The Division of Labor, Coordination Costs, and Knowledge," *Quarterly Journal of Economics* 107, no. 4 (1992): 1137–60; L. Borghans and B. Weel, "The Division of Labour, Worker Organisation, and Technological Change," *The Economic Journal* 116, no. 509 (2006): F45–F72.

6. H. Mintzberg, *The Structuring of Organizations* (Englewood Cliffs, NJ: Prentice Hall, 1979), chap. 1; D. A. Nadler and M. L. Tushman, *Competing by Design: The Power of Organizational Architecture* (New York: Oxford University Press, 1997), chap. 6; J. R. Galbraith, *Designing Organizations: An Executive Guide to Strategy, Structure, and Process* (San Francisco: Jossey-Bass, 2002), chap. 4.

7. J. Stephenson Jr., "Making Humanitarian Relief Networks More Effective: Operational Coordination, Trust and Sense Making," *Disasters* 29, no. 4 (2005): 337.

8. A. Willem, M. Buelens, and H. Scarbrough, "The Role of Inter-Unit Coordination Mechanisms in Knowledge Sharing: A Case Study of a British MNC," *Journal of Information Science* 32, no. 6 (2006): 539–61; R. R. Gulati, "Silo Busting," *Harvard Business Review* 85, no. 5 (2007): 98–108.

9. L. Borghans and B. Weel, "The Division of Labour, Worker Organisation, and Technological Change," *The Economic Journal* 116, no. 509 (2006): F45–F72.

10. T. Van Alphen, "Magna in Overdrive," *Toronto Star*, July 24, 2006.

11. J. R. Galbraith, *Designing Organizations: An Executive Guide to Strategy, Structure, and Process* (San Francisco, CA: Jossey-Bass, 2002), 66–72; D. Aaker, *Spanning Silos: The New CMO Imperative* (Cambridge, MA: Harvard Business Press, 2008), 95–96; A. Pike, *Brands and Branding Geographies* (Cheltenham, UK: Edward Elgar, 2011), 133.

12. S. M. Sapuan, M. R. Osman, and Y. Nukman, "State of the Art of the Concurrent Engineering Technique in the Automotive Industry," *Journal of Engineering Design* 17, no. 2 (2006): 143–57; D. M. Anderson, *Design for Manufacturing: How to Use Concurrent Engineering to Rapidly Develop Low-Cost, High-Quality Products for Lean Management* (Boca Raton, FL: CRC Press/Taylor & Francis, 2014), chap. 2.

13. A. H. Van De Ven, A. L. Delbecq, and R. J. Koenig Jr., "Determinants of Coordination Modes within Organizations," *American Sociological Review* 41, no. 2 (1976): 322–38.

14. T. Gould, "How Employees Really Feel about Their Bosses," *HR Morning*, July 2, 2011; Kelly Services, *Effective Employers: The Evolving Workforce*, Kelly Global Workforce Index (Troy, MI: Kelly Services, November 2011); Society for Human Resource Management, *SHRM Poll: Intergenerational Conflict in the Workplace* (Alexandria, VA: Society for Human Resource Management, April 29, 2011); Accountemps, "Something to Talk about," news release (Toronto: Accountemps, October 22, 2013); Accountemps, "Survey: More Than Half of Employees Have Worked for a Micromanager," news release (Menlo Park, CA: PR Newswire, July 1, 2014).

15. Y. M. Hsieh and A. T. Hsieh, "Enhancement of Service Quality with Job Standardisation," *Service Industries Journal* 21 (2001): 147–66.

16. B. Davison, "Management Span of Control: How Wide Is Too Wide?," *Journal of Business Strategy* 24, no. 4 (2003): 22–29; N. A. Theobald and S. Nicholson-Crotty, "The Many Faces of Span of Control: Organizational Structure across Multiple Goals," *Administration Society* 36, no. 6 (2005): 648–60; R. M. Meyer, "Span of Management: Concept Analysis," *Journal of Advanced Nursing* 63, no. 1 (2008): 104–12.

17. D. D. Van Fleet and A. G. Bedeian, "A History of the Span of Management," *Academy of Management Review* 2 (1977): 356–72; H. Fayol, *General and Industrial Management*, trans. C. Storrs (London: Pitman, 1949); D. A. Wren, A. G. Bedeian, and J. D. Breeze, "The Foundations of Henri Fayol's Administrative Theory," *Management Decision* 40, no. 9 (2002): 906–18.

18. D. Drickhamer, "Lessons from the Leading Edge," *IndustryWeek*, February 21, 2000, 23–26.

19. D. Thompson, "More on the Span of Control Issue," *Statesman Journal Blog* (Oregon), May 16, 2011; Iowa State Legislative Services Agency, *Span of Control*, Fiscal Note, Iowa State (Des Moines: Iowa Legislature, March 10, 2011); Western Management Consultants, *Service Efficiency Study Program Management Span of Control Review Report to the City Manager* (Toronto: City of Toronto, October 31, 2012); U.S. Postal Service, *Supervisor Workhours and Span of Control: Management Advisory* (Washington, DC: U.S. Postal Service, April 4, 2013); N. Fish and S. Novick, *FY 2013-14 Budget Subcommittee #1 Final Report* (Portland, Oregon: City of Portland, April 8, 2013); E. Schmidt and J. Rosenberg, *How Google Works* (New York: Grand Central, 2014), 42–44; S. Stoll, *Accenture Update: Progress Report through August 31, 2015* (Bowling Green, OH: Bowling Green State University, September 18, 2015); WMC Consultants, *Toronto Transit Commission Organizational Review Report* (Toronto: Toronto Transit Commission, July 2015); *The New Organization: Different by Design*, Global Human Capital Trends 2016 (New York: Deloitte University Press, 2016).

20. T. B. Filipski, "Best Bosses of 2015," *PPB Magazine*, September 24, 2015.

21. J. Greenwald, "Ward Compares the Best with the Rest," *Business Insurance*, August 26, 2002, 16. One recent article also emphasized that claims managers require a narrow span of control. See M. T. Murdock, "Getting Claim Costs under Control: Improve Your Loss Ratio Using These Proven Fundamentals," *Claims Journal*, March 1, 2016.

22. J. H. Gittell, "Supervisory Span, Relational Coordination and Flight Departure Performance: A Reassessment of Postbureaucracy Theory," *Organization Science* 12, no. 4 (2001): 468–83.

23. T. D. Wall, J. L. Cordery, and C. W. Clegg, "Empowerment, Performance, and Operational Uncertainty: A Theoretical Integration," *Applied Psychology: An International Review* 51 (2002): 146–69.

24. S. Marchionne, "Navigating the New Automotive Epoch," *Vital Speeches of the Day* (2010): 134–37.

25. C. Pellegrini, "BCE's George Cope Named Canada's Outstanding CEO of the Year," *Financial Post Magazine*, November 10, 2015; Conagra Foods, "Conagra Brands Investor Day," news release (Chicago: CQ FD Disclosure, October 18, 2016); McDonald's Corp., "McDonald's Corp at Sanford C Bernstein Strategic Decision Conference," news release (Oak Brook, IL: Bloomberg, May 31, 2017).

26. Q. N. Huy, "In Praise of Middle Managers," *Harvard Business Review* 79 (2001): 72–79; C. R. Littler, R. Wiesner, and R. Dunford, "The Dynamics of Delayering: Changing Management Structures in Three Countries," *Journal of Management Studies* 40, no. 2 (2003): 225–56; H. J. Leavitt, *Top Down: Why Hierarchies Are Here to Stay and How to Manage Them More Effectively* (Cambridge: Harvard Business School Press, 2005); L. McCann, J. Morris, and J. Hassard, "Normalized Intensity: The New Labour Process of Middle Management," *Journal of Management Studies* 45, no. 2 (2008): 343–71; "Why Middle Managers May Be the Most Important People in Your Company," *Knowledge @ Wharton*, May 25, 2011.

27. H. Furness, "BBC to Cut 1,000 Jobs in Management Cull," *The Telegraph* (London), July 2, 2015; "A Simpler and Leaner BBC," news release (London: BBC, July 2, 2015); "Speech by Tony Hall to the Media & Telecoms Conference," news release (London: BBC, March 8, 2016).

28. The variations of decentralization within a company are discussed in G. Masada, "To Centralize or Decentralize?," *Optimize*, May 2005, 58–61. The 7-Eleven example is described in J. G. Kelley, "Slurpees and Sausages: 7-Eleven Holds School," *Richmond* (VA) *Times-Dispatch*, March 12, 2004, C1; S. Marling, "The 24-Hour Supply Chain," *InformationWeek*, January 26, 2004, 43.

29. H. Mintzberg, *The Structuring of Organizations* (Englewood Cliffs, NJ: Prentice Hall, 1979), chap. 5.

30. W. Dessein and T. Santos, "Adaptive Organizations," *Journal of Political Economy* 114, no. 5 (2006): 956–95; A. A. M. Nasurdin et al., "Organizational Structure and Organizational Climate as Potential Predictors of Job Stress: Evidence from Malaysia," *International Journal of Commerce and Management* 16, no. 2 (2006): 116–29; C. J. Chen and J. W. Huang, "How Organizational Climate and Structure Affect Knowledge Management—The Social Interaction Perspective," *International Journal of Information Management* 27, no. 2 (2007): 104–18.

31. T. Burns and G. Stalker, *The Management of Innovation* (London: Tavistock, 1961).

32. J. Tata, S. Prasad, and R. Thom, "The Influence of Organizational Structure on the Effectiveness of TQM Programs," *Journal of Managerial Issues* 11, no. 4 (1999): 440–53; A. Lam, "Tacit Knowledge, Organizational Learning and Societal Institutions: An Integrated Framework," *Organization Studies* 21 (2000): 487–513.

33. W. D. Sine, H. Mitsuhashi, and D. A. Kirsch, "Revisiting Burns and Stalker: Formal Structure and New Venture Performance in Emerging Economic Sectors," *Academy of Management Journal* 49, no. 1 (2006): 121–32.

34. H. Mintzberg, *The Structuring of Organizations* (Englewood Cliffs, NJ: Prentice Hall, 1979), 106.

35. H. Mintzberg, *The Structuring of Organizations* (Englewood Cliffs, NJ: Prentice Hall, 1979), chap. 17; R. M. Burton, B. Obel, and G. DeSanctis, *Organizational Design: A Step-by-Step Approach*, 2nd ed. (Cambridge, UK: Cambridge University Press, 2011), 61–63.

36. J. R. Galbraith, *Designing Organizations: An Executive Guide to Strategy, Structure, and Process* (San Francisco: Jossey-Bass, 2002), 23–25; R. M. Burton, B. Obel, and G. DeSanctis, *Organizational Design: A Step-by-Step Approach*, 2nd ed. (Cambridge, UK: Cambridge University Press, 2011), 63–65.

37. E. E. Lawler III, *Rewarding Excellence: Pay Strategies for the New Economy* (San Francisco: Jossey-Bass, 2000), 31–34.

38. The evolutionary development of the divisional structure is described in J. R. Galbraith, "The Evolution of Enterprise Organization Designs," *Journal of Organization Design* 1, no. 2 (2012): 1–13.

39. These structures were identified from corporate websites and annual reports. The organizations typically rely on a mixture of structures (typically functional units along with the divisional units shown here), so the charts shown have been adapted and simplified for learning purposes.

40. M. Goold and A. Campbell, "Do You Have a Well-Designed Organization?," *Harvard Business Review* 80 (2002): 117–24. Others have added factors such as economies of scale and what resources need to be controlled the most. See G. Kesler and A. Kates, *Leading Organization Design: How to Make Organization Design Decisions to Drive the Results You Want* (San Francisco: Jossey-Bass, 2011), chap. 3.

41. J. R. Galbraith, "Structuring Global Organizations," in *Tomorrow's Organization*, ed. S. A. Mohrman et al. (San Francisco: Jossey-Bass, 1998), 103–29; C. Homburg, J. P. Workman Jr., and O. Jensen, "Fundamental Changes in Marketing Organization: The Movement toward a Customer-Focused Organizational Structure," *Academy of Marketing Science Journal* 28 (2000): 459–78; T. H. Davenport, J. G. Harris, and A. K. Kohli, "How Do They Know Their Customers So Well?," *Sloan Management Review* 42 (2001): 63–73; J. R. Galbraith, "Organizing to Deliver Solutions," *Organizational Dynamics* 31 (2002): 194–207.

42. R. M. Burton, B. Obel, and G. DeSanctis, *Organizational Design: A Step-by-Step Approach,* 2nd ed. (Cambridge, UK: Cambridge University Press, 2011), 65–68.

43. J. R. Galbraith, E. E. Lawler III, and Associates, *Organizing for the Future: The New Logic for Managing Complex Organizations* (San Francisco: Jossey-Bass, 1993); R. Bettis and M. Hitt, "The New Competitive Landscape," *Strategic Management Journal* 16 (1995): 7–19.

44. P. C. Ensign, "Interdependence, Coordination, and Structure in Complex Organizations: Implications for Organization Design," *Mid-Atlantic Journal of Business* 34 (1998): 5–22.

45. M. M. Fanning, "A Circular Organization Chart Promotes a Hospital-Wide Focus on Teams," *Hospital & Health Services Administration* 42 (1997): 243–54; L. Y. Chan and B. E. Lynn, "Operating in Turbulent Times: How Ontario's Hospitals Are Meeting the Current Funding Crisis," *Health Care Management Review* 23 (1998): 7–18.

46. R. Cross, "Looking before You Leap: Assessing the Jump to Teams in Knowledge-Based Work," *Business Horizons* 43, no. 5 (2000): 29–36; M. Fenton-O'Creevy, "Employee Involvement and the Middle Manager: Saboteur or Scapegoat?," *Human Resource Management Journal* 11 (2001): 24–40; C. Douglas and W. L. Gardner, "Transition to Self-Directed Work Teams: Implications of Transition Time and Self-Monitoring for Managers' Use of Influence Tactics," *Journal of Organizational Behavior* 25 (2004): 47–65; G. Garda, K. Lindstrom, and M. Dallnera, "Towards a Learning Organization: The Introduction of a Client-Centered Team-Based Organization in Administrative Surveying Work," *Applied Ergonomics* 34 (2003): 97–105.

47. S. M. Davis and P. R. Lawrence, *Matrix* (Reading, MA: Addison-Wesley, 1977); J. R. Galbraith, *Designing Matrix Organizations That Actually Work* (San Francisco: Jossey-Bass, 2009); G. Kesler and A. Kates, *Leading Organization Design: How to Make Organization Design Decisions to Drive the Results You Want* (San Francisco: Jossey-Bass, 2011), chap. 7.

48. H&M's matrix structure is illustrated and described in *Corporate Governance Report 2016* (Stockholm: H & M Hennes & Mauritz AB, March 2017). Shiseido's recently introduced matrix structure is described in *Our Global Management Organization Is Fully Operational*, Annual Report 2015 (Tokyo: Shiseido, May 2016).

49. Deloitte U.S. Chinese Services Group, *Balancing Flexibility and Control: Optimizing Your Organizational Structure in China*, Board Brief China (New York: Deloitte, 2008).

50. R. C. Ford and W. A. Randolph, "Cross-Functional Structures: A Review and Integration of Matrix Organization and Project Management," *Journal of Management* 18 (1992): 267–94.

51. R. Muzyka and G. Zeschuk, "Managing Multiple Projects," *Game Developer*, March 2003, 34–42.

52. J. X. J. Qiu and L. Donaldson, "Stopford and Wells Were Right! MNC Matrix Structures *Do* Fit a 'High-High' Strategy," *Management International Review (MIR)* 52, no. 5 (2012): 671–89; D. Ganguly and M. Mitra, "Survive the Matrix," *Economic Times* (Mumbai, India), March 29, 2013.

53. D. Ciampa and M. Watkins, "Rx for New CEOs," *Chief Executive*, January 2008.

54. G. Calabrese, "Communication and Co-operation in Product Development: A Case Study of a European Car Producer," *R&D Management* 27 (1997): 239–52; T. Sy and L. S. D'Annunzio, "Challenges and Strategies of Matrix Organizations: Top-Level and Mid-Level Managers' Perspectives," *Human Resource Planning* 28, no. 1 (2005): 39–48; J. Wolf and W. G. Egelhoff, "An Empirical Evaluation of Conflict in MNC Matrix Structure Firms," *International Business Review* 22, no. 3 (2013): 591–601.

55. D. Ganguly, "Matrix Evolutions," *Economic Times* (Mumbai, India), February 18, 2012.

56. D. A. Nadler and M. L. Tushman, *Competing by Design: The Power of Organizational Architecture* (New York: Oxford University Press, 1997), chap. 6; M. Goold and A. Campbell, "Structured Networks: Towards the Well-Designed Matrix," *Long Range Planning* 36, no. 5 (2003): 427–39.

57. L. Donaldson, *The Contingency Theory of Organizations* (Thousand Oaks, CA: Sage, 2001); J. Birkinshaw, R. Nobel, and J. Ridderstråle, "Knowledge as a Contingency Variable: Do the Characteristics of Knowledge Predict Organizational Structure?," *Organization Science* 13, no. 3 (2002): 274–89.

58. P. R. Lawrence and J. W. Lorsch, *Organization and Environment* (Homewood, IL: Irwin, 1967); H. Mintzberg, *The Structuring of Organizations* (Englewood Cliffs, NJ: Prentice Hall, 1979), chap. 15.

59. T. Burns and G. Stalker, *The Management of Innovation* (London: Tavistock, 1961); P. R. Lawrence and J. W. Lorsch, *Organization and Environment* (Homewood, IL: Irwin, 1967).

60. H. Mintzberg, *The Structuring of Organizations* (Englewood Cliffs, NJ: Prentice Hall, 1979), 282.

61. D. S. Pugh and C. R. Hinings, *Organizational Structure: Extensions and Replications* (Farnborough, UK: Lexington Books, 1976); H. Mintzberg, *The Structuring of Organizations* (Englewood Cliffs, NJ: Prentice Hall, 1979), chap. 13.

62. J. R. Galbraith, *Designing Matrix Organizations That Actually Work* (San Francisco: Jossey-Bass, 2009), 52–55; G. Hertel, S. Geister, and U. Konradt, "Managing Virtual Teams: A Review of Current Empirical Research," *Human Resource Management Review* 15 (2005): 69–95.

63. C. Perrow, "A Framework for the Comparative Analysis of Organizations," *American Sociological Review* 32 (1967): 194–208; D. Gerwin, "The Comparative Analysis of Structure and Technology: A Critical Appraisal," *Academy of Management Review* 4, no. 1 (1979): 41–51; C. C. Miller et al., "Understanding Technology-Structure Relationships: Theory Development and Meta-Analytic Theory Testing," *Academy of Management Journal* 34, no. 2 (1991): 370–99.

64. R. H. Kilmann, *Beyond the Quick Fix* (San Francisco: Jossey-Bass, 1984), 38.

65. A. D. Chandler, *Strategy and Structure* (Cambridge, MA: MIT Press, 1962).

66. D. Miller, "Configurations of Strategy and Structure," *Strategic Management Journal* 7 (1986): 233–49.

13 | Organizational Culture

©Jacob Lund/Shutterstock

Learning Objectives

After you read this chapter, you should be able to:

LO13-1 Describe the elements of organizational culture and discuss the importance of organizational subcultures.

LO13-2 Describe four categories of artifacts through which corporate culture is deciphered.

LO13-3 Discuss the importance of organizational culture and the conditions under which organizational culture strength improves organizational performance.

LO13-4 Compare and contrast four strategies for merging organizational cultures.

LO13-5 Describe five strategies for changing and strengthening an organization's culture, including the application of attraction–selection–attrition theory.

LO13-6 Describe the organizational socialization process and identify strategies to improve that process.

organizational culture
the values and assumptions
shared within an organization

he phrase "organizational culture" was rarely uttered before 1982.[1] Today, the concept is on the minds of most executives and is almost daily the subject of popular-press articles. Whenever a company is in deep trouble or very successful, its organizational culture is usually implicated as a key part of the explanation. The following recent newspaper and magazine headlines illustrate this point.[2]

- "Amazon and Whole Foods Are Headed for a Culture Clash." This article from *Fortune* magazine warns that employees at Whole Foods will experience conflict and stress because its culture contrasts sharply from the culture at Amazon, which recently acquired the food retailer.

- "Uber Pays a $26 Billion Price for Its Toxic Corporate Culture." The respected author of this article in the *Sydney Morning Herald* explains that Uber's organizational culture caused the numerous scandals (sexual harassment, alleged software theft, bullying) that have plagued the "ride-sharing" company and led to the departure of its founder and more than 70 executives.

- "Lax Corporate Culture Set Up Takata's Fall." This piece in the *Nikkei Asian Review* outlines how air bag manufacturer Takata's corporate culture created a "breeding ground" for misconduct (falsifying safety data) and lax quality standards, which led to its recent bankruptcy.

> ## The thing I have learned at IBM is that culture is everything.[6]
> —Louis V. Gerstner, Jr., former CEO of IBM and RJR Nabisco

Organizational culture consists of the values and assumptions shared within an organization.[3] It defines what is important and unimportant in the company and, consequently, directs everyone in the organization toward the "right way" of doing things. You might think of organizational culture as the company's DNA—invisible to the naked eye, yet a powerful template that shapes what happens in the workplace.

This chapter begins by identifying the elements of organizational culture and then describing how culture is deciphered through artifacts. Next, we examine the relationship between organizational culture and organizational effectiveness, including the effects of cultural strength, fit, and adaptability. Our attention then turns to the challenges of and solutions to merging organizational cultures. The latter part of this chapter examines ways to change and strengthen organizational culture and looks more closely at the related topic of organizational socialization.

LO13-1 Describe the elements of organizational culture and discuss the importance of organizational subcultures.

ELEMENTS OF ORGANIZATIONAL CULTURE

Organizational culture consists of shared values and assumptions. Exhibit 13.1 illustrates how these shared values and assumptions relate to each other and are associated with artifacts, which are discussed in the next section of this chapter. *Values* are stable, evaluative beliefs that guide our preferences for outcomes or courses of action in a variety of situations (see Chapters 1 and 2).[4] They are conscious perceptions about what is good or bad, right or wrong. In the context of organizational culture, values are discussed as *shared values*, which are values that people within the organization or work unit have in common and place near the top of their hierarchy of values.[5]

Organizational culture also consists of *shared assumptions*—a deeper element that some experts believe is the essence of corporate culture. Shared assumptions are nonconscious, taken-for-granted perceptions or ideal prototypes of behavior that are considered the correct way to think and act toward problems and opportunities. Shared assumptions are so deeply ingrained that you probably wouldn't discover them by surveying employees. Only by observing employees, analyzing their decisions, and debriefing them on their actions would these assumptions rise to the surface.

Espoused versus Enacted Values

Most corporate websites have "Careers" web pages for job candidates, and many of these sites proudly list the company's core values. Do these values really represent the organization's culture? Some do, but these pages more likely describe *espoused values*—the values that corporate leaders hope will eventually become the organization's culture, or at least the values they want others to believe guide the organization's decisions and actions.[7] Espoused values are usually socially desirable, so they present a positive public image. Even if top management acts

Exhibit 13.1 Organizational Culture Assumptions, Values, and Artifacts

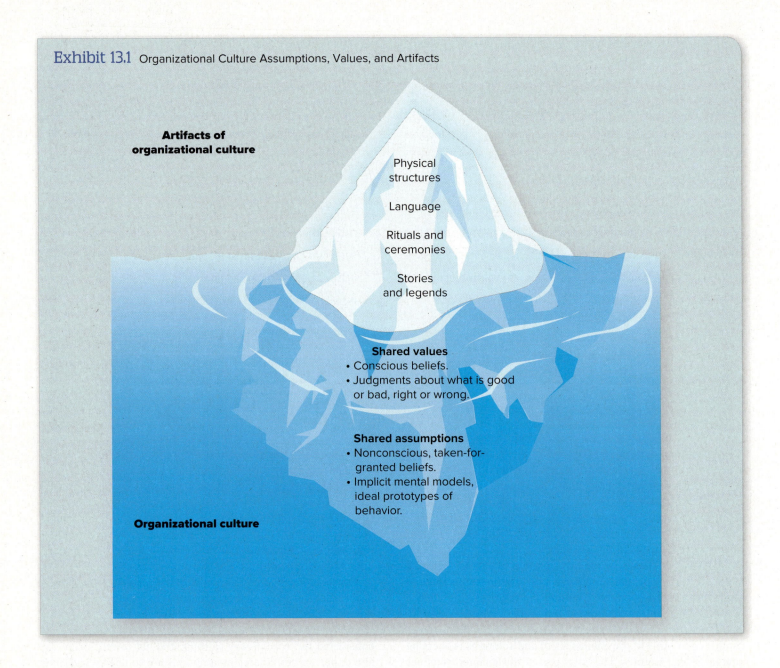

Artifacts of organizational culture

Physical structures

Language

Rituals and ceremonies

Stories and legends

Shared values
• Conscious beliefs.
• Judgments about what is good or bad, right or wrong.

Shared assumptions
• Nonconscious, taken-for-granted beliefs.
• Implicit mental models, ideal prototypes of behavior.

Organizational culture

consistently with the espoused values, lower-level employees might not do so. Employees bring diverse personal values to the organization, some of which might conflict with the organization's espoused values.

An organization's culture is defined by its *enacted values*, not its espoused values. Values are *enacted* when they actually guide and influence decisions and behavior. They are values put into practice. Enacted values are apparent when watching executives and other employees in action, including their decisions, where they focus their attention and resources, how they behave toward stakeholders, and the outcomes of those decisions and behavior.

Content of Organizational Culture

Organizations differ considerably in their cultural content, that is, the relative ordering of shared values.[9] Consider Netflix and PPL Corporation. Netflix seems to prioritize individual performance with undertones of internal competitiveness. For instance, the online streaming media provider points out that "We're a team, not a family"; that "Netflix leaders hire, develop, and cut smartly"; and that "adequate performance gets a generous severance package." In contrast, electrical utility PPL seems to prioritize fulfillment of stakeholder needs, such as employee safety, customer service, and community support. It emphasizes mutual respect rather than competitive performance. PPL's six values include ensuring safety/health, delivering customer service, valuing each other and appreciating differences, getting the job done right, doing the right thing, and investing in communities.[10]

How many corporate cultures are there? Several models and measures classify organizational culture into a handful of easy-to-remember categories. One of these, shown in Exhibit 13.2,

Corporate Culture Alignments and Misalignments[8]

90% of nearly 2,000 CEOs and CFOs surveyed say organizational culture is important at their company.

82% of more than 7,000 business leaders across 130 countries say that an organization's culture is a potential competitive advantage.

58% of 812 managers (majority in human resources) in the UK say their organization's espoused values generally reflect the actual values practiced by management.

51% of 2,219 executives and employees surveyed across several countries think their organization's culture is in need of a major overhaul.

15% of nearly 2,000 CEOs and CFOs surveyed say their own corporate culture is exactly where it needs to be.

12% of more than 7,000 business leaders across 130 countries say their company is driving the "right" corporate culture.

©Flying Colours Ltd/Getty Images

Unfortunately, the models oversimplify the diversity of cultural values in organizations. There are dozens of individual values, and many more combinations of values, so the number of organizational cultures that these models describe likely falls considerably short of the full set.

The diversity of corporate cultures is evident in a recent study of espoused values at the top 500 American companies.[12] The study distilled these values down to nine categories. Integrity appeared most often, followed by teamwork, innovation, respect, quality, safety, community, communication, and hard work. But each of these categories includes a large number of specific values. The "respect" category, for instance, includes the specific values of diversity, inclusion, development, empowerment, and dignity. Because there are dozens of espoused values, there would be an equally long list of enacted values.

Another concern is that organizational culture models and measures typically ignore the shared assumptions aspect of culture. This oversight likely occurs because measuring shared assumptions is even more difficult than measuring shared values. A third concern is that many organizational culture models incorrectly assume that organizations have a fairly clear, unified culture that is easily decipherable.[13] In reality, an organization's culture is typically blurry and fragmented. As we discuss next, organizations consist of diverse subcultures in which clusters of employees across the organization have different experiences and backgrounds that influence their preferred values. Furthermore, an organization's culture is founded on the values of its employees. Employees have diverse hierarchies of values, so an organization's culture necessarily has noticeable variability.

identifies seven corporate cultures. Another popular model identifies four organizational cultures organized in a two-by-two table representing internal versus external focus and flexibility versus control. Other models organize cultures around a circle with 8 or 12 categories. These circumplex models suggest that some cultures are opposite to others, such as an avoidance culture versus a self-actualization culture, or a power culture versus a collegial culture.[11]

These organizational culture models and surveys are popular with corporate leaders faced with the messy business of diagnosing their company's culture and identifying what kind of culture they want to develop.

Exhibit 13.2 Organizational Culture Profile Dimensions and Characteristics

Organizational Culture Dimension	Characteristics of the Dimension
Innovation	Experimenting, opportunity seeking, risk taking, few rules, low cautiousness
Stability	Predictability, security, rule-oriented
Respect for people	Fairness, tolerance
Outcome orientation	Action-oriented, high expectations, results-oriented
Attention to detail	Precise, analytic
Team orientation	Collaboration, people-oriented
Aggressiveness	Competitive, low emphasis on social responsibility

Source: Based on information in C. A. O'Reilly III, J. Chatman, and D. F. Caldwell, "People and Organizational Culture: A Profile Comparison Approach to Assessing Person–Organization Fit," *Academy of Management Journal* 34, no. 3 (1991): 487–518.

artifacts the observable symbols and signs of an organization's culture

Thus, many of the popular organizational culture models and measures oversimplify the variety of organizational cultures and falsely presume that organizations can easily be identified within these categories.

Organizational Subcultures

When discussing organizational culture, we are really referring to the *dominant culture*, that is, the values and assumptions shared most consistently and widely by the organization's members. The dominant culture is usually supported by senior management, but not always. Cultural values and assumptions also can persist in spite of senior management's desire for another culture. Furthermore, organizations are composed of *subcultures* located throughout their various divisions, geographic regions, and occupational groups.[14] Some subcultures enhance the dominant culture by espousing parallel assumptions and values. Others differ from but do not conflict with the dominant culture. Still others are called *countercultures* because they embrace values or assumptions that directly oppose the organization's dominant culture. It is also possible that some organizations (including some universities, according to one study) consist of subcultures with no decipherable dominant culture at all.[15]

Some subcultures enhance the dominant culture, whereas others are called *countercultures* because their values or assumptions oppose the organization's dominant culture.
©Mediaphotos/iStock/Getty Images Plus

Subcultures, particularly countercultures, potentially create conflict and dissension among employees, but they also serve two important functions.[16] First, they maintain the organization's standards of performance and ethical behavior. Employees who hold countercultural values are an important source of surveillance and critical review of the dominant order. They encourage constructive conflict and more creative thinking about how the organization should interact with its environment. Subcultures potentially support ethical conduct by preventing employees from blindly following one set of values. Subculture members continually question the "obvious" decisions and actions of the majority, thereby making everyone more mindful of the consequences of their actions.

Subcultures serve a second valuable function: they are spawning grounds for emerging values that keep the firm aligned with the evolving needs and expectations of customers, suppliers, communities, and other stakeholders. Companies eventually need to replace their existing dominant values with ones that are more appropriate for the changing environment. Those emerging cultural values and assumptions usually exist in subcultures long before they are ideal for the organization. If subcultures are suppressed, the organization may take longer to discover, develop, and adopt the emerging desired culture.

LO13-2 Describe four categories of artifacts through which corporate culture is deciphered.

DECIPHERING ORGANIZATIONAL CULTURE THROUGH ARTIFACTS

Shared values and assumptions are not easily measured through surveys and might not be accurately reflected in the organization's values statements. Instead, as Exhibit 13.1 illustrated earlier, an organization's culture needs to be deciphered through a detailed investigation of artifacts. **Artifacts** are the observable symbols and signs of an organization's culture, such as the way visitors are greeted, the organization's physical layout, and how employees are rewarded.[17] A few experts suggest that artifacts are the essence of organizational culture, whereas most others (including the authors of this book) view artifacts as symbols or indicators of culture. In other words, culture is cognitive (values and assumptions inside people's heads) whereas artifacts are observable manifestations of

An organization's culture needs to be deciphered through a detailed investigation of artifacts, such as workplace behavior, everyday conversations, documents, and physical settings.
©View Pictures/REX/Shutterstock

that culture. Either way, artifacts are important because they represent and reinforce an organization's culture.

Artifacts provide valuable evidence about a company's culture.[18] An organization's ambiguous (fragmented) culture is best understood by observing workplace behavior, listening to everyday conversations among staff and with customers, studying written documents and emails, viewing physical structures and settings, and interviewing staff about corporate stories. In other

words, to truly understand an organization's culture, we need to sample information from a variety of organizational artifacts.

The Mayo Clinic conducted such an assessment a few years ago. An anthropologist was hired to decipher the medical organization's culture at its headquarters in Minnesota and to identify ways of transferring that culture to its two newer sites in Florida and Arizona. For six weeks, the anthropologist shadowed employees, posed as a patient in waiting rooms, did countless interviews, and accompanied physicians on patient visits. The final report outlined Mayo's dominant culture and how its satellite operations varied from that culture.[19] Over the next few pages, we review four broad categories of artifacts: organizational stories and legends, language, rituals and ceremonies, and physical structures and symbols.

Organizational Stories and Legends

Stories and legends about the company's founders and past events permeate strong organizational cultures. Some tales

recount heroic deeds, whereas others ridicule incidents that deviated from the firm's core values. Organizational stories and legends serve as powerful social prescriptions of the way things should (or should not) be done. They add human realism to corporate expectations, individual performance standards, and the criteria for getting fired. Stories also produce emotions in listeners, and these emotions tend to improve listeners' memory of the lesson within the story.[20] Stories communicate corporate culture most effectively when they describe real people, are assumed to be true, and are known by employees throughout the organization. Stories are also prescriptive—they advise people what to do or not to do.[21]

Organizational Language

The language of the workplace speaks volumes about the company's culture. How employees talk to each other, describe customers, express anger, and greet stakeholders are all verbal symbols of shared values and assumptions. An organization's culture particularly stands out when employees habitually use customized phrases and labels.

Employees at DaVita HealthCare Partners, Inc., refer to their company as the "village" and its chief executive is the "mayor." Employees (called teammates) at the Denver-based provider of kidney care and dialysis services become "citizens" of the village as they "cross the bridge," meaning that they embrace the company's culture. These aren't contrived slogans. The language symbolizes DaVita's deeply held cultural beliefs that employee

> ## "What we say—and how we say it—can deeply affect a company's culture.[22]
>
> —Tom Kelley and David Kelley, partner (Tom) and founder (David) of IDEO

well-being and performance depend on the human connection of workplace community that, in turn, translates into superior service to DaVita's patients.[23]

Language also captures less complimentary cultural values. At Goldman Sachs, "elephant trades" are apparently large investment transactions with huge profit potential, so the investment firm allegedly encourages its salespeople to go "elephant hunting" (seeking out these large trades from clients). A former Goldman Sachs manager reported that some employees at the investment firm also routinely described their clients as "muppets." "My muppet client didn't put me in comp on the trade we just printed," said one salesperson, meaning that the client was a fool because he didn't compare prices, so the salesperson overcharged him. The "muppet" label seems to reveal a culture with a derogatory view of clients. When this language use became public, Goldman Sachs scanned its internal emails for the "muppet" label and warned employees not to use the term.[24]

Rituals and Ceremonies

Rituals are the programmed routines of daily organizational life that dramatize an organization's culture.[25] They include how visitors are greeted, how often senior executives visit subordinates, how people communicate with each other, how much time employees take for lunch, and so on. These rituals are repetitive, predictable events that have symbolic meaning of underlying cultural values and assumptions. For instance, BMW's fast-paced culture is quite literally apparent in the way employees walk around the German automaker's offices. "When you move through the corridors and hallways of other companies' buildings, people kind of crawl, they walk slowly," observes a BMW executive. "But BMW people tend to move faster."[26] **Ceremonies** are more formal artifacts than rituals. Ceremonies are planned activities conducted specifically for the benefit of an audience. This would include publicly rewarding (or punishing) employees or celebrating the launch of a new product or newly won contract.

Physical Structures and Symbols

The size, shape, location, and age of buildings both reflect and influence an organization's culture. Buildings might support a company's emphasis on teamwork, environmental friendliness, hierarchy, or any other set of values.[27] Even if the building doesn't make much of a statement, there is a treasure-trove of physical artifacts inside. Desks, chairs, office space, and wall hangings (or lack of them) are just a few of the items that might convey cultural meaning.[28] Each physical artifact alone might not say much, but put enough of them together and an image begins to form of how they symbolize the organization's culture.

For example, one prominent workspace design and manufacturing company recently identified the workspace features typically found at companies with several different cultures. Exhibit 13.3

> ## We shape our buildings; thereafter, they shape us.[29]
> —Winston Churchill, former Prime Minister of the United Kingdom

---

Exhibit 13.3 Workspace Design and Organizational Culture

Collaborative and creative cultures

- More team space
- Informal space
- Low/medium enclosure
- Flexible environment
- Organic layout

Controlling and competitive cultures

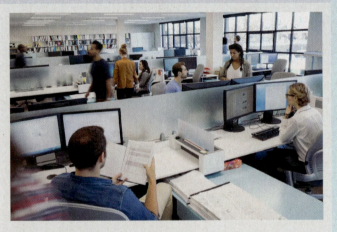

- More individual space
- More formal than informal space
- High/medium enclosure
- More fixed environment
- More structured, symmetrical layout

Photos: (Left) ©Robert Daly/Getty Images; (Right) ©Hero Images/Getty Images

Source: Based on information in *How to Create a Successful Organizational Culture: Build It—Literally* (Holland, MI: Haworth Inc., June 2015).

summarizes the physical space design of collaborative and creative cultures compared to cultures that emphasize efficiency (control) and competition. Collaborative and creative cultures value more teamwork and flexibility, so space design is informal and enables spontaneous group discussion. Controlling and competitive cultures tend to have more structural office arrangements and provide more space for individual work than teamwork.

LO13-3 Discuss the importance of organizational culture and the conditions under which organizational culture strength improves organizational performance.

IS ORGANIZATIONAL CULTURE IMPORTANT?

Does organizational culture improve organizational effectiveness? Launi Skinner thinks so. "You can have the best strategy in the world, but culture will kill strategy," warns the CEO of First West Credit Union in Vancouver, Canada, and former senior executive at Starbucks in the United States. Bill Emerson, Vice Chair of Rock Holdings Inc. (parent company of Quicken Loans), agrees. When asked why the Detroit-based finance company has grown so quickly, Emerson replied: "The No. 1 thing is culture. It allows us to move very quickly and react very quickly in making business decisions."[30]

Launi Skinner, Bill Emerson, and many other leaders believe that an organization's success partly depends on its culture. Several popular-press management books similarly assert that the most successful companies have strong cultures. In fact, one popular management book, *Built to Last*, suggests that successful companies are "cultlike" (although not actually cults, the authors are careful to point out).[32] Does OB research support this view that companies are more effective when they have a strong culture? Yes, potentially, but the evidence indicates that the relationship depends on a few conditions.[33]

Meaning and Potential Benefits of a Strong Culture

Before discussing these contingencies, let's examine the meaning of a "strong" organizational culture and its potential benefits. The strength of an organization's culture refers to how widely and deeply employees hold the company's dominant values and assumptions. In a strong organizational culture, most employees across all subunits understand and embrace the dominant values. These values and assumptions are also institutionalized through well-established artifacts, which further entrench the culture. In addition, strong cultures tend to be long-lasting; some can be traced back to the values and assumptions established by the company's founder. In contrast, companies have weak cultures when the dominant values are held mainly by a few people at the top of the organization, the culture is difficult to interpret from artifacts, and the cultural values and assumptions are unstable over time or highly varied across the organization.

Under specific conditions, companies are more effective when they have strong cultures because of the three important functions listed in Exhibit 13.4 and described below:

- *Control system.* Organizational culture is a deeply embedded form of social control that influences employee decisions and behavior.[34] Culture is pervasive and operates nonconsciously. Think of it as an automatic pilot, nonconsciously directing employees so their behavior is consistent with organizational expectations. For this reason, some writers describe organizational culture as a compass that points everyone in the same direction.

- *Social glue.* Organizational culture is the social glue that bonds people together and makes them feel part of the organizational experience.[35] Employees are motivated to internalize the organization's dominant culture because it fulfills their need for social identity. This social glue attracts new staff and retains top performers. It also becomes the common thread that holds employees together in global organizations.

- *Sense making.* Organizational culture helps employees to make sense of what goes on and why things happen in the company.[36] Corporate culture also makes it easier for them to understand what is expected of them. For instance, research has found that sales employees in companies with stronger organizational cultures have clearer role perceptions and less role-related stress.[37]

Contingencies of Organizational Culture and Effectiveness

Studies have found only a moderately positive relationship between culture strength and organizational effectiveness. The reason for this weak link is that strong cultures improve organizational effectiveness only under specific conditions (see Exhibit 13.4). The three main contingencies are (1) whether the culture content is aligned with the environment; (2) whether the culture is moderately strong, not cultlike; and (3) whether the culture incorporates an adaptive culture.

Exhibit 13.4 Potential Benefits and Contingencies of Culture Strength

Benefits of culture strength depend on . . .
- Whether culture content fits the environment.
- Moderate strength (not a cult).
- An adaptive culture.

Functions of strong cultures
- Control system.
- Social glue.
- Sense making.

Organizational outcomes
- Organizational performance.
- Employee well-being.

> ❝ **The values of the company are really the bedrock—the glue which holds the firm together.**[38] ❞
>
> —Nandan Nilekani, co-founder and former CEO of Infosys

Culture Content Is Aligned with the External Environment The benefits of a strong culture depend on whether its content—the culture's dominant values and assumptions—is aligned with the external environment. Companies require an employee-centric culture in environments where business success depends mainly on employee talent, whereas an efficiency-focused culture may be more critical for companies in environments with strong competition and standardized products. If the dominant values are congruent with the environment, then employees are more likely to engage in decisions and behaviors that improve the organization's interaction with that environment. But when the dominant values are misaligned with the environment, a strong culture encourages decisions and behaviors that can undermine the organization's connection with its stakeholders.

For example, Coles became a successful competitor in the Australian retail food industry after it was acquired by Wesfarmers, which injected a strong culture around performance and customer service. Wesfarmers is a highly successful Australian conglomerate, but it doesn't nurture the same culture in all of its businesses (food, hardware, clothing, office supplies, fertilizers, mining, etc.). Instead, Wesfarmers' executive team encourages each company to maintain a strong culture around the values that matter most for that industry and its stakeholders. "It would be a huge mistake if we tried to impose one culture over all these businesses," explains Richard Goyder, who recently stepped down as Wesfarmers CEO. "Bunnings (Australia's largest home improvement retailer) and Coles have to be customer-centric, whereas our coal business has to be absolutely focused on safety."[39]

Culture Strength Is Not the Level of a Cult A second contingency is the degree of culture strength. Various experts suggest that companies with very strong cultures (i.e., corporate "cults") may be less effective than companies with moderately strong cultures.[40] One reason why corporate cults may undermine organizational effectiveness is that they lock people into mental models, which can blind them to new opportunities and unique problems. The effect of these very strong cultures is that people overlook or incorrectly define subtle misalignments between the organization's activities and the changing environment.

The other reason why very strong cultures may be dysfunctional is that they suppress dissenting subcultures. The challenge for organizational leaders is to maintain not only a strong culture but one that allows subcultural diversity. Subcultures

adaptive culture an organizational culture in which employees are receptive to change, including the ongoing alignment of the organization to its environment and continuous improvement of internal processes

Corporate cults tend to undermine organizational effectiveness by locking people into mental models, which can blind them from seeing new opportunities and unique problems.
©Mediaphotos/iStock/Getty Images Plus

encourage task-oriented conflict, which improves creative thinking and offers some level of ethical vigilance over the dominant culture. In the long run, a subculture's nascent values could become important dominant values as the environment changes. Corporate cults suppress subcultures, thereby undermining these benefits.

Culture Is an Adaptive Culture A third condition influencing the effect of cultural strength on organizational effectiveness is whether the culture content includes an **adaptive culture**.[41] In an adaptive culture, employees are receptive to change, including the ongoing alignment of the organization to its environment and continuous improvement of internal processes. Thus, employees in adaptive cultures see things from an open systems perspective and take responsibility for the organization's performance and alignment with the external environment.

In an adaptive culture, receptivity to change extends to internal processes and roles. Employees believe that satisfying stakeholder needs requires continuous improvement of internal work processes. They also recognize the importance of remaining flexible in their own work roles. The phrase "That's not my job" is found in nonadaptive cultures. Finally, an adaptive culture has a strong *learning orientation* because being receptive to change necessarily means that the company also supports action-oriented discovery. With a learning orientation, employees welcome new learning opportunities, actively experiment with new ideas and practices, view reasonable mistakes as a natural part of the learning process, and continuously question past practices (see Chapter 6).[43]

Organizational Culture and Business Ethics

An organization's culture influences the ethical conduct of its employees. This makes sense because good behavior is driven by ethical values, and ethical values become embedded in an organization's dominant culture. For example, AIA Group, Hong Kong's largest life insurance company (by number of policies), has a strong culture focused on "doing the right thing, in the right way, with the right people, and the results will come." This means that employees are expected to think through the ramifications of their actions (right thing) and ensure they always work with integrity and teamwork (right way).[44]

The opposite is equally true. There are numerous instances where an organization's culture has been the apparent cause of unethical conduct. For example, critics suggest that Uber's "toxic culture" explains many of the ride-sharing company's public embarrassments, including allegations of sexual harassment, bullying, privacy violations, anti-competitive activities, and theft of proprietary technology.[45] Uber has 14 espoused

Uber's recent problems illustrate the principle that leaders create an ethical organization by actively working on the enacted culture that steers employee behavior.
©Vincenzo Mancuso/Shutterstock

> **You have to create a culture that not only accepts change but seeks out how to change.**[42]
>
> —Dan Akerson, former GM CEO

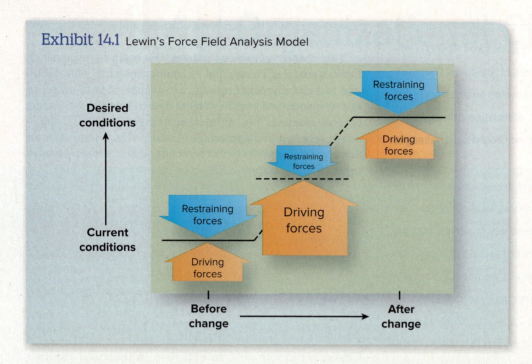

Exhibit 14.1 Lewin's Force Field Analysis Model

Desired conditions

Restraining forces

Driving forces

Restraining forces

Restraining forces

Driving forces

Current conditions

Driving forces

Before change → After change

and restraining forces are roughly in equilibrium—that is, they are of approximately equal strength in opposite directions.

Lewin's force field model emphasizes that effective change occurs by **unfreezing** the current situation, moving to a desired condition, and then **refreezing** the system so it remains in the desired state. Unfreezing involves producing disequilibrium between the driving and restraining forces. As we will describe later, this may occur by increasing the driving forces, reducing the restraining forces, or doing a combination of both. Refreezing occurs when the organization's systems and structures are aligned with the desired behaviors. They must support and reinforce

> I've always believed that when the rate of change inside an institution becomes slower than the rate of change outside, the end is in sight. The only question is when.[3]
>
> —Jack Welch, former General Electric CEO

model to describe this process using the metaphor of a force field (see Exhibit 14.1).[4] Although it was developed more than 50 years ago, recent reviews affirm that Lewin's **force field analysis** model remains one of the most widely respected ways of viewing the change process.[5]

One side of the force field model represents the *driving forces* that push organizations toward a new state of affairs. These might include new competitors or technologies, evolving client expectations, or a host of other environmental changes. Corporate leaders also produce driving forces even when external forces for change aren't apparent. For instance, some experts call for "divine discontent" as a key feature of successful organizations, meaning that leaders continually urge employees to strive for higher standards or better practices. Even when the company outshines the competition, employees believe they can do better. "We have a habit of divine discontent with our performance," says creative agency Ogilvy & Mather about its corporate culture. "It is an antidote to smugness."[6]

The other side of Lewin's model represents the *restraining forces* that maintain the status quo. These restraining forces are commonly called "resistance to change" because they appear to block the change process. Stability occurs when the driving

the new role patterns and prevent the organization from slipping back into the old way of doing things. Over the next few pages, we use Lewin's model to understand why change is blocked and how the process can evolve more smoothly.

L014-2 Discuss the reasons why people resist organizational change and how change agents should view this resistance.

UNDERSTANDING RESISTANCE TO CHANGE

United Airlines struggled to resolve operational and customer service problems after its merger with Continental Airlines. United executives say the poor results were partly due to the challenges of combining complex reservation and operational systems. But they also were frustrated by subtle forms of employee resistance to change. Some Continental employees opposed United Airlines' operational practices, while some

Resistance to change takes many forms, ranging from overt work stoppages to subtle attempts to continue the old ways.
©Jacob Wackerhausen/iStock/Getty Images Plus; ©McGraw-Hill Education/ Mark Dierker, photographer

United Airlines employees failed to adopt Continental's customer service standards. "You know, the cultural change takes time," explained the former United Airlines CEO who orchestrated the merger. "And people resist change. People are sort of set in their ways."[7]

Executives at United Airlines experienced considerable *resistance to change* following the merger with Continental Airlines. Resistance to change takes many forms, ranging from overt work stoppages to subtle attempts to continue the old ways.[8] A study of bank employees reported that subtle resistance is much more common than overt resistance. Some employees in that study avoided the desired changes by moving into different jobs. Others continued to perform tasks the old way as long as management didn't notice. Even when employees complied with the planned changes, they showed resistance by performing the new task while letting customers know that they disapproved of these changes forced on them![9]

Most change agents are understandably frustrated by passive or active resistance to their planned change. However, resistance is a common and natural human response. Even when people support change, they typically assume that it is others— not themselves—who need to do the changing. Resistance is a form of conflict, but change agents unfortunately sometimes

> Faced with the choice between changing one's mind and proving that there is no need to do so, almost everyone gets busy on the proof.[10]
>
> —John Kenneth Galbraith, economics scholar, U.S. ambassador, author

interpret that disagreement as relationship conflict (see Chapter 10). They describe the people opposing change as unreasonable, dysfunctional, and irrational reactionaries to a beneficial initiative. This perspective shapes the change agent's response to resistance. Perversely, the change agent's conflict-oriented response to resistance tends to escalate the conflict, which often generates even stronger resistance to the change initiative.

A more productive approach is to view resistance to change as task conflict. From the task conflict perspective, resistance is a signal either that the change agent has not sufficiently prepared employees for change or that the change initiative should be altered or improved.[11] Employees might not feel a sufficiently strong urgency to change, or they might feel the change strategy is ill-conceived. Even if they recognize the need for change and agree with the strategy, employees might resist because they lack confidence to change or believe the change will make them worse off than the current situation. Resistance takes many forms, and change agents need to decipher those different types of resistance to understand their underlying causes.[12]

Resistance is also a form of voice, so discussion potentially improves procedural justice through voice (see Chapter 5) as well as decision making (see Chapter 6). By redirecting initial forms of resistance into constructive conversations, change agents can generate a feeling of fairness among employees. Furthermore, resistance is motivated behavior; it potentially engages people to think about the change strategy and process. Change agents can harness that motivational force to ultimately strengthen commitment to the change initiative.

Why Employees Resist Change

Change management experts have developed a long list of reasons why people resist change.[13] Some people inherently oppose change because of their personality and values.[14] Aside from these dispositional factors, employees typically oppose organizational change because they lack sufficient motivation, ability, role clarity, or situational support to change their attitudes, decisions, and behavior.[15] In other words, an employee's readiness for change depends on all four elements of the MARS model. These

force field analysis Kurt Lewin's model of systemwide change that helps change agents diagnose the forces that drive and restrain proposed organizational change

unfreezing the first part of the change process, in which the change agent produces disequilibrium between the driving and restraining forces

refreezing the latter part of the change process, in which systems and structures are introduced that reinforce and maintain the desired behaviors

Opp, K. D., 183
Orbell, S., 99
Ordoñez, L. D., 132, 133
Oreg, S., 318, 336, 337
Organ, D. W., 49
Ormiston, M., 74
Ortiz de Guinea, A., 184
Ortman, J. M., 23
Osborn, Alex, 185
Osborn, R. N., 275
Oslanld, J. S., 74
Osman, M. R., 295
Osorio, J., 180, 205
Ossip, David, 260, 273
Osterman, P., 134
Ostroff, C., 24, 316, 319
Oswick, C., 24
Otondo, R. F., 207
Ott, J. S., 316
Ouchi, W., 180, 209
Ovsey, D., 272
Oyserman, D., 46, 53
Ozer, M., 49
Ozgen, C., 23

P

Paihountas, D., 23
Paine, Lynn S., 26
Pakrashi, M., 75
Palanski, M. E., 276
Pals, J. L., 50
Palvia, P., 205
Panaccio, A., 103
Panchak, P., 184
Panteli, N., 206
Paquin, A. R., 273
Parisot, F., 181
Park, M., 101
Park, T. -Y., 50, 74
Parker, M., 75
Parker, S. K., 49
Parks-Leduc, L., 51
Parks, L., 51, 130
Parmar, B. L., 25
Parmar, P., 26
Paroush, J., 158
Parr, A. D., 276
Parry, E., 23, 206
Pasa, S. F., 230
Pascale, R. T., 180
Passmann, H., 99
Passmore, J., 132
Passyn, K., 130
Paswan, A. K., 228
Patel, P. C., 23, 182
Pathak, R. D., 273
Patient, D. L., 52
Paukert, M., 102
Paustian-Underdahl, S., 277
Pawar, B. S., 274
Peach, M., 184
Pearce, C. L., 272, 274, 275
Pearce, J., 22
Pearson, C. M., 104
Peart, F. M., 100
Pedersen, J. S., 316
Pedersen, L. J. T., 52
Pedersen, Z., 339
Peiro, J. M., 229
Pelled, L. H., 251
Pellegrini, C., 295
Pelloni, O., 103

Pelton, L. E., 231
Peng, A. C., 73
Penke, L., 50
Penney, L. M., 51
Pennington, C. R., 75
Pennington, R., 208
Pepper, E. M., 181
Perkel, C., 229
Perlis, Mike, 260
Perrewé, P. L., 104
Perri, D. F., 253
Perrow, C., 134, 297
Perry, V. G., 73
Perryman, S., 129
Perschke, K., 206
Pervin, L. A., 51
Pescuric, A., 132
Peter, Laurence J., 142, 155
Peters, L. H., 49
Peters, R. S., 129
Peters, Thomas J., 209, 231, 283, 316
Petersen, L. E., 276
Petersen, R., 316
Peterson, M. F., 317
Peterson, S. J., 273, 274
Pettigrew, A. M., 228, 229
Pettigrew, T. F., 77, 254
Petty, R., 230
Peus, C., 73, 77
Pexman, P. M., 206
Peyrefitte, J., 205
Pfaff, D. W., 129
Pfanner, E., 53
Pfau, B. N., 134
Pfau, M., 230
Pfeffer, Jeffrey, 24, 26, 104, 129, 156, 228, 231, 276
Pham, M. T., 100, 156
Phelps, C., 230
Phillips, J. M., 319
Phillips, L. T., 75
Phipps, K. A., 253
Piccolo, R. F., 274, 275
Pickett, C. L., 74
Picone, P. M., 73
Piekkar, R., 208
Piening, E. P., 22
Pierce J. L., 103
Pierce, J. L., 74, 158, 337
Pierrett, M., 208
Pietroni, D., 255
Pike, A., 295
Pike, K., 319
Pilavin, J. A., 26, 51, 130, 316
Pillet, J. C., 22
Pillutla, A., 273
Pindek, S, 104
Pinder, C. C., 49, 129, 131, 132, 133
Pinfari, M., 255
Pinsonneault, A., 185
Piper, W., 183
Pirson, M., 184
Pitt, D. C., 275
Pizarro, D. A., 130
Plank, R. E., 49
Plato, 4, 61, 75, 125, 138
Platow, M. J., 273
Plaut, V. C., 53
Plimmer, G., 133
Ployhart, R. E., 22, 49
Pluess, M., 50

Podsakoff, N. P., 49
Podsakoff, P. M., 228, 266, 275
Poff, D., 52
Pohling, R., 50
Poitras, J., 254
Polderman, T. J. C., 50
Pollock. T. G., 276
Pondy, L., 252
Pondy, L. R., 317
Poole, M. S., 183
Porath, C. L., 104
Porras, D., 23
Porras, J. I., 26, 317
Porter, L. M., 103, 131
Porter, L. W., 21, 48, 131, 231, 319
Porter, S., 101
Portes, A., 229
Portillo, M., 228
Portman, J., 155
Posner, B. Z., 77, 184, 272, 276, 317
Postmes, T., 75, 253
Poteet, M. L., 229
Potter, R. E., 316
Powell, G. N., 277
Powell, S., 158
Power, M., 99
Pownall, I., 154
Prasad, S., 296
Pratt, M. G., 156, 231
Preece, C., 74
Preiss, R. W., 254
Prelc, A., 155
Premeaux, S. F., 102
Prencipe, A., 24
Prentice, K., 156
Preston, R., 336
Preuss, L., 52
Priem, R. L., 22
Prietula, M. J., 25
Prislin, R., 230
Pritchard, R. D., 49
Pugh, D. S., 297
Pugh, S. D., 101
Pullins, E. B., 104
Purvis, R. L., 131
Putnam, L., 254

Q

Qin, J., 23
Qiu, J. X. J., 297
Quarter, J., 22
Quarto, T., 101
Quick, J.C., 103
Quigley, T. J., 22
Quinn, K. A., 75
Quinn, R. E., 273, 338
Quinn, R. T., 90

R

Rabung, S., 207
Raelin, J. A., 272
Rafferty, A. E., 337
Ragins, B. R., 230
Ragu-Nathan, T. S., 104
Rahim, A., 251
Rahim, M. A., 251
Rai, A., 157
Raiborn, C. A., 318

Rain, J. S., 77
Raisinghani, D., 154
Ramarajan, L., 74
Ramsoy, T. Z., 99
Randolph, A., 275
Randolph, W. A., 296
Ranson, S., 294
Rao, A., 230
Rao, H., 316
Rauthmann, J. F., 49
Raven, B., 228
Raven, B. H., 229
Ravlin, E. C., 26, 51, 316
Raymond, L., 25
Raynor, M. E., 24
Read, S., 155
Ready, D. A., 276
Real, J. C., 25
Reason, P., 338
Reed, A., II, 52
Reeskens, T., 133
Reich, A., 336
Reicher, S., 205
Reid, D. A., 49
Reid, E., 104
Reid, Ipsos, 101
Reider, M. H., 182
Reiley, D. H., 129
Reilly, M. D., 5151
Reilly, R. R., 133
Reiman, J., 26
Reimann, M., 130
Reinsch, N. L., Jr., 207
Reio, T. G., Jr, 130
Reisenzein, R., 99
Reitzschel, E. F., 23
Rempel, M., 183
Rench, T. A., 49
Rensoin, J., 157
Rentfrow, P. J., 53, 74
Rentsch, J. R., 103, 272
Repetti, R. L., 104
Resick, C. J., 318
Restburg, S. L. D., 337
Reyna, V. F., 155
Reynolds, S. J., 52
Rezaeinia, A., 154
Rhodes, N., 230
Riccomini, B., 209
Rice, R. E., 207
Rico, R., 182
Ridderstrale, J., 297
Rietzschel, E. F., 185
Riggio, R. E., 272, 317
Riketta, M., 103
Rindova, V. P., 276
Rink, F., 183
Rips, L. J., 75
Risberg, A., 253
Rispens, S., 251
Ritchey, Sharon, 220, 230
Ritchey, T., 158
Ritchie, T. D., 73
Ritov, I., 155
Rivera, M. T., 183, 229
Roan, A. M., 100
Roberge, M. -E., 23
Robert, C., 100
Robert, L. P., 184, 207
Roberto, M. A., 155, 338
Roberts, B. W., 50, 73
Roberts, K., 134
Roberts, L. M., 73

Wuinn, R. W., 207
Wünerlich, N. V., 103

CHAPTER SUMMARY

LO1-1 Define organizational behavior and organizations, and discuss the importance of this field of inquiry.

Organizational behavior is the study of what people think, feel, and do in and around organizations. Organizations are groups of people who work interdependently toward some purpose. OB theories help us (a) comprehend and predict work events, (b) adopt more accurate personal theories, and (c) influence organizational events. OB knowledge is for everyone, not just managers. OB theories and practices are highly beneficial for an organization's survival and success.

LO1-2 Debate the organizational opportunities and challenges of technological change, globalization, emerging employment relationships, and workforce diversity.

Technological change has improved efficiency, interactivity, and well-being, but it also has been a disruptive force in organizations. Information technology has altered communication patterns and power dynamics at work, and has affected our nonwork time, attention span, and techno-stress. Globalization, which refers to various forms of connectivity with people in other parts of the world, has become more intense than ever before because of information technology and transportation systems. It has brought more complexity and new ways of working to the workplace, requiring additional knowledge and skills. It may be an influence on work intensification, reduced job security, and lessening of the work–life balance.

An emerging employment relationship trend is the blurring of work and nonwork time and the associated call for more work–life balance (minimizing conflict between work and nonwork demands). Another employment trend is telecommuting, whereby employees work from home one or more workdays per month rather than commute to the office. Telecommuting potentially benefits employees and employers, but there are also disadvantages and its effectiveness depends on the employee, job, and organization. An organization's workforce has both surface-level diversity (observable demographic and other overt differences in people) and deep-level diversity (differences in personalities, beliefs, values, and attitudes). Diversity may improve creativity and decision making, and provide better awareness and response to diverse communities. However, diversity also poses challenges, such as dysfunctional conflict and slower team development.

LO1-3 Discuss the anchors on which organizational behavior knowledge is based.

The multidisciplinary anchor states that the field should develop from knowledge in other disciplines (e.g., psychology, sociology, economics), not just from its own isolated research base. The systematic research anchor states that OB knowledge should be based on systematic research, consistent with evidence-based management. The contingency anchor states that OB theories generally need to consider that there will be different consequences in different situations. The multiple levels of analysis anchor states that OB topics may be viewed from the individual, team, and organization levels of analysis.

LO1-4 Compare and contrast the four perspectives of organizational effectiveness.

The open systems perspective views organizations as complex organisms that "live" within an external environment, depend on it for resources, then use organizational subsystems to transform those resources into outputs, which are returned to the environment. Organizations receive feedback to maintain a good "fit" with that environment. Fit occurs by adapting to the environment, influencing the environment, or moving to a more favorable environment. Effective transformation processes are efficient, adaptable, and innovative. The

KEY TERMS

corporate social responsibility (CSR) organizational activities intended to benefit society and the environment beyond the firm's immediate financial interests or legal obligations

deep-level diversity differences in the psychological characteristics of employees, including personalities, beliefs, values, and attitudes

ethics the study of moral principles or values that determine whether actions are right or wrong and outcomes are good or bad

evidence-based management the practice of making decisions and taking actions based on research evidence

globalization economic, social, and cultural connectivity with people in other parts of the world

high-performance work practices (HPWPs) a perspective that holds that effective organizations incorporate several workplace practices that leverage the potential of human capital

human capital the stock of knowledge, skills, and abilities among employees that provide economic value to the organization

intellectual capital a company's stock of knowledge, including human capital, structural capital, and relationship capital

learning orientation beliefs and norms that support the acquisition, sharing, and use of knowledge as well as work conditions that nurture these learning processes

open systems a perspective that holds that organizations depend on the external environment for resources, affect that environment through their output, and consist of internal subsystems that transform inputs to outputs

organizational behavior (OB) the study of what people think, feel, and do in and around organizations

organizational effectiveness a broad concept represented by several perspectives, including the organization's fit with the external environment, internal subsystems' configuration for high performance, emphasis on organizational learning, and ability to satisfy the needs of key stakeholders

organizational learning a perspective that holds that organizational effectiveness depends on the organization's capacity to acquire, share, use, and store valuable knowledge

organizations groups of people who work interdependently toward some purpose

relationship capital the value derived from an organization's relationships with customers, suppliers, and others

stakeholders individuals, groups, and other entities that affect, or are affected by, the organization's objectives and actions

structural capital knowledge embedded in an organization's systems and structures

surface-level diversity the observable demographic or physiological differences in people, such as their race, ethnicity, gender, age, and physical disabilities

telecommuting an arrangement whereby, supported by information technology, employees work from home one or more work days per month rather than commute to the office

values relatively stable, evaluative beliefs that guide a person's preferences for outcomes or courses of action in a variety of situations

work–life balance the degree to which a person minimizes conflict between work and nonwork demands

organizational learning perspective states that organizations are effective when they find ways to acquire, share, use, and store knowledge. Intellectual capital consists of human capital, structural capital, and relationship capital. Knowledge is retained in the organizational memory; companies also selectively unlearn.

The high-performance work practices (HPWP) perspective identifies a bundle of systems and structures to leverage workforce potential. The most widely identified HPWPs are employee involvement, job autonomy, employee competency development, and performance- and skill-based rewards. HPWPs improve organizational effectiveness by building human capital, increasing adaptability, and strengthening employee motivation and attitudes. The stakeholder perspective states that organizations are more effective when they understand, manage, and satisfy stakeholder needs and expectations. Leaders manage the interests of diverse stakeholders by relying on their personal and organizational values for guidance. Ethics and corporate social responsibility (CSR) are natural variations of values-based organizations. CSR consists of organizational activities intended to benefit society and the environment beyond the firm's immediate financial interests or legal obligations.

chapter two

Individual Behavior, Personality, and Values

CHAPTER SUMMARY

LO2-1 Describe the four factors that directly influence individual behavior and performance.

Four variables—motivation, ability, role perceptions, and situational factors—which are represented by the acronym MARS, directly influence individual behavior and performance. Motivation represents the forces within a person that affect his or her direction, intensity, and persistence of voluntary behavior; ability includes both the natural aptitudes and the learned capabilities required to successfully complete a task; role perceptions are the extent to which people understand the job duties (roles) assigned to them or expected of them; and situational factors include conditions beyond the employee's immediate control that constrain or facilitate behavior and performance.

LO2-2 Summarize the five types of individual behavior in organizations.

There are five main types of workplace behavior. Task performance refers to goal-directed behaviors under the individual's control that support organizational objectives. It includes proficiency, adaptivity, and proactivity. Organizational citizenship behaviors consist of various forms of cooperation and helpfulness to others that support the organization's social and psychological context. Counterproductive work behaviors are voluntary behaviors that have the potential to directly or indirectly harm the organization. Joining and staying with the organization refers to agreeing to become an organizational member and remaining with the organization. Maintaining work attendance includes minimizing absenteeism when capable of working and avoiding scheduled work when not fit (i.e., low presenteeism).

LO2-3 Describe personality and discuss how the "Big Five" personality dimensions and four MBTI types relate to individual behavior in organizations.

Personality refers to the relatively enduring pattern of thoughts, emotions, and behaviors that characterize a person, along with the psychological processes behind those characteristics. Personality is formed through hereditary (nature) as well as socialization (nurture). The "Big Five" personality dimensions include conscientiousness, agreeableness, neuroticism, openness to experience, and extroversion. Conscientiousness and extraversion are the best overall predictors of job performance in most job groups. Extraversion and openness to experience are the best predictors of adaptive and proactive performance. Emotional stability (low neuroticism) is also associated with better adaptivity. Conscientiousness and agreeableness are the two best personality predictors of organizational citizenship and (negatively) with counterproductive work behaviors.

Based on Jungian personality theory, the Myers-Briggs Type Indicator (MBTI) identifies competing orientations for getting energy (extraversion versus introversion), perceiving information (sensing versus intuiting), processing information and making decisions (thinking versus feeling), and orienting to the external world (judging versus perceiving). The MBTI improves self-awareness for career development and mutual understanding but is more popular than valid.

LO2-4 Summarize Schwartz's model of individual values and discuss the conditions where values influence behavior.

Values are stable, evaluative beliefs that guide our preferences for outcomes or courses of action in a variety of situations. Compared to personality traits, values are evaluative (rather than descriptive), more likely to conflict, and formed more from socialization than heredity. Schwartz's model organizes 57 values into a circumplex of 10 dimensions along two bipolar

Key Terms

ability the natural aptitudes and learned capabilities required to successfully complete a task

achievement-nurturing orientation cross-cultural value describing the degree to which people in a culture emphasize competitive versus cooperative relations with other people

agreeableness a personality dimension describing people who are trusting, helpful, good-natured, considerate, tolerant, selfless, generous, and flexible

collectivism a cross-cultural value describing the degree to which people in a culture emphasize duty to groups to which they belong and to group harmony

conscientiousness a personality dimension describing people who are organized, dependable, goal-focused, thorough, disciplined, methodical, and industrious

counterproductive work behaviors (CWBs) voluntary behaviors that have the potential to directly or indirectly harm the organization

extraversion a personality dimension describing people who are outgoing, talkative, sociable, and assertive

five-factor (Big Five) model (FFM) the five broad dimensions representing most personality traits: conscientiousness, emotional stability, openness to experience, agreeableness, and extraversion

individualism a cross-cultural value describing the degree to which people in a culture emphasize independence and personal uniqueness

mindfulness a person's receptive and impartial attention to and awareness of the present situation as well as to one's own thoughts and emotions in that moment

moral intensity the degree to which an issue demands the application of ethical principles

moral sensitivity a person's ability to recognize the presence of an ethical issue and determine its relative importance

motivation the forces within a person that affect his or her direction, intensity, and persistence of voluntary behavior

Myers-Briggs Type Indicator (MBTI) an instrument designed to measure the elements of Jungian personality theory, particularly preferences regarding perceiving and judging information

neuroticism a personality dimension describing people who tend to be anxious, insecure, self-conscious, depressed, and temperamental

openness to experience a personality dimension describing people who are imaginative, creative, unconventional, curious, nonconforming, autonomous, and aesthetically perceptive

organizational citizenship behaviors (OCBs) various forms of cooperation and helpfulness to others that support the organization's social and psychological context

personality the relatively enduring pattern of thoughts, emotions, and behaviors that characterize a person, along with the psychological processes behind those characteristics

power distance a cross-cultural value describing the degree to which people in a culture accept unequal distribution of power in a society

role perceptions the degree to which a person understands the job duties assigned to or expected of him or her

task performance the individual's voluntary goal-directed behaviors that contribute to organizational objectives

uncertainty avoidance a cross-cultural value describing the degree to which people in a culture tolerate ambiguity (low uncertainty avoidance) or feel threatened by ambiguity and uncertainty (high uncertainty avoidance)

dimensions: openness to change to conservation and self-enhancement to self-transcendence. Values influence behavior in three ways: (1) shaping the attractiveness of choices, (2) framing perceptions of reality, and (3) aligning behavior with self-concept and self-presentation. However, the effect of values on behavior also depends on whether the situation supports or prevents that behavior and on how actively we think about them and understand their relevance to the situation. Values congruence refers to how similar a person's values hierarchy is to the values hierarchy of another source (organization, team, etc.).

LO2-5 Describe three ethical principles and discuss three factors that influence ethical behavior.

Ethics refers to the study of moral principles or values that determine whether actions are right or wrong and outcomes are good or bad. Three ethical principles are utilitarianism (greatest good for the greatest number), individual rights (upholding natural rights), and distributive justice (same or proportional benefits and burdens). Ethical behavior is influenced by the degree to which an issue demands the application of ethical principles (moral intensity), the individual's ability to recognize the presence and relative importance of an ethical issue (moral sensitivity), and situational forces. Ethical conduct at work is supported by codes of ethical conduct, mechanisms for communicating ethical violations, the organization's culture, and the leader's behavior.

LO2-6 Describe five values commonly studied across cultures.

Five values often studied across cultures are individualism (valuing independence and personal uniqueness); collectivism (valuing duty to in-groups and group harmony); power distance (valuing unequal distribution of power); uncertainty avoidance (tolerating or feeling threatened by ambiguity and uncertainty); and achievement-nurturing orientation (valuing competition versus cooperation).

CHAPTER SUMMARY

LO3-1 Describe the elements of self-concept and explain how each affects an individual's behavior and well-being.

Self-concept includes an individual's self-beliefs and self-evaluations. It has three structural characteristics—complexity, consistency, and clarity—all of which influence employee well-being, behavior, and performance. People are inherently motivated to promote and protect their self-concept (self-enhancement) and to verify and maintain their existing self-concept (self-verification). Self-evaluation consists of self-esteem, self-efficacy, and locus of control. Self-concept also consists of both personal identity and social identity. Social identity theory explains how people define themselves by the groups to which they belong or have an emotional attachment.

LO3-2 Outline the perceptual process and discuss the effects of categorical thinking and mental models in that process.

Perception involves selecting, organizing, and interpreting information to make sense of the world around us. Perceptual organization applies categorical thinking—the mostly nonconscious process of organizing people and objects into preconceived categories that are stored in our long-term memory. Mental models—knowledge structures that we develop to describe, explain, and predict the world around us—also help us make sense of incoming stimuli.

LO3-3 Discuss how stereotyping, attribution, self-fulfilling prophecy, and the halo, false-consensus, primacy, and recency effects influence the perceptual process.

Stereotyping occurs when people assign traits to others based on their membership in a social category. This assignment economizes mental effort, fills in missing information, and enhances our self-concept, but it also lays the foundation for stereotype threat as well as systemic and intentional discrimination. The attribution process involves deciding whether an observed behavior or event is caused mainly by the person (internal factors) or the environment (external factors). Attributions are decided by the perceived consistency, distinctiveness, and consensus of the behavior. This process is subject to self-serving bias and fundamental attribution error. A self-fulfilling prophecy occurs when our expectations about another person cause that person to act in a way that is consistent with those expectations. This effect is stronger when employees first join the work unit, when several people hold these expectations, and when the employee has a history of low achievement. Four other perceptual errors commonly noted in organizations are the halo effect, false-consensus effect, primacy effect, and recency effect.

LO3-4 Discuss three ways to improve perceptions, with specific application to organizational situations.

One way to minimize perceptual biases is to become more aware of their existence. Awareness of these biases makes people more mindful of their thoughts and actions, but this training sometimes reinforces rather than reduces reliance on stereotypes and tends to be ineffective for people with deeply held prejudices. A second strategy is to become more aware of biases in our own decisions and behavior. Self-awareness increases through formal tests such as the Implicit Association Test (IAT) and by applying the Johari Window, which is a process in which others provide feedback to you about your behavior, and you offer disclosure to them about yourself. The third strategy is meaningful interaction, which applies the contact hypothesis that people who interact will be less prejudiced or perceptually biased

KEY TERMS

attribution process the perceptual process of deciding whether an observed behavior or event is caused largely by internal or external factors

categorical thinking organizing people and objects into preconceived categories that are stored in our long-term memory

confirmation bias the process of screening out information that is contrary to our values and assumptions, and to more readily accept confirming information

contact hypothesis a theory stating that the more we interact with someone, the less prejudiced or perceptually biased we will be against that person

empathy a person's understanding of and sensitivity to the feelings, thoughts, and situations of others

false-consensus effect a perceptual error in which we overestimate the extent to which others have beliefs and characteristics similar to our own

fundamental attribution error the tendency to see the person rather than the situation as the main cause of that person's behavior

global mindset an individual's ability to perceive, appreciate, and empathize with people from other cultures, and to process complex cross-cultural information

halo effect a perceptual error whereby our general impression of a person, usually based on one prominent characteristic, colors our perception of other characteristics of that person

Johari Window a model of mutual understanding that encourages disclosure and feedback to increase our own open area and reduce the blind, hidden, and unknown areas

locus of control a person's general belief about the amount of control he or she has over personal life events

mental models knowledge structures that we develop to describe, explain, and predict the world around us

perception the process of receiving information about and making sense of the world around us

positive organizational behavior a perspective of organizational behavior that focuses on building positive qualities and traits within individuals or institutions as opposed to focusing on what is wrong with them

primacy effect a perceptual error in which we quickly form an opinion of people based on the first information we receive about them

recency effect a perceptual error in which the most recent information dominates our perception of others

selective attention the process of attending to some information received by our senses and ignoring other information

self-concept an individual's self-beliefs and self-evaluations

self-efficacy a person's belief that he or she has the ability, motivation, correct role perceptions, and favorable situation to complete a task successfully

self-enhancement a person's inherent motivation to have a positive self-concept (and to have others perceive him or her favorably), such as being competent, attractive, lucky, ethical, and important

self-fulfilling prophecy the perceptual process in which our expectations about another person cause that person to act more consistently with those expectations

self-serving bias the tendency to attribute our favorable outcomes to internal factors and our failures to external factors

self-verification a person's inherent motivation to confirm and maintain his or her existing self-concept

social identity theory a theory stating that people define themselves by the groups to which they belong or have an emotional attachment

stereotype threat an individual's concern about confirming a negative stereotype about his or her group

stereotyping the process of assigning traits to people based on their membership in a social category

toward one another. Meaningful interaction is strongest when people work closely and frequently with relatively equal status on a shared meaningful task that requires cooperation and reliance on one another. Meaningful interaction helps improve empathy, which is a person's understanding and sensitivity to the feelings, thoughts, and situations of others.

LO3-5 Outline the main features of a global mindset and justify its usefulness to employees and organizations.

A global mindset refers to an individual's ability to perceive, know about, and process information across cultures. This includes (1) an awareness of, openness to, and respect for other views and practices in the world; (2) the capacity to empathize and act effectively across cultures; (3) an ability to process complex information about novel environments; and (4) the ability to comprehend and reconcile intercultural matters with multiple levels of thinking. A global mindset enables people to develop better cross-cultural relationships, to digest huge volumes of cross-cultural information, and to identify and respond more quickly to emerging global opportunities. Employees develop a global mindset through self-awareness, opportunities to compare their own mental models with people from other cultures, formal cross-cultural training, and immersion in other cultures.

chapter four

Workplace Emotions, Attitudes, and Stress

CHAPTER SUMMARY

LO4-1 Explain how emotions and cognition (conscious reasoning) influence attitudes and behavior.

Emotions are physiological, behavioral, and psychological episodes experienced toward an object, person, or event that create a state of readiness. Emotions differ from attitudes, which represent a cluster of beliefs, feelings, and behavioral intentions toward a person, object, or event. Beliefs are a person's established perceptions about the attitude object. Feelings are positive or negative evaluations of the attitude object. Behavioral intentions represent a motivation to engage in a particular behavior toward the target.

Attitudes have traditionally been described as a purely rational process in which beliefs predict feelings, which predict behavioral intentions, which predict behavior. We now know that emotions have an influence on behavior that is equal to or greater than that of cognition. This dual process is apparent when we internally experience a conflict between what logically seems good or bad and what we emotionally feel is good or bad in a situation. Emotions also affect behavior directly. Behavior sometimes influences our subsequent attitudes through cognitive dissonance.

LO4-2 Discuss the dynamics of emotional labor and the role of emotional intelligence in the workplace.

Emotional labor consists of the effort, planning, and control needed to express organizationally desired emotions during interpersonal transactions. It is more common in jobs requiring a variety of emotions and more intense emotions, as well as in jobs in which interactions with clients are frequent and long in duration. Cultures also differ on the norms of displaying or concealing a person's true emotions. Emotional dissonance is the psychological tension experienced when the emotions people are required to display are quite different from the emotions they actually experience at that moment. Deep acting can minimize this dissonance, as can the practice of hiring people with a natural tendency to display desired emotions.

Emotional intelligence is the ability to perceive and express emotion, assimilate emotion in thought, understand and reason with emotion, and regulate emotion in oneself and others. This concept includes four components arranged in a hierarchy: awareness of one's own emotions, management of one's own emotions, awareness of others' emotions, and management of others' emotions. Emotional intelligence can be learned to some extent, particularly through personal coaching.

LO4-3 Summarize the consequences of job dissatisfaction, as well as strategies to increase organizational (affective) commitment.

Job satisfaction represents a person's evaluation of his or her job and work context. Four types of job dissatisfaction consequences are quitting or otherwise getting away from the dissatisfying situation (exit), attempting to change the dissatisfying situation (voice), patiently waiting for the problem to sort itself out (loyalty), and reducing work effort and performance (neglect). Job satisfaction has a moderate relationship with job performance and with customer satisfaction. Affective organizational commitment (loyalty) is the employee's emotional attachment to, identification with, and involvement in a particular organization. This form contrasts with continuance commitment, which is a calculative bond with the organization. Companies build loyalty through justice and support, shared values, trust, organizational comprehension, and employee involvement.

KEY TERMS

affective organizational commitment an individual's emotional attachment to, involvement in, and identification with an organization

attitudes the cluster of beliefs, assessed feelings, and behavioral intentions toward a person, object, or event (called an attitude object)

cognitive dissonance an emotional experience caused by a perception that our beliefs, feelings, and behavior are incongruent with one another

continuance commitment an individual's calculative attachment to an organization

emotional dissonance the psychological tension experienced when the emotions people are required to display are quite different from the emotions they actually experience at that moment

emotional intelligence (EI) a set of abilities to perceive and express emotion, assimilate emotion in thought, understand and reason with emotion, and regulate emotion in oneself and others

emotional labor the effort, planning, and control needed to express organizationally desired emotions during interpersonal transactions

emotions physiological, behavioral, and psychological episodes experienced toward an object, person, or event that create a state of readiness

exit–voice–loyalty–neglect (EVLN) model the four ways, as indicated in the name, that employees respond to job dissatisfaction

general adaptation syndrome a model of the stress experience, consisting of three stages: alarm reaction, resistance, and exhaustion

job satisfaction a person's evaluation of his or her job and work context

service profit chain model a theory explaining how employees' job satisfaction influences company profitability indirectly through service quality, customer loyalty, and related factors

stress an adaptive response to a situation that is perceived as challenging or threatening to the person's well-being

LO4-4 **Describe the stress experience and review four major stressors.**

Stress is an adaptive response to a situation that is perceived as challenging or threatening to a person's well-being. The stress experience, called the general adaptation syndrome, involves moving through three stages: alarm, resistance, and exhaustion. Stressors are the causes of stress and include any environmental conditions that place a physical or emotional demand on a person. Four of the most common workplace stressors are organizational constraints, interpersonal conflict, work overload, and low task control.

LO4-5 **Identify five ways to manage workplace stress.**

Many interventions are available to manage work-related stress, including removing the stressor, withdrawing from the stressor, changing stress perceptions, controlling stress consequences, and receiving social support.

CHAPTER SUMMARY

LO5-1 Define employee engagement.

Employee engagement is defined as an individual's emotional and cognitive (rational) motivation, particularly a focused, intense, persistent, and purposive effort toward work-related goals. It is emotional involvement in, commitment to, and satisfaction with the work, as well as a high level of absorption in the work and sense of self-efficacy about performing the work.

LO5-2 Explain how drives and emotions influence employee motivation, and discuss the employee motivation implications of four-drive theory, Maslow's needs hierarchy, intrinsic and extrinsic motivation, and learned needs theory.

Motivation consists of the forces within a person that affect his or her direction, intensity, and persistence of voluntary behavior in the workplace. Drives (also called primary needs) are neural states that energize individuals to correct deficiencies or maintain an internal equilibrium. They generate emotions, which put us in a state of readiness to act. Needs—goal-directed forces that people experience—are shaped by the individual's self-concept (including personality and values), social norms, and past experience.

Four-drive theory states that everyone has four innate drives: acquire, bond, comprehend, and defend. These drives activate emotions that people regulate through social norms, past experience, and personal values. The main recommendation from four-drive theory is to ensure that individual jobs and workplaces provide a balanced opportunity to fulfill the four drives. Maslow's needs hierarchy theory groups needs into a hierarchy of five levels and states that the lowest needs are initially most important, but higher needs become more important as the lower ones are satisfied. Although very popular, the theory lacks research support, mainly because it wrongly assumes that everyone has the same hierarchy. The emerging evidence suggests that needs hierarchies vary from one person to the next, according to their personal values.

Intrinsic motivation refers to motivation controlled by the individual and experienced from the activity itself, whereas extrinsic motivation occurs when people are motivated to receive something that is beyond their personal control for instrumental reasons. Intrinsic motivation is anchored in the innate drives for competence and autonomy. Some research suggests that extrinsic motivators may reduce existing intrinsic motivation to some extent and under some conditions, but the effect is often minimal. McClelland's learned needs theory argues that needs can be strengthened through learning. The three needs studied in this respect have been need for achievement, need for power, and need for affiliation.

LO5-3 Discuss the expectancy theory model, including its practical implications.

Expectancy theory states that work effort is determined by the perception that effort will result in a particular level of performance (E-to-P expectancy), the perception that a specific behavior or performance level will lead to specific outcomes (P-to-O expectancy), and the valences that the person feels for those outcomes. The E-to-P expectancy increases by improving the employee's ability and confidence to perform the job. The P-to-O expectancy increases by measuring performance accurately, distributing higher rewards to better performers, and showing employees that rewards are performance-based. Outcome valences increase by finding out what employees want and using these resources as rewards.

KEY TERMS

distributive justice perceived fairness in the individual's ratio of outcomes to contributions relative to a comparison of other's ratio of outcomes to contributions

drives hardwired characteristics of the brain that correct deficiencies or maintain an internal equilibrium by producing emotions to energize individuals

employee engagement individual emotional and cognitive motivation, particularly a focused, intense, persistent, and purposive effort toward work-related goals

equity theory a theory explaining how people develop perceptions of fairness in the distribution and exchange of resources

expectancy theory a motivation theory based on the idea that work effort is directed toward behaviors that people believe will lead to desired outcomes

four-drive theory a motivation theory based on the innate drives to acquire, bond, learn, and defend that incorporates both emotions and rationality

goal setting the process of motivating employees and clarifying their role perceptions by establishing performance objectives

job characteristics model a job design model that relates the motivational properties of jobs to specific personal and organizational consequences of those properties

job design the process of assigning tasks to a job, including the interdependency of those tasks with other jobs

job enlargement the practice of adding more tasks to an existing job

job enrichment the practice of giving employees more responsibility for scheduling, coordinating, and planning their own work

job specialization the result of a division of labor, in which work is subdivided into separate jobs assigned to different people

Maslow's needs hierarchy theory a motivation theory of needs arranged in a hierarchy, whereby people are motivated to fulfill a higher need as a lower one becomes gratified

motivation the forces within a person that affect his or her direction, intensity, and persistence of voluntary behavior

need for achievement (nAch) a learned need in which people want to accomplish reasonably challenging goals and desire unambiguous feedback and recognition for their success

need for affiliation (nAff) a learned need in which people seek approval from others, conform to their wishes and expectations, and avoid conflict and confrontation

need for power (nPow) a learned need in which people want to control their environment, including people and material resources, to benefit either themselves (personalized power) or others (socialized power)

needs goal-directed forces that people experience

organizational behavior modification (OB Mod) a theory that explains employee behavior in terms of the antecedent conditions and consequences of that behavior

procedural justice perceived fairness of the procedures used to decide the distribution of resources

scientific management the practice of systematically partitioning work into its smallest elements and standardizing tasks to achieve maximum efficiency

self-reinforcement reinforcement that occurs when an employee has control over a reinforcer but doesn't "take" it until completing a self-set goal

skill variety the extent to which employees must use different skills and talents to perform tasks within their jobs

social cognitive theory a theory that explains how learning and motivation occur by observing and modeling others as well as by anticipating the consequences of our behavior

strengths-based coaching a positive organizational behavior approach to coaching and feedback that focuses on building and leveraging the employee's strengths rather than trying to correct his or her weaknesses

task identity the degree to which a job requires completion of a whole or an identifiable piece of work

task interdependence the extent to which team members must share materials, information, or expertise in order to perform their jobs

task significance the degree to which a job has a substantial impact on the organization and/or larger society

LO5-4 Outline organizational behavior modification (OB Mod) and social cognitive theory, and explain their relevance to employee motivation.

Organizational behavior modification takes the behaviorist view that the environment teaches people to alter their behavior so that they maximize positive consequences and minimize adverse consequences. Antecedents are environmental stimuli that provoke (not necessarily cause) behavior. Consequences are events following behavior that influence its future occurrence. Consequences include positive reinforcement, punishment, negative reinforcement, and extinction. The schedules of reinforcement also influence behavior.

Social cognitive theory states that much learning and motivation occur by observing and modeling others, as well as by anticipating the consequences of our behavior. It suggests that people typically infer (rather than only directly experience) cause-and-effect relationships, anticipate the consequences of their actions, develop self-efficacy in performing behavior, exercise personal control over their behavior, and reflect on their direct experiences. The theory emphasizes self-regulation of individual behavior, including self-reinforcement, which is the tendency of people to reward and punish themselves as a consequence of their actions.

LO5-5 Describe the characteristics of effective goal setting and feedback.

Goal setting is the process of motivating employees and clarifying their role perceptions by establishing performance objectives. Goals are more effective when they are SMARTER (specific, measurable, achievable, relevant, time-framed, exciting, and reviewed). Effective feedback is specific, relevant, timely, credible, and sufficiently frequent. Strengths-based coaching (also known as *appreciative coaching*) maximizes employee potential by focusing on their strengths rather than weaknesses. Employees usually prefer nonsocial feedback sources to learn about their progress toward goal accomplishment.

LO5-6 Summarize equity theory and describe ways to improve procedural justice.

Organizational justice consists of distributive justice (perceived fairness in the outcomes we receive relative to our contributions and the outcomes and contributions of others) and procedural justice (fairness of the procedures used to decide the distribution of resources). Equity theory has four elements: outcome/input ratio, comparison other, equity evaluation, and consequences of inequity. The theory also explains what people are motivated to do when they feel inequitably treated. Companies need to consider not only equity in the distribution of resources but also fairness in the process of making resource allocation decisions.

LO5-7 List the advantages and disadvantages of job specialization and explain how to improve employee motivation through job design.

Job design is the process of assigning tasks to a job, including the interdependency of those tasks with other jobs. Job specialization subdivides work into separate jobs for different people. This increases work efficiency because employees master the tasks quickly, spend less time changing tasks, require less training, and can be matched more closely with the jobs best suited to their skills. However, job specialization may reduce work motivation; create mental health problems; lower product or service quality; and increase costs through discontentment, absenteeism, and turnover.

The job characteristics model is a template for job redesign that specifies core job dimensions, psychological states, and individual differences. The five core job dimensions are skill variety, task identity, task significance, autonomy, and job feedback. Jobs also vary in their required social interaction (task interdependence), predictability of work activities (task variability), and procedural clarity (task analyzability). Contemporary job design strategies try to motivate employees through job rotation, job enlargement, and job enrichment. Organizations introduce job rotation to reduce job boredom, develop a more flexible workforce, and reduce the incidence of repetitive strain injuries. Job enlargement involves increasing the number of tasks within the job. Two ways to enrich jobs are clustering tasks into natural groups and establishing client relationships.

chapter SiX

Decision Making and Creativity

CHAPTER SUMMARY

LO6-1 Describe the elements of rational choice decision making.

Decision making is a conscious process of making choices among one or more alternatives with the intention of moving toward some desired state of affairs. Rational choice decision making identifies the best choice by calculating the expected valence of numerous outcomes and the probability of those outcomes. It also follows the logical process of identifying problems and opportunities, choosing the best decision style, developing alternative solutions, choosing the best solution, implementing the selected alternative, and evaluating decision outcomes.

LO6-2 Explain why people differ from rational choice decision making when identifying problems/opportunities, evaluating/choosing alternatives, and evaluating decision outcomes.

Solution-focused problem identification, decisive leadership, stakeholder framing, perceptual defense, and mental models affect our ability to objectively identify problems and opportunities. We can minimize these challenges by being aware of the human limitations and discussing the situation with colleagues.

Evaluating and choosing alternatives is often challenging because organizational goals are ambiguous or in conflict, human information processing is incomplete and subjective, and people tend to satisfice rather than maximize. Decision makers also short-circuit the evaluation process when faced with an opportunity rather than a problem. People generally make better choices by systematically evaluating alternatives. Scenario planning can help make future decisions without the pressure and emotions that occur during real emergencies.

Confirmation bias and escalation of commitment make it difficult to evaluate decision outcomes accurately. Escalation is mainly caused by the self-justification effect, self-enhancement effect, prospect theory effect, and sunk costs effect. These problems are minimized by separating decision choosers from decision evaluators, establishing a preset level at which the decision is abandoned or reevaluated, relying on more systematic and clear feedback about the project's success, and involving several people in decision making.

LO6-3 Discuss the roles of emotions and intuition in decision making.

Emotions shape our preferences for alternatives and the process we follow to evaluate alternatives. We also listen in on our emotions for guidance when making decisions. This latter activity relates to intuition—the ability to know when a problem or opportunity exists and to select the best course of action without conscious reasoning. Intuition is both an emotional experience and a rapid, nonconscious, analytic process that involves pattern matching and action scripts.

LO6-4 Describe employee characteristics, workplace conditions, and specific activities that support creativity.

Creativity is the development of original ideas that make a socially recognized contribution. The four creativity stages are preparation, incubation, illumination, and verification. Incubation assists divergent thinking, which involves reframing the problem in a unique way and generating different approaches to the issue.

Four of the main features of creative people are intelligence, persistence, expertise, and independent imagination. Creativity also is strengthened for everyone when the work environment supports a learning orientation, the job has high intrinsic motivation, the

KEY TERMS

anchoring and adjustment heuristic a natural tendency for people to be influenced by an initial anchor point such that they do not sufficiently move away from that point as new information is provided

availability heuristic a natural tendency to assign higher probabilities to objects or events that are easier to recall from memory, even though ease of recall is also affected by nonprobability factors (e.g., emotional response, recent events)

bounded rationality the view that people are bounded in their decision-making capabilities, including access to limited information, limited information processing, and tendency toward satisficing rather than maximizing when making choices

cognitive dissonance an emotional experience caused by a perception that our beliefs, feelings, and behavior are incongruent with one another

confirmation bias the process of screening out information that is contrary to our values and assumptions, and to more readily accept confirming information

creativity the development of original ideas that make a socially recognized contribution

decision making the conscious process of making choices among alternatives with the intention of moving toward some desired state of affairs

design thinking a human-centered, solution-focused creative process that applies both intuition and analytical thinking to clarify problems and generate innovative solutions

divergent thinking reframing a problem in a unique way and generating different approaches to the issue

employee involvement the degree to which employees influence how their work is organized and carried out

escalation of commitment the tendency to repeat an apparently bad decision or allocate more resources to a failing course of action

implicit favorite a preferred alternative that the decision maker uses repeatedly as a comparison with other choices

intuition the ability to know when a problem or opportunity exists and to select the best course of action without conscious reasoning

learning orientation beliefs and norms that support the acquisition, sharing, and use of knowledge as well as work conditions that nurture these learning processes

mental models knowledge structures that we develop to describe, explain, and predict the world around us

prospect theory effect a natural tendency to feel more dissatisfaction from losing a particular amount than satisfaction from gaining an equal amount

representativeness heuristic a natural tendency to evaluate probabilities of events or objects by the degree to which they resemble (are representative of) other events or objects rather than on objective probability information

satisficing selecting an alternative that is satisfactory or "good enough," rather than the alternative with the highest value (maximization)

scenario planning a systematic process of thinking about alternative futures and what the organization should do to anticipate and react to those environments

self-enhancement a person's inherent motivation to have a positive self-concept (and to have others perceive him or her favorably), such as being competent, attractive, lucky, ethical, and important

organization provides a reasonable level of job security, and project leaders provide appropriate goals, time pressure, and resources. Four types of activities that encourage creativity are redefining the problem, associative play, cross-pollination, and design thinking. Design thinking is a human-centered, solution-focused creative process that applies both intuition and analytical thinking to clarify problems and generate innovative solutions.

LO6-5 Describe the benefits of employee involvement and identify four contingencies that affect the optimal level of employee involvement.

Employee involvement refers to the degree that employees influence how their work is organized and carried out. The level of participation may range from an employee providing specific information to management without knowing the problem or issue, to complete involvement in all phases of the decision process. Employee involvement may lead to higher decision quality and commitment, but several contingencies need to be considered, including the decision structure, source of decision knowledge, decision commitment, and risk of conflict.

CHAPTER SUMMARY

LO7-1 Explain why employees join informal groups, and discuss the benefits and limitations of teams.

Teams are groups of two or more people who interact and influence one another, are mutually accountable for achieving common goals associated with organizational objectives, and perceive themselves as a social entity within an organization. All teams are groups because they consist of people with a unifying relationship; not all groups are teams because some groups do not exist to serve organizational objectives.

People join informal groups (and are motivated to be on formal teams) for four reasons: (1) They have an innate drive to bond, (2) group membership is an inherent ingredient in a person's self-concept, (3) some personal goals are accomplished better in groups, and (4) individuals are comforted in stressful situations by the mere presence of other people. Teams have become popular because they tend to make better decisions, support the knowledge management process, and provide superior customer service. Teams are not always as effective as individuals working alone. Process losses and social loafing drag down team performance.

LO7-2 Outline the team effectiveness model and discuss how task characteristics, team size, and team composition influence team effectiveness.

Team effectiveness includes the team's ability to achieve its objectives, fulfill the needs of its members, and maintain its survival. The model of team effectiveness considers the team and organizational environment, team design, and team processes. Three team design elements are task characteristics, team size, and team composition. Teams tend to be better suited for situations in which the work is complex yet tasks are well-structured and have high task interdependence. Teams should be large enough to perform the work yet small enough for efficient coordination and meaningful involvement. Effective teams are composed of people with the competencies and motivation to perform tasks in a team environment. Team member diversity has advantages and disadvantages for team performance.

LO7-3 Discuss how the four team processes—team development, norms, cohesion, and trust—influence team effectiveness.

Teams develop through the stages of forming, storming, norming, performing, and eventually adjourning. Within these stages are two distinct team development processes: developing team identity and developing team mental models and coordinating routines. Team development can be accelerated through team building—any formal activity intended to improve the development and functioning of a work team. Teams develop norms to regulate and guide member behavior. These norms may be influenced by initial experiences, critical events, and the values and experiences that team members bring to the group.

Team cohesion—the degree of attraction people feel toward the team and their motivation to remain members—increases with member similarity, smaller team size, higher degree of interaction, somewhat difficult entry, team success, and external challenges. Cohesion increases team performance when the team has high interdependence and its norms are congruent with organizational goals. Trust refers to positive expectations one person has toward another person in situations involving risk. People trust others on the basis of three foundations: calculus, knowledge, and identification.

KEY TERMS

brainstorming a freewheeling, face-to-face meeting where team members aren't allowed to criticize but are encouraged to speak freely, generate as many ideas as possible, and build on the ideas of others

brainwriting a variation of brainstorming whereby participants write (rather than speak about) and share their ideas

Brooks's law the principle that adding more people to a late software project only makes it later

electronic brainstorming a form of brainstorming that relies on networked computers for submitting and sharing creative ideas

evaluation apprehension a decision-making problem that occurs when individuals are reluctant to mention ideas that seem silly because they believe (often correctly) that other team members are silently evaluating them

nominal group technique a variation of brainwriting consisting of three stages in which participants (1) silently and independently document their ideas, (2) collectively describe these ideas to the other team members without critique, and then (3) silently and independently evaluate the ideas presented

norms the informal rules and shared expectations that groups establish to regulate the behavior of their members

process losses resources (including time and energy) expended toward team development and maintenance rather than the task

production blocking a time constraint in team decision making due to the procedural requirement that only one person may speak at a time

role a set of behaviors that people are expected to perform because they hold certain positions in a team and organization

self-directed teams (SDTs) cross-functional work groups that are organized around work processes, complete an entire piece of work requiring several interdependent tasks, and have substantial autonomy over the execution of those tasks

social loafing the problem that occurs when people exert less effort (and usually perform at a lower level) when working in teams than when working alone

task interdependence the extent to which team members must share materials, information, or expertise in order to perform their jobs

team building a process that consists of formal activities intended to improve the development and functioning of a work team

team cohesion the degree of attraction people feel toward the team and their motivation to remain members

team efficacy the collective belief among team members in the team's capability to successfully complete a task

teams groups of two or more people who interact with and influence each other, are mutually accountable for achieving common goals associated with organizational objectives, and perceive themselves as a social entity within an organization

virtual (remote) teams teams whose members operate across space, time, and organizational boundaries and are linked through information technologies to achieve organizational tasks

LO7-4 **Discuss the characteristics and factors required for the success of self-directed teams and virtual (remote) teams.**

Self-directed teams (SDTs) complete an entire piece of work requiring several interdependent tasks, and they have substantial autonomy over the execution of their tasks. Members of virtual teams operate across space, time, and organizational boundaries and are linked through information technologies to achieve organizational tasks. Virtual (remote) teams are more effective when the team members have certain competencies, the team has the freedom to choose the preferred communication channels, and the members meet face-to-face fairly early in the team development process.

LO7-5 **Identify four constraints on team decision making and discuss the advantages and disadvantages of four structures aimed at improving team decision making.**

Team decisions are impeded by time constraints, evaluation apprehension, conformity to peer pressure, and overconfidence. Teams minimize these issues with critical thinking norms, diverse team membership, optimal team size, and procedures that prevent the leader and others from dominating. Four structures also potentially improve decision making in team settings: brainstorming, brainwriting, electronic brainstorming, and nominal group technique.

chapter eight

Communicating in Teams and Organizations

CHAPTER SUMMARY

LO8-1 Explain why communication is important in organizations, and discuss four influences on effective communication encoding and decoding.

Communication refers to the process by which information is transmitted and *understood* between two or more people. Communication supports work coordination, organizational learning, decision making, the changing of others' behavior, and employee well-being. The communication process involves forming, encoding, and transmitting the intended message to a receiver, who then decodes the message and provides feedback to the sender. Effective communication occurs when the sender's thoughts are transmitted to and understood by the intended receiver. The effectiveness of this process depends on whether the sender and receiver have similar codebooks, the sender's proficiency at encoding that message to the audience, the sender's and receiver's motivation and ability to transmit messages through that particular communication channel, and their common mental models of the communication context.

LO8-2 Compare and contrast the advantages of and problems with electronic mail, other verbal communication media, and nonverbal communication.

The two main types of communication channels are verbal and nonverbal. Various forms of Internet-based communication are widely used in organizations, with email being the most popular. Although efficient and a useful filing cabinet, email (and most other forms of written digital communication) is relatively poor at communicating emotions; it tends to reduce politeness and respect; it is an inefficient medium for communicating in ambiguous, complex, and novel situations; and it contributes to information overload. Social media, which are Internet- or mobile-based channels that allow users to generate and interactively share information, are slowly replacing or supplementing email in organizations. Social media are more conversational and reciprocally interactive than traditional channels. They are "social" by encouraging collaboration and the formation of virtual communities. Nonverbal communication includes facial gestures, voice intonation, physical distance, and even silence. Unlike verbal communication, nonverbal communication is less rule-bound and is mostly automatic and nonconscious. Some nonverbal communication is automatic through a process called emotional contagion.

LO8-3 Discuss the relevance of synchronicity, social presence, social acceptance, and media richness when choosing the preferred communication channel.

The most appropriate communication medium depends on several factors. Synchronicity refers to the channel's capacity for the sender and receiver to communicate at the same time (synchronous) or at different times (asynchronous). Synchronous channels are better when the issue is urgent or the topic is complex. Asynchronous channels are better when it is costly for both parties to communicate at the same time or when the receiver should have time to reflect before responding. A channel has high social presence when it creates psychological closeness to the other party and awareness of their humanness. This is valuable when the parties need to empathize or influence each other. Social acceptance refers to how well the communication medium is approved and supported by others. This acceptance depends on organization or societal norms, each party's preferences and skills with the channel, and the symbolic meaning of a channel. Media richness refers to a channel's data-carrying capacity. Nonroutine and ambiguous situations require rich media. However, technology-based lean media may be possible where users can multicommunicate, have high proficiency with that technology, and don't have social distractions.

KEY TERMS

communication the process by which information is transmitted and *understood* between two or more people

emotional contagion the nonconscious process of "catching" or sharing another person's emotions by mimicking that person's facial expressions and other nonverbal behavior

grapevine an unstructured and informal communication network founded on social relationships rather than organizational charts or job descriptions

information overload a condition in which the volume of information received exceeds the person's capacity to process it

management by walking around (MBWA) a communication practice in which executives get out of their offices and learn from others in the organization through face-to-face dialogue

media richness a medium's data-carrying capacity—that is, the volume and variety of information that can be transmitted during a specific time

persuasion the use of facts, logical arguments, and emotional appeals to change another person's beliefs and attitudes, usually for the purpose of changing the person's behavior

social presence the extent to which a communication channel creates psychological closeness to others, awareness of their humanness, and appreciation of the interpersonal relationship

synchronicity the extent to which the channel requires or allows both sender and receiver to be actively involved in the conversation at the same time (synchronous) or at different times (asynchronous)

LO8-4 Discuss various barriers (noise) to effective communication, including cross-cultural and gender-based differences in communication.

Several barriers create noise in the communication process. People misinterpret messages because of misaligned codebooks due to different languages, jargon, and the use of ambiguous phrases. Filtering messages and information overload are two other communication barriers. These problems are often amplified in cross-cultural settings, where these problems occur, along with differences in the meaning of nonverbal cues, silence, and conversational overlaps. There are also some communication differences between men and women, such as the tendency for men to exert status and engage in report talk in conversations, whereas women use more rapport talk and are more sensitive to nonverbal cues.

LO8-5 Explain how to get your message across more effectively, and summarize the elements of active listening.

To get a message across, the sender must learn to empathize with the receiver, repeat the message, choose an appropriate time for the conversation, and be descriptive rather than evaluative. Listening includes sensing, evaluating, and responding. Active listeners support these processes by postponing evaluation, avoiding interruptions, maintaining interest, empathizing, organizing information, showing interest, and clarifying the message.

LO8-6 Summarize effective communication strategies in organizational hierarchies, and review the role and relevance of the organizational grapevine.

Some companies try to encourage communication across the organization through workspace design as well as through Internet-based communication channels. Some executives also meet directly with employees by engaging in management by walking around (MBWA) and by holding town-hall meetings.

In any organization, employees rely on the grapevine, particularly during times of uncertainty. The grapevine is an unstructured and informal network founded on social relationships rather than organizational charts or job descriptions. Although early research identified several unique features of the grapevine, some of these features may be changing as the Internet plays an increasing role in grapevine communication.

chapter nine

Power and Influence in the Workplace

REVIEW CARD

CHAPTER SUMMARY

LO9-1 Describe the dependence model of power and the five sources of power in organizations.

Power is the capacity to influence others. It exists when one party perceives that he or she is dependent on the other for something of value. However, the dependent person also must have countervailing power—some power over the dominant party—to maintain the relationship, and the parties must have some level of trust.

There are five power bases. Legitimate power is an agreement among organizational members that people in certain roles can request certain behaviors of others. This power has restrictions, represented by the target person's zone of indifference. It also includes the norm of reciprocity (a feeling of obligation to help someone who has helped you), as well as control over the flow of information to others. Reward power is derived from the ability to control the allocation of rewards valued by others and to remove negative sanctions. Coercive power is the ability to apply punishment. Expert power is the capacity to influence others by possessing knowledge or skills that they value. An important form of expert power is the (perceived) ability to manage uncertainties in the business environment. People have referent power when others identify with them, like them, or otherwise respect them.

LO9-2 Discuss the four contingencies of power.

Four contingencies determine whether these power bases translate into real power. Individuals and work units are more powerful when they are nonsubstitutable. Employees, work units, and organizations reduce substitutability by controlling tasks, knowledge, and labor and by differentiating themselves from competitors. A second contingency is centrality. People have more power when they have high centrality, which means that many people are quickly affected by their actions. The third contingency, visibility, refers to the idea that power increases to the extent that a person's or work unit's competencies are known to others. Discretion, the fourth contingency of power, refers to the freedom to exercise judgment. Power increases when people have the freedom to use their power.

LO9-3 Explain how people and work units gain power through social networks.

Social networks are social structures of individuals or social units (e.g., departments, organizations) that connect to one another through one or more forms of interdependence. People receive power in social networks through social capital, which is the goodwill and resulting resources shared among members in a social network. Three main resources from social networks are information, visibility, and referent power.

Employees gain social capital through their relationship in the social network. Social capital tends to increase with the number of network ties. Strong ties (close-knit relationships) also can increase social capital because these connections offer more resources more quickly. However, having weak ties with people from diverse networks can be more valuable than having strong ties with people in similar networks. Weak ties provide more resources that we do not already possess. Another influence on social capital is the person's centrality in the network. Network centrality is determined in several ways, including the extent to which you are located between others in the network (betweenness), how many direct ties you have (degree), and the closeness of these ties. People also gain power by bridging structural holes—linking two or more clusters of people in a network.

KEY TERMS

centrality a contingency of power pertaining to the degree and nature of interdependence between the power holder and others

charisma a personal characteristic or special "gift" that serves as a form of interpersonal attraction and referent power over others

coalition a group that attempts to influence people outside the group by pooling the resources and power of its members

countervailing power the capacity of a person, team, or organization to keep a more powerful person or group in the exchange relationship

impression management actively shaping through self-presentation and other means the perceptions and attitudes that others have of us

influence any behavior that attempts to alter someone's attitudes or behavior

inoculation effect a persuasive communication strategy of warning listeners that others will try to influence them in the future and that they should be wary of the opponent's arguments

legitimate power an agreement among organizational members that people in certain roles can request certain behaviors of others

Machiavellian values the beliefs that deceit is a natural and acceptable way to influence others and that getting more than one deserves is acceptable

norm of reciprocity a felt obligation and social expectation of helping or otherwise giving something of value to someone who has already helped or given something of value to you

organizational politics behaviors that others perceive as self-serving tactics at the expense of other people and possibly the organization

persuasion the use of facts, logical arguments, and emotional appeals to change another person's beliefs and attitudes, usually for the purpose of changing the person's behavior

power the capacity of a person, team, or organization to influence others

referent power the capacity to influence others on the basis of an identification with and respect for the power holder

social capital the knowledge and other resources available to people or social units (teams, organizations) from a durable network that connects them to others

social networks social structures of individuals or social units that are connected to each other through one or more forms of interdependence

structural hole an area between two or more dense social network areas that lacks network ties

upward appeal a type of influence in which someone with higher authority or expertise is called on in reality or symbolically to support the influencer's position

LO9-4 **Describe eight types of influence tactics, three consequences of influencing others, and three contingencies to consider when choosing an influence tactic.**

Influence refers to any behavior that attempts to alter someone's attitudes or behavior. The most widely studied influence tactics are silent authority, assertiveness, information control, coalition formation, upward appeal, impression management, persuasion, and exchange. "Soft" influence tactics such as friendly persuasion and subtle ingratiation are more acceptable than "hard" tactics such as upward appeal and assertiveness. However, the most appropriate influence tactic also depends on the influencer's power base; whether the person being influenced is higher, lower, or at the same level in the organization; and personal, organizational, and cultural values regarding influence behavior.

LO9-5 **Identify the organizational conditions and personal characteristics associated with organizational politics, as well as ways to minimize organizational politics.**

Organizational politics refer to influence tactics that others perceive to be self-serving behaviors, sometimes contrary to the interests of the organization. It is more common when ambiguous decisions allocate scarce resources and when the organization tolerates or rewards political behavior. Individuals with a high need for personal power and strong Machiavellian values have a higher propensity to use political tactics. Organizational politics can be minimized by providing clear rules for resource allocation, establishing a free flow of information, using education and involvement during organizational change, supporting team norms and a corporate culture that discourages political behavior, and having leaders who role model organizational citizenship rather than political savvy.

CHAPTER SUMMARY

LO10-1 Define conflict and debate its positive and negative consequences in the workplace.

Conflict is the process in which one party perceives that its interests are being opposed or negatively affected by another party. The earliest view of conflict was that it was dysfunctional for organizations. Even today, we recognize that conflict sometimes or to some degree consumes productive time, increases stress and job dissatisfaction, discourages coordination and resource sharing, undermines customer service, fuels organizational politics, and undermines team cohesion. But conflict also can be beneficial. It is known to motivate more active thinking about problems and possible solutions, encourage more active monitoring of the organization in its environment, and improve team cohesion (where the conflict source is external).

LO10-2 Distinguish task from relationship conflict and describe three strategies to minimize relationship conflict during task conflict episodes.

Task conflict occurs when people focus their discussion around the issue while showing respect for people with other points of view. Relationship conflict exists when people view each other, rather than the issue, as the source of conflict. It is apparent when people attack each other's credibility and display aggression toward the other party. It is difficult to separate task from relationship conflict. However, three strategies or conditions that minimize relationship conflict during constructive debate are (1) emotional intelligence and emotional stability of the participants, (2) team cohesion, and (3) supportive team norms.

LO10-3 Diagram the conflict process model and describe six structural sources of conflict in organizations.

The conflict process model begins with the six structural sources of conflict: incompatible goals, differentiation (different values and beliefs), interdependence, scarce resources, ambiguous rules, and communication problems. These sources lead one or more parties to perceive a conflict and to experience conflict emotions. This produces manifest conflict, such as behaviors toward the other side. The conflict process often escalates through a series of episodes.

LO10-4 Outline the five conflict-handling styles and discuss the circumstances in which each would be most appropriate.

There are five known conflict-handling styles: problem solving, forcing, avoiding, yielding, and compromising. People who use problem solving have a win–win orientation. Other styles, particularly forcing, assume a win–lose orientation. In general, people gravitate toward one or two preferred conflict-handling styles that match their personality, personal and cultural values, and past experience.

The best style depends on the situation. Problem solving is best when interests are not perfectly opposing, the parties trust each other, and the issues are complex. Forcing works best when you strongly believe in your position, the dispute requires quick action, and the other party would take advantage of a cooperative style. Avoidance is preferred when the conflict has become emotional or the cost of resolution is higher than its benefits. Yielding works well when the other party has substantially more power, the issue is less important to you, and you are not confident in the logical soundness of your position. Compromising is preferred when the parties have equal power, they are under time pressure, and they lack trust.

KEY TERMS

best alternative to a negotiated settlement (BATNA) the best outcome you might achieve through some other course of action if you abandon the current negotiation

conflict the process in which one party perceives that its interests are being opposed or negatively affected by another party

negotiation the process whereby two or more conflicting parties attempt to resolve their divergent goals by redefining the terms of their interdependence

relationship conflict a type of conflict in which people focus on characteristics of other individuals, rather than on the issues, as the source of conflict

superordinate goals goals that the conflicting parties value and whose attainment requires the joint resources and effort of those parties

task conflict a type of conflict in which people focus their discussion around the issue while showing respect for people who have other points of view

third-party conflict resolution any attempt by a relatively neutral person to help conflicting parties resolve their differences

win–lose orientation the belief that conflicting parties are drawing from a fixed pie, so the more one party receives, the less the other party will receive

win–win orientation the belief that conflicting parties will find a mutually beneficial solution to their disagreement

LO10-5 Apply the six structural approaches to conflict management and describe the three types of third-party dispute resolution.

Structural approaches to conflict management include emphasizing superordinate goals, reducing differentiation, improving communication and understanding, reducing interdependence, increasing resources, and clarifying rules and procedures.

Third-party conflict resolution is any attempt by a relatively neutral person to help the parties resolve their differences. The three main forms of third-party dispute resolution are mediation, arbitration, and inquisition. Managers tend to use an inquisition approach, though mediation and arbitration often are more appropriate, depending on the situation.

LO10-6 Discuss activities in the negotiation preparation, process, and setting that improve negotiation effectiveness.

Negotiation occurs whenever two or more conflicting parties attempt to resolve their divergent goals by redefining the terms of their interdependence. Effective negotiators engage in several preparation activities. These include determining their initial, target, and resistance positions; understanding their needs behind these goals; and knowing their alternatives to the negotiation (BATNA). They set higher initial offer and target positions, which anchor the negotiation at a higher level.

During the negotiation process, effective negotiators devote more attention to gathering than giving information. They try to determine the other party's underlying needs rather than just their stated positions. They make fewer and smaller concessions but use concessions strategically to discover the other party's priorities and to maintain trust. They try to avoid time traps (negotiating under deadlines set by the other side), and they engage in practices to maintain a positive relationship with the other party. Characteristics of the setting—including location, physical setting, and audience characteristics—are also important in successful negotiations.

chapter eleven

Leadership in Organizational Settings

CHAPTER SUMMARY

LO11-1 Define leadership and shared leadership.

Leadership is defined as the ability to influence, motivate, and enable others to contribute to the effectiveness and success of the organizations of which they are members. Leaders use influence to motivate followers and arrange the work environment so they do the job more effectively. Shared leadership views leadership as a role rather than a formal position, so employees throughout the organization act informally as leaders as the occasion arises. These situations include serving as champions for specific ideas or changes, as well as filling leadership roles where it is needed.

LO11-2 Describe the four elements of transformational leadership and explain why they are important for organizational change.

Transformational leadership begins with a strategic vision, which is a positive representation of a future state that energizes and unifies employees. A vision is values-based, a distant goal, abstract, and meaningful to employees. Transformational leaders effectively communicate the vision by framing it around values; showing sincerity and passion toward the vision; and using symbols, metaphors, and other vehicles that create richer meaning for the vision. Transformational leaders model the vision (walk the talk) and encourage employees to experiment with new behaviors and practices that are potentially more consistent with the visionary future state. They also build employee commitment to the vision through the preceding activities, as well as by celebrating milestones to the vision. Transformational leaders are not necessarily charismatic, and charismatic leaders do not necessarily apply transformational leadership behaviors.

LO11-3 Compare managerial leadership with transformational leadership, and describe the features of task-oriented, people-oriented, and servant leadership.

Managerial leadership includes the daily activities that support and guide the performance and well-being of individual employees and the work unit to achieve current objectives and practices. Transformational and managerial leadership are dependent on each other, but they differ in their assumptions of stability versus change and their micro versus macro focus.

Task-oriented behaviors include assigning employees to specific tasks, clarifying their work duties and procedures, ensuring they follow company rules, and pushing them to reach their performance capacity. People-oriented behaviors include showing mutual trust and respect for subordinates, demonstrating a genuine concern for their needs, and having a desire to look out for their welfare.

Servant leadership defines leadership as serving others to support their need fulfillment and personal development and growth. Servant leaders have a natural desire or "calling" to serve others. They maintain a relationship with others that is humble, egalitarian, and accepting. Servant leaders also anchor their decisions and actions in ethical principles and practices.

KEY TERMS

authentic leadership the view that effective leaders need to be aware of, feel comfortable with, and act consistently with their values, personality, and self-concept

implicit leadership theory a theory stating that people evaluate a leader's effectiveness in terms of how well that person fits preconceived beliefs about the features and behaviors of effective leaders (leadership prototypes) and that people tend to inflate the influence of leaders on organizational events

leadership influencing, motivating, and enabling others to contribute toward the effectiveness and success of the organizations of which they are members

leadership substitutes theory a theory identifying conditions that either limit a leader's ability to influence subordinates or make a particular leadership style unnecessary

managerial leadership a leadership perspective stating that effective leaders help employees improve their performance and well-being toward current objectives and practices

path–goal leadership theory a leadership theory stating that effective leaders choose the most appropriate leadership style(s), depending on the employee and situation, to influence employee expectations about desired results and their positive outcomes

servant leadership the view that leaders serve followers, rather than vice versa; leaders help employees fulfill their needs and are coaches, stewards, and facilitators of employee development

shared leadership the view that leadership is a role, not a position assigned to one person; consequently, people within the team and organization lead each other

transformational leadership a leadership perspective that explains how leaders change teams or organizations by creating, communicating, and modeling a vision for the organization or work unit and inspiring employees to strive for that vision

LO11-4 Discuss the elements of path–goal leadership theory and leadership substitutes theory.

The path–goal theory of leadership takes the view that effective managerial leadership involves diagnosing the situation and using the most appropriate style for it. The core model identifies four leadership styles—directive, supportive, participative, and achievement-oriented—and several contingencies related to the characteristics of the employee and of the situation. Leadership substitutes theory identifies contingencies that either limit the leader's ability to influence subordinates or make a particular leadership style unnecessary.

LO11-5 Describe the two components of the implicit leadership perspective.

According to the implicit leadership perspective, people have leadership prototypes, which they use to evaluate the leader's effectiveness. Furthermore, people form a romance of leadership; they want to believe that leaders make a difference, so they engage in fundamental attribution error and other perceptual distortions to support this belief in the leader's impact.

LO11-6 Identify eight personal attributes associated with effective leaders and describe authentic leadership.

The personal attributes perspective identifies the characteristics of effective leaders. Recent writing suggests that leaders have specific personality characteristics, positive self-concept, leadership motivation, drive, integrity, knowledge of the business, cognitive and practical intelligence, and emotional intelligence. Authentic leadership refers to how well leaders are aware of, feel comfortable with, and act consistently with their self-concept. This concept consists mainly of two parts: self-awareness and engaging in behavior that is consistent with one's self-concept.

LO11-7 Discuss cultural and gender similarities and differences in leadership.

Cultural values influence the leader's personal values, which in turn influence his or her leadership practices. Women generally do not differ from men in the degree of people-oriented or task-oriented leadership. However, female leaders more often adopt a participative style. Research also suggests that people evaluate female leaders on the basis of gender stereotypes, which may result in higher or lower ratings.

CHAPTER SUMMARY

LO12-1 Describe three types of coordination in organizational structures.

Organizational structure is the division of labor as well as the patterns of coordination, communication, workflow, and formal power that direct organizational activities. All organizational structures divide labor into distinct tasks and coordinate that labor to accomplish common goals. The primary means of coordination are informal communication, formal hierarchy, and standardization.

LO12-2 Discuss the role and effects of span of control, centralization, and formalization, and relate these elements to organic and mechanistic organizational structures.

The four basic elements of organizational structure are span of control, centralization, formalization, and departmentalization. The optimal span of control—the number of people directly reporting to the next level in the hierarchy—depends on what coordinating mechanisms are present other than formal hierarchy, whether employees perform routine tasks, and how much interdependence there is among employees within the department.

Centralization occurs when formal decision authority is held by a small group of people, typically senior executives. Many companies decentralize as they become larger and more complex, but some sections of the company may remain centralized while other sections decentralize. Formalization is the degree to which organizations standardize behavior through rules, procedures, formal training, and related mechanisms. Companies become more formalized as they get older and larger. Formalization tends to reduce organizational flexibility, organizational learning, creativity, and job satisfaction.

Span of control, centralization, and formalization cluster into mechanistic and organic structures. Mechanistic structures are characterized by a narrow span of control and a high degree of formalization and centralization. Companies with an organic structure have the opposite characteristics.

LO12-3 Identify and evaluate five types of departmentalization.

Departmentalization specifies how employees and their activities are grouped together. It establishes the chain of command, focuses people around common mental models, and encourages coordination through informal communication among people and subunits. A simple structure employs few people, has minimal hierarchy, and typically offers one distinct product or service. A functional structure organizes employees around specific knowledge or other resources. This structure fosters greater specialization and improves direct supervision, but it weakens the focus on serving clients or developing products.

A divisional structure groups employees around geographic areas, clients, or outputs. This structure accommodates growth and focuses employee attention on products or customers rather than tasks. However, this structure also duplicates resources and creates silos of knowledge. Team-based structures are very flat, with low formalization, and organize self-directed teams around work processes rather than functional specialties. The matrix structure combines two structures to leverage the benefits of both types. However, this approach requires more coordination than functional or pure divisional structures, may dilute accountability, and increases conflict.

KEY TERMS

centralization the degree to which formal decision authority is held by a small group of people, typically those at the top of the organizational hierarchy

divisional structure an organizational structure in which employees are organized around geographic areas, outputs (products or services), or clients

formalization the degree to which organizations standardize behavior through rules, procedures, formal training, and related mechanisms

functional structure an organizational structure in which employees are organized around specific knowledge or other resources

matrix structure an organizational structure that overlays two structures (such as a geographic divisional and a product divisional structure) in order to leverage the benefits of both

mechanistic structure an organizational structure with a narrow span of control and a high degree of formalization and centralization

organic structure an organizational structure with a wide span of control, little formalization, and decentralized decision making

organizational strategy the way the organization positions itself in its environment in relation to its stakeholders, given the organization's resources, capabilities, and mission

organizational structure the division of labor as well as the patterns of coordination, communication, workflow, and formal power that direct organizational activities

span of control the number of people directly reporting to the next level above in the hierarchy

team-based organizational structure an organizational structure built around self-directed teams that complete an entire piece of work

LO12-4 Explain how the external environment, organizational size, technology, and strategy are relevant when designing an organizational structure.

The best organizational structure depends on whether the environment is dynamic or stable, complex or simple, diverse or integrated, and hostile or munificent. Another contingency is the organization's size. Larger organizations need to become more decentralized and more formalized. The work unit's technology—including variability of work and analyzability of problems—influences whether it should adopt an organic or mechanistic structure. These contingencies influence but do not necessarily determine structure. Instead, corporate leaders formulate and implement strategies that shape both the characteristics of these contingencies and the organization's resulting structure.

chapter thirteen

Organizational Culture

CHAPTER SUMMARY

LO13-1 Describe the elements of organizational culture and discuss the importance of organizational subcultures.

Organizational culture consists of the values and assumptions shared within an organization. Shared assumptions are nonconscious, taken-for-granted perceptions or beliefs that have worked so well in the past that they are considered the correct way to think and act toward problems and opportunities. Values are stable, evaluative beliefs that guide our preferences for outcomes or courses of action in a variety of situations.

Organizations differ in their cultural content, that is, the relative ordering of values. There are several classifications of organizational culture, but they tend to oversimplify the wide variety of cultures and completely ignore the underlying assumptions of culture. Organizations have subcultures as well as the dominant culture. Subcultures maintain the organization's standards of performance and ethical behavior. They are also the source of emerging values that replace misaligned core values.

LO13-2 Describe four categories of artifacts through which corporate culture is deciphered.

Artifacts are the observable symbols and signs of an organization's culture. Four broad categories of artifacts include organizational stories and legends, rituals and ceremonies, language, and physical structures and symbols. Understanding an organization's culture requires the assessment of many artifacts because they are subtle and often ambiguous.

LO13-3 Discuss the importance of organizational culture and the conditions under which organizational culture strength improves organizational performance.

Organizational culture has three main functions: a form of social control, the "social glue" that bonds people together, and a way to help employees make sense of the workplace. Companies with strong cultures generally perform better than those with weak cultures, but only when the cultural content is appropriate for the organization's environment. Also, the culture should not be so strong that it drives out dissenting values, which may form emerging values for the future. Organizations should have adaptive cultures in which employees support ongoing change in the organization and their own roles.

LO13-4 Compare and contrast four strategies for merging organizational cultures.

Organizational culture clashes are common in mergers and acquisitions. This problem can be minimized by performing a bicultural audit to diagnose the compatibility of the organizational cultures. The four main strategies for merging different corporate cultures are integration, deculturation, assimilation, and separation.

KEY TERMS

adaptive culture an organizational culture in which employees are receptive to change, including the ongoing alignment of the organization to its environment and continuous improvement of internal processes

artifacts the observable symbols and signs of an organization's culture

attraction–selection–attrition (ASA) theory a theory that states that organizations have a natural tendency to attract, select, and retain people with values and personality characteristics that are consistent with the organization's character, resulting in a more homogeneous organization and a stronger culture

bicultural audit a process of diagnosing cultural relations between companies and determining the extent to which cultural clashes will likely occur

ceremonies planned displays of organizational culture, conducted specifically for the benefit of an audience

organizational culture the values and assumptions shared within an organization

organizational socialization the process by which individuals learn the values, expected behaviors, and social knowledge necessary to assume their roles in the organization

realistic job preview (RJP) a method of improving organizational socialization in which job applicants are given a balance of positive and negative information about the job and work context

reality shock the stress that results when employees perceive discrepancies between their preemployment expectations and on-the-job reality

rituals the programmed routines of daily organizational life that dramatize the organization's culture

LO13-5 Describe five strategies for changing and strengthening an organization's culture, including the application of attraction–selection–attrition theory.

An organization's culture begins with its founders and leaders because they use personal values to transform the organization. The founder's activities are later retold as organizational stories. Companies also introduce artifacts as mechanisms to maintain or change the culture. A related strategy is to introduce rewards and recognition practices that are consistent with the desired cultural values. A fourth method to change and strengthen an organization's culture is to support workforce stability and communication. Stability is necessary because culture exists in employees. Communication activities improve sharing of the culture. Finally, companies strengthen and change their culture by attracting and selecting applicants with personal values that fit the company's culture, by encouraging those with misaligned values to leave the company, and by engaging in organizational socialization—the process by which individuals learn the values, expected behaviors, and social knowledge necessary to assume their roles in the organization.

LO13-6 Describe the organizational socialization process and identify strategies to improve that process.

Organizational socialization is the process by which individuals learn the values, expected behaviors, and social knowledge necessary to assume their roles in the organization. It is a process of both learning and adjustment. Employees typically pass through three socialization stages: preemployment, encounter, and role management. To manage the socialization process, organizations should introduce realistic job previews (RJPs) and recognize the value of socialization agents in the process. These RJPs give job applicants a realistic balance of positive and negative information about the job and work context. Socialization agents provide information and social support during the socialization process.

CHAPTER SUMMARY

LO14-1 Describe the elements of Lewin's force field analysis model.

Lewin's force field analysis model states that all systems have driving and restraining forces. Change occurs through the process of unfreezing, changing, and refreezing. Unfreezing produces disequilibrium between the driving and restraining forces. Refreezing realigns the organization's systems and structures with the desired behaviors.

LO14-2 Discuss the reasons why people resist organizational change and how change agents should view this resistance.

Restraining forces are manifested as employee resistance to change. The main reasons people resist change are the negative valence of change, fear of the unknown, not-invented-here syndrome, breaking routines, incongruent team dynamics, and incongruent organizational systems. Resistance to change should be viewed as a resource, not an inherent obstacle to change. Change agents need to view resistance as task conflict rather than relationship conflict. Resistance is a signal that the change agent has not sufficiently strengthened employee readiness for change. It is also a form of voice, so discussion potentially improves procedural justice.

LO14-3 Outline six strategies for minimizing resistance to change, and debate ways to effectively create an urgency to change.

Organizational change requires employees to have an urgency for change. This typically occurs by informing them about driving forces in the external environment. Urgency to change also develops by putting employees in direct contact with customers. Leaders often need to create an urgency to change before the external pressures are felt, and this can occur through a vision of a more appealing future.

Resistance to change may be minimized by keeping employees informed about what to expect from the change effort (communicating); teaching employees valuable skills for the desired future (learning); involving them in the change process; helping employees cope with the stress of change; negotiating trade-offs with those who will clearly lose from the change effort; and using coercion (sparingly and as a last resort).

LO14-4 Discuss how leadership, coalitions, social networks, and pilot projects assist organizational change.

Every successful change requires transformational leaders with a clear, well-articulated vision of the desired future state. They also need the assistance of several people (a guiding coalition) who are located throughout the organization. In addition, change occurs more informally through social networks. Viral change operates through social networks using influencers.

Many organizational change initiatives begin with a pilot project. The success of the pilot project is then diffused to other parts of the organization. This occurs by motivating employees to adopt the pilot project's methods, training people to know how to adopt these practices, helping clarify how the pilot can be applied to different areas, and providing time and resources to support this diffusion.

KEY TERMS

action research a problem-focused change process that combines action orientation (changing attitudes and behavior) and research orientation (testing theory through data collection and analysis)

appreciative inquiry an organizational change strategy that directs the group's attention away from its own problems and focuses participants on the group's potential and positive elements

force field analysis Kurt Lewin's model of systemwide change that helps change agents diagnose the forces that drive and restrain proposed organizational change

positive organizational behavior a perspective of organizational behavior that focuses on building positive qualities and traits within individuals or institutions as opposed to focusing on what is wrong with them

refreezing the latter part of the change process, in which systems and structures are introduced that reinforce and maintain the desired behaviors

unfreezing the first part of the change process, in which the change agent produces disequilibrium between the driving and restraining forces

LO14-5 Describe and compare action research and appreciative inquiry as formal approaches to organizational change.

Action research is a highly participative, open systems approach to change management that combines an action orientation (changing attitudes and behavior) with research orientation (testing theory). It is a data-based, problem-oriented process that diagnoses the need for change, introduces the intervention, and then evaluates and stabilizes the desired changes.

Appreciative inquiry embraces the positive organizational behavior principle by focusing participants on the positive and possible. This approach to change also applies the constructionist, simultaneity, poetic, and anticipatory principles. The four stages of appreciative inquiry include discovery, dreaming, designing, and delivering.

LO14-6 Discuss two cross-cultural and three ethical issues in organizational change.

One significant concern is that organizational change theories developed with a Western cultural orientation potentially conflict with cultural values in some other countries. Also, organizational change practices can raise one or more ethical concerns, including increasing management's power over employees, threatening individual privacy rights, and undermining individual self-esteem.